Bruckner Studies presents the latest musicological and theoretical research on the life and music of Anton Bruckner. It is the most important English-language book on the composer since Robert Simpson's *The Essence of Bruckner*. The essays provide new biographical insights into his enigmatic personality, working procedures, and circle of students and friends; consider the fascinating history of the dissemination of his music during his lifetime and in this century, including its reception in Nazi Germany; and provide new analytical perspectives on his musical style and its origins. The volume challenges the reader to reassess the man and his music in a new light, unencumbered by decades of special interest and propaganda which have colored perceptions of Bruckner for more than a century.

BRUCKNER STUDIES

Bruckner Studies

EDITED BY

Timothy L. Jackson
Connecticut College

AND

Paul Hawkshaw
School of Music, Yale University

PUBLISHED BY THE PRESS SYNDICATE OF THE UNIVERSITY OF CAMBRIDGE
The Pitt Building, Trumpington Street, Cambridge CB2 1RP, United Kingdom

CAMBRIDGE UNIVERSITY PRESS
The Edinburgh Building, Cambridge CB2 2RU, United Kingdom
40 West 20th Street, New York, NY 10011–4211, USA
10 Stamford Road, Oakleigh, Melbourne 3166, Australia

First published 1997

Printed in the United Kingdom at the University Press, Cambridge

Typeset in Adobe Minion 10.75/14pt, using QuarkXpress™ [SE]

A catalogue record for this book is available from the British Library

Library of Congress cataloguing in publication data
Bruckner studies / edited by Timothy L. Jackson and Paul Hawkshaw.
    p. cm.
  Includes index.
  ISBN 0 521 57014 X (hardback)
    1. Bruckner, Anton, 1824–1896 – Criticism and interpretation.
  I. Jackson, Timothy L., 1958– II. Hawkshaw, Paul, 1950–.
  ML410.B88B785 1997
  780′.92 – dc20   96-36248 CIP

ISBN 0 521 57014 X hardback

Contents

CONTENTS

Plates

Preface

When Anton Bruckner died in October 1896, the musical world lost a composer, theorist, teacher, and performer who had stood at the cutting edge of the avant-garde of his generation. The contrasting views of this enigmatic and controversial figure ranged from adulation to disparagement and were reflected in the large number of obituaries. In the *Wiener Allgemeine Zeitung*, Bruckner was praised as an "unpretentious, modest man" and, as a musician, he was eulogized as "the most daring innovator who shied away from no enterprise and constantly developed new musical weapons." The *Neue Freie Presse* was much less flattering:

> One of the most original and unique figures in the musical life of Vienna, Professor Dr. Anton Bruckner, passed away yesterday afternoon at the age of seventy-two after a long illness. For decades Anton Bruckner had to fight for his musical existence; he never established himself as a composer and not even in his chosen field of church music was he able to create anything of value. As an elderly man, during the last ten years of his life, he was a figurehead for a lamentable and equally excessive cult. The Wagnerian School, which, after the death of its Master, needed a new visible leader, dragged the modest Viennese musician, who lived a solitary, dreamlike existence without ambition, out of the darkness.

By identifying prejudices which have colored perceptions and which continue to be influential in many quarters, the present essays challenge us, on the centenary of his death, to consider Bruckner, his music, and its sources from a fresh perspective. Four interrelated historical articles (Margaret Notley, Bryan Gilliam, Benjamin Korstvedt, Stephen McClatchie) address different aspects of Bruckner reception by German ultra-nationalists in the later nineteenth century and by the Nazis. Documentary studies of Bruckner's private diaries (Elisabeth Maier) and working methods (Paul Hawkshaw) reveal aspects of Bruckner's personal and compositional "inner worlds." Bruckner's theoretical ideas and their impact are then examined in Robert Wason's discussion of an unpublished treatise by Joseph Schalk (a Bruckner pupil). The final group of analytical essays examines individual works from contrasting perspectives, focusing on problems of form (Warren Darcy), rhythm (Joseph Kraus), the "reversed recapitulation" (Timothy Jackson), and the motivic organization of the middleground in late Bruckner (Edward Laufer).

Both during his lifetime and throughout most of this century, generations of admirers have enlisted Bruckner's music in support of heterogeneous political, religious, and personal agendas, including Austrian nationalism, Catholicism, and Nazism. As early as 1867 Kapellmeister Johann Herbeck and critic Eduard Hanslick urged Bruckner to move to Vienna because they believed they had found the contemporary Austrian symphonist to counter the pernicious influence of Richard Wagner. Bruckner's unabashed admiration for Wagner's music soon turned Hanslick into a most powerful adversary. For the next thirty years he and his followers, in a segment of the Viennese press representing a strange combination of political liberalism and musical conservatism, vituperatively condemned the "uncontrolled Wagnerism" and "decadence" of Bruckner's "music of the future."

Hanslick's critical stance played perfectly into the hands of Viennese Wagnerites. The Wiener akademischer Wagner-Verein placed Bruckner on a pedestal, and he became the darling of the local anti-Brahms, politically conservative, and often anti-Semitic press. Young Wagnerites including Gustav Mahler (ironically, a Jew), Hugo Wolf, August Göllerich, Ferdinand Löwe, and the brothers Franz and Josef Schalk were among his staunchest supporters and often responsible for the early publication of his works. Bruckner received much of his contemporary critical acclaim from Wagnerian fundamentalists, many of whom belonged to what Notley describes as "the most extreme part of the *völkisch* fringe" of Vienna.

Wagnerian ideology and politics have influenced the dissemination of Bruckner's musical legacy well into this century. Nowhere is this more evident than in the area of text criticism. The controversy over the validity of the first editions is perhaps the most high-profile issue in the Bruckner literature. The editions and the myriad of revisions, which Bruckner left in his autograph manuscripts, have combined to pose some of the thorniest text-critical problems in the history of western music. Korstvedt points out that a major impetus for the first important attempt to address fundamental editorial issues came from Nazism. In 1937, a Bruckner bust was consecrated in Regensburg's Valhalla shrine to German cultural, scientific, and political leaders. As Gilliam observes, Bruckner had become a paragon of Wagnerian virtue, a prototypical German composer, and a cultural icon of the Third Reich. It was now propitious to publish Bruckner's music in a new, politically correct *Gesamtausgabe* edited by Robert Haas and Alfred Orel.

Any benefits which accrued as a result of the appearance of the new scores were more than offset in many parts of the world by the negative implications of Bruckner's adoption by the Third Reich. After the war, with a few notable exceptions such as Robert Simpson, Hans Ferdinand Redlich, and Deryck Cooke, English-speaking scholars published little on

Bruckner. In Austria, the editorial process continued with a second *Gesamtausgabe* under Leopold Nowak. This edition provided a number of welcome new scores of the symphonies and the choral music. While Nowak attempted to rectify his predecessors' most glaring *faux pas*, he reissued the Haas–Orel editions of the symphonies supported by an incomplete and sometimes unreliable editorial apparatus. In the past fifteen years, scholars from the international community have begun to participate in the systematic investigation of surviving biographical materials and musical sources for Bruckner's music – with fascinating results; this book presents some of the fruits of their research.

Deciphering the complex Bruckner manuscripts, in which many revisions may be superimposed, is a difficult task. Issues of authenticity will have to be decided on the basis of a careful reexamination of the primary sources – composition by composition, manuscript by manuscript, print by print, and document by document. A century after Bruckner's death, an astonishing amount of this primary research remains to be done. Hawkshaw untangles, for example, an intricate web of variants in reconstructing the chronology of Bruckner's revisions to his F Minor Mass. These alterations – many extremely subtle – testify to the composer's attention to practical performance issues as well as to the internal, self-critical dialogue concerning "good and bad, good and better" as described by Joseph Kerman. They also document an evolution in Bruckner's aesthetics and theoretical ideas with regard to the voice-leading and metrical aspects of his own and other composers' music. In Maier's study of the Bruckner diaries, excerpts are presented and discussed for the first time. Her contribution elucidates Bruckner's "inner" autobiography as revealed by the diaries' cryptic annotations concerning the composer and significant events in his life.

It is also time to reassess the music. That Bruckner remains cloaked in an almost exclusively Wagnerian mantle is no longer justifiable. There is no question that Bruckner admired the "Meister aller Meister" and often made references to his music; aesthetically, politically, philosophically, and often *musically*, the two men were far apart. Bruckner knew his Mozart, Beethoven, and Schubert; all evidence indicates that, during periods of self-analysis, he turned to these composers rather than to Wagner. In view of the classical roots of Bruckner's symphonic and choral styles, Edward Laufer, Warren Darcy, and Timothy Jackson explain Brucknerian compositional techniques in relation to classical precedents. For example, Laufer elucidates Bruckner's unusual treatment of elision through comparison with classical usage. Jackson and Darcy demonstrate that Bruckner's unique handling of sonata form both conforms to and deviates from classical models. Laufer and Kraus explode the myth – a by-product of the dispute between pro- and anti-Wagnerian camps – that Bruckner's music is incoherent and metrically foursquare. Questioning Schenker's harsh condemnation of Bruckner as incapable of achieving large-scale unity (Schenker's critique must also be understood in the context of the Wagnerian conflict), Laufer argues that Bruckner's middlegrounds are as motivically "organic" and unified as those of his classical models. Identifying various types of expansions in the Scherzi of the early symphonies, Kraus demonstrates that some metrical symmetries are, in fact, expansions of underlying asymmetries.

The original versions of these chapters were presented at the first international symposium on the music of Anton Bruckner ever held in North America: *Perspectives on Anton Bruckner: Composer, Theorist, Teacher, Performer*, 21–24 February 1994, at Connecticut College, New London, Connecticut, coorganized by the editors of the present volume. The editors wish to express their gratitude to the faculty, staff, and students of the College, especially to Claire Gaudiani (President of the College), Professor Noel Zahler (Chair of the Music Department), and Mr. Christopher Cory (Director of College Relations), without whose encouragement, wisdom, and boundless energy the conference could never have taken place. Special thanks are also due to Professors Robert Bailey (New York University), Leon Botstein (Bard College), Christopher Hailey (Franz Schreker Foundation, Inc.), Janet Schmalfeldt (Tufts University), and Christoph Wolff (Harvard University), who chaired sessions at the conference. The following people granted permission to reproduce documents from their archives: Hofrat Dr. Günter Brosche (Österreichische Nationalbibliothek, Musiksammlung, Vienna), Pater Dr. Alfons Mandorfer (Musikarchiv des Benediktinerstiftes, Kremsmünster), and Dr. Elisabeth Maier (Anton Bruckner Institut Linz). The cover reproduction is from the Österreichische Nationalbibliothek, Musiksammlung, Mus. Hs. 2106.

Finally the editors wish to convey their deepest appreciation to the Albert Goldman Memorial Bruckner Fund for its generous financial support of the present publication. The fund was established in Mr. Goldman's memory by his friends. A well-known writer on popular music, Mr. Goldman was also a passionate admirer of Bruckner. He owned a large collection of recordings of Bruckner's music, including many rare early performances, to which he listened constantly. Only a final illness prevented Mr. Goldman from attending the Connecticut College Bruckner Conference. This book is gratefully dedicated to his memory.

TIMOTHY L. JACKSON *Connecticut College*
PAUL HAWKSHAW *Yale School of Music*

Abbreviations

Kr   Kremsmünster: Benediktinerstift, Musikarchiv

Wgm   Vienna: Library of the Gesellschaft der Musikfreunde

Wn   Vienna: Österreichische Nationalbibliothek, Musiksammlung

Wst   Vienna: Wiener Stadt- und Landesbibliothek, Musiksammlung

Auer, *Bruckner gesammelte Briefe*   Auer, Max, ed. *Anton Bruckner. Gesammelte Briefe. Neue Folge.* Regensburg: Gustav Bosse, 1924.

Göllerich–Auer   Göllerich, August and Auer, Max. *Anton Bruckner. ein Lebens- und Schaffensbild.* 4 vols. in 9. Regensburg: Gustav Bosse, 1922–37.

Gräflinger, *Bruckner gesammelte Briefe*   Gräflinger, Franz, ed. *Anton Bruckner. Gesammelte Briefe.* Regensburg: Gustav Bosse, 1924.

Bruckner Sämtliche Werke A   Haas, Robert and Orel, Alfred, eds. *Anton Bruckner Sämtliche Werke, Kritische Gesamtausgabe*, im Auftrage der Generaldirektion der Österreichischen Nationalbibliothek und der Internationalen Bruckner-Gesellschaft. Various publishers, 1930–53.

Bruckner Sämtliche Werke B   Nowak, Leopold, ed. *Anton Bruckner Sämtliche Werke, Kritische Gesamtausgabe*, herausgeben von der Generaldirektion der Österreichischen Nationalbibliothek und der Internationalen Bruckner-Gesellschaft. Vienna: Musikwissenschaftlicher Verlag der Internationalen Bruckner-Gesellschaft, 1951–.

1 An anatomy of change: Anton Bruckner's revisions to the Mass in F Minor

Paul Hawkshaw

Anton Bruckner's revisions and his students' tampering have been a source of editorial distress for most of this century. He was an inveterate reviser throughout much of his career and, late in his life, relied upon his students in preparations for publication. Most of his major works survive in more than one manuscript version and many exist in early editions which are different yet again. As a result this century has witnessed the publication of an imposing array of scores including not one, but two Collected Works Editions, and a substantial portion of the secondary literature on the composer has been devoted to assessing the relative merits of various versions and speculating as to their *raison d'être*.[1] In particular the battle over the reliability of early prints as opposed to the manuscripts has been hard-fought, often on terrain far removed from music.[2] Although the manuscript versions have achieved supremacy in the eyes of performers and scholars in recent years, many text-critical aspects of the Bruckner legacy remain shrouded in mystery. Crucial sources, especially *Stichvorlagen* for many early editions, have disappeared, and an

---

[1] For lists of published scores of major works see Arthur D. Walker, "Bruckner's Works: A List of the Published Scores of the Various Versions," *Brio* 3 (Autumn 1966), 4–9 and Renate Grasberger, *Werkverzeichnis Anton Bruckner* (Tutzing: Hans Schneider Verlag, 1977), pp. 246–53. For selected points of view see Max Auer, "Der Streit um den 'echten' Bruckner im Licht biographischer Tatsachen," *Zeitschrift für Musikwissenschaft* 103 (May and October 1936), 538–45 and 1191–96; Deryck Cooke, "The Bruckner Problem Simplified," *Musical Times* 110 (January, February, April, May, and August 1969), 20–22, 142–44, 362–65, 479–82, and 828; Franz Grasberger, *Anton Bruckner zwischen Wagnis und Sicherheit*, (Graz: Akademische Druck- und Verlagsanstalt, 1977); Grasberger, *Anton Bruckner in Wien. Eine kritische Studie zu seiner Persönlichkeit*, Anton Bruckner Dokumente und Studien, no. 2 (Graz: Akademische Druck- und Verlagsanstalt, 1980); *Bruckner-Symposion Bericht "Die Fassungen,"* ed. Grasberger (Graz: Akademische Druck- und Verlagsanstalt, 1981); Max Morold, "Der wahre Bruckner?", *Zeitschrift für Musikwissenschaft* 103 (May 1936), 533–37; Morold, "Noch einiges zur Bruckner-Frage," *Zeitschrift für Musikwissenschaft* 103 (October 1936), 1187–90; Leopold Nowak, "Urfassung und Endfassung bei Bruckner," *Bericht über den Internationalen Musikwissenschaftlichen Kongress. Wien. Mozartjahr 1956*, ed. Erich Schenk (Graz: Hermann Bölhaus Nachf., 1958), pp. 448–51; and Geoffrey Sharp, "Anton Bruckner: Simpleton or Mystic?", *Music Review* 3 (February 1942), 46–54.

[2] See Benjamin Korstvedt's study in the present volume for a history of this debate. He believes there is reason to reconsider these issues.

enormous amount of source-critical analysis remains to be done on those which are available. Why Bruckner revised, when he did it (numerous autograph dates notwithstanding), what he altered on specific occasions, and the extent of his involvement in the preparation of published scores are lingering questions for many of his works.

On the premise that present-day Bruckner scholarship must address these questions one work at a time, the exclusive concern of this article is the Mass in F Minor. The Mass is a useful case study because its history touches upon every controversial and problematic aspect of the "versions" question. Often cited for its numerous revisions and foreign incursions, not to mention the stormy provenance of its autograph score, it was first published in 1894 by Doblinger, in a much altered form, the product of solicitous efforts on the part of Josef Schalk.[3] Schalk's alterations have been purged from two different publications (manuscript versions) in the *Gesamtausgabe*, one by Robert Haas and one by Leopold Nowak.[4] Both transmit mixed stages of the composer's own revisions, and neither contains the "original" version of 1868. That score has yet to be published.[5]

The present study traces the chronology of Bruckner's revisions as they are preserved in the primary sources for his Mass in F Minor. What did *he* change, when, and why? The alterations occurred in four stages which are not always easy to discern – early revisions, 1877/81, the 1890s, and the first edition. The process of separating the layers and analyzing them in this order leads to three conclusions:

1. Haas and Nowak were correct to use Bruckner's manuscripts, rather than the first print, as the basis for their modern editions of the F Minor Mass. The first print contains an "arrangement" of the score and not a

[3] Thomas Leibnitz, *Die Brüder Schalk und Anton Bruckner* (Tutzing: Hans Schneider, 1988), p. 192, cites a letter dated 24 May 1894 from Josef to Franz Schalk in which the former indicates that the Doblinger edition (title page undated) was in preparation. The autograph manuscript was at the center of a well-publicized dispute between the Music Collection of the Austrian National Library and Lilly Schalk. Robert Haas, "Die Originalpartitur von Bruckners Messe in F-moll," *Der Auftakt* 4 (1924), 106–09. Haas, "Die neue Bruckner-Bewegung," *Zeitschrift für Musikwissenschaft* 103 (October 1936), 1185.

[4] Robert Haas, ed., *Bruckner Sämtliche Werke A*, XIV (published 1944); Leopold Nowak, ed., *Bruckner Sämtliche Werke B*, XVIII (published 1960). Neither editor prepared a critical

report. Leopold Nowak, "Die Messe in F-moll von Anton Bruckner," *Österreichische Musik Zeitschrift* 15 (September 1960), 429–31 provides an overview of the revisions as well as a discussion of the differences between his and Haas's editions. A third modern edition, by Hans Ferdinand Redlich, is also available: *Anton Bruckner: Mass in F Minor* (London: Ernst Eulenburg, 1967). Redlich's score is the same as the Haas edition. He provided an often perceptive, but vituperative introduction lamenting that Leopold Nowak, then Director of the Music Collection of the Austrian National Library, had denied him access to the primary sources.

[5] It will appear along with detailed descriptions of the sources discussed in this chapter in Paul Hawkshaw, ed., *Bruckner Sämtliche Werke B*, XVIII, Revisionsbericht.

legitimate version for which the composer was responsible. This article will demonstrate that Bruckner disapproved of its content and criticized it, in writing, for its editors' failure to recognize the very things he had devoted years of revision to correcting in his manuscripts.

2. Many of Bruckner's revisions in the manuscripts were the practical results of years of professional performances in the Viennese Hofkapelle – performances in which Bruckner himself participated as organist.

3. His other revisions were influenced by detailed studies of music of his predecessors, particularly of Mozart's Requiem.

Of principal concern in this study are alterations in pitch, orchestration, and structure which Bruckner made after his initial completion of the score.[6] What emerges is *not* a picture of an insecure, adulation-seeking composer with a counting mania, as Bruckner has often been portrayed. Rather, the process of analyzing his layers of change in the Mass sources reveals a professional composer at work systematically "fine-tuning" his score throughout a quarter century of performances and meticulous self-analyses.

I

First some chronological facts about the Mass: Bruckner began the work in Linz in late summer 1867 and finished his first version approximately one year later. The earliest surviving autograph date, 14 September 1867, appears on a Kyrie sketch, and the end of the autograph score is dated 9 September 1868.[7] Although rehearsals began in November 1868, the first performance did not take place until 16 June 1872 in the Augustinerkirche, Vienna, with Bruckner conducting.[8] He conducted the Mass again on 8 December 1873, this time in the Hofkapelle where the work remained in the repertoire throughout his career.[9] The first

[6] With the exception of an early score draft discussed in the first example, the sketch process as well as discrepancies between surviving sketches and the score are not considered. See Paul Hawkshaw, "Weiteres über die Arbeitsweise Anton Bruckners während seiner Linzer Jahren. Der Inhalt von Kremsmünster C56. 2," in *Bruckner-Symposion Bericht 1992* (Vienna: Musikwissenschaftlicher Verlag, 1995), pp. 143–52. Also discrepancies in dynamics and other performance directions are not discussed, even though many of these eminated from Bruckner himself and coincided (both in time as well as in their location in the sources) with alterations described here.

[7] Wn Mus. Hs. 2106, fols. 123r. and 120v. respectively.
[8] Performer's rehearsal date, 20 November 1868, Viola 1 part, Wn Mus. Hs. 6075, fol. 401v. Bruckner's annotation in the autograph score re. date of the first performance is found on Wn Mus. Hs. 2106, fol. 120v.
[9] Theophil Antonicek, *Anton Bruckner und die Wiener Hofmusikkapelle*, Anton Bruckner. Dokumente und Studien, vol. I (Graz: Akademische Druck- und Verlagsanstalt, 1979), p. 142. By the end of the century the work had also found its way into the repertories of major choruses throughout Europe. Göllerich–Auer IV/4, p. 255.

Table 1.1. *Manuscript sources for the Mass in F Minor*

Source	Description	Date
1. Wn Mus. Hs. 2106, fols. 123r.–124v.	Autograph Kyrie sketches	14 Sept.–19 Oct. 1867
2. Kr C56.2, fols. 6r.–12v.	Autograph Gloria, Credo sketches	21 Nov. 1867 (Credo)
3. Wn Mus. Hs. 2106, fols. 9r.–10v.	Autograph Kyrie score bifolio 4	before 1 Mar. 1868
4. Kr C56.2, fols. 13r.–18v.	Autograph Credo score bifolios 10, 17, 18	21 Nov. 1867 (bif. 10); completed 15 Feb. 1868 (bif. 18)
5. Wn Mus. Hs. 2106, fols. 79r.–80v.	Autograph Credo score bifolio 16	before 15 Feb. 1868
6. Wn Mus. Hs. 2106	Autograph score (entries by Johann Noll)	completed 9 Sept. 1868; revised Aug. 1876, 1877, and 1881
7. Wn Mus. Hs. 31.246	Copy score (autograph entries)	before 1 Oct. 1868
8. Wn Mus. Hs. 6075	Copy parts (autograph entries)	before 20 Nov. 1868; additions before 30 Jul. 1876
9. Wn Mus. Hs. 6015	Copy score	between 1877 and 1881; revised 1881 and 1893/94
10. Wn Mus. Hs. 29.302	Copy score by Johann Noll (Entries by Josef Schalk)	Nov. 1883
11. Wgm I57.583	Copy parts	1889–93

concert performance took place with the chorus of the Wiener akademischer Wagner-Verein and the Capelle Eduard Strauss under Josef Schalk in the Grosser Musikvereinsal, Vienna, on 23 March 1893.[10] The surviving primary manuscript sources for the Mass are listed in table 1; they date from 1867 to 1893.

Strictly speaking plate 1 falls outside the purview of a study of Bruckner's *revisions* because it involves a bifolio removed during the initial composition of the Mass. It concerns a passage which Bruckner

---

[10] Wgm I57.583 parts: trumpet 1, horns 2, 3, and 4 have performers' signatures and dates referring to the 1893 performance.

was still changing as late as 1881 and illustrates a very important distinction between Bruckner's compositional and revisionist activities as they are reflected in sources for the F Minor Mass. In large works such as Masses or symphonies, Bruckner composed in layers on bifolios arranged successively and numbered by movement. If he was unhappy with a particular passage, excessive emendation led to his discarding an entire bifolio and replacing it with a new one.[11] He often followed the same procedure revising a work. Extensive alteration caused him to replace or, later in his career, paste over original bifolios in both autograph and copy scores. As a result a proliferation of discarded score bifolios in varying states of completion survives for many Bruckner pieces including the F Minor Mass.

The bifolio reproduced, in part, in plate 1.1 (table 1, no. 4) stems from the earliest stages of work on the Mass and is described best as a score sketch. It is an incomplete Credo bifolio 10; the wind staves are blank waiting for either music or rests. A comparison with the published scores illustrates that the complete version is quite different. It has a clearer Bb–Db harmonic axis on its way to the F which closes the section; relies on Alberti-like figurations as opposed to arpeggios; and its vocal parts place more textual emphasis on "judicare" rather than "vivos et mortuos."[12] Evidence that Bruckner replaced the bifolio of plate 1.1 at an early stage is provided by the dedication copy, Wn Mus. Hs. 31.246 (table 1.1, no. 7). This manuscript contains the reading of the bifolio as it existed in the autograph score prior to revisions which Bruckner made in 1881.[13] Prepared by Bruckner's most important anonymous Linz copyist, Wn Mus. Hs. 31.246 was signed and dated by the composer 1 October 1868.[14] The Kremsmünster tenth Credo bifolio had already been replaced by that date.

---

[11] Paul Hawkshaw, "The Manuscript Sources for Anton Bruckner's Linz Works: A Study of his Working Methods from 1856 to 1868" (Ph.D. diss., Columbia University, 1984), pp. 185–203. His copyists were often involved in the replacement process.

[12] Compare, for example, Leopold Nowak, *Bruckner Sämtliche Werke B*, XVIII, 105ff. Because it is the most accessible, measure and page numbers in this edition will serve as the point of reference for the remainder of the chapter. A point of interest as far as Bruckner's working procedures are concerned: the manuscript page in plate 1.1 has an autograph date, "21. Nov." The same date is found on a sketch for the same music (table 1.1, no. 2) as well as on the present tenth bifolio of the autograph score, Kr C56.2, fol. 12r. and Wn

Mus. Hs. 2106, fol. 67r. respectively. At this point in the movement Bruckner must have worked on a sketch, started, and restarted the score all on the same day. 21 November is also the date of Karl Waldeck's anecdote about Bruckner improvising parts of the Credo at the piano. Göllerich–Auer, III/1, pp. 472–73.

[13] To be discussed as plate 1.9, a revision which affected the same section of the movement.

[14] Wn Mus. Hs. 31.246, fol. 97v. Antonicek, *Bruckner und die Hofmusikkapelle*, pp. 148f., contains a facsimile of the signature page. For more on Bruckner's Linz copyists see Paul Hawkshaw, "Die Kopisten Anton Bruckners während seines Aufenthaltes in Linz," in *Bruckner-Symposion Bericht 1990* (Vienna: Musikwissenschaftlicher Verlag, 1993), pp. 225–40.

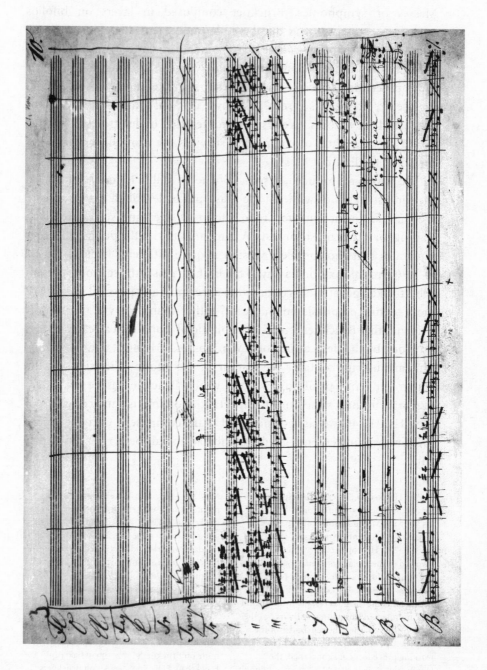

Plate 1.1a   Kr C56.2, fol. 13r. (Credo mm. 255ff, score sketch)

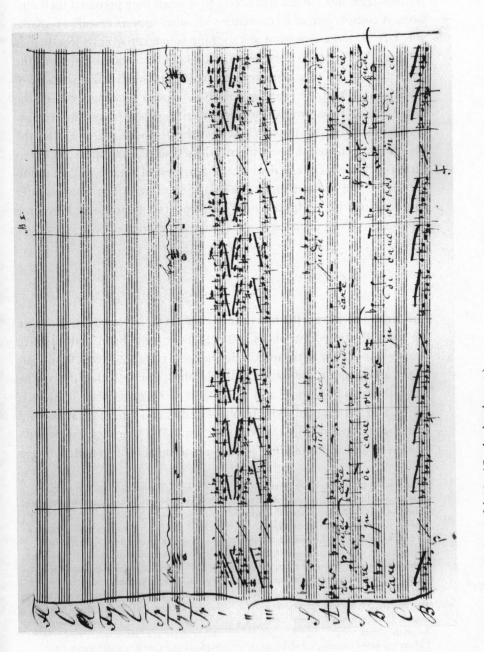

Plate 1.1b Kr C56.2, fol. 13v. (Credo sketch cont.)

The copy score, Wn Mus. Hs. 31.246, is of critical importance to understanding the genesis of the F Minor Mass and its revisions because it contains the only surviving reading of the earliest complete version.[15] Neither Haas nor Nowak had access to it when they prepared their editions. A comparison of its contents with other sources reveals a remarkable fact: with the exception of a soprano solo taken over by woodwinds at the end of the Credo (table 1.2, no. 10), for all intents and purposes, the vocal parts of the Mass were never altered after 1868.[16] The discussion of plate 1.1 demonstrated that, as was to be expected, changes during the initial composition process included rewriting vocal parts. The remainder of this investigation will show that the revisions did not. After the Mass was completed in 1868, the vocal parts were, so to speak, its structural skeleton which remained intact regardless of what Bruckner did to the rest of the body of the score. The 1868 score differs from its later counterparts in orchestration, instrumental figuration, harmonic content of orchestral passages, and phrase structure.

II

The earliest revisions which Bruckner made to his Mass are listed in table 1.2 and illustrated in plates 1.2–1.5. Following his usual practice Bruckner made the Kyrie and Credo changes (table 1.2, nos. 2, 9, and 10) in the autograph score by removing bifolios and replacing them. The original Credo bifolios 17 and 18 are now in Kremsmünster (table 1.1, no. 4), and the original Kyrie bifolio 4 and Credo bifolio 16 are bound with the autograph score (table 1, nos. 3 and 5).[17] The autograph Credo bifolios 13 and 14 containing the earlier reading of no. 9 in table 1.2 were

[15] Wn Mus. Hs. 31.246 probably came into the possession of the dedicatee, Anton Ritter Imhof von Geisslinghof, soon after Bruckner signed it. Antonicek, *Bruckner und die Hofmusikkapelle*, pp. 148ff. It almost certainly did not remain with the composer because, unlike the autograph and other materials to which Bruckner had access during his Vienna years, it was not subject to later revision. It came into the possession of the Austrian National Library from a Professor Louis Dité in the 1960s.

[16] There was a nine-measure cut of the entire ensemble in the Gloria (table 1.2, no. 5). Also the vocal parts of the Credo were affected, on occasion, by the addition and removal of individual measures during the metrical revisions of the 1870s and 1880s as will be

discussed below. See also note 39 concerning the eventual deletion of an alternative version of the Soprano solo in the Agnus Dei, mm. 76–78.

[17] Redlich, *Mass F Minor*, pp. 40ff., contains a discussion and facsimile of Kremsmünster bifolio 18. The two Vienna bifolios are bound in their respective places in the autograph score as though they had never been superseded. Their replacements are presently located at the end of the autograph, fols. 125r.–126v. and 127r.–128v. respectively. How this arrangement came about is a mystery. Without question Bruckner intended the reading in the replacement bifolios to prevail because it is found in all surviving sources (other than Wn Mus. Hs 31.246) including the instrumental parts which had to be corrected as a result of the changes (see below).

Table 1.2. *Distinguishing features of the first version of the Mass in F Minor preserved in the copy score, Wn Mus. Hs. 31.246, and altered during early revision stages*

A. Passages altered prior to 20 Nov. 1868.
B. Passages altered between Nov. 1868 and Apr. 1873.
C. Subsequent alterations copied with the 1877 revisions in Wn Mus. Hs. 6015.

Kyrie

1.	66–71	A	solos are more independent of the chorus (compare Haas with Nowak. See note 20).
2.	101–21	B	violin figurations continue as sixteenths throughout (plate 1.2).

Gloria

3.	100–11	C	upper pitch of violin trills is unspecified.
4.	157–59	C	soprano and alto are chorus, not solo.
5.	169–77	B	these measures are in Wn 31.246; cut from later sources.
6.	301 and 303, beat 3	C	oboe 1 has c^2 and b^1 respectively.
7.	238–end	B	less instrumental doubling of the fugue subject and its inversion (plate 1.3).

Credo

8.	186–89	A	trombone chorale is not doubled by French horns.
9.	349–58 and 377–97	B	violin and viola figurations recall a trill motive which originates in the Kyrie, m. 22, and plays a rôle in the Gloria, mm. 100–15 (see note 18). Texture is more contrapuntal (plate 1.4).
10.	437–end	B	violin figurations in the fugal sections again rely on the trill motive, this time combined with a triplet (plate 1.5). Wn 31.246 (mm. 479–515) has an extensive soprano solo which, in later scores, is largely given over to oboes and flutes. What survived in the voice part (mm. 509–514) is less chromatic and less virtuosic.

Benedictus

11.	52, beat 4	C	violin 2 is $b\flat^1$ quarter note.

mentioned by Göllerich–Auer as being in Bruckner's *Nachlass* but are now lost.[18] Bruckner wrote the remaining alterations, including the additional Gloria fugue doublings (table 1.2, no. 7), directly into the autograph score as illustrated in plate 1.3 where new flute parts cover the original measure rests.

Precisely when Bruckner made each of these changes is difficult to determine. That they were not all made at the same time is illustrated by the manuscript parts which, with the exception of four later additions – altos 2 and 5, second violin part 3, and cello – were prepared for the first rehearsal of 20 November 1868.[19] The two alterations designated by the letter "A" in table 1.2 (nos. 1 and 8) had been made by then because the new readings were copied directly into their respective parts.[20] All remaining alterations came later because the original parts had to be pasted over or otherwise corrected in the affected measures. Plate 1.6 illustrates a page of the second trombone part which had to be changed in order to accommodate the additional doubling in the Gloria fugue and the rehearsal letters (Plate 1.6, lines 2 and 9) absent from Wn Mus. Hs. 31.246.

Some assistance in differentiating chronological layers among the later changes listed in table 1.2 is provided by the four additions to the original set of parts. Their copyists omitted the nine measures (table 1.2, no. 5) which had to be crossed out of the Gloria in the other parts (see plate 1.6, lines 3–4). Yet both new alto parts had to be emended in order to accommodate the change from chorus to solo, Gloria mm. 157–59 (table 1.2, no. 4); this revision must have post-dated the Gloria cut. A Viennese copyist, Tenschert, added the second violin part 3 and cello.[21] He was able to copy all changes affecting these parts except the Gloria trill clarifications and the adjustment from a quarter to two eighths in the Benedictus (table 1.2, nos. 3 and 11).[22] Another relatively late change occurred in the first oboe, Gloria mm. 301–03 (table 1.2, no. 6); the new reading was

[18] Göllerich–Auer III/1, pp. 468, provides an example of the violin trill motive which permeated the original version at this point.
[19] Wn Mus. Hs. 6075 (table 1.1, no. 8). See note 8.
[20] In the autograph Wn Mus. Hs. 2106, fol. 62r., the new horn parts, Credo mm. 186–89 (table 1.2, no. 8), are added in pencil. Haas was mistaken in his assertion that this change was made in 1881 (*Bruckner Sämtliche Werke A*, XIV, 93). Nowak failed to correct this misconception in his edition, *Bruckner Sämtliche Werke B*, XVIII, 93. The other alteration copied directly into the parts occurred in the soprano and bass solos in the Kyrie, mm. 66–71 (table 1.2, no. 1). (Wn Mus. Hs. 6075, fol. 2r., for example.)

Bruckner also made this change in pencil in the autograph, Wn Mus. Hs. 2106, fol. 7r. Robert Haas incorrectly included the earliest reading in his edition, *Bruckner Sämtliche Werke A*, XIV, 13–14; Nowak has the later version, *Bruckner Sämtliche Werke B*, XVIII, 13–14. Because its third bifolio is missing, it is impossible to know whether this alteration predated the preparation of Wn Mus. Hs. 31.246.
[21] Hawkshaw, "Manuscript Sources," pp. 330–31.
[22] The original reading of the second violin part, which would have clashed with the second soprano, was almost certainly an error on Bruckner's part in the autograph score. Why it took so long to correct is a mystery.

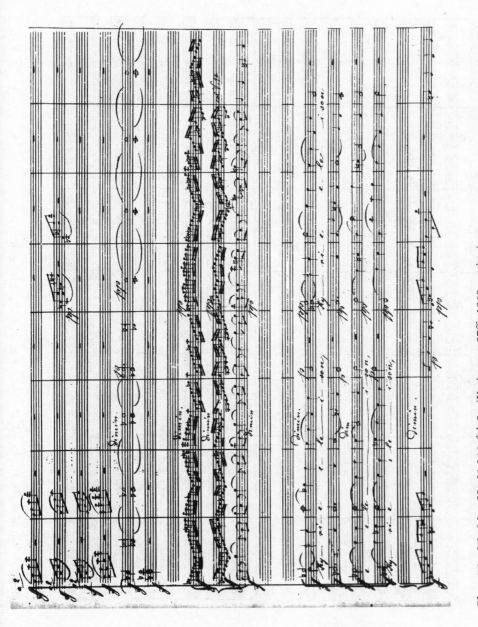

Plate 1.2   Wn Mus. Hs. 31.246, fol. 5v. (Kyrie mm. 97ff., 1868 version)

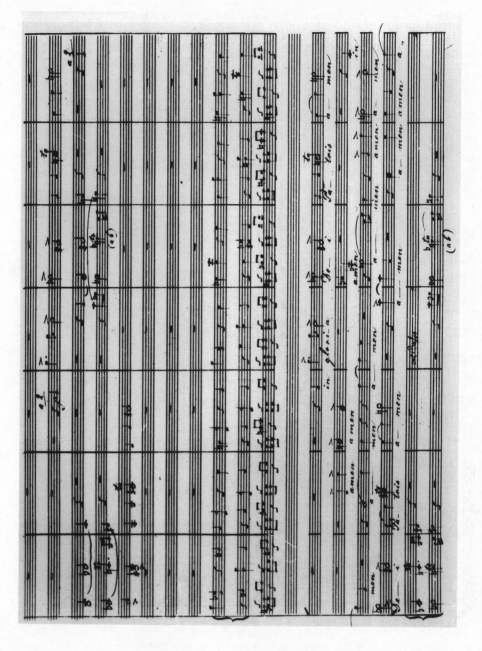

Plate 1.3a Wn Mus. Hs. 31.246, fol. 28v. (Gloria mm. 244ff., 1868 version)

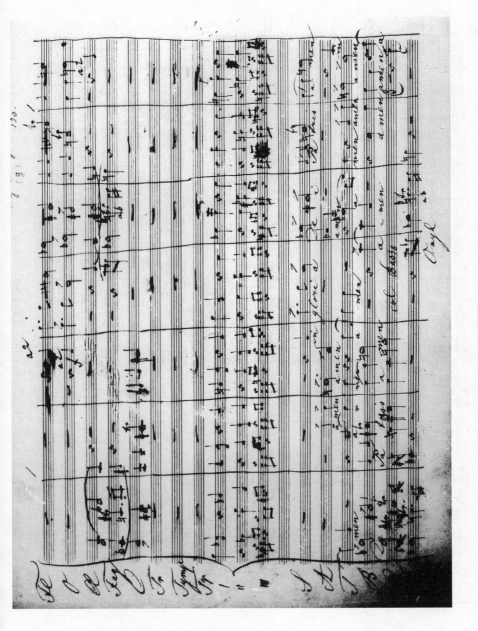

Plate 1.3b Wn Mus. Hs. 2106, fol. 36v. (Gloria mm. 244ff., early revision)

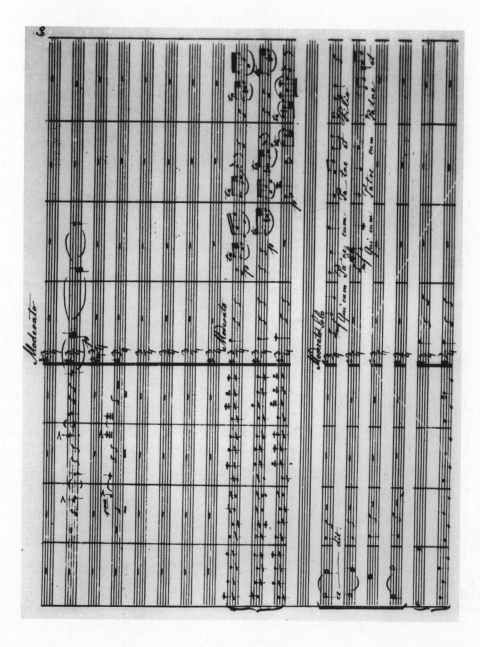

Plate 1.4   Wn Mus. Hs. 31.246, fol. 60r. (Credo mm. 344ff, 1868 version)

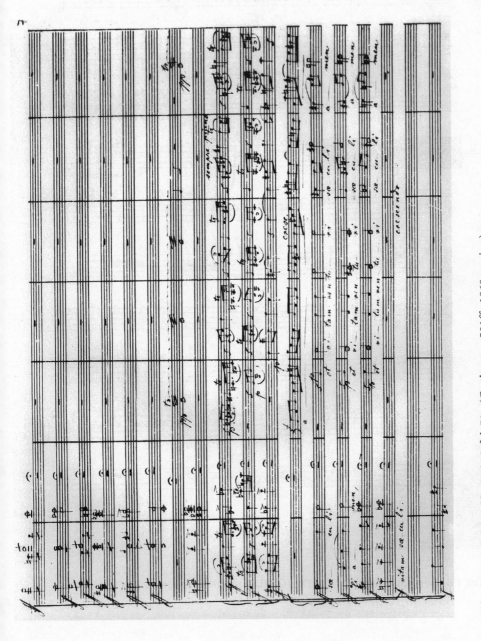

Plate 1.5 Wn Mus. Hs. 31.246, fol. 71r. (Credo mm. 501ff., 1868 version)

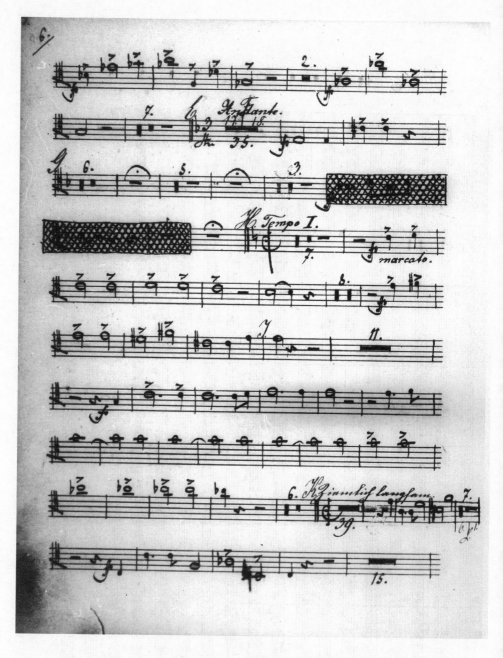

Plate 1.6   Wn Mus. Hs. 6075, fol. 597v. (Gloria mm. 101ff.), Trombone 2

added in the part to the insert containing the additional fugue doublings (table 1.2, no. 7).[23] The four late changes (nos. 3, 4, 6, and 11) are designated in table 1.2 by the letter "C".

All other revisions which post-dated the first rehearsal of November 1868 are denoted with the letter "B." There is no question that Bruckner had made these intermediate changes by the summer of 1876 because Tenschert's violin part has a performer's date, 30 July of that year.[24] As well, the bifolios Bruckner removed from the autograph score in the course of making these alterations contain neither the annotations nor the metrical numbers he added in pencil to the manuscript when he returned to work on it during August 1876.[25]

The alto part 5, with the Gloria cut, has a performer's signature and date, 27 April 1873.[26] Although it cannot be demonstrated conclusively, it is tempting to assume that Bruckner had made his other "B" changes by that date as well, in conjunction with rehearsals in 1868–69 or the performances of 1872–73.[27] Their net result was to render the piece easier to perform, something he may well have wanted to do as a consequence of, or in preparation for, the early hearings. The most extensive revisions (table 1.2, nos. 2, 9, and 10), for example, produced accompanimental textures which are more transparent, less hectic, and simpler to play; no. 10 also resulted in a far less formidable solo; soprano and alto choristers will be forever grateful for being relieved of the responsibility of singing the soft, high notes in the Gloria (no. 4); and the lines in the Gloria fugue (no. 7) and Credo chorale (no. 8) are more secure with the extra doubling. Late in his life, reminiscing about the history of the F Minor Mass to August Göllerich, Bruckner remarked:

> In January 1869 there was a second rehearsal after which Herbeck came to me and said, "I liked the D Minor Mass – but this one I cannot perform

[23] Wn Mus. Hs. 6075, fol. 495v.

[24] Wn Mus. Hs. 6075, fol. 363r.

[25] In Wn. Mus. Hs. 2106, the Kyrie (fol. 1r.), Sanctus (fol. 87r.), Benedictus (fol. 95r.), and Agnus Dei (fol. 111r.) have the autograph remark, "rythmisch gut"; on the Gloria (fol. 47r.) Bruckner wrote "rythmisch geändert" and on the Credo (fol. 87r.) "rythmisch fertig." The Kyrie annotation is dated 13 August 1876, and the Gloria 16 August of the same year; although the others have no dates, they almost certainly stem from the same period. They refer to metrical numbers Bruckner wrote under the measures throughout the autograph. How Bruckner used these numbers to analyze and, in some cases, alter metrical grids operating in his

music are questions only beginning to be answered. See, for example, Timothy L. Jackson, "Bruckner's Metrical Numbers," in *Nineteenth Century Music* (Spring 1990), 101–31. Indications are that, in 1876 in the F minor Mass, the numbers served primarily analytical purposes; I have been unable to identify any place which Bruckner rhythmically or metrically altered as a result of their addition to the autograph score. He did not add or delete measures as he did in later revisions (see below). What he intended by the phrase "rythmisch geändert" in reference to the Gloria is a mystery.

[26] Wn Mus. Hs. 6075, fol. 129v.

[27] Wn Mus. Hs. 6075, fol. 401v. also has rehearsal dates 16 and 18 January 1869.

because it is too long and unsingable!" He wanted me to double the voice parts with the violins. Then I also made substantial changes.[28]

III

In 1877 and again in 1881 Bruckner made further alterations to the Credo of the Mass. Both dates are found in the autograph score of that movement.[29] After the 1877 revisions he ordered a new copy score, Wn Mus. Hs. 6015 (table 1.1, no. 9); its copyists also included the four late changes listed in table 1.2.[30] Bruckner had to make the 1881 alterations in this manuscript himself. The Mass was performed in the Hofkapelle on 30 July 1876, 17 June 1877, and 30 April 1882.[31] Again there can be little doubt that the correspondence between performance and revision dates was more than coincidence.

Alterations during these years were not nearly so extensive as the earlier ones. They included:

1. Pitch changes in the violins and violas mm. 61–68 and m. 372, beats 1–2, as a result of concerns over doubling the vocal parts (1877).
2. Adding or removing individual measures as part of further metrical analyses. In 1877 he added five measures; in 1881 he added twelve more and deleted five others.[32]
3. Delicate harmonic adjustments approaching the close of the "descendit de coelis" (mm. 105–16) and "judicare" (mm. 285–96) sections.

A major factor in the 1877 revisions was Bruckner's analyses of meter and voice leading in music by Beethoven and Mozart. His notes on works by

[28] Göllerich–Auer, IV/1, p. 78. There is no physical evidence to indicate that Herbeck had a direct hand in any of the alterations. Redlich, *Mass F Minor*, p. 41, was of the view that Bruckner had completed the revisions to the end of the Credo in time for the 1872 performance.
[29] Wn Mus. Hs. 2106, fol. 53r., for example, has the autograph date 1877 and 54v., 1881.
[30] How Wn Mus. Hs. 6015 came to be assembled in its present configuration is mysterious. Pagination and foliation numbers and the confluence of handwriting of two copyists suggests that the Credo and Benedictus once belonged to a different

manuscript or, at least, were prepared separately from the other movements. See Hawkshaw, "Manuscript Sources," pp. 333–34.
[31] Antonicek, *Bruckner und die Hofmusikkapelle*, p. 142.
[32] These will be listed and described in detail in the forthcoming Critical Report. The additions and deletions were almost always repeated measures as in plates 1.8d and 1.9b. The 1868 reading in plate 1.4 is also missing Credo m. 344 which was added in 1881. With the exception of the passages in plates 1.8 and 1.9, these metrical alterations seldom involved rewriting of the surrounding measures.

both composers can be found in his calendars of 1876 and 1877.[33] Of particular importance for the F Minor Mass were his studies of Mozart's Requiem. Timothy Jackson has observed that Bruckner was especially interested in Mozart's doubling of the vocal parts with the upper strings.[34] At the top of fol. 36v. of the autograph score of the Mass, for example, Bruckner referred to pages 30, 41, 127, and 130 in the Breitkopf und Härtel (Leipzig: [1800]) edition of the Requiem and noted that, on page 127, Mozart had doubled the first violins with the tenor (see plate 1.3b). In the F Minor Mass, the most extensive revision to result from these studies took place in the Credo mm. 61–68. (Compare the 1868 reading of plate 1.7 with Nowak's score.) As Jackson observed, Bruckner changed the violins and violas to reinforce the sopranos in octaves, mm. 63–64, and eliminate parallels, especially with the tenors and basses in mm. 61–63. An interesting aside to Bruckner's interest in the Mozart work in the mid 1870s is that he began his own unfinished Requiem in D minor on 18 September 1875.[35]

The next two examples illustrate a fascinating series of remarkably subtle alterations from the year 1881 in the approaches to two cadences in the Credo. These are not major structural changes; they are delicate adjustments to the harmonic and metrical *Klang* which result from subtle shifts in pitch emphases. Plates 1.8a–d concern the closing measures of the "judicare." Plates 1.8a and b contain the 1868 reading; plates 1.8c and d have the 1881 revision in the autograph score. On the surface the deletion of the bar on fol. 69r. of the autograph (plate 1.8d) serves to regularize the nine-measure phrase which Bruckner had numbered in 1876 in pencil and again in 1877 in ink. One wonders why the metrical structure required correcting in 1881 when it had passed muster, not once, but twice a few years earlier. In fact, as indicated by Bruckner's final (1881) ink set of numbers identifying two phrases of six bars (plates 1.8c–d), concern for eight-measure periodicity had no bearing on the decision-making process.

In 1881, in this passage, Bruckner adjusted the aural weight of the

[33] Alfred Orel, "Eine Mozartstudie Anton Bruckners," *Mozart-Almanach* (1941), pp. 105–11 and Göllerich-Auer IV/1, pp. 443f. Bruckner's pocket calendar for the year 1876, for example, contains his notes on the metrical structure of Beethoven symphonies 3, 4, and 9. Wn Mus. Hs. 3181, fols. 11v., 13r., and 15r.

[34] Timothy L. Jackson, "Bruckner's *Oktaven*: A Study of his Notes on Mozart's Requiem," *Music and Letters* 78/3, forthcoming. The article includes a detailed description of analyses Bruckner made in 1877, in conjunction with his Mozart and Beethoven studies, of the voice leading in the vocal and string parts of the Gloria fugue and Credo of the F Minor Mass. Jackson observes that Bruckner was especially concerned with parallels which sometimes resulted from string doubling of the vocal parts.

[35] Wn Mus. Hs. 2105 is an autograph eighteen-measure sketch for the beginning of a Requiem.

Plate 1.7 Wn Mus. Hs. 31.246, fol. 40r. (Credo mm. 58ff., 1868 version)

pitches of B♭ and F, the latter serving as the cadential point of the section (plates 1.8b and d, m. 296). In m. 285 he changed the violas, cellos, and basses to coincide with the violins. In the next measure the presence of F was ameliorated by the delay of the trombone entry by a bar (compare plates 1.8a and c, mm. 286–87). Then it was reinforced for four measures by the trombones whose harmonic changes – most notably the moves to B♭ in mm. 287 and 289 – were eliminated in favor of octave Fs. Bruckner also eliminated the B♭s in the tenor and bass voices in the second half of m. 289. In the next measure, as though he wished to restore some vigor to the now-subdued B♭, he gave it a stronger presence in the revised string figurations. B♭ here closes, albeit in a transitory manner given the prevailing tempo and downward trajectory of the bass line to F, the first of Bruckner's six-measure phrases. The elimination of the repeated bar with its passing reference to B♭ on the next page (plates 8b and d, mm. 291–92) hastens the emergence of F (itself on its way to E to open the "cujus regni", m. 297) and results in a second six-measure phrase. As a final touch, Bruckner repeated the bass F, m. 296.[36]

An equally fascinating, aurally more perceptible, revision took place in 1881 in a similar passage preceding the cadence before the "Et incarnatus" (plates 1.9a–b). Again the alteration concerned the pitches F and B♭ before a move to E. Here the E (major) of the new section is much stronger, and the cadential pitch is G. Bruckner added mm. 105 and 114 (plate 1.9b; m. 105 cannot be seen in the facsimile) strengthening the G. In the revision the clear G major quality of the cadence was eliminated in favor of a stronger presence of B♭ and F and, ultimately, unison Gs. Bruckner emphasized the distinction between the two sections (as opposed to smoothing the transition as he did with the extra F in plate 1.8) by putting a fermata on the final rest.[37]

IV

In November 1883 another copyist, Johann Noll, prepared a new score of the F Minor Mass, Wn Mus. Hs. 29.302 (table 1.1, no. 10), which incorporated all the changes Bruckner had made by the end of 1881.[38] Robert Haas published this version but restored the nine-measure Gloria cut (table 1.2, no. 5) noted with an editorial "VI-DE" and, for some

---

[36] This is part of the same passage Bruckner rewrote when he removed his original bifolio 10 from the Credo in November 1867 (see plate 1.1). The relative importance of B♭ was an issue at that point as well.

[37] Haas mistakenly did not include this fermata in his edition.
[38] Noll signed and dated the score on fol. 43v., 19 November 1883 (end of the Gloria) and fol. 89v., 29 November 1883 (end of the Credo).

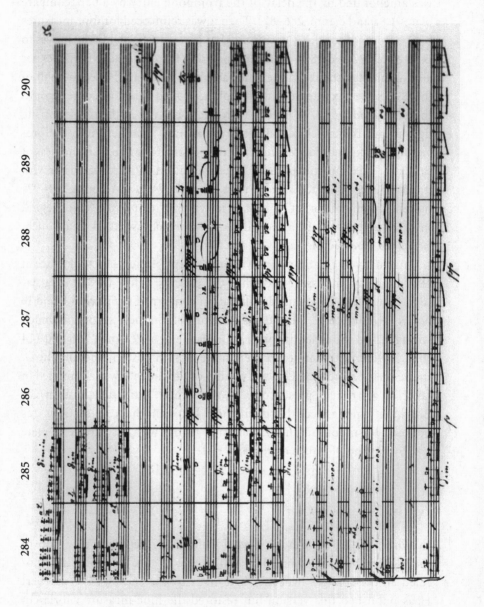

Plate 1.8a   Wn Mus. Hs. 31.246, fol. 56r. (Credo mm. 284ff., 1868 version)

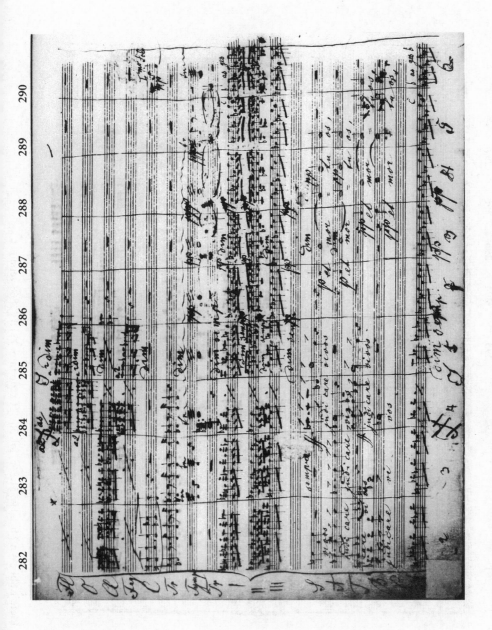

Plate 1.8c Wn Mus. Hs. 2106, fol. 68v. (Credo mm. 282ff., 1881 revision)

Plate 1.8b Wn Mus. Hs. 31.246, fol. 56v. (Credo mm. 291ff., 1868 version)

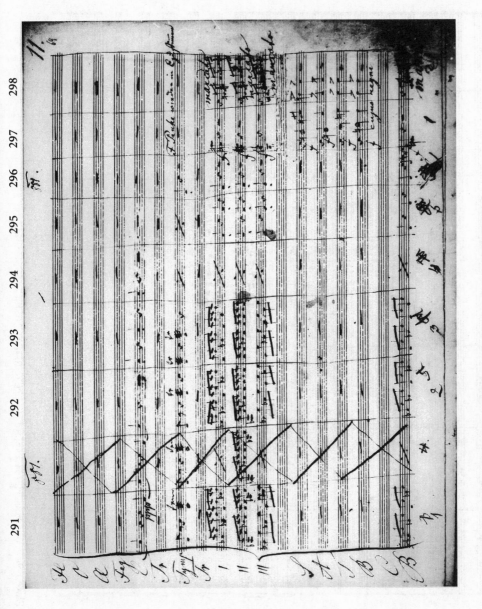

Plate 1.8d Wn Mus. Hs. 2106, fol. 69r. (Credo mm. 291ff., 1881 revision)

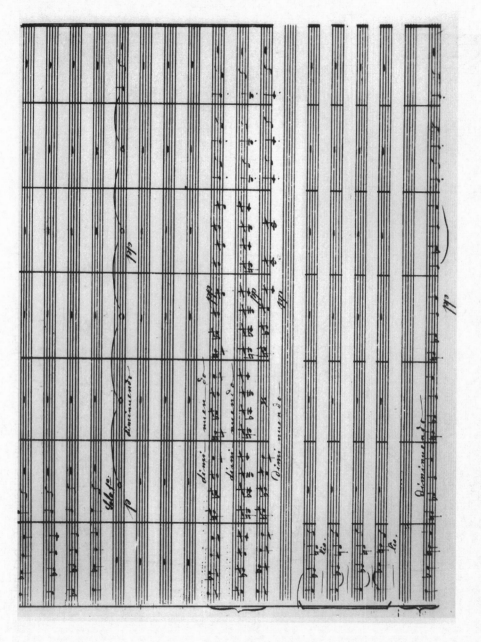

Plate 1.9a Wn Mus. Hs. 31.246, fol. 43v. (Credo mm. 109ff., 1868 version)

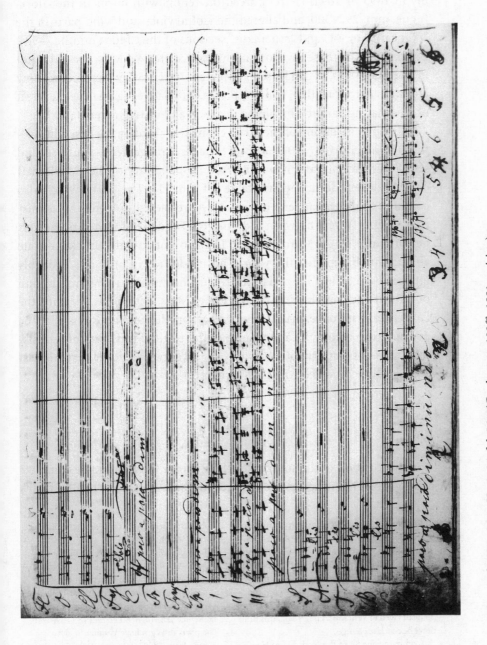

Plate 1.9b   Wn Mus. Hs. 2106, fol. 56v. (Credo mm. 109ff., 1881 revision)

unexplained reason, the earliest reading of the soprano and bass solos, Kyrie, mm. 66–71 (table 1.2, no. 1).[39] Leopold Nowak's edition includes further changes which Bruckner made to the Mass late in his life, probably in 1893 or 1894. He reinforced the tenors with horns in the Gloria fugue, mm. 292–300, and altered the violin, viola, and wind parts in the "et incarnatus est" and "crucifixus" sections of the Credo (mm. 117–90). Bruckner made these revisions in the copy score, Wn Mus. Hs. 6015, not in the autograph, as can be seen in plate 1.10. Timothy Jackson drew my attention to the fact that, in many places, the changes again have the effect of eliminating parallels involving the vocal and instrumental parts.[40]

More precise dating of these late changes is aided by the first edition – the Doblinger print (1894) of Josef Schalk's arrangement – and a second set of manuscript parts now preserved in the library of the Gesellschaft der Musikfreunde in Vienna (table 1.1, no. 11). The parts, which also contain Schalk's arrangement, were prepared for the Wiener akademischer Wagner-Verein between 1889 and 1893 and used for the first concert performance on 23 March 1893.[41] They do not contain Bruckner's late alterations. Except for the Gloria horn addition, which was probably ignored by Schalk in his zeal to rewrite the horns (including the addition of a third and fourth part) for the entire Mass, with a few variants, the Doblinger print does. Bruckner must have made these revisions after the performance before the appearance of the edition. It is certainly consistent with his pattern of revision over twenty-five years that his last changes also coincided with a performance.

V

No investigation of the sources for the F Minor Mass would be complete without commenting on the first edition and the extent of Bruckner's

---

[39] See note 20. Haas also incorrectly eliminated an ossia in the soprano solo in the Agnus Dei, mm. 76–78. In all readings up to and including the 1883 Noll score, the soloist had the option of singing a on m. 76, beat 3, and f♯[1] on m. 78, beats 1–2. The option was removed from the autograph and Wn Mus. Hs. 6015. Given that it had survived in Wn. Mus. Hs. 29.302, this must have been a late change.

[40] Compare page 88 in the Nowak and Haas editions. At this point, if I were to express a musical preference, it would be for the 1881 version printed by Haas. In 1893–94, Bruckner's quest to remove parallels resulted in more angular and disjunct solo violin and

viola parts. Redlich was of a similar mind: *Mass F Minor*, p. 38.

[41] *Jahresbericht des Wiener akademischen Wagner-Vereines* 17 (1889), p. 51 indicates that the society owned choral parts for the Kyrie and Gloria at that point. The Credo was added a year later: *Jahresbericht des Wiener akademischen Wagner-Vereines* 18 (1890), 46. The parts in Wgm have Wagner Society stamps from 1890, 1892, and 1893. The first trumpet and horns 2, 3, and 4 have performers' signatures and dates referring to the 1893 performance. The chorus and orchestra of the first performance are identified by the fourth horn player.

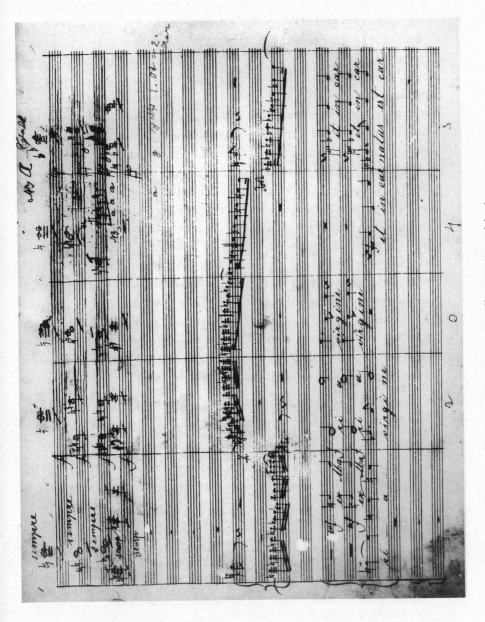

Plate 1.10 Wn Mus. Hs. 6015, fol. 51v. (Credo mm. 135ff., 1893–94 revision)

involvement in its preparation. It contains numerous spurious performance directions and articulations as well as a massive reorchestration, particularly of the winds.[42] Josef Schalk – not Bruckner – was responsible for this arrangement of the Mass. Schalk began work on his score as early as 1890; his pencil sketches for it are preserved in Noll's copy, Wn Mus. Hs. 29.302.[43] Bruckner was aware of Schalk's efforts and cognizant of their results because he attended the rehearsals and performance of 1893.[44] Any comments he may have made about the arrangement have not survived. A few weeks after the concert, writing to his brother, Franz, Josef Schalk tempered his report of its success with a statement that Bruckner had been difficult during rehearsals and behaved as if he had not noticed the reorchestration.[45] Preparations for the first edition were overseen by another Bruckner pupil, Max von Oberleithner, who was in close contact with the Schalks.[46] It has already been observed that Bruckner supplied the editors with his 1893–94 revisions. At present it is impossible to verify whether he expected these to be inserted into an edition of the 1881 version (as he had put them himself into the manuscript, Wn Mus. Hs 6015) or into the Schalk arrangement, as they were eventually printed.[47] Whatever his intentions, during its preparation, the edition was altered *without Bruckner's knowledge*. His suspicions in this regard caused him to have a severe falling out with Oberleithner and demand that the Mass score be returned. At first the composer was unaware of the nature of the unauthorized alterations, as Josef Schalk reported to his brother on 24 May 1894; one can surmise from Josef's subsequent remarks that the tampering had been extensive:

> Fortunately the printed score has not yet appeared. In the meantime we can only hope that Bruckner forgets the matter again. Otherwise there is going to be a hell of a scandal.[48]

Given the admission of tampering and Josef Schalk's testimony that the composer had failed to acknowledge the existence of the arrangement, in

---

[42] See Redlich, *Mass F Minor*, pp. 40ff. for a description of Schalk's editorial alterations.
[43] Leibnitz, *Brüder Schalk*, pp. 152ff. and Nowak, "Messe in F-moll," 429.
[44] Göllerich–Auer, IV/3, p. 315 and Leibnitz, *Brüder Schalk*, pp. 177–78.
[45] Leibnitz, *Brüder Schalk*, pp. 177–78. Letter dated 15 April 1893.
[46] Ibid., 192.
[47] Or into some combination thereof. The *Stichvorlage* has been lost. None of the surviving manuscripts could have served as a source for the engraver. Wn Mus. Hs. 6015 does not have the Schalk changes, and the

only manuscript which does, Wn Mus. Hs. 29.302, is missing Bruckner's 1893–94 revisions and contains no printer's markings. The *Stichvorlage* and the autograph score were absent from Bruckner's library in 1895 when he wrote on the page facing the month of May in his pocket calendar:

"Mir fehlt: / I[.] die Originalpartitur / der F. Messe ~~did zum~~ / II[.] Die Partitur der F. / Messe die zum Druck / verwendet worden ist"

Wn Mus. Hs. 3179, Bd. 6, fol. 724r.
[48] Leibnitz, *Brüder Schalk*, p. 192.

the absence of a *Stichvorlage*, there is no choice but to write off the first edition as an anomaly of history. The last version of the F Minor Mass which Bruckner can be shown to have left for posterity is preserved in Wn Mus. Hs. 6015.

Bruckner's anger with his editors must have subsided somewhat because, so far as is known, the scandal Schalk feared failed to materialize. The composer did not forget the matter entirely. After the print appeared he compared it with Wn Mus. Hs. 6015, writing critical annotations in the margins of the manuscript.[49] Among other things he observed, probably much to his chagrin, that his student had failed to avoid the ubiquitous parallels he himself had labored so hard over many years to eliminate. For example, very late in his life, as evidenced by the shaky handwriting, on fol. 77r. (Credo m. 138–39), he wrote "a g Schalk 1. Ob – 2. / Clar" lamenting the fact that, in the print, Schalk had failed to follow the final revision of the second clarinet and held the concert a^1 for the entire m. 138 (see plate 1.10). The result was a set of parallel octaves with the first oboe moving to g^2 in the next measure.

Bruckner's revisions to the sources for the F Minor Mass began soon after the initial completion of the score and continued almost until the end of his life. Each alteration demonstrates the work of a professional composer confronting a specific performance or analytical issue. Throughout his career there was a pattern of revisions coinciding with performances of the Mass. As a general rule changes prompted by concerns over difficulties of execution occurred during the late 1860s and early 1870s. Later alterations tended to be products of harmonic, metrical, or contrapuntal (voice-leading) analyses. None of these revisions should be confused with Josef Schalk's "arrangement" in the first print. While this edition is an interesting phenomenon of its time, it should not be viewed as a cherished component of Bruckner's legacy.

---

[49] These will be listed in the Critical Report.

2 A hidden personality: access to an "inner biography" of Anton Bruckner

Elisabeth Maier

The sources

On 10 November 1893 Anton Bruckner placed his signature on a will which contained the following passage:

> I bequeath the original manuscripts of my compositions as follows: the Symphonies, of which there are eight so far – the Ninth will, God willing, soon be finished – the three large Masses, the Quintet, the Te Deum, the 150th Psalm and the choral work, *Helgoland*, to the Imp[erial] and Roy[al] Court Library in Vienna and request the I[mperial] and R[oyal] Direction of that institute to take the necessary steps for the preservation of those manuscripts.[1]

As executor of his estate Bruckner appointed Court and Public Solicitor, Dr. Theodor Reisch, who together with Ferdinand Löwe and Cyrill Hynais also witnessed the will.[2] After Bruckner's death on 11 October 1896, his earthly possessions were inspected and listed in a "death protocol" of 16 October 1896. Compiled by Victor Czerny, this document, which bears the signatures of Dr. Reisch and two further witnesses, contains the following:

> In 2 wall-closets and 1 chest were diverse original manuscripts and copies of Bruckner's compositions. Of the original manuscripts a portion of the recent compositions was given to the executor for inspection. The remaining manuscripts were left in the cupboards which were sealed with the seal of the Senior Court Marshal's Office.[3]

Unfortunately, the seal was put in place four or five fateful days too late. In the interim friends and pupils received – perhaps from Bruckner's housekeeper Katharina Kachelmaier, who could not foresee the consequences of her actions – presents of manuscripts, sketches, and single

[1] Rolf Keller, "Die letztwilligen Verfügungen Anton Bruckner," in *Bruckner-Jahrbuch 1982/83* (1984), p. 98.

[2] Unless otherwise indicated, biographical information can be found in *Anton Bruckner. Ein Handbuch* (Salzburg and Vienna: Residenz Verlag, 1996).

[3] Rolf Keller, "Verfügungen," p. 102.

sheets as keepsakes; others simply took possession of such mementos. For example, as late as 1921 the autograph manuscript of the Mass in F Minor, which had been missed by Dr. Reisch when carrying out the provisions of the will, made headlines when it was brought to the National Library for an expert evaluation.[4] It had been in the possession of Bruckner's pupil, Dr. Max Oberleithner, who had given it to the Viennese drawing teacher Fritz Winkler. It was then passed on to the Austrian National Library, in part, with the help of Franz Gräflinger. The affair came to an end when the manuscript was impounded by the Director of the Music Collection, Robert Haas; his action was followed by an amicable settlement. This event made the public aware that other manuscripts intended for the Library had been missing at the execution of the will. A reporter summarized:

> An inquiry into the whereabouts of these manuscripts is in progress, and there is already evidence to indicate in whose possession can be found the other lost Bruckner manuscripts to which the National Library lays legal claim.[5]

Naturally the entire blame must not be laid on the shoulders of "relic-collectors." At least equally at fault was the interpretation of the will by Dr. Reisch, who was of the opinion that only the final versions of the works should be handed over to the Court Library, as can be seen from a newspaper report from the year 1926, when the issue was still attracting attention:

> The late Court and Public Solicitor, Dr. Ferdinand [sic] Reisch, who was supposed to secure the inheritance, allowed himself to be persuaded by someone that, by "original manuscripts," Bruckner only meant the "last version." As a result, from among the piles of autograph music in the composer's apartment, such "last versions" as could be found were extracted in the presence of the conductor Ferdinand Löwe, who has likewise since died. However, a number of things were missing. The manuscripts of the F Minor Mass, the E Minor Mass, and a symphony were not found. The executors were satisfied with the promise of the administrators that they would search and find and surely not let the Library be cheated. However, the matter was dropped.[6]

The mementos, in the course of time, were scattered to the four corners of the earth. If this brief excursion illustrates the magnitude of the problem of the provenance of Bruckner's original music manuscripts, it is easy to imagine how much more complicated the situation is with

---

[4] *Österreichische Volks-Zeitung*, 22, 24 and 26 February, 1 and 13 March 1921.
[5] Ibid., 13 March 1921.

[6] Ernst Friedman, "Ein verschollenes Bruckner-Manuskript," *Neues Wiener Journal*, 22 June 1926.

personal documents, letters, and notes which came under no legal protection.[7]

Anton Bruckner lived in a society which took great pleasure in writing: memoirs, diaries, and an enormous quantity of letters by his contemporaries, often written with a sidelong glance at later publication, have been preserved. One need only think of Adalbert Stifter, who wrote and edited his letters with a constant view to publication.[8] Bruckner's attitude was far removed from this. His correspondence demonstrates that, as Othmar Wessely has observed,

> The literary quality of musicians' letters has a totally different value in
> the genre of "letters" than that of the writings of a poet or writer. A poet,
> a writer communicates in his letters through the same medium of
> speech as he uses in his creative works.[9]

Bruckner rarely expressed himself freely in his correspondence; rather he hid behind the formulae of his time and environment. Wessely continues:

> The observation is . . . correct that whoever expects from Bruckner's letters
> fresh insights into the master's artistic personality or analytical perceptions
> about his works will be disappointed. Bruckner obviously wrote his letters
> neither from a personal need to communicate nor with an unconscious
> intention to provide biographical material. Bruckner's statements to his
> authorized biographer August Göllerich that the contents of conversations
> should not be mentioned since they were of no interest to anyone; and that
> this or that intimate fact of his life must not be printed for he was no "fop,"
> point in the same direction. What seemed to him worth communicating
> almost exclusively concerned his works.[10]

In contrast to Carl Dahlhaus, who referred to Bruckner's letters as "impotent stutterings," Wessely sees the reason for their meager personal contents in the composer's upbringing during the Vormärz period and its formal constrictions, which Bruckner was never able to escape.[11] There are subtle differentiations in the salutation and closing: "The expression of a feeling for form almost lost today," according to Wessely. In some cases the mode of address was carefully calculated – e.g. in addressing Cosima Wagner as "Your Grace".[12] With the exception of a few really personal statements – e.g. the offer of marriage to Josefine Lang or the letters

---

[7] The Anton Bruckner Institut Linz is presently involved in the often difficult task of locating these along with the many important musical sources which are still missing.

[8] Contrary to popular belief, there is no evidence that Bruckner and Stifter ever met.

[9] Othmar Wessely, "Anton Bruckner als Briefschreiber," in *Bruckner-Symposion Bericht*

"*Johannes Brahms und Anton Bruckner*" (Graz: Akademische Druck- und Verlagsanstalt, 1984), p. 90.

[10] Ibid., 91.

[11] Carl Dahlhaus, "Bruckner und der Barock," *Neue Zeitschrift für Musik* 124 (1963), 335.

[12] Wessely, "Bruckner als Briefschreiber," p. 92.

to his benefactor, Johann Herbeck – the correspondence offers few insights into Bruckner's personality.[13] In this connection his pocket calendars are of much greater value.

It is almost a miracle that these private notebooks were not completely purloined by the souvenir hunters. A total of twenty-three diaries with personal entries have survived complete or in fragments.[14] They are listed on pp. 35–36. They date, at first with gaps of several years, from 1860 to immediately before Bruckner's death.

Bruckner's calendars

1. *Brieftaschen-Kalender für das Jahr 1860.* Wn Mus. Hs. 28.253

2. *Krippen-Kalender für das Jahr 1872.* Wn Mus. Hs. 3180

3. *Oesterreichischer Volks- und Wirtschafts-Kalender für das Schaltjahr 1876.* Wn Mus. Hs. 3181

4. [Travel Notebook 1876–89]. Linz (private possession)

5. *Neuer Krakauer Schreib-Kalender für das Jahr 1877.* Wn Mus. Hs. 3182/1

6. *Neuer Krakauer Schreib-Kalender für das Jahr 1878.* Wn Mus. Hs. 3182/2

7. *Akademischer Kalender der Österreichischen Hochschulen für das Studienjahr 1879.* Wn Mus. Hs. 3178/1

8. *Akademischer Kalender der Österreichischen Hochschulen für das Studienjahr 1880.* Switzerland (private possession)

9. *Akademischer Kalender der Oesterreichischen Hochschulen für das Studienjahr 1882.* Wn Mus. Hs. 3178/2

10. *Neuer Krakauer Schreib-Kalender für das Jahr 1883.* Wn Mus.Hs. 3182/3

11. *Fromme's Neuer Auskunfts-Kalender für Geschäft und Haus 1884.* Wn Mus. Hs. 3183. Fols. 11, 13, 15, 17, and 18 missing. Fol. 17 is in private possession in Braunschweig. Fol. 13 was found in 1995 by Renate Grasberger in the estate of the journalist Theodor Altwirth (Elimar).

12. [Notebook 1884/85, "Leipzig"] Lost notice-book that Bruckner is known to have used during his stay in Leipzig. After his death, it was first in the possession of Max Auer who gave it to Ferdinand Armbruster. Perhaps Armbruster gave it to the Leipzig Stadtbibliothek. Today only four pages are known as photographs.[15]

13. *Fromme's Oesterreichischer Hochschulen-Kalender für Professoren und Studirende für das Studienjahr 1884/85.* Wn Mus. Hs. 3178b/1

14. [Notebook ca. 1885/86] Wn Mus. Hs. 28.255

---

[13] Auer, *Bruckner gesammelte Briefe*, pp. 73–74. Bruckner wrote a love letter to Josefine Lang in the summer of 1866.

[14] A complete edition, with commentary, of all the calendars is in preparation by the present author. It will contain a concordance of all foliations, numbered, and unnumbered pages and will facilitate more precise citations than can be made here.

[15] The photographs are in the Leipzig Stadtbibliothek and the Anton Bruckner Institut Linz.

15. *Fromme's Oesterreichischer Hochschulen-Kalender für Professoren und Studirende für das Studienjahr 1885/86.* Wn Mus. Hs. 3178b/2

16. *Fromme's Oesterreichischer Professoren- und Lehrer-Kalender für das Studienjahr 1886/87.* Wn Mus. Hs. 3179/1

17. *Fromme's Oesterreichischer Professoren- und Lehrer-Kalender für das Studienjahr 1887/88.* Wn Mus. Hs. 3179/2

18. *Fromme's Österreichischer Professoren- und Lehrer-Kalender für das Studienjahr 1888/89.* Wn Mus. Hs. 3179/3

19. *Fromme's Österreichischer Professoren- und Lehrer-Kalender für das Studienjahr 1889/90.* Wn Mus. Hs. 3179/4

20. *Fromme's Österreichischer Professoren- und Lehrer-Kalender für das Studienjahr 1890/91.* Wn Mus. Hs. 3179/5

21. *Fromme's . . . Professoren- und Lehrer-Kalender für das . . . Jahr 1893/94.* This calendar was formerly in possession of Prof. Mairecker, a member of the Vienna Philharmonic Orchestra. Today it must be considered as missing. Its contents may be reconstructed with reference to an article by Julius Bistron.[16]

22. *Fromme's Österreichischer Professoren- und Lehrer-Kalender für das Studienjahr 1894/95.* Wn Mus. Hs. 3179/6. A single page is in private possession in Braunschweig.

23. [Undated notebook] Wn Mus. Hs. 28.254. This notice-book incorrectly contains a page that belonged to the [Reise-Notizbüchlein 1876–1889].

24. [Prayer records] Linz, Oberösterreichisches Landesmuseum, Bibliothek Inv. Nr. MSi 5/1962. Only half of the page is in Linz; an illustration of the other half can be seen in Abendroth's biography.[17]

Another diary, formerly in the possession of Professor Mairecker (see No. 21) of Vienna, is missing, as are those for the years 1861–71, 1873–75, 1881, 1891–92 and 1895–96; all or most of these may well have existed, although at this point it is impossible to be certain.

It was Bruckner's habit – which became more pronounced with advancing age – to use his notebooks in various temporal phases or layers. When a diary was new, it served to record appointments, lessons, addresses, household notes, bills, and personal encounters that had impressed him. At a later date, empty pages were used for further annotations, usually in conjunction with a new, up-to-date diary. Finally, when listing prayers (a unique pastime of Bruckner's), there was another layer of annotations, often added on vacation.

---

[16] Julius Bistron, "Das Notizbuch Anton Bruckners. Ein musikhistorischer Fund," *Neues Wiener Journal*, 12 April 1925.

[17] Walther Abendroth, *Bruckner. Eine Bildbiographie* (Munich: Kindler Verlag, 1958) p. 105.

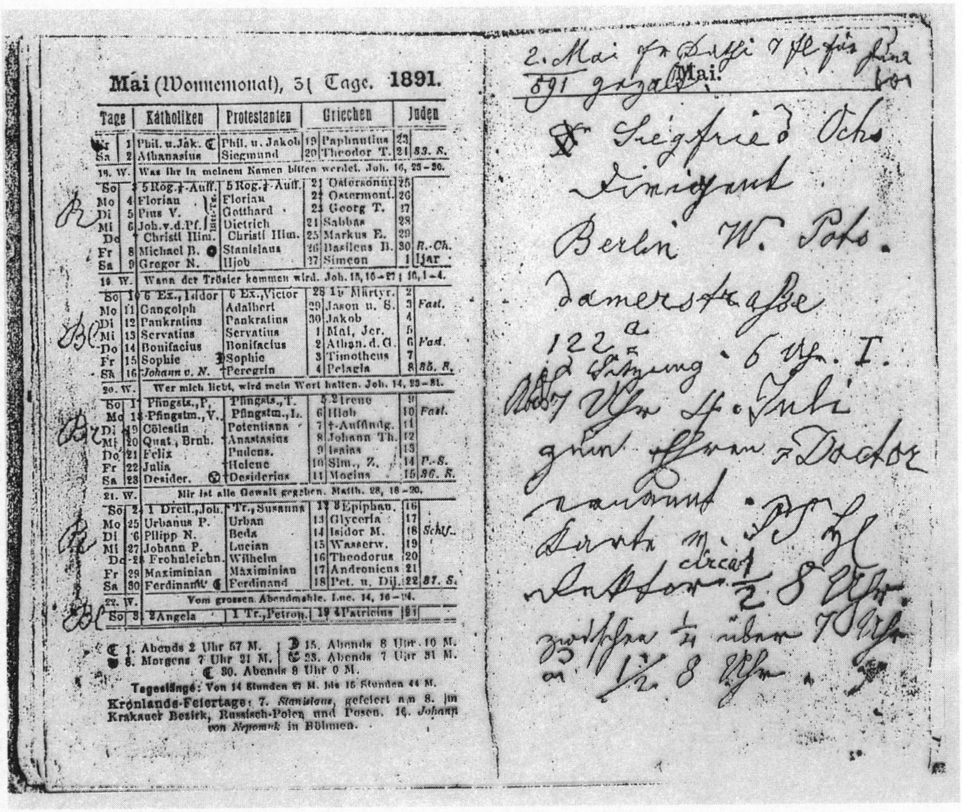

Plate 2.1   Fromme's Österreichischer Professoren- und Lehrer-Kalender für das Studienjahr 1890/91. Wn Mus. Hs. 3179/5, fols. 14v.–15r.

Plate 2.1 illustrates two facing pages from the diary section of *Fromme's Kalender . . . 1890/91* where Bruckner entered engagements and events from this period. On the left-hand page, next to the week's dates, are entries related to duties in the Hofkapelle. "R" stands for Pius Richter; "Bl" for Rudolf Bibl; and "Br" for Bruckner himself. Each entry covers an entire week. On fol. 15r. he noted the monthly wages for his housekeeper, Kathi Kachelmaier; the address of the Berlin conductor Siegfried Ochs; and Bruckner's award of an honorary doctorate from the University of Vienna. With their mixture of the everyday, the professional, and the unusual, these pages are characteristic of the contents of the pocket diaries and illustrate the private nature of the notes as purely an *aide-mémoire*. Nothing of the inner satisfaction that may have moved Bruckner, when at last he was able to receive recognition of the long-desired doctorate from the highest academic authority in the country, can be seen here. The only clue to the importance of this honor for

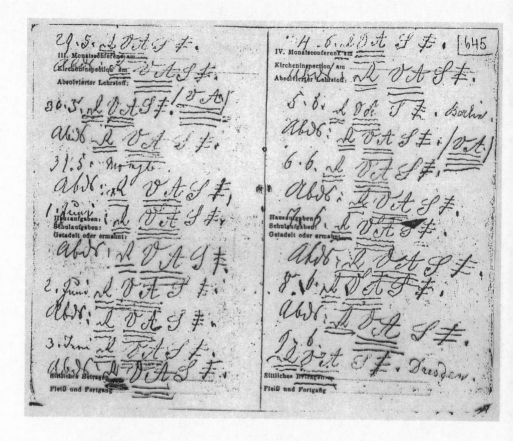

Plate 2.2   *Fromme's Österreichischer Professoren- und Lehrer-Kalender für das Studienjahr 1890/91.* Wn Mus. Hs. 3179/5, fols. 59v.–60r.

Bruckner is the care with which he recorded the moment when the postcard with the news reached him: "Card from P. T. H. Rector about 7:30, between 7:15 and 7:30."

On fols. 58v.–59r., the prayer notes in this diary begin. As illustrated in plate 2.2, Bruckner noted the date, sometimes the time of day (morning and evening), and the type and number of prayers:

"R"   the rosary or at least a decade of it
"V"   *Vater Unser*
"A"   Ave Maria
"S"   probably Salve Regina
"≢"   probably the Doxology
"Gl"   (rare) is the *Glaubensbekenntnis* (Creed) or Gloria

The lines under the prayers record the number of repetitions. Occasionally a change of location is noted between the prayer annotations, as on fol. 60r.: "Berlin" and "Dresden." On 31 May 1891 Bruckner attended the Berlin performance of his Te Deum, conducted by Siegfried Ochs, and visited Dresden on the way home.[18] Far more frequently Bruckner did not take the diary in current use on a journey; rather he used another notebook, with the result that there are gaps in the prayer records. Sometimes these gaps can be closed with entries in other diaries. On special occasions of the church year, special prayers were added, such as a "Lent Prayer" about whose text we are not informed.

Prayer notes have survived from the year 1876 (11–22 December) and, to an increased degree, after 25 September 1880.[19] They continue until Bruckner's death.

An "inner biography"

To what extent can an "inner biography" of Bruckner be discerned through a chronological overview of the diary entries in the calendars? I use the term "inner biography" to refer to internalized feelings, impressions, and perceptions etc. which may be inferred from the laconic day-to-day annotations. For a biographer this is a difficult area of inquiry touching upon subtle distinctions between discretion and trenchancy, between documentation and interpretation. The exploration requires not only philological accuracy but also an equal amount of interpretive sensitivity. In making the following observations, we must remember that Bruckner's private notes – especially those concerning prayers – were not intended for public scrutiny.

The earliest surviving calendar, the *Brieftaschen-Kalender . . . 1860*, belonged to the thirty-six-year-old cathedral and parish organist in Linz. Bruckner had reached the first pinnacle of his career: a respected position with pupils from well-situated Linz circles, for example Emil, the son of Mayor Fink, and Helene and Pauline Hoffmann.[20] Nevertheless, he strove

---

[18] Göllerich–Auer, IV/3, pp. 149–59.
[19] An undated page acquired by the Library of the Upper Austrian Provincial Museum in 1962 (list, p. 36 above, no. 24) has been incorrectly described as a "prayer from the last year of life." Catalogue No. 81, Musikantiquariat Hans Schneider, Tutzing, No. 17. [ca. 1962]. Its handwriting clearly dates from an earlier period than 1895–96.

[20] Vinzenz Fink was mayor from 1856. He was active in the administration of the Liedertafel Frohsinn between 1850 and 1854 and served on the search committee for Bruckner's organist position. His son Emil was Bruckner's first piano student in Linz. Bruckner dedicated his songs *Im April* and *Mein Herz und deine Stimme* to the Hoffman sisters.

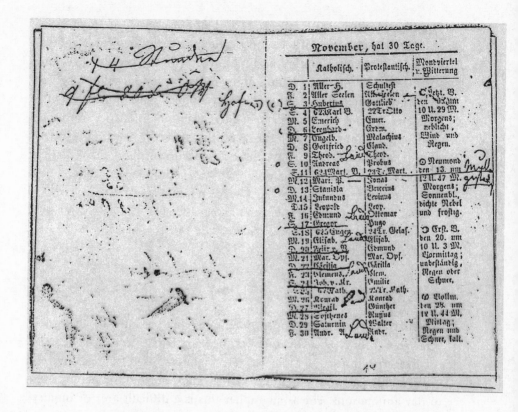

Plate 2.3   *Brieftaschen-Kalender für das Jahr 1860.* Wn Mus. Hs. 28.253, fols. 13v.–14r.

to break out of what, for him, was still too narrow a sphere of activity: "write to Sechter" is noted on the diary page for October. The letter itself has not been preserved but, on 30 December, Sechter expressed his thanks for "two friendly letters" from Bruckner, who was in the midst of his systematic counterpoint studies.[21] During this period of self-advancement and hope, Bruckner was smitten by a severe blow. "Mother died" is noted on 11 November 1860 (plate 2.3) – only these two words, nothing more. From numerous reports we know that Bruckner kept a photograph of his mother on her deathbed in his room. He is not known to have had a photograph made of her while she was alive. Therefore someone must have traveled with the Linz photographer posthaste to Ebelsberg to record her features. His mother, from whom he is thought to have inherited his melancholy temperament, meant a great deal to Bruckner; yet the fateful blow is recorded in only two words.

In the *Krippen-Kalender . . . 1872*, we meet Bruckner as an organist

---

[21] Auer, *Bruckner gesammelte Briefe*, p. 354.

whose reputation has extended beyond the boundaries of his country. He has written the address of August Manns[22] in London, and the famous dedication of his Third Symphony to Richard Wagner appears on fol. 40r.[23] A brief entry on the page for May in the *Volks- und Wirthschafts-Kalender . . . 1876* reads: "Miss Wagner Elise, Donaustraße No. 2, Döbling. (like Lang in Linz)." Here too, a few lines testify to a major wound: the sight of a Viennese girl had reminded Bruckner of his Linz beloved, Josefine Lang, who had rejected his offer of marriage in 1866. Bruckner had proposed to her – not as a buffoon, but with deep emotion:

> May I hope for you and ask your dear parents for your hand? Or is it not possible for you from a lack of affection for me to undertake the step of marriage?[24]

A presumably accidental meeting with an unknown woman – from whom Bruckner, as was his wont, requested her name and address – brought the memory to life again.

In the *Neuer . . . Schreib-Kalender . . . 1877* there is a page (fol. 7r., plate 2.4) with entries which illustrate the extent of Bruckner's physical and mental workload. He notes no less than twenty-eight lessons – University, Conservatory, and private students. Added to this were the services in the Hofkapelle, totaling about forty working hours per week. Reports of his nervousness and impatience when teaching are therefore not surprising. The decade from 1870 to 1880 also saw the creation of the Second to Sixth Symphonies, the String Quintet, and important church works including *Os justi* and *Tota pulchra es*, as well as the revision of the three Masses and Second to Fifth Symphonies.

Because the notes in this diary are typical in the variety of their content, I shall discuss them more exhaustively. Private and professional matters, everyday joys and financial difficulties, triumphs and aggravations, everything is side by side. For example, there are notes on attendance at balls (with the names of dancing partners) immediately adjacent to entries about pupils' debts. Migraine attacks, which seem to have been very frequent at this time, are noted alongside household bills. There are also important insights into artistic matters: "30 April 1st time counterpoint at the University. 1877. A[nton] Br[uckner]mp." is noted with obvious satisfaction in a large, self-assured hand. At last he is receiving academic recognition and attesting to this himself by signing the annotation with the additional abbreviation for "manu propria" on fol. 11r.

[22] August Manns, Music Director at the Crystal Palace.
[23] For a facsimile see Abendroth, *Bruckner*, p. 58. There is in fact some doubt about whether this is Bruckner's handwriting.
[24] Auer, *Bruckner gesammelte Briefe*, pp. 73–74.

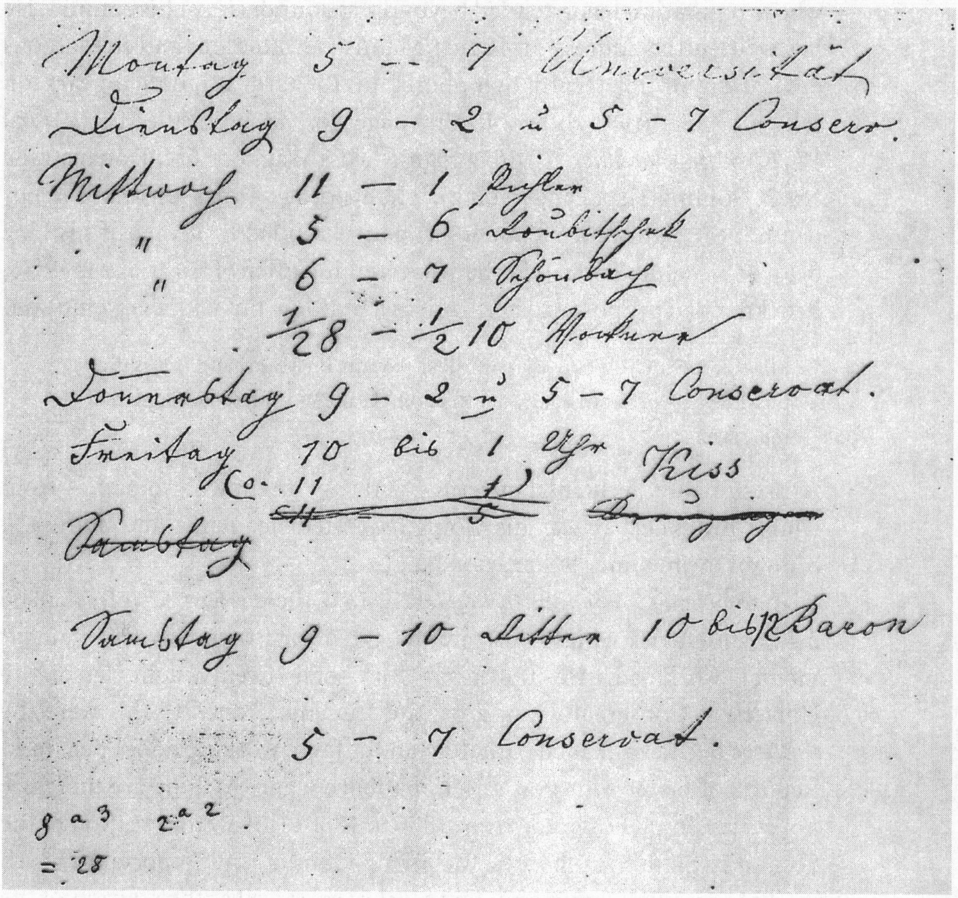

Plate 2.4 *Neuer Krakauer Schreib-Kalender für das Jahr 1877.* Wn Mus. Hs. 3182/1, fol. 7r.

The same diary contains an analysis of the voice leading in Mozart's Requiem: in 1876 and 1877 Bruckner revised his three Masses thoroughly and, in the course of this work, studied Mozart's piece.[25] In another place (fol. 15v.), in an irregular hand (perhaps reflecting his depressed mood), Bruckner records (plate 2.5):

> Thursday 27 September 1877 3rd rejection[:] of my Wagner Symphony No. 3
> 1st rejection fall 1872 C Minor Symph[ony] No. 2
> 2nd rejection by the Philharmonic in the fall 1875. Symphony No. 3

To Bruckner's further pain and dismay his patron and benefactor, Johann Herbeck, died on 28 October 1877. The composer's despair must have been very great since, without his protector, he now saw himself totally

[25] See Paul Hawkshaw, "Anatomy of change," pp. 18–19 in the present volume.

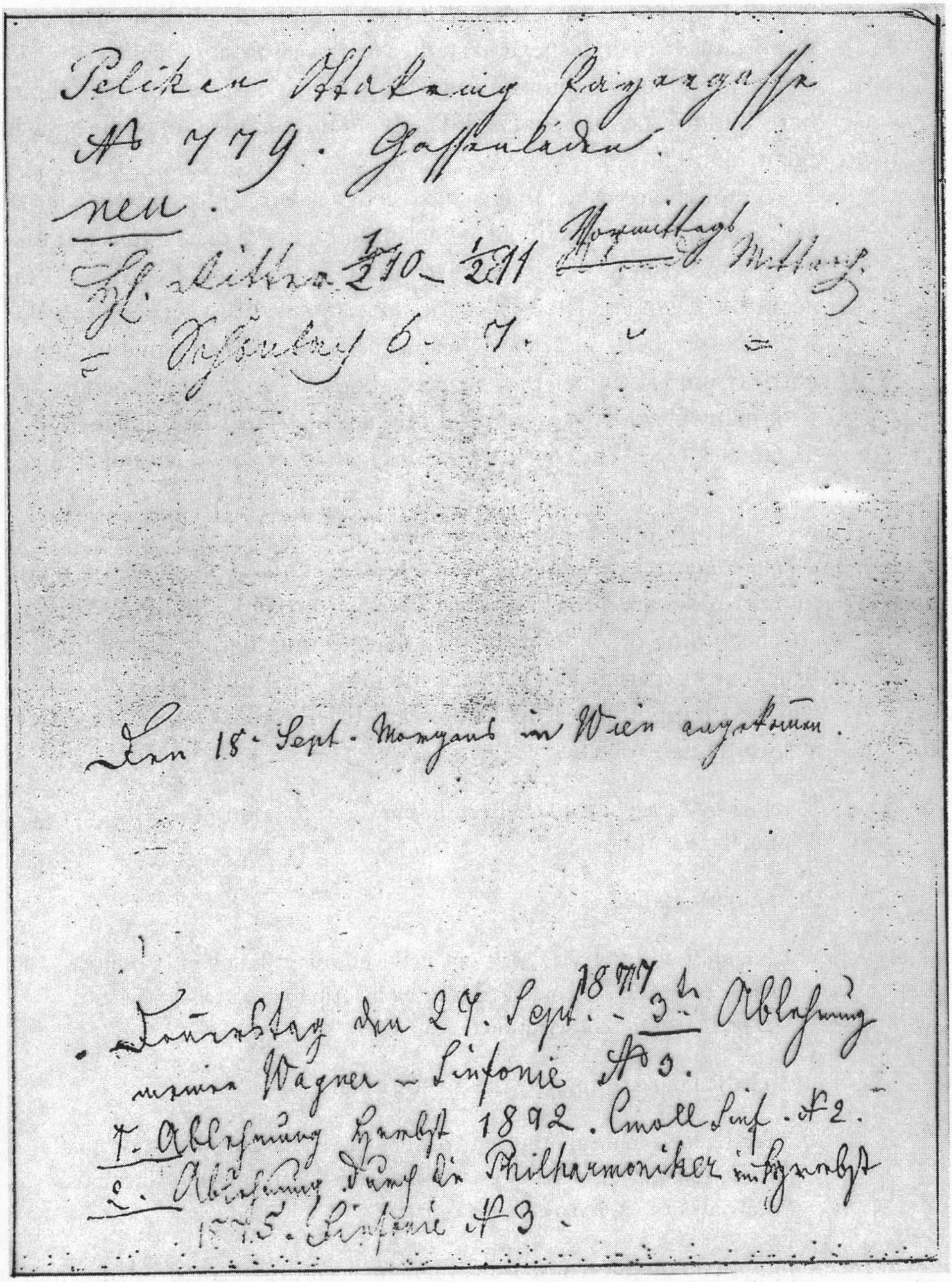

Plate 2.5 *Neuer Krakauer Schreib-Kalender für das Jahr 1877.* Wn Mus. Hs.
3182/1, fol. 15v.

exposed to the artistic intrigues of the Viennese music scene. The most important entry in the next diary, the *Neuer . . . Schreib-Kalender . . . 1878*, can be found on fol. 15r.: two students, good friends, entered their names here: Rudolf Krzyzanowski and "Gustav Mahler, student of philosophy in Iglau, Mähren."

As though he wished to give his recent academic recognition external expression, later in his life Bruckner usually used a diary typical of university and college professors, with the year arranged according to the academic calendar. The earliest of these to survive is an *Akademischer Kalender der Österreichischen Hochschulen . . . 1879*. It contains topical entries from November 1878 to December 1879 and, in an appendix and with many periodic gaps, prayer notes dating from 1 November 1883 to 31 January 1887. The character of the entries from 1879 has not changed from those of the previous year; they are all mixed together and are intended primarily as an *aide-mémoire*.

The *Akademischer Kalender . . . 1880* is similar, except that a major journey is documented here: the trip to Switzerland at the end of August and beginning of September. Anyone expecting literary descriptions of Bruckner's experience of some of the most beautiful scenery in Europe will be disappointed. These notes are brief, lapidary, and sometimes awkward linguistically:

> return to Zurich by the Lake by steamship. Fearful storm[.] 1 Sept[ember] Mont blanc Grotto

then more detailed:

> Lausanne Cathedral. Viewed at 7:00 in the morning. Rudolf of Habsburg (whose castle was seen on the left during the trip from Zurich to Geneva) was present at the consecration.

and a little later, completely the professional:

> 7 Sept[ember] in the morning to Freiburg. Played the cathedral organ and attended an organ concert by cathedral organist Vogt: (D Minor Toccata) Pedal only to C. I played after the concert.

A judgment on the cathedral organ in Freiburg seemed to him more important than crossing Lake Geneva; he dedicated more time to a reminiscence about Rudolf von Habsburg than to the Lucerne sunset which he found "magnificent." "Miss Babette," sister of the hotelier Schreiber in Küssnacht, impressed him just as much as the more massive natural beauties; as did a "Miss Wisbauer," a hotelier's daughter from Salzburg whom he met on the return journey and found "very pretty." Another girl's name appears: "Oberammergau Miss Marie Bartl." This again is a remembrance of a budding love affair which did not go beyond an initial stage. The young woman played a "daughter of Jerusalem" in the Oberammergau Passion Play, which Bruckner saw on 22 and 23 August 1880. Her resolute mother brought what was, to her, an absurd matter to a relatively rapid close. The girl's and her mother's letters up to June 1881 have survived.[26]

The *Akademischer Kalender . . . 1882* contains an observation on the victims of the Ring Theater fire of 8 December 1881. A striking entry describes the scene: "on both sides numerous corpses. Most between the second and third floors" is noted with choking horror.

Bruckner's prayer notes, which are unique in the history of biography, have been subjected to the most contradictory interpretations. For example, they have been linked to the tradition of St. Ignatius Loyola's "Spiritual Exercises"[27] or described as an "additive, mathematical piety . . ."[28] The latter author, who also diagnoses "religious theatricality" and "hysteria," interprets the repetitions of the prayers as a sign of scrupulosity:

> Every clergyman has had the experience that many such sufferers tend to repeat prayers incessantly because they are always afraid of an imperfection that could render the prayer ineffectual.[29]

I tend to the much less spectacular view that the prayer records were a private means of keeping track, certainly not intended for the eyes of outsiders. They can be found not only in the diaries (and there, as already seen, in complex temporal layers) but also, though less often, in musical manuscripts which Bruckner happened to have available. The latter especially can hardly be intended as a measure of "additive, mathematical piety"; that would surely require as continuous a record as possible. Rather prayer annotations bear witness to the same comprehensive discipline which Bruckner applied to his studies and his composing, areas which are more accessible to us as a result of the publication of the various versions of his works and the critical reports. Perhaps people are

---

[26] They are now preserved in the Monastery of St. Florian.
[27] Kosch, "Der Beter Anton Bruckner," 69.
[28] Leopold M. Kantner, "Die Frömmigkeit Anton Bruckners," in *Anton Bruckner in Wien.* *Eine kritische Studie zu seiner Persönlichkeit,* Anton Bruckner. Dokumente und Studien, vol. II (Graz: Akademische Druck- und Verlagsanstalt, 1980) p. 250.
[29] Kantner, "Frömmigkeit," p. 259.

too ready to resort to psychological explanations in the more sensitive area of personal prayer.[30]

On fol. 10v. of the next diary, the *Neuer . . . Schreib-Kalender . . . 1883,* there is an entry of particular interest for the English-speaking world:

> Dr. Vincent 1882 60 fl for London
> Ditto 21 February 10 fl ditto
> In Summer 1882 a few Gulden as well

This apparently unimportant note is connected with a partly tragic, partly tragi-comic episode in which Bruckner's efforts to obtain further academic recognition caused someone else to fall victim to already ominous German Nationalist currents. Since the awarding of honorary doctorates to Johannes Brahms by the Universities of Cambridge (1876) and Breslau (1879), Bruckner's desire for a doctorate of his own had intensified: "this man [Bruckner] envies nothing about his rival Brahms more than the latter's title of doctor."[31] Bruckner took great pains over unsuccessful applications to Cambridge University and, three years later, to two American universities, Philadelphia and Cincinnati.[32] Whether Bruckner actually submitted these petitions is not known; in any case, no such honor was forthcoming from the universities in question.

Evidence of the extent of the composer's efforts is provided by numerous surviving documents in officially attested translation.[33] Although the petition presents "an official, serious impression"; is "precisely constructed [and] carefully documented"; and is "[in] form and content" in accordance with "the official requirements," the person of the compiler and translator, "Dr. Erard Vincent, English Professor at the Imperial Court of Vienna" has been portrayed in an extremely dubious light.[34] He was described by Bruckner's circle and the first generation of biographers as an unscrupulous swindler who had cheated the composer out of a great deal of money. One reads that Dr. Vincent was just "a Jew," as were the civil servants, Kohn and Nathan, who were also concerned with the translation. That was enough to explain their moral shamelessness.[35] Subsequent commentators repeatedly upheld this distorted view.[36]

[30] In extreme situations Bruckner may well have retained a neurotic anxiety, a tendency to pedanticism, to scrupulosity, and to compulsive counting as a remnant of his severe nervous breakdown. This is not enough to explain the real meaning of the prayer notes. Psychology and philology are not enough here.
[31] Friedrich Klose, *Meine Lehrjahre bei Bruckner. Erinnerungen und Betrachtungen* (Regensburg: Gustav Bosse Verlag, 1927), p. 113.
[32] Göllerich–Auer IV/2, p. 10.

[33] Wn Mus. Hs. 6009.
[34] Rolf Keller, "Das 'amerikanische Ehrendoktorat' für Anton Bruckner," *Bruckner-Symposion Bericht 1992* (Linz: Linzer Veranstaltungsgesellschaft, 1995), pp. 73–92.
[35] Friedrich Klose, *Lehrjahre,* pp. 15f.
[36] I, too knew nothing about the anti-Semitic background of this story. See Elisabeth Maier, "Zur Eröffnung der Bruckner-Ausstellung in Schwäbisch Hall," *Mitteilungsblatt der Internationalen Bruckner-Gesellschaft* 35 (December 1990), 17–20.

The truth is that Dr. Vincent, although not formally engaged at court, was well-known there and in the highest Viennese society as an English teacher; for example, he taught Landgrave Vinzenz Fürstenberg, who was related to the Bavarian royal house. The costs of Bruckner's application resulted from the necessary translation and notary's fees. Dr. Vincent, who had worked correctly and charged by no means exorbitant fees, was in no way responsible for the collapse of the composer's plans to obtain an honorary American doctorate. The besmirching of Dr. Vincent, because he was a Jew, is a reminder once again of how ideology can undermine serious research.

The next diaries document Bruckner's growing fame. We find addresses in Munich and Leipzig including that of the painter Hermann Kaulbach, who produced an imposing, if not completely successful, portrait in oils of Bruckner; a list of sacred compositions forwarded to the publisher Rättig;[37] notes about newspaper reports and reviews, among them a citation of a precedent for a music professorship at a university;[38] and the draft dedication of the Seventh Symphony to King Ludwig II of Bavaria.

In subsequent years, for example in *Fromme's . . . Hochschulen-Kalender . . . 1885/86,* the number of day-to-day annotations decreases while the frequency of prayer entries increases; here notes appear on fifteen pages as opposed to thirty-six for prayer entries. As mentioned above, the diaries were written in at different times; there was usually an intervening period of two to three years. In this case the topical entries date from October 1885 to December 1886 and the prayer records from 1 February 1887 to 28 July 1888.

As can be seen from his correspondence, Bruckner's fame continued to grow during these years. Letters are sent to Graz, Hamburg, Munich, Bayreuth, and Leipzig.[39] A special event is the awarding of the Franz Joseph Order. As recorded in the diary, Bruckner received the Order on 9 July 1886 from Prince Konstantin Hohenlohe-Schillingsfürst at "circa 1 o'clock." Members of the highest society are now numbered among Bruckner's pupils, including the German attaché, Count Carl Pückler; and finally (plate 2.6) he has on

> 23 September at 11:15[a.m.] (after 11:00) an audience with His Majesty, the Emperor

[37] *Fromme's . . . Hochschulen-Kalender . . . 1884/85,"* pp. 31 and 35. Hermann Kaulbach (1846–1909) was a painter of genre and historical scenes in Munich. His portrait of Bruckner was finished 11 March 1885. See Renate Grasberger, *Bruckner Ikonographie* (Graz: Akademische Druck- und Verlagsanstalt, 1990), p. 19.

[38] *Notizbüchlein* (list, p. 35 above, no. 14) fols. 2v.–3v, 8r., and 13r. respectively. The annotation on fol. 8r. reads: "12 July 1885, *Deutsche Zeitung.* The academic and city Music Director, Leonhard Wolf, in Bonn has been named Professor at the local university."
[39] *Fromme's . . . Hochschulen-Kalender . . . 1885/86,* pp. 15 and 24.

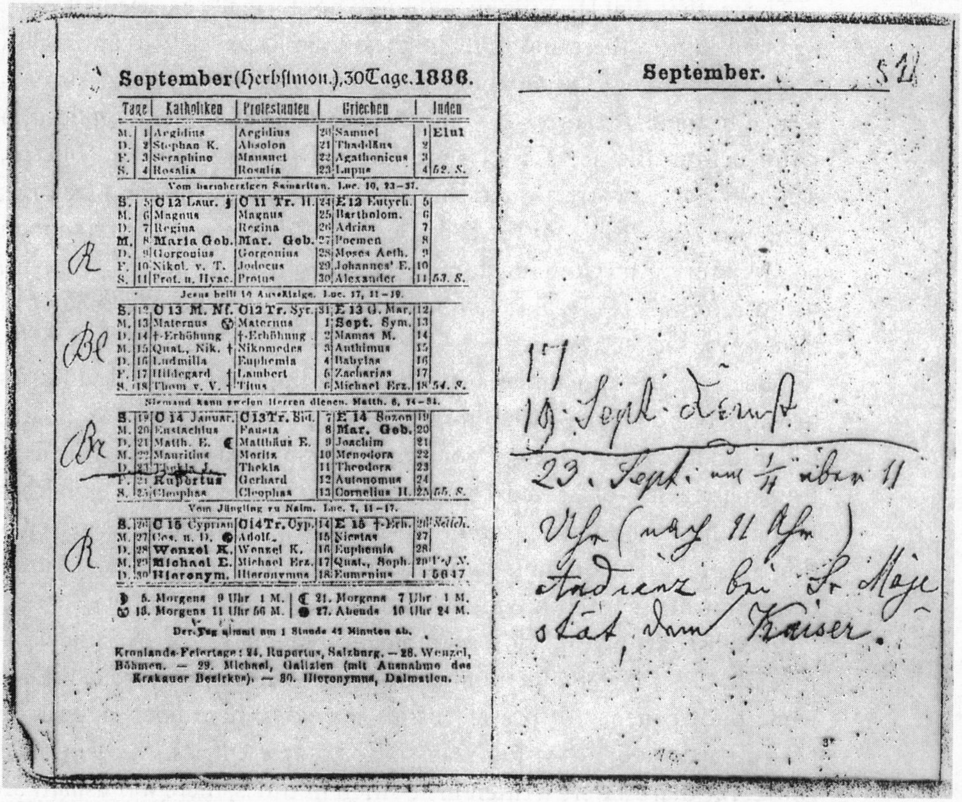

Plate 2.6 *Fromme's Œsterreichischer Hochschulen-Kalender für Professoren und Studirende für das Studienjahr 1885/86*, Wn Mus. Hs. 3178b/2, pp. 34f.

The next diary (list, p. 36 above, no. 16) continues to document Bruckner's social ascent with its mention of the Court ball and those present interspersed with the usual notes on his daily routine.[40] On fol. 17r. a small, easily overlooked note, though proudly signed "manu propria," announces the completion of the Eighth Symphony:

1 July 8th Symphony finished. 9 August 1887 copy complete. Anton Brucknermp

He still appreciates social pleasures such as making the acquaintance of the pretty glovemaker's daughter, Miss Bielohaubek, whom he met at the "Anna Festival."[41] Many of the diary pages remain empty in contrast to the tightly filled forty-eight pages of prayer notes from the years 1888–89.[42] At this time the emphases in Bruckner's life are his work and his relationship with God.

[40] *Fromme's . . . Professoren- und Lehrer-Kalender . . . 1886/87*, fol. 11r.
[41] *Fromme's . . . Professoren- und Lehrer-Kalender . . . 1887/88*, fol. 17v.
[42] The entries run from 3 March 1888, evening, to 17 August 1889, evening.

In December 1889 Bruckner applied for the post of conductor at the Burgtheater. This application should be seen as an indication of his ever-increasing anxiety about his future material security – by this time unfounded – and not as a desire to extend his sphere of activity. On 12 July 1890 he took leave of his duties at the Conservatory for health reasons. After a serious illness, he terminated his service in the Hofkapelle on 28 October 1892; finally, in November 1894 he gave his last lecture at the University. Late honors gave him pleasure – the honorary doctorate from Vienna University (7 November 1891) and the bronze bust by the Viennese sculptor Viktor Tilgner – as did honorary member-ships of the Gesellschaft der Musikfreunde (15 January 1891) and of the Vienna Male Chorus Society (22 September 1893), and an honorary citizenship of the City of Linz (11 July 1894), etc.

Financial support from the Upper Austrian Provincial Diet, Vienna University, and the Ministry of Education, as well as lodging granted by the Emperor in the Custodian's Building of the Belvedere Palace (to which he moved on 4 July 1895) eased the external circumstances of the seriously ill composer. His creative life was dominated by difficult work on the Ninth Symphony, begun on 21 September 1887 and continually interrupted by reworking, revisions, and "improvements" of other compositions. The 150th Psalm and *Helgoland* were among the new works of this period.

In Bruckner's last calendars, the shift in emphasis towards the prayer notes is even more evident. The ratios are as follows:

1889/90	16 pages notes	19 pages prayers (dating from 1890–91)
1890/91	13 pages notes	65 pages prayers (dating from 1891–95)
1894/95	14 pages notes	21 pages prayers (dating from 1896)

In *Fromme's . . . Kalendar . . . 1889/90* at first the notes document the daily routine of the Court organist and teacher: schedules, pupils' addresses and Court Chapel services are entered in the same way as in earlier diaries, as are the usual notes about domestic affairs. There is also an abbreviated medical report (fol. 13r.): "chronic catarrh of the throat and larynx. Chiari" and "intense nervousness. Riehl" which must have led to the cessation of his work at the Conservatory. A draft of a request to be released from his duties as organ teacher is also found here (fol. 20r.). He also notes acquaintances with young women and an excursion and (fols. 18r.–19r.), full of pride, praise:

> H. H. [presumably the Court Conductor, Hellmesberger]: No-one has ever played as beautifully as Bruckner did today in the Hofkapelle

Another Sunday of service that year was less edifying:

> 26 April heard a Mass in A by Cherubini in the Hofkapelle.
> Terrible composition !!!Performance!!!

On 7 November, after the ceremony when Bruckner was awarded the honorary doctorate from the University of Vienna, he again had an audience with the Emperor. His Majesty was "extremely gracious," as noted by Bruckner together with the names of people who had waited with him for the audience. Among them a "Miss Diebl," whose name he not only noted but also underlined, appears especially to have appealed to him.

Among the lost diaries is *Fromme's . . . Professoren- und Lehrer-Kalender . . . 1893/94.* We are familiar with its contents because Julius Bistron examined and described the diary in 1925.[43] As usual it is a kaleidoscope of Bruckner's daily rounds and artistic successes: the last attempt at a relationship with a girl much too young for him;[44] notes about his works; trivial matters such as the date of a pedicure and the New Year's tip to the concierge; a complaint about the bite of a mad dog; and an interesting note on his last organ improvisation (in St. Florian on 25 March 1894):

> End of High Mass freely improvised. At the beginning of the High Mass
> from my 150th Psalm. Then free Holy Thursday

with the very characteristic theme noted alongside (example 2.1).

A quotation from the famous anatomist, Josef Hyrtl, is especially revealing of Bruckner's inner world:[45]

> Prof[essor] Hyrtl 1864.
> Is the soul a product of the brain, which functions according to immutable organic laws, or is this brain rather one of those prerequisites through which the interaction of an immaterial soul-being with the world-in-space is transmitted?[46]

Julius Bistron makes the unnecessary attempt to protect Bruckner from what he calls such a "scientifically based perception of God."[47] He is of the opinion that Bruckner "only wrote out the quotation from Hyrtl . . . in order to argue against it or to discuss it with other people." This inter-

[43] Bistron, "Notizbuch."
[44] Ida Buhz, whom Bruckner met in Berlin.
[45] Josef Hyrtl (Eisenstadt, 7 December 1810 – Perchtoldsdorf, 17 July 1894). Choir boy at the Viennese Hofkapelle; studied medicine and became a doctor in 1835; professor in Prague in 1837 and Vienna in 1845. He was the Rector during the academic year 1864–65, the five-hundredth anniversary celebration of the University of Vienna. He was famous for his spiritual lectures. His inauguration address was a rejection of materialism. In his speech at the anniversary celebration of the university, he stressed the relationship between faith and science and, in so doing, belittled the sympathies of liberal "enlightened" Vienna.
[46] Joseph Hyrtl, *Die materialistische Weltanschauung unserer Zeit* (Vienna: Holzhausen, 1865).
[47] Bistron, "Notizbuch."

Ex. 2.1   The theme for Bruckner's improvisation at St. Florian, 25 March 1894

pretation would, in fact, stamp Bruckner as narrow-mindedly naive, and he certainly was not that.

Bruckner's circle and later writers have reported, with a mixture of horror and mockery, his touching and kissing the skulls of Beethoven and Schubert at their exhumation; the attempt to keep the skull of his cousin, Johann Baptist Weiss, who died tragically; and his efforts to see the body of Emperor Maximilian of Mexico, whom he esteemed. Because of these things Bruckner has been described as having a tendency to necrophilia, which is utter nonsense. One should think rather of the much greater familiarity with death of an Austrian country child in the nineteenth century and of the veneration of relics in the Catholic Church. In this context a skull could have been nothing unusual or frightening for Bruckner. Two years before his own death we find him meditating on the words of the anatomist Hyrtl: "Is that which Faith calls the immortal soul of man only an organic reaction of the brain?" A hermeneutic connection between this quotation from Hyrtl and the Ninth Symphony (which Bruckner was composing at the time) cannot be lightly dismissed. In both cases we can detect existential questioning and wrestling with final statements.

The last of the extant diaries, *Fromme's . . . Professoren- und Lehrer-Kalender . . . 1894/95* (plate 2.7), shows the shaky handwriting of a seriously ill old man. Bruckner organizes his scores and packs them up in preparation for their removal to Belvedere. Assisted by his secretary, Meissner, he makes a list of valuables – ring, watchchain, golden box, diamond pin – and notes the addresses of his physician, Dr. Heller, and his executor, Dr. Reisch. The prayer entries are of varying clarity, painful witnesses of an unstable physical condition; they become increasingly confused. Bruckner strives to keep his orientation in time; brief improvements alternate with even deeper relapses; dates, prayer notes, and musical references are all alike and are evidence of an increasing removal from temporal existence. In his last days his handwriting again becomes a little clearer. On two different diary pages Bruckner enters his prayers; on the second we find the annotation "D.D.D." which Franz Kosch interprets

52   Elisabeth Maier

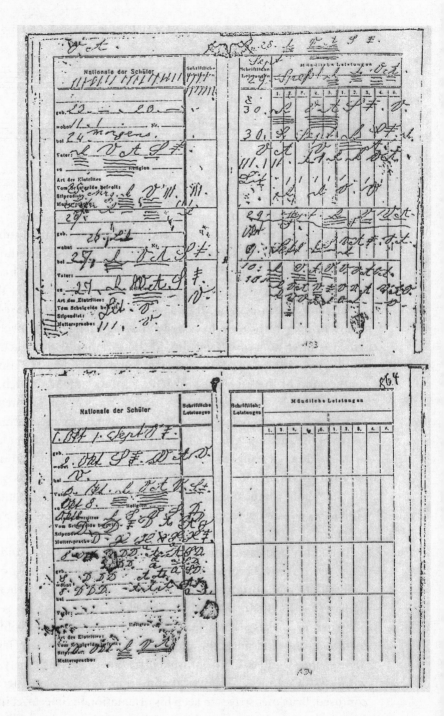

Plate 2.7   *Fromme's Österreichischer Professoren- und Lehrer-Kalender für das Schuljahr 1894/95, Wn Mus. Hs. 3179/6, fols. 153v.–155r.*

as (possibly) "Deus Deus Deus" or as a sign for the Trinity.[48] On 10 October 1896, the day before his death, Bruckner prayed at three different times; it is one of the longest, if not *the* longest of all his prayer entries. Then the man, Bruckner, withdraws into silence.

Can the historian draw conclusions about an "inner biography" from Bruckner's personal notes? Perhaps the answer must be that Bruckner's personal annotations present – from the biographical-philological point of view – completely unique material which, in many cases, can shed light on the life and works of a great composer. It is only a little light; the secrets of a human being and the works of art created by him can never be fully explained. To cite Nikolaus Harnoncourt:

> All our research only opens doors behind which there are further closed
> doors, we can never find the final reason . . . There is undoubtedly
> something behind things – about which we know and yet remain ignorant –
> the "thoughts of the heart" provide us with an unprovable certainty.[49]

Not long ago in the reflections of the Russian director Andrei Tarkovsky, who sought in his films and texts "the lost spirituality of our world," I found a remark which is particularly appropriate to Anton Bruckner and the two poles of his existence, faith and artistic creativity:

> At any rate, for me there can be no doubt that the goal of any art is . . . to
> explain to oneself and one's environment the meaning of life and human
> existence. To make clear to human beings the sense and goal of their being
> on this planet. Or perhaps not to explain it to them, but only to present
> them with this question.[50]

[48] Kosch, "Der Beter Anton Bruckner," 70.
[49] Nikolaus Harnoncourt, "Vom Denken des Herzens," *Die Macht der Musik. Zwei Reden*

(Salzburg–Vienna: Residenz Verlag, 1993), p.22.
[50] Andrei Tarkovsky, *Die versiegelte Zeit*, 3rd ed. (Berlin, 1988), dust cover and p. 41.

3 Bruckner and Viennese Wagnerism

Margaret Notley

The death of his beloved "Meister aller Meister" in 1883 ironically coincided with a turn for the better in Anton Bruckner's fortunes. A confluence of events, including the brilliant successes of the String Quintet and the Seventh Symphony in the 1884–85 season, served to bring him long-delayed recognition as a composer of instrumental music. As Liberalism waned in Vienna during the mid 1880s, Wagnerian aesthetics and "the politics of Wagnerism" flourished, a change that favored a composer of his background and artistic inclinations.[1] During these same years a group of Viennese journalists began a campaign to cement the position of Bruckner and his symphonies in the Wagnerian world-view.

Bruckner's relationship with Richard Wagner and certain Wagnerites as well as the support he received from the anti-Liberal, anti-Semitic press in the final decade of his life have been discussed in a number of recent studies. Egon Voss has described, with painstaking care, the one-sidedness of the personal relationship between the two composers: Wagner paid little attention to the reverential symphonist.[2] Yet, as Thomas Leibnitz has shown, after "the Master's" death, Josef Schalk intensified efforts to advance Bruckner's music through the Wiener akademischer Wagner-Verein.[3] Along with Leibnitz, Manfred Wagner and Matthias Hansen see a direct connection between Bruckner's growing prestige in these years and the decline of Viennese Liberalism.[4] In an exploration of links between Bayreuth and radical German nationalists in Austria who favored the

I would like to thank Dr. Andrea Harrandt and Dr. Elisabeth Maier for making the resources of the Anton Bruckner-Institut Linz available to me.

[1] For this phrase, see *Wagnerism in European Culture and Politics*, ed. David C. Large and William Weber (Ithaca and London: Cornell University Press, 1984), p. 18.
[2] Egon Voss, "Wagner und Bruckner. Ihre persönlichen Beziehungen anhand der überlieferten Zeugnisse (mit einer Dokumentation der wichtigsten Quellen)," in *Anton Bruckner: Studien zu Werk und Wirkung. Walter Wiora zum 30. Dezember 1986*, ed. Christoph-Hellmut Mahling (Tutzing: Hans Schneider, 1988), pp. 219–33.
[3] Thomas Leibnitz, *Die Brüder Schalk und Anton Bruckner dargestellt an den Nachlaßbeständern der Musiksammlung der Österreichischen Nationalbibliothek* (Tutzing: Hans Schneider, 1988).
[4] Leibnitz, *Die Brüder Schalk*, p. 162; Manfred Wagner, *Bruckner. Leben–Werke–Dokumente* (Mainz and Munich: Wilhelm Goldmann, 1983), p. 189; Matthias Hansen, *Anton*

breakup of the Empire, Susanna Grossmann-Vendrey has pointed out that they "concurred in their conscious opposition to the politically customary ...and not least in their anti-Semitism."[5]

This chapter will provide a more comprehensive picture of the relationship between Bruckner and Viennese Wagnerism by addressing two questions: (1) Since Wagner himself had taken almost no interest in the symphonist, how did Viennese Wagnerites effect Bruckner's transformation into the symbolic standard bearer of the movement in the mid 1880s? and (2) Did Bruckner have personal connections with Wagner-influenced political groups in the city? Viennese Wagnerites consistently promoted Bruckner and his symphonies through rhetorical strategies grounded in "the Master's" writings. As will become apparent, his relations with the lunatic fringe of Wagnerian politics were, in fact, more direct than has been suspected. The activities of Bruckner's biographer, August Göllerich, a surprisingly overlooked figure, will provide a key to a more complete understanding of Bruckner and Wagnerism in the city. As a consequence of the orientation of Göllerich and other early commentators, Wagnerian ideology in large part shaped the traditional image of Bruckner.

Wagnerism and Viennese politics (1)

Since his early years in Vienna, the reception of Bruckner's music had been linked with Wagner's name. The music historian A. W. Ambros, Bruckner's colleague at the University, had raised the issue as early as 1873 in a review of the Second Symphony, writing that during a visit the previous year Wagner "had expressed his warmly sympathetic opinion of Bruckner's talent."[6] In his mostly negative assessment, Ambros regretted "that a man of such talent, rather than going boldly and bravely to the temple of fame on his own two feet, preferred to jump on the servants' board of Wagner's triumphal wagon and have himself be driven upward in this way."[7] No doubt the perceived connection with Wagner continued

Bruckner (Leipzig: Philipp Reclam jun., 1987), pp. 280–85. Wagner and Hansen quote reviews from the anti-Semitic *Ostdeutsche Rundschau*; both neglect August Göllerich's contributions to the *Deutsches Volksblatt*. See also Manfred Wagner, "Bruckner in Wien. Ein Beitrag zur Apperzeption und Rezeption des oberösterreichischen Komponisten in der Hauptstadt der k. k. Monarchie," in *Anton Bruckner in Wien. Eine Kritische Studie zu seiner Persönlichkeit*, Anton Bruckner: Dokumente und Studien, vol. II (Graz:

Akademische Druck- und Verlagsanstalt, 1980), pp. 9–74.
[5] Susanna Grossmann-Vendrey, "Bayreuth und Österreich," in *Bruckner-Symposion Bericht: Bruckner, Wagner und die Neudeutschen*, ed. Othmar Wessely (Graz: Akademische Druck- und Verlagsanstalt, 1986), p. 104.
[6] This review, which appeared originally in the *Wiener Abendpost* of 28 October 1873, is reprinted with modernized spelling in Göllerich–Auer, IV/1, p. 251.
[7] Ibid., 253.

to play a role in Bruckner's critical failures in subsequent years. With increasing polarization in both the musical and the political spheres in Vienna during the 1880s, the virulence of the attacks on Bruckner increased.[8] At the same time more favorable critics became unreserved advocates of his music, their efforts playing into an intensifying cult of "the Master."

In the Göllerich–Auer biography, Max Auer disputed an observation by Max Kalbeck that the Wagner faction in Vienna did not take up the symphonist's cause until after 1883.[9] Auer argued that the composer's ascendancy among Viennese Wagnerites had begun in 1881 when the Wiener akademischer Wagner-Verein made Bruckner an honorary member and sponsored the premiere of his Fourth Symphony. Auer had one of his dates wrong: the Akademischer Wagner-Verein made Bruckner an honorary member in 1885.[10] And he sidestepped another, more important part of Kalbeck's claim: that, after Wagner's death, "music got mixed up with politics" and that Bruckner began to get significant support from radically right-wing Wagnerites.[11]

The change in Bruckner's fortunes and the enhanced prestige of Wagnerian ideas accompanied a fundamental political shift. An electoral reform in 1882 initiated a gradual transition to universal male suffrage, followed by the eventual formation, in 1889, of parties to represent the interests of the lower middle and working classes.[12] From mid-century the established political groups had been the Liberals, the party of educated German and German-Jewish middle and upper middle classes (there was a special bond between the Liberal Party and Vienna's Jews), and the Conservatives, associated with the Church, Slavs, and aristocracy. Even after a Conservative coalition gained control of the central government in 1879, Vienna itself had remained a stronghold of the Liberal Party. By the end of the century the new mass parties would succeed in virtually destroying Viennese Liberalism.[13]

---

[8] Margaret Notley, "Brahms as Liberal: Genre, Style, and Politics in Late Nineteenth-Century Vienna," *19th-Century Music* 17 (1993), 107–23.

[9] Göllerich–Auer, IV/1, p. 630; Max Kalbeck, *Johannes Brahms,* rev. ed., 4 vols. (Berlin: Deutsche Brahms-Gesellschaft, 1912–21), III, pp. 402–04.

[10] *Dreizehnter Jahres-Bericht des Wiener akademischen Wagner-Vereines für das Jahr 1885* (Vienna: Verlag des Wiener akademischen Wagner-Vereines, 1886), p. 5. Manfred Wagner perpetuates this mistake in *Bruckner,* p. 144.

[11] Notley, "Brahms as Liberal," 107–08.

[12] Lower-middle-class men received the vote on the national level in 1882 and on the local level in 1885. Working-class men could not vote until 1907. John Boyer, *Political Radicalism in Late Imperial Vienna: Origins of the Christian Social Movement 1848–1897* (Chicago and London: University of Chicago Press, 1981), pp. 64, 211, and 324. On the formation of the Christian Social Party see ibid., 224–25.

[13] Peter Pulzer, *The Rise of Political Anti-Semitism in Germany and Austria,* rev. ed. (London: P. Halban, 1988), pp. 123 and 159; also, Robert S. Wistrich, *The Jews of Vienna in the Age of Franz Joseph* (Oxford and New York: Oxford University Press, 1989), p. 145.

While the dominance of the Liberals had played a crucial part in establishing the preeminence of Johannes Brahms in the city, the fresh challenges to the Liberal establishment in the 1880s on both the right and left worked to Bruckner's advantage.[14] He, of course, had strong ties to the Church and received warm praise from the ultra-conservative Catholic newspaper *Das Vaterland*; the resurgence of Catholicism attending the rise of the right-wing Christian Socials helped his cause (the Liberals had always been antagonistic to the Church).[15] His humble background made him an attractive figure not only to the Christian Socials, a party that appealed to the lower middle classes, but also to the leftist workers' party, the Social Democrats. Certain founders of the Social Democratic Party, most notably Viktor Adler and Engelbert Pernerstorfer, were passionate Wagnerites. According to William McGrath, "there is little evidence that Wagnerian cultural theory penetrated deeply into the Austrian socialist movement or that it retained a lasting influence on Austrian socialist tradition," although Johann Seidl has presented considerable evidence to the contrary.[16] In any case, the party's newspaper, the *Arbeiter-Zeitung*, founded in 1889, did not feature music reviews or other coverage of cultural events until 1895.

Wagnerian aesthetics and populist politics converged most naturally in the outlook of a third party, like the Christian Socials anti-Semitic and reactionary: the Pan-Germans led by Georg von Schönerer. As young men Adler and Pernerstorfer had followed Schönerer; they broke with him in 1883 when he veered to the right and openly espoused racist views. Bruckner himself had close professional and personal ties to a group of musicians and critics whose peculiar idealism combined a commitment to reforming the musical life of the city with the anti-Semitism, radical German nationalism, and crackpot populism of the Pan-Germans.

Much of the positive reception of Bruckner was refracted through Wagnerian ideologies. In a number of essays Wagner had challenged basic assumptions of German and Austrian Liberals, their rationalism, worldliness, and emphasis on a *Bildung* that he found superficial.[17] After

[14] Notley, "Brahms as Liberal."

[15] For more on this newspaper, see Wistrich, *The Jews of Vienna*, pp. 224–25, and Franz Grasberger, "Das Bruckner-Bild der Zeitung 'Das Vaterland' in den Jahren 1870–1900," in *Festschrift Hans Schneider zum 60. Geburtstag*, ed. R. Elvers and E. Vogel (Munich: Ernst Vogel, 1981), pp. 113–32.

[16] William J. McGrath, *Dionysian Art and Populist Politics in Austria* (New Haven and London: Yale University Press, 1974), p. 237; Johann W. Seidl, *Musik und Austromarxismus.*

Zur Musikrezeption der österreichischen Arbeiterbewegung im späten Kaiserreich und in der ersten Republik (Vienna, Cologne, and Graz: Böhlau, 1989).

[17] See, for example, Richard Wagner, *Oper und Drama* (1851), in *Gesammelte Schriften und Dichtungen*, 3rd ed., 10 vols. (Leipzig: C. F. W. Siegel's Musikalienhandlung, 1897), vols. III–IV; "Modern" (1878), in ibid., X, pp. 54–60; "Publikum und Popularität" (1878), in ibid., X, pp. 61–90.

his death, Wagner's writings attained near-Biblical status among his disciples, who took them as a frame of reference for cultural criticism and music-historical interpretation, as well as a program for political change. Their exegeses often hinged on the German-versus-Jewish polarity found throughout "the Master's" writings. Bruckner emerged repeatedly from the Wagnerites' interpretations as a quintessential "German" composer. In order for the Austrian organist to achieve such status his supporters first had to deal with Wagner's own problematic stance toward Bruckner's symphonies.

Bruckner as Wagnerian symphonist

In 1884, articles about Bruckner by Joseph Schalk and August Göllerich appeared in two prominent Wagnerian periodicals, the *Bayreuther Blätter* and the *Deutsche Worte* respectively. Reconciling the work of any latter-day symphonist with the prescripts of Wagner's writings posed almost insurmountable difficulties. Especially thorny for Bruckner partisans was the essay "Über die Anwendung der Musik auf das Drama," which had appeared in the *Bayreuther Blätter* only five years earlier. Wagner's purpose had been to explain "the necessary difference in musical style for dramatic, as opposed to symphonic, compositions."[18] He managed along the way to condemn, on several grounds, post-Beethoven symphonic production.

Wagner found modern symphonists to have forgone Beethoven's symphonic "gaiety" (*Heiterkeit*) in favor of an inappropriate "world-weary and catastrophic" tone: "we are dark and wrathful, then once again brave and bold . . . competent, sturdy, upright, Hungarian or Scottish – for others, unfortunately, boring." He refused to believe that "a favorable future has been secured for instrumental music through the creations of its most recent masters."[19] Vague throughout most of the essay about his intended targets, Wagner censured symphonists of the "let us say, Romantic-Classical school" – certainly including Mendelssohn, Schumann, and Brahms – for having transplanted into their symphonies a melodic style suitable only for chamber music, a criticism inapplicable to Bruckner.[20]

But Wagner also complained about the excessive, un-Beethovenian use of modulation by later symphonists. Bruckner could have been seen as the object of this charge with more justification than most other

---

[18] *Bayreuther Blätter* 2/11 (November 1879), 313.

[19] Ibid., 317–18.

[20] Ibid., 318.

composers. Wagner concluded his essay with a blanket condemnation of contemporary symphonies:

> as the first rule . . . never leave a key so long as what you have to say can still be said in it. If this rule were followed, then perhaps we would once again get to hear noteworthy symphonies, whereas there is absolutely nothing to be said about our most recent symphonies.[21]

The stickiest aspect of this essay for Bruckner's supporters may have been Wagner's refusal to make an exception or use an obvious opportunity to speak out publicly on his behalf. In their articles of 1884, Schalk and Göllerich confronted the problem boldly. Schalk chose to use reports of Wagner's *spoken* words, anecdotes much invoked in the older literature on Bruckner, that demonstrated "the Master's" high regard for him as a symphonist. According to these stories Wagner, recognizing the greatness of the symphonies, promised to arrange for performances of them. Voss has shown that these stories exist only in the Bruckner literature.[22] Wagner is not known to have tried to help Bruckner either by a show of support in his writings or by approaching any conductors for him.

One of the earliest appearances in print of some of these anecdotes was Schalk's essay of 1884, directed, like Wagner's article five years earlier, at the audience of the *Bayreuther Blätter*. Schalk began:

> In what place other than these pages could it more trustingly be attempted to show readers the image of a man whose artistic strivings as a musician have – as a consequence of their seriousness and purity – relied on only one true and understanding friend, that same one to whom we look as the protector of our German art, as of all our loftiest treasures: Richard Wagner.[23]

Interweaving Wagner's reported comments about Bruckner's symphonies into an account of the latter's trials and accomplishments, Schalk created a narrative of considerable cumulative power. His description of the First Symphony as a work "worthy of the spirit of the Master" is followed by the first Wagner quotation: "Why is this work not known? How is it possible that it has never been performed?"[24] A description of the occasions the two composers met led naturally to the story in which

---

[21] Ibid., 325.

[22] Voss provides the most systematic examination of the sources, but a number of other writers have come to the same conclusion. See, for example, Leibnitz, *Die Brüder Schalk*, p. 54; Klaus Kropfinger, *Wagner and Beethoven: Richard Wagner's Reception of Beethoven*, trans. Peter Palmer (Cambridge University Press, 1991), p. 253;

Rudolf Stephan, "Bruckner–Wagner," in *Bruckner, Wagner und die Neudeutschen*, 60–61.

[23] Josef Schalk, "Anton Bruckner," *Bayreuther Blätter* 7/10 (October 1884), 329. Leibnitz, too, notes that in this essay "Schalk created a close connection between Bruckner and Wagner." Leibnitz, *Die Brüder Schalk*, p. 71.

[24] Schalk, "Anton Bruckner," 330.

Wagner accepted the dedication of the Third Symphony: "Well then, dear Bruckner, the dedication is a fact; you give me uncommonly great pleasure with this work."[25] Schalk's tale of the inadequate performances and hostile reception of Bruckner's symphonies closed with one final anecdote:

> Only the One remained always staunchly sympathetic to him, and . . . it was he who, in his singularly tender manner toward Bruckner, spoke friendly words of consolation: "Depend on me; I myself will still perform your work!"[26]

At the end, Schalk addressed the issues of Wagner's 1879 essay by assuring his readers that Bruckner's music was, "in the distinguished sense, symphonic throughout [and] does not give rise to fears of a freedom of expression and construction bewildering without dramatic clues," and posing a rhetorical question: "should the liberties of complicated harmonies and modulations remain excluded from symphonic style, if their use is produced and justified by masterful thematic or contrapuntal development?"[27]

With this article Schalk continued his long-standing support of Bruckner, as his student and then as a member of the Wiener akademischer Wagner-Verein. Since Bruckner had been convinced that Wagner would some day help him, "the Master's" death had made him despair about his own future. In response to Bruckner's dark mood Schalk became even more active on the composer's behalf.[28] The article in the *Bayreuther Blätter*, in fact, greatly benefited Bruckner's cause. According to Auer, it inspired the editor of the journal and most committed Wagnerite of all, Hans von Wolzogen, acquainted for many years with Bruckner, "henceforth also to intercede for him with his great influence."[29]

In contrast to Schalk, Göllerich's conversion to Bruckner's cause almost coincided with the death of Wagner. "Enthusiastically absorbed" in Wagner's writings from an early age, Göllerich rivaled Wolzogen in his devotion to "the Master's" world-view.[30] He had known about Bruckner as well since childhood, but the performance by the Vienna Philharmonic of the middle movements of the Sixth Symphony on 11 February 1883 (two days before Wagner's death) gave him "the occasion . . . to be more intensively engaged with Bruckner."[31] In 1884, he began to attend the composer's University lectures and then became his official biographer.[32]

Göllerich described his article in the *Deutsche Worte* as a tribute "to the

---

[25] Ibid., 332.
[26] Ibid., 333.
[27] Ibid., 333–34.
[28] Leibnitz, *Die Brüder Schalk*, pp. 54–55.
[29] Göllerich-Auer, IV/2, p. 196.
[30] Ibid., II/1, p. 5.
[31] Ibid., IV/2, p. 85.
[32] Ibid., 162–63.

seventy-first birthday of Richard Wagner."[33] A daring reinterpretation of
Wagner's reception of Beethoven began with a quotation from the 1870
centennial essay:

> "[Beethoven] never fundamentally changed any of the established forms
> of instrumental music; the same structure is to be detected unequivocally
> in his last works as in his first . . . Here emerges again the peculiarity of the
> German nature, which is so intrinsically deep and richly talented that it can
> imprint its essence on every form, transforming from within and therefore
> spared the necessity of external revolution."[34]

Göllerich immediately applied Wagner's words to Bruckner, likewise "so
intrinsically deep and richly talented, so German and therefore so specifically a musician, that it is completely natural that he is satisfied by the
outward form of the symphony."[35]

Turning to that most problematic essay, "Über die Anwendung der
Musik auf das Drama" (1879), Göllerich cited both Wagner's claim that
Beethoven had changed nothing in the form as found in Haydn and his
comparison of the symphony's formal constraints to structural "pillars."
Göllerich asserted that "Bruckner, too, has not changed the pillars of the
symphonic structure, but rather has shown for the first time – and that is
his place in music history – the expansion and enrichment still possible
in the symphonic form with the new resources after Wagner and Liszt,
what splendors can be created in it . . . without its having to become a
Lisztian 'symphonic poem.'"[36]

Göllerich finally quoted Wagner from the same essay on the historical
absence of "the right Beethoven" who would have known how to proceed
in the earlier, Classical symphonic style using recent harmonic and thematic innovations. He then identified Bruckner as "that second Beethoven
longed for by Wagner," an astonishing claim since Wagner already knew of
Bruckner and his symphonies in 1879: he had looked at the Second and
Third Symphonies in 1873 and accepted the dedication to himself of the
Third – a story of no little importance to Bruckner's Wagnerian devotees.
Despite the cavernous hole in his argument, Göllerich seems to have been
proud of this article, as he reprinted it in his biography of Bruckner and
used it again in a review of a performance of the Seventh Symphony in
1889.[37] The immediate aim of this exegesis was to justify Bruckner's

---

[33] August Göllerich, "Anton Bruckner. Zum
71. Geburtstage Richard Wagners," *Deutsche
Worte* 4, 22 May 1884, 145–50. Reprinted in
Göllerich–Auer, I, pp. 14–29; page references
are to this reprint.
[34] Ibid., 18.
[35] Ibid., 19.
[36] Ibid., 19–20.

[37] "Ein Fest musikalischen Fortschrittes" [*sic*]
Deutsches Volksblatt, 6 March 1889. (This was
a review of a performance of works by Liszt,
Wagner, and Bruckner sponsored by the
Wiener akademischer Wagner-Verein.) For
another example of Göllerich's propensity for
this kind of reinterpretation, see Notley,
"Brahms as Liberal," 121 and note 85.

cultivation of the symphony rather than the symphonic poem; its ultimate objective was to claim, using the full weight of Wagner's authority, a truly exalted place in music history for the symphonist.

Bruckner as archetypal German

Although reconciling his symphonies with Wagner's words required some finesse, Bruckner was otherwise admirably suited to Wagnerian strategies. His perceived artistic idealism, his roots in the Austrian peasantry, and even his uncultivated demeanor fitted naturally with the Germanic ideology projected in "the Master's" essays. Within the Wagnerian world-view, the implicit "un-German" opposites of these attributes were artistic careerism, rootlessness, and shallow cultivation. The German/un-German dichotomy that permeated Wagner's writings lends itself to tabular representation, as in the following summation by the historian Ernst Hanisch, who notes that all the "negative, non-German qualities came together in one figure of hate: the Jew":

German	Not German
province	city
culture	civilization
inwardness	superficiality
nonpolitical orientation	political orientation
conservatism	revolution
authority	democracy
idealism	materialism
depth of feeling	superficial distractedness
creativity and originality	imitation and exploitation
morality	intellect[38]

Bruckner's background and personality, as described by most commentators, perfectly matched Wagner's "German" archetype. Bruckner's advocates stressed such qualities as "idealism," "depth of feeling," and "creativity and originality" using themes and language from Wagner's essays to explain his experiences in Vienna. Schalk, for example, attributed much of the incomprehension that Bruckner encountered to his unconventional deportment and "lack of that makeshift today called 'liberal education.'"[39] In their rejection of many features of the modern "civilized" world, Wagner's writings offered a positive view of Bruckner's

[38] Ernst Hanisch, "The Political Influence and Appropriation of Wagner," trans. Paul Knight, in *Wagner Handbook*, ed. Ulrich Müller and Peter Wapnewski (Cambridge, Mass.: Harvard University Press, 1992), p. 191.
[39] Schalk, "Anton Bruckner," 333.

eccentricities and the narrow range of his intellectual interests. Wagner had asserted that persons of true culture and education (*Bildung*) were "superior to all," but had decried superficial polish or "educated-ness" (*Gebildetheit*), ascribing this especially to Jews (including Mendelssohn).[40] In the same vein, Göllerich wrote in 1891 that, while Bruckner had been found to lack that "splendid 'educatedness'" prized in Liberal-Jewish circles, he in truth possessed a "genuine culture not only in the domain of learning but also in that of the heart . . . Modest and simple all his life [he] had sought only true culture, and avoided an artificial, deforming educatedness" (*künstliche Verbildetheit*).[41]

Wagnerian ideology lent dignity to Bruckner's character and background and, with its emphasis on "inner necessity" as the only valid motivation for artistic endeavors, ennobled his failure to achieve much critical or popular success as a symphonist: he did not pander to public taste.[42] "Inner necessity" and related Wagnerian motifs – for instance, the idea borrowed from Kant that "only the purposeless is beautiful" – became central critical *topoi* for Bruckner's supporters.[43] One of the most notable for his seriousness and integrity was Theodor Helm, who wrote for the *Deutsche Zeitung* and the *Musikalisches Wochenblatt*. Göllerich claimed he had convinced Helm of Bruckner's greatness shortly after he himself had been converted to the composer's cause in 1883. Helm's reviews confirm this assertion. While his reactions to Bruckner's earlier compositions had been at best mixed, he wrote enthusiastically about a private performance of the String Quintet in 1884 and remained a valuable advocate thereafter.[44]

In 1886, a long article by Helm about Bruckner appeared in the *Musikalisches Wochenblatt*. It touched on his resemblance as an artist to both Beethoven and Wagner, a familiar theme in the early literature on Bruckner, framing part of the discussion in terms taken directly from Wagner:

> Bruckner has written seven symphonies and, with youthful ardor, is
> presently at work on an eighth! This unbroken and tireless freshness in
> creation, this ceaseless devotion to an artistic genre chosen as a favorite

[40] Richard Wagner, "Über das Dirigieren," *Gesammelte Schriften* VIII, pp. 313–16.
[41] From an article to be discussed at length below, "Anton Bruckner. Die beim Bruckner-Commers nicht gehaltene Festrede von August Göllerich," *Deutsches Volksblatt*, 13 and 15 December 1891.
[42] There are a number of possible sources for the term "innere Notwendigkeit" favored by Wagner; see *Oper und Drama*, ed. Klaus Kropfinger (Stuttgart: Philipp Reclam jun.,

1984), p. 405.
[43] Richard Wagner, "Deutsche Kunst und deutsche Politik," *Gesammelte Schriften*, VIII, p. 97.
[44] Even Helm's review of the Vienna Philharmonic's performance of two movements from Bruckner's Sixth Symphony in February 1883 is mixed: *Musikalisches Wochenblatt* 14 (1883), 216. For the review of the Quintet, see *Musikalisches Wochenblatt* 15 (1884), 296–97.

form, with such relatively little outward recognition, speaks for the inner necessity of the composer, for his true calling. One thinks involuntarily of the deaf Beethoven, who, in his last quartets, "undisturbed by the sounds of life listens only to the harmonies inside himself" . . . and of Richard Wagner, who, when far away from his beloved homeland, laid away one completed "Nibelungen"-score after the other with no hope of any performance whatsoever.[45]

At times Helm and the pianist-critic Hans Paumgartner used their reviews as a forum for criticizing aspects of the modern concert world that made the success of a composer like Bruckner improbable. Both took aim at such familiar Wagnerian targets as subscription concerts, inconsequential or conservative programs, fashionable audiences, and irresponsible critics.[46] They found an occasion to denounce several of these in their reviews of the Viennese premiere of Bruckner's Seventh Symphony in 1886. Helm wrote that "a part of the parquet audience which appears at the Philharmonic Concerts only for the sake of fashion left the hall after the sublime but very long Adagio to provide for their hungry stomachs, a process that was repeated, as well, after the Scherzo."[47] Paumgartner, like Helm and Josef Schalk closely associated with the Wiener akademischer Wagner-Verein, concurred about the behavior of the audience and went on to place some of the blame on certain unnamed critics:

> The audience for the Philharmonic concerts has degenerated increasingly from year to year into a fashionable public. They come to see and be seen, just as they do on the Ringstrasse or in the Stadtpark. They come and go freely as they wish; the whole thing is truly a kind of promenade with music . . . Of course critics, too, have professional responsibilities. One of the most salient is surely, while maintaining full freedom in their personal judgment, to hear a new work through to the end, so that by departing prematurely, they do not give that elegant, modern part of the public . . . an excuse to leave at the same time.[48]

[45] Theodor Helm, "Biographisches. Anton Bruckner," *Musikalisches Wochenblatt* 17 (1886), 46; the internal citation is from Wagner's essay "Beethoven" of 1870. Helm, a long-time admirer of Wagner, is an ambiguous figure. He continued to write for the Viennese newspaper *Deutsche Zeitung* after it dismissed its editor, Heinrich Friedjung, in 1887 because he was Jewish. Helm's reviews suggest, however, that he was not as doctrinaire in his anti-Semitism as the newspaper eventually became. For additional information on Helm, see Henry-Louis de la Grange, *Gustav Mahler, Volume 2. Vienna: The Years of*

Challenge (1897–1904) (Oxford and New York: Oxford University Press, 1995).
[46] See, especially, Richard Wagner, "Bericht an Seine Majestät König Ludwig II. von Bayern über eine in München zu errichtende deutsche Musikschule," (1865) in *Gesammelte Schriften* VIII, 125–76 and "Wollen wir hoffen?" (1879) in ibid., X, pp. 118–36.
[47] Most of this review, which originally appeared in the *Deutsche Zeitung*, was reprinted in *Kastner's Wiener Musikalische Zeitung*, 15 April 1886.
[48] *Wiener Abendpost*, 27 March 1886.

In 1885 Schalk devoted an entire article in the *Deutsche Worte* to a consideration of contemporary musical life in Germany and Vienna. He addressed the question: "How is it possible in our musically blessed age that an artist of such significance [i.e. Bruckner] could remain unrecognized into his sixties?"[49] In this essay, originally a lecture delivered to the Wiener akademischer Wagner-Verein, Schalk criticized artistic careerism, taking aim at technically proficient but uninspired orchestral performances and at institutions of music education that emphasized mechanical skills at the expense of spiritual understanding:

> It may, after all, have even been an impediment to the appreciation of Bruckner that his music is more German than anything else that we have had until now in purely instrumental music. To be sure, not more German than Bach or Beethoven in so far as their basic character and that of their work is concerned, but more German in the form of expression.[50]

Noting that Wagner had made many Germans conscious of themselves as a people for the first time, Schalk asserted that many others continued to be alienated from the German spirit and concluded that Bruckner's

> power must seem like shapelessness to them; his warmth like childish ingenuousness. For the most un-German thing about us is precisely our artistic activity. To be German means, as our Master splendidly explained: to do a thing for its own sake.[51]

Wagnerism and Viennese politics (2)

Schalk dwelt upon Bruckner's "German" artistic idealism; he did not refer to the "Other" of German. Indeed, the Wiener akademischer Wagner-Verein, the original audience for his address, included many Jews. This organization, which Helm likened in 1891 to "a miniature Bayreuth for Bruckner," declined to support the anti-Semitic politics that began to pose a serious threat to Viennese Liberalism in the 1880s.[52] According to the critic Josef Stolzing, the Society went so far as to force out members like himself "who reminded the directorate whether in a subtle or blunt manner that Wagner was an anti-Semite until the end of his life."[53] Still, a covert anti-Semitism can be discerned in the reviews of

[49] Schalk, "Anton Bruckner und die moderne Musikwelt. Vortrag, gehalten im Wiener Akademischen Wagner-Verein," *Deutsche Worte* 5 (1885), 470. Leibnitz does not discuss this article.
[50] Ibid., 474.
[51] Ibid., 476. See note 42.

[52] Review in the *Deutsche Zeitung*, 17 December 1891, of a performance by the Vienna Philharmonic of Bruckner's First Symphony.
[53] Review in the *Ostdeutsche Rundschau*, 11 January 1891, of a performance by the Vienna Philharmonic of Bruckner's Third Symphony.

so eminent and steadfast an associate as Paumgartner, for as Stolzing's remark suggests, anti-Semitism was an inevitable part of the Wagnerian world-view.[54] As is well known, this often took the form of rejecting cultural traits considered "Jewish," but accepting as "German" Jews who did not exhibit the objectionable traits: an ambiguous formulation that allowed for Jewish Wagnerites.

A group of young Wagnerites with a number of Jews in prominent positions had, in fact, envisioned and developed the emotional or "sharper-key" style of politics that later became a powerful tool of the anti-Semites. Under Pernerstorfer's leadership, these Wagnerian idealists had espoused radical social reform and extreme German nationalism.[55] I noted earlier that Pernerstorfer's circle initially backed Schönerer as their representative in Parliament, but that his fanatical anti-Semitism caused many of his followers, including Pernerstorfer himself in June 1883, to fall away.[56] Schönerer eventually lost his right to participate in politics for five years after he and some associates assaulted the staff of the *Neues Wiener Tagblatt* in 1888 for issuing a premature report of the German Kaiser's death.[57] Following Schönerer's disgrace, the government cracked down on German-nationalist groups, and most of the Pan-Germans transferred their support for the time being to the candidates of the emerging Christian Social Party.[58]

In March 1890 Schönerer and a splinter group of Pan-German sympathizers left the Wiener akademischer Wagner-Verein. They formed the Neuer Richard-Wagner-Verein, in the words of the Pan-German leader's hagiographer, Eduard Pichl, "to free German art from adulteration and Jewish influence." Pichl wrote that "because the national rebirth of Germanness in Austria is connected in perpetuity with his [Schönerer's] cherished name," the Society took an oath to conduct itself in his spirit and to associate only with other Wagnerites and followers of Schönerer; needless to say, it excluded Jews. The founding members included Göllerich, Stolzing, Camillo Horn, and Hans Puchstein, all of whom wrote music criticism for anti-Semitic newspapers: the already existing *Deutsches Volksblatt* and the *Ostdeutsche Rundschau*, which began publication two weeks after the Society's inaugural meeting. During that meeting the Society declared its guiding principle: "Since Richard Wagner, as a nationalistic artist, was himself an anti-Semite,

[54] Notley, "Brahms as Liberal," 120–21. Although Paumgartner was a pianist for the Wagner-Verein from at least 1877 and became its musical director after Felix Mottl moved to Karlsruhe in 1880, he does not appear on the roster of members until 1887.
[55] McGrath, *Populist Politics and Dionysian Art*, pp. 165–207.

[56] Herwig [Eduard Pichl], *Georg Schönerer und die Entwicklung des Alldeutschtumes in der Ostmark. Ein Lebensbild*, 4 vols. (1912–23; reprint, Oldenburg, Berlin: Gerhard Stalling, 1938), II, p. 59.
[57] Wistrich, *The Jews of Vienna*, pp. 219–20.
[58] Pulzer, *The Rise of Political Anti-Semitism*, p. 153; Wistrich, *The Jews of Vienna*, p. 219.

every Wagner society must also be unadulteratedly German, so as not to become a caricature of an artistic association bearing the name Wagner." Bruckner was named honorary member and Göllerich, the "spiritual creator" of the group, its honorary chairman.[59]

The *Deutsches Volksblatt*, of course, gave an approving account of the founding of the Neuer Richard-Wagner-Verein; both it and the *Ostdeutsche Rundschau* continued, moreover, to make use of Bruckner's growing fame in their reports on the Society's activities.[60] In April 1893, for instance, the *Deutsches Volksblatt* reported that he might attend a meeting set to feature a performance of his String Quintet and a talk by the notorious Houston Stewart Chamberlain, "On Wagner's Relationship to the Social-Religious Question":

> The Society looks forward to a large turnout of members and guests, especially since Professor Bruckner himself has held out the prospect of appearing at the interesting evening, which through the master's presence might lay claim in more than one respect to being called a Bruckner evening.[61]

The fact that political radicals had taken up Bruckner's cause did not pass unnoticed, and it complicated matters for his more moderate supporters.[62] When Bruckner received an honorary doctorate from the University of Vienna in 1891, Göllerich had been his official biographer for some time. As such, he was an obvious choice to speak at a celebratory gathering of students (*Commers*) on 11 December. Because Göllerich's outspoken anti-Semitism made him too controversial, the University eventually asked him to withdraw. Having already prepared a speech, he published it in the *Deutsches Volksblatt* as "Anton Bruckner. The formal address by August Göllerich not given at the Bruckner celebration."[63]

Beginning with its paean to the German spirit, Göllerich's speech was a tribute that a Wagnerian fundamentalist might be expected to conjure up for such an occasion. Peppering his presentation with unattributed quotations from "the Master" – for instance, "only the purposeless is

[59] Pichl, *Schönerer und die Entwicklung des Alldeutschtumes*, IV, p. 586. The *Siebzehnter Jahresbericht des Wiener akademischen Wagner-Vereines für das Jahr 1889*, pp. 8–9, lists members who left the society during that year: Stolzing, Göllerich, Horn, Puchstein, and Schönerer. The report discusses the departure of members who wanted the organization to be actively political, inaccurately calling them students. Helmut Kowar misidentifies the newly formed organization in "Vereine für die Neudeutschen in Wien," in *Bruckner, Wagner und die Neudeutschen*, p. 84.

[60] *Deutsches Volksblatt*, 27 March 1890.
[61] *Deutsches Volksblatt*, 9 April 1893. By now Chamberlain, too, was an Honorary Member of the Society. The composer became gravely ill and was unable to attend this meeting.
[62] Robert Hirschfeld noted in a review (*Die Presse*, 24 December 1890) that Bruckner had "fallen into the hands of political partisans" because of the constant "scorn and ridicule" of musically conservative reviewers.
[63] See note 41.

beautiful" – and with such Wagnerian keywords as "educatedness" (*Gebildetheit*), "guilelessness" (*Harmlosigkeit*), and "necessity" (*Nothwendigkeit*) he exposed the topics in a straightforward discursive manner. But when he began to discuss the historical significance of Bruckner's symphonies, he suddenly started to make a Wagnerian montage, splicing together excerpts from at least six different essays with little connecting material between them. In 1884 Göllerich had made an elaborate exegesis on the vulnerable key issue of Bruckner's symphonies; this time he chose to create a distracting barrage of Wagneriana:

It would have been a rational process if he had consciously overthrown the received architectural forms of music; we find, however, not a trace of that in his works. His rebellion against every constraint of convention lay in nothing but the unfolding of his inner genius – exuberantly free, not to be restrained by anything, even those forms[a] – which allowed us to approach a completely new world in almost completely identical, merely amplified forms. For the same reason that an architect cannot move the pillars of his building at his discretion, nor indeed use the horizontal parts as vertical,[b] Bruckner, too, changed nothing in the structure of the Beethovenian symphony; in that he simply installed expanded and sundry themes and counterthemes on that legitimate foundation, out of which he built increasingly majestic buildings. At the same time he took these apart into their smallest components, to which he gave now predominantly rhythmic, now harmonic significance, allowed them to grow here like a stream in ever new patterns, to disperse there in a whirlpool – always, however, so enthralling through their vivid movement, that the hearer can at no moment avoid its effect, but rather, strained with the most intense interest, must recognize a melodic significance in every harmonic tone, indeed every rhythmic pause.[c] Wagner says that often the real essence of art today is only industry; its moral purpose, the acquisition of money; its aesthetic pretext, the entertainment of the bored.[d] And many of today's composers follow quite intentionally the maxim, "the world wants to be deceived," which Liszt once delightfully rendered as "the world wants trash,"[e] and which we see observed sometimes by even the truly thoughtful with the aim of achieving the desired popularity. Since, moreover, nowadays there is a great deal of traveling, many of the most estimable current symphonists bring back unpliable melodies that have made no impression on others. And we are on our fine way toward having our painting and art exhibitions or our newspaper articles set flatly in music, and downright peculiar instrumental effects and surprising harmonizations based on such a foundation, so that stolen melodies are made unrecognizable and played to the astonished world as classical-vivid music[f] [underlining indicates phrases taken verbatim from Wagner's essays].[64]

Bruckner's position

Wagner's essays thus served as the ideological framework for many of Bruckner's early supporters.[65] Göllerich stands out for his "strict constructionist" approach to the writings, as well as his political extremism. As a result of the split in the Wiener akademischer Wagner-Verein, Bruckner was receiving separate support from middle-of-the-road Wagnerites such as Schalk and the lunatic fringe led by Göllerich. After Göllerich withdrew, under pressure, from the planned *Commers*, he traveled to Nuremberg. Bruckner wrote to him on 5 December 1891:

> To see you or even only to be able to be nearby you is indescribable joy and bliss! Thus away with diabolical influences now and forever in the future. You know my attitude now and from such a long time ago; you know, as well, my character.
>
> Untruth – insinuation – estrangement are the weapons of my enemies! But you have pity on me, you noble one who have gone so far away!!!
>
> Were you nevertheless to come, I would naturally be extremely pleased. (I have been in Vienna 23 years.)
>
> I entrust everything to you; further particulars orally.[66]

The locutions are classic Bruckner, a mixture of caginess and *non sequitur* ("I have been in Vienna 23 years"). The letter seems to suggest both sympathy with Göllerich's point of view ("you know my attitude," "the weapons of my enemies," "further particulars") as well as relief at his apparent decision to stay away from the celebration ("you have pity on me, you noble one who have gone so far away").[67]

We know Göllerich's political position; where did Bruckner stand? Göllerich reported in his biography that, toward Jews, Bruckner felt an

[64] Göllerich used passages from (a) "Beethoven" (Gesammelte Schriften IX, p. 85); (b) "Über die Anwendung der Musik auf das Drama" (ibid., X, p. 232); (c) "Zukunftsmusik" (ibid., VII, p. 127); (d) "Die Kunst und die Revolution" (ibid., III, p. 25); (e) "Publikum und Popularität" (ibid., X, pp. 103–04); f) "Über die Anwendung der Musik auf das Drama" (ibid., X, 238–39). In the immediately preceding sentence he borrowed a phrase from "Über das Opern-Dichten und Komponieren im Besonderen" (ibid., X, p. 227).
[65] The themes established in these early sources recur in later commentaries; see, for example, Göllerich–Auer, IV/3, pp. 9–10. There are other continuities: at least two of Bruckner's students, Max Millenkovich-Morold and Josef Czerny-Stolzing (or Stolzing-Cerny), were active first as Pan-Germans in the late nineteenth century and

then as supporters of the Nazis in the twentieth. (Both men had added names of Wagnerian characters to their original family names.) For Millenkovich-Morold, see his memoir, *Vom Abend zum Morgen: Aus dem alten Österreich ins neue Deutschland. Mein Weg als österreichischer Staatsbeamter und deutscher Schriftsteller* (Leipzig: Philipp Reclam jun., 1940). For Czerny-Stolzing, see Winfried Schüler, *Der Bayreuther Kreis von seiner Entstehung bis zum Ausgang der Wilhelminischen Ära. Wagnerkult und Kulturreform im Geiste völkischer Weltanschauung* (Münster: Aschendorff, 1971), pp. 85 and 127.
[66] Auer, *Bruckner gesammelte Briefe*, pp. 252–53.
[67] According to Auer, Göllerich ended up attending the celebration. Göllerich–Auer, IV/3, p. 198.

"aversion" which, through his piety, he transformed into "profound compassion."[68] The well-known connection the composer made between the Scherzo of the Eighth Symphony and the sleeping "deutscher Michael" had clear political implications: this traditional folkloristic rendering of the Archangel Michael served, within Pan-German circles, as the personification of the German-Austrian people.[69] Bruckner confirmed the significance of this reference in a letter of March 1892 to Helm; he stated that "the Austrian Germans are meant, and certainly not a joke."[70] In a review of the symphony in the *Deutsches Volksblatt*, Camillo Horn noted that, beyond its other more narrowly aesthetic qualities, Bruckner's composition manifested "an additional virtue . . . his German feeling and thinking, which endowed the second movement that he himself had christened 'the German Michael,' with an eloquent expression."[71]

Was Bruckner simply trying to please his Pan-German friends in choosing the title for his Scherzo and allowing the Neuer Richard-Wagner-Verein to use his name? Bruckner's reputation for being a perpetual outsider suggests that he might not have rejected *any* offer of support. An obvious contradiction exists between his Catholic piety and Schönerer's rabid anti-Church stance (*los von Rom* would later be his motto). Nevertheless, the incompatibility of the religious views of the Christian Socials and those of the Pan-Germans did not prevent the two groups from forming a temporary coalition after Schönerer's banishment from politics.[72]

Bruckner did not completely accept the views of the Neuer Richard-Wagner-Verein because he continued to associate with Jews. In January 1891 Stolzing excused this behavior on the grounds that the composer was "so little affected by the influence of the Jewish element." He added that Bruckner "has no 'Judenthum in der Musik,' no 'Modern,' no 'Erkenne dich selbst' on his conscience!" This cryptic passage catches

[68] Göllerich–Auer, IV/1, p. 532: "His aversion to Jews differed from the indiscriminate hatred of the anti-Semites, in that on account of his true and deep piety he changed this feeling into profound compassion."
[69] See, for example, the quotation from Schönerer's organ, the *Unverfälschte Deutsche Worte*, 16 December 1895; quoted in Pichl, *Schönerer und die Entwicklung des Alldeutschtumes* IV, p. 142. Martin Geck, too, has recently noted this connection in his book *Von Beethoven bis Mahler. Die Musik des deutschen Idealismus* (Stuttgart and Weimar: J. B. Metzler, 1993), pp. 396–97.
[70] Gräflinger, *Bruckner gesammelte Briefe*,

pp. 42–43; also, Göllerich–Auer, IV/3, p. 16. The letter is different in the two sources.
[71] *Deutsches Volksblatt*, 20 December 1892.
[72] Both the *Deutsches Volksblatt* and the *Ostdeutsche Rundschau* sympathized with Schönerer although they supported Karl Lueger, the Christian Social candidate, for mayor. Schönerer himself bitterly opposed both newspapers. (He had founded his own *Unverfälschte Deutsche Worte* after the split with Pernerstorfer in 1883.) Kurt Paupié, *Handbuch der österreichischen Pressegeschichte 1848–1959*, 2 vols. (Vienna and Stuttgart: Wilhelm Braumüller, 1960), I, pp. 106–07.

Stolzing in a complicated balancing act. He attributed critical attacks on Bruckner to his having dedicated the Third Symphony to Wagner: "woe to those Austrians [like Bruckner] who proclaim their allegiance as full-blooded Wagnerites, as Wolzogen so admirably names them!"[73] Yet by dissociating Bruckner from Wagner's most polemical anti-Semitic writings, Stolzing denied him status as a "full-blooded Wagnerite."

Why did the radicals treat Bruckner with such caution? One possible explanation is that he did not allow more extensive exploitation of his name. Apart from any possible personal ambivalence he may have felt toward their extremism, he was employed by the Court. It would have been unwise for him to be identifed with German nationalists advocating the dissolution of the Empire. Another possibility is that they did not want to involve him too much in their activities. Their politics stemmed from Wagner for whom the ideal "German" was, paradoxically, supposed to be apolitical. Bruckner's Wagnerian advocates, like his Liberal critics, had an interest in presenting him unidimensionally, in suppressing any suggestion of complexity or contradiction in his character. In several important respects the image of Bruckner was purified, and the ideological filters through which it passed were Wagnerian.

[73] *Ostdeutsche Rundschau*, 11 January 1891.

4 The annexation of Anton Bruckner: Nazi revisionism and the politics of appropriation

Bryan Gilliam

The infamous photograph of 1937 in Regensburg (see plate 4.1) is diffi-cult to forget: Adolf Hitler, in full Nazi military dress, stands gazing rever-ently at a marble bust of the Austrian composer.[1] This likeness, created by Adolf Rothenberger in a style consonant with National Socialist realism, is placed on a dark pedestal bordered in gold and topped with the Nazi seal, an eagle clutching the swastika. Bruckner had at long last joined the other luminaries of German culture in Regensburg's Valhalla, a marble replica of the Parthenon completed in 1841 under the direction of King Ludwig I of Bavaria and filled with images of German cultural heroes of the past. A central goal of the Bruckner occasion was the Austrian com-poser's "elevation" to the status of a full-fledged German composer brought into the embrace of the Third Reich, a step that no doubt fore-shadowed the *Anschluss* of Austria eight months later.[2]

The Regensburg ceremony – which included speeches and remarks by Peter Raabe (president of the Reichsmusikkammer), Max Auer (presi-dent of the International Bruckner Society), Joseph Goebbels, and others – served as a centerpiece for various musical-political events, including a series of concerts, a convention of the International Bruckner Society, and a meeting of the Bavarian District Nazi Party Congress. Through the narrow lens of Bruckneriana this celebration could be interpreted merely as an event capping the festivities of the previous year commemorating the fortieth anniversary of Bruckner's death. From the wider perspective of Nazi political strategies of the late 1930s, this event should, more cor-rectly, be recognized as a launching point.

[1] A full report of the ceremony appeared in Paul Ehlers, "Das Regensburg Bruckner-Erlebnis," *Zeitschrift für Musik* 104 (1937), 745–48. For more recent commentary see Joseph Wulf, *Musik im Dritten Reich* (Gütersloh: Rowohlt, 1966), pp. 155–57; and Albert Dümling, "Entartete Musik," in *Entartete Musik. Eine kommentierte Rekonstruktion*, ed. Albrecht Dümling and Peter Girth (Catalogue for the 1988 Düsseldorf Exhibition), pp. 9–18.

[2] Remarks made by the Bavarian minister at the ceremony make the connection quite clear: "The longing of true Germans for their past, their longing for the great, proud, *united* [my emphasis] Germany has been fulfilled by our Führer." Ehlers, "Regensburg Bruckner-Erlebnis," 747.

Plate 4.1   Adolf Hitler at the Bruckner ceremony in the Valhalla shrine in Regensburg, 6 June 1937. Photo: Ullstein Bilderdienst. Used with permission.

Beyond this Bruckner anniversary, 1936 marked a time when, according to Goebbels, the "chains" of Versailles had finally been "stripped off"; Germany had once again become a formidable military power, and it was time to expand toward Austria, Czechoslovakia, and Poland.[3] Though it may seem far-fetched to mention Nazi military strategy within the context of a Bruckner essay, we shall see how the image of the composer was manipulated in a complex domestic propaganda campaign synchronized with the post-1936 era, a period of mobilization that Goebbels himself characterized as the "danger zone."[4]

Bruckner's importance as a cultural icon for National Socialism goes far beyond marble statuary, banners, swastikas, or even Teutonic cultural chauvinism. Forty years after his death he had become an integral part of a reinvigorated *Gleichschaltung* for post-1936 German culture, a campaign launched in the press and sustained through concerts, music festivals, and even political rallies. The threads that connect Bruckner to the cultural-political aims of the Third Reich are manifold, ranging from the openly banal to the artfully subtle, where words sounding innocent enough to present-day ears were encoded with different meanings to audiences of the 1930s and 1940s.

Hitler's personal interest

The Nazi propaganda campaign glorifying Bruckner would never have taken place were it not for Hitler's personal interest in and identification with Bruckner as a man, a composer, and a fellow Upper Austrian. Indeed, the future dictator had been infatuated with Bruckner's music from the days of his youth. Hitler's early struggles as an artist are well known: the young, mediocre artist from Braunau had tried and failed to enter the Viennese artistic establishment, and he doubtless identified with Bruckner who, decades earlier, found himself outside the Viennese bourgeois musical mainstream.[5] An excerpt from Goebbels's diary from 13 March 1941 suggests both the longevity of Hitler's wounded feelings with regard to Vienna and the direct connection with Bruckner:

[3] Ralf Georg Reuth, *Goebbels*, trans. Krishna Winston (New York: Harcourt Brace, 1993), p. 220.
[4] Ibid., 220.
[5] Hitler twice tried to enter the Academy of Fine Arts in Vienna (1907 and 1908). He also sought admission to the Vienna Architectural School but did not have sufficient credentials.

He would remain in the Austrian capital for another five years, years that Hitler himself discussed in *Mein Kampf*. In *Hitler and the Artists* (New York: Holmes and Meier, 1983), Henry Grosshans surveys this Viennese period as an important context for his later artistic opinions and political policies. "The Viennese Experience," 31–46.

Drive to St. Florian. To the monastery where Bruckner used to compose.
What a beautiful baroque building. We intend to turn the priests out of here
and found a music college and a home for the Bruckner society. A marvelous
plan . . . A farm boy who conquered the world with his music. How rich this
district is in culture, history, and artistic power even today . . . [Hitler]
intends to establish a center of culture here. As a counterweight to Vienna,
which will have to be gradually phased out of the picture. He does not like
Vienna . . . Linz is his darling . . . He intends to make alterations to St.
Florian at his own expense.[6]

An illuminating monograph by Hanns Kreczi chronicles Hitler's preoccupation with Bruckner up to the end of the war – specifically the plan
(dating from around 1941) to convert St. Florian into a Bruckner-
Stiftung under the personal protection of the Führer. This so-called
"Brucknerian Bayreuth" would serve a threefold purpose: St. Florian
would become a "sacred shrine for the immortal works of Bruckner" (to
promote and to maintain a "Bruckner tradition"); it would be the site of
an annual Bruckner festival not unlike Bayreuth; and it would become
the site of a music institute.[7]

But beyond the Bruckner-Stiftung project, the composer's music was
exploited ceremonially, both in live concert and on the radio. Albert
Speer recalled how a movement from a Bruckner symphony preceded
"each of his 'cultural speeches' at the Nuremberg Party Rallies."[8] The infamous 30 June 1937 *Tag der deutschen Kunst*, a massive Nazi-organized
parade celebrating "healthy" German art, opened with a fanfare from
Bruckner's Third Symphony. Granted, the Bruckner melody displays a
certain solemn, ceremonial quality; more importantly, it was the very
theme cited by Wagner himself in connection with the dedication of the
Third Symphony to the Bayreuth master. Wagner and Bayreuth had been
politicized by the new regime within the first year of Hitler's takeover,
and the Nazis saw much to gain by reinforcing the cliché of Bruckner as
"Wagner-symphonist." Such a view is exemplified by a critique of an SS
concert that appeared in *Die Musik* (1934); the commentator even
managed to include Beethoven as a precursor to the Third Reich:

The Bayreuth master, one of the most important pioneers of the German
transformation and one of the boldest oracles of the Third Reich, was
represented by the overture to the *Flying Dutchman*, the "Grail Monologue,"
and "Am stillen Herd." And Bruckner's monumental Seventh, which could

[6] Fred Taylor, trans. and ed., *The Goebbels Diaries* (New York: G. P. Putnam's Sons, 1983), pp. 265–66.
[7] Hanns Kreczi, *Das Bruckner-Stift St. Florian und das Linzer Reichs-Bruckner-Orchester (1942–1945)*, Anton Bruckner. Dokumente und Studien, V (Graz: Akademische Druck- und Verlagsanstalt, 1986).
[8] Albert Speer, *Inside the Third Reich*, trans. Clara and Robert Winston (New York: Macmillan, 1970), p. 130.

be called his "Eroica," is heroically related to Beethoven's Third Symphony not only in the tone of the entire work but also in the *Trauermusik* of the slow movement. It [Bruckner's slow movement] also has as its subject the lament over the death of a hero – in this case it relates to Richard Wagner.[9]

In April 1945 Bruckner's music would be used to commemorate the death of another "hero" when the Adagio of the Seventh Symphony followed the news of Hitler's death on German radio.[10]

Bruckner, Wagner, and the International Bruckner Society

The early, close relationship between Bayreuth and the Third Reich drew minor friction between the International Bruckner Society (IBS) and the National Socialists, despite their friendly ties. Before Hitler's takeover, the aims of the Society were simple enough: to promote the works of Anton Bruckner and to argue for authentic editions of those works. But there was an unofficial twofold agenda as well: to present Bruckner as a rational, logical composer along the lines of the prevailing Brahmsian paradigm and to counter the stereotype of Bruckner as a "Wagner-symphonist." The IBS was delighted with promises of financial support by the Nazis (Goebbels openly pledged money for authentic Bruckner editions in his Regensburg speech), yet beneath this surface of mutual satisfaction lay an unresolved element of tension with regard to Bruckner and Wagner.

This tension would surface in the May 1937 issue of the *Zeitschrift für Musik*, just a month before the Regensburg ceremony, when Auer published an article drawing clear stylistic distinctions between the two composers. Auer's goal was to contrast Wagner's roots in the world of the theater from Bruckner's as a church organist.[11] The fundamental difference concerned orchestration; the *Bruckner-Klang* grew out of his experience as an organist – a sound far removed from Wagner, notwithstanding the Wagner tubas in Bruckner's late symphonies. Most curious in Auer's article is a odd footnote that asserts (in letters double spaced for emphasis) that neither he nor the IBS "had or have" anti-Wagnerian aims. The

[9] Oskar von Pander, "SS-Konzert," *Die Musik* 26 (1934), 206.
[10] H. C. Robbins Landon, "The Baffling Case of Anton Bruckner," *High Fidelity*, February 1963, 47.
[11] Max Auer, "Anton Bruckner, die Orgel und Richard Wagner," *Zeitschrift für Musik* 104 (1937), 477–81. "It is unthinkable [to ponder] Bach's entire output excluding his experience as an organist, Haydn's and Mozart's music without their courtly collaborations, Beethoven's work without his liberal ideals, and Wagner's creations without the role of the theater in his formative years. Bruckner's earliest musical experience was that of the organ at St. Florian."

political overtones to this disclaimer are obvious, for music commentators who criticized Wagner during the Third Reich risked running afoul of the regime itself. Auer was admittedly swimming against the stream in his effort to separate Bruckner and Wagner, an effort undercut by a report in the very same issue in which a contributor suggested that the Bayreuth Festival might well incorporate a Bruckner festival by performing his symphonies on the days when operas were not being staged.[12]

Goebbels straddled the fence in his Regensburg address, for he neither wanted to insult the IBS, who cosponsored the event, nor did he want to undermine prevailing National Socialist cultural views which sought to link the two composers. He twice alluded to Wagner in his address. Early in his speech he criticized those who viewed Bruckner's music as a "symphonic distortion of Wagner's art" – a remark that few could gainsay.[13] But Auer, promoter of the Bruckner organist-orchestrator paradigm, must have swallowed hard when Goebbels continued: "[Bruckner's Wagner] experience had an almost revolutionary effect on the sonority of his musical language [*die klangliche Gestalt seiner Tonsprache*], which only then assumed *that* character that we recognize as the true Brucknerian style ... From that moment onwards the church musician at once retreats almost entirely, and out of him emerges the distinctive symphonist."[14] What Goebbels suggests is a metamorphosis – galvanized by Wagner – from church musician to symphonist, from *Kantor* to *Symphoniker*. This image of Bruckner's elevation to the loftier *secular* realm was integral to Goebbels's post-1936 domestic propaganda campaign.

Bruckner's music and National Socialist "aesthetics"

Beyond Hitler's personal interest and the Wagner connection, what was Bruckner's musical attraction for the Nazis? Was there anything inherently German about his works? The question of "Germanness" in music preoccupied music commentators throughout the Third Reich. It is a question with a significant history in German culture, an issue insepara-

[12] Heinrich Lemacher, "Bruckner in Bayreuth", *Zeitschrift für Musik* 104 (1937), 530–31. Auer replied to Lemacher's suggestion in the next issue, *Zeitschrift für Musik* 104 (1937), 675. The diplomacy of the reply still reflects Auer's desire not to be confused with anti-Wagnerians. Without getting bogged down in the substance and meaning of such a suggestion, Auer merely pointed to practical problems: the sunken orchestra pit and the excessive fatigue it would cause musicians who might need a break on those days when an opera was not being performed.
[13] Helmut Heiber, ed., *Goebbels Reden 1932–1939* (Düsseldorf: Droste, 1971), I, 282.
[14] Ibid., 284.

ble from its racial subtext, and with roots in the anti-Mendelssohn campaign around the mid nineteenth century and the Brahms-Bruckner controversy later on in the century.[15] The issue resurfaced in a slightly different form at the end of the First World War, when wounded national pride catalyzed a search among scholars and journalists alike for cultural identity.[16] And though some of this early postwar nationalism was benign and unreflective, most of it had become strongly ideological and openly racial by the 1930s.[17] By then the conclusions were fairly easy to summarize: Aryan music was heroic, lofty, organic, uplifting, philosophical, and spiritual; non-Aryan music (foreign or domestic) was viewed as trivial, superficial, epigonic (considered a particularly Jewish trait), ornamental without substance, eclectic, and rootless.

Friedrich W. Herzog ("Was ist deutsche Musik?") offers specific examples for the Teutonic paradigm: Bach's *Well-Tempered Clavier* and *Art of Fugue*, Beethoven's Ninth Symphony and Third Leonore Overture, Wagner's *Tristan und Isolde*, and Bruckner's Fifth and Ninth Symphonies.[18] He specifically cites the fugal Finale of the Fifth and the slow movement of the Ninth. Herzog's essay lays particular emphasis on fugue, which had had such a noble German history and which, after the First World War, had allegedly lost its "heroic character." Fugue and chorale, the twin towers of Holy German Art, had been degraded during the "Golden 20s"; they had even been parodied in such works as Kurt Weill's *Die Dreigroschenoper*. Against this perceived backdrop of Weimar pessimism, even cynicism, where cultural values of the metropolis seemed to prevail over those of the village, where the chamber symphony became the new orchestral paradigm, Bruckner's music must have appeared as an enormous anachronism. Bruckner, the schoolteacher from Upper Austria, served as an ideal symbol for *Blut und Boden*; fugue and chorale were essential to his musical expression, and his epic symphonic designs were conceived on a scale unprecedented even for their

---

[15] Leon Botstein surveys the anti-Mendelssohn campaign and its cultural context in "The Aesthetics of Assimilation and Affirmation: Reconstructing the Career of Felix Mendelssohn," in *Mendelssohn and His World*, ed. R. Larry Todd (Princeton University Press, 1991), pp. 5–42. For a contemporary political perspective on the Brahms–Bruckner controversy see Margaret Notley's "Brahms as Liberal: Genre, Style, and Politics in Late 19th-Century Vienna," *19th-Century Music* 17 (1993), 107–23.

[16] Pamela Potter surveys this important issue in "German Musicology and Early Music Performance in the 1920s", in *Music and Performance during the Weimar Republic*, ed. Bryan Gilliam (Cambridge University Press, 1994), pp. 94–106. In the same volume Peter Williams discusses the nationalist agenda underlying the *Orgelbewegung* of the 1920s. "The Idea of *Bewegung* in the German Organ Reform Movement in the 1920s", pp. 135–53.

[17] See Potter's chapter "From National Difference to Nationalism" in *German Musicology and Society from the Weimar Republic to the End of Hitler's Reich* (Yale University Press, forthcoming).

[18] Friedrich W. Herzog, "Was ist deutsche Musik? Erkenntnisse und Folgerungen," *Die Musik* 26 (1934), 802.

own time. It was this very monumental scale – with its grandiosity, lavishness, and spirituality – that appealed to the National Socialists. Moreover, Herzog was hardly alone in recognizing fugue as a cultural-political phenomenon. Hitler himself savored the fugal Finale of the Fifth Symphony, which he specifically selected to close the Nuremberg Party Congress of October 1937.[19]

But was Bruckner the only nineteenth-century composer to write deep, weighty music; to score for a large orchestra; or to compose fugues? Didn't Brahms compose a weighty, grandiose passacaglia for orchestra in the final movement of his Fourth Symphony? Brahms was far too connected with the dreaded Viennese bourgeois mainstream to fit the Nazi model; he was too intellectual and urbane to conform with *Blut und Boden* imagery. Could a great living composer of large-orchestral music, such as Richard Strauss, serve Nazi propaganda? The well-documented rocky relationship between Strauss and the National Socialists during the mid 1930s exemplified the difficulties in dealing with world-famous living composers. They were too independent, too egotistical, and too undependable. Even the nationalist, anti-Semitic Hans Pfitzner was deemed unreliable and ultimately unfriendly to the political aims of the Third Reich.[20] Only a deceased composer could be effectively manipulated by the Nazi Propaganda Ministry, and Bruckner would be ideal.

He would be ideal since the man behind the music had always eluded his biographers, despite the many anecdotes, letters, and a wealth of published material. "Nature may abhor a vacuum," Richard Taruskin observes, "but nothing better suits a historical fictioneer."[21] Bruckner's fictioneer would be Goebbels, whose seventeen-minute speech in Regensburg served as a cornerstone of the campaign to reinvent the composer. The address presented the fundamental imagery and intoned the vital code words that would help prepare for a wartime domestic propaganda campaign.

Goebbels's Regensburg address

Hitler chose not to speak at the ceremony that morning; the burden of recreating Bruckner was left to the propaganda minister, who succeeded in doing so in a remarkably concise, efficient address: a three-part narrative first romanticizing Bruckner's peasant roots, then offering him as a case study in the condemnation of music criticism, and finally characterizing Bruckner as a composer whose genius and spirituality "frees itself of

[19] Wulf, *Musik im dritten Reich*, 249.
[20] See "Der Fall Hans Pfitzner," ibid., pp. 334–41.
[21] Richard Taruskin, "Of Kings and Divas," *The New Republic*, 13 December 1993, 43.

all ties to the church."[22] This last part was the most important, directly coinciding with the breakdown of relations between the Nazis and the Vatican in 1936.

The peasant symphonist

Goebbels exploits various clichés in his sentimental portrait of the composer: the man of humble origins whose childlike purity remained untainted by intellectual doubt, a composer who, despite his "lowly office," succeeded and prevailed through the power of his "German musical creativity."[23] He also stresses Bruckner's rural farmer lineage, his link to the soil, his "mystical affinity with nature," and his undamaged peasant roots – roots he shared with Hitler. This peasant-genius paradox, accordingly, can only be solved by comprehending the "elemental forces of blood and race."[24]

An integral part of Bruckner's "lowly office," beyond his peasant roots, was his work as a schoolteacher, a fact stressed by Goebbels. Hitler recognized that, if the Thousand-Year Reich were to succeed, the frontline for National Socialist indoctrination would be education. Teachers sympathetic to Nazi doctrine soon found themselves in elevated positions of responsibility, but their task was far from what it had been during the Republic. Rather than focus on intellectual development, the National Socialist teacher was expected to mold a personality, which included Aryan racial indoctrination. Education journals served to reinforce racial-political dogma. Indeed, an entire issue of *Der Deutsche Erzieher* (The German Educator) was dedicated to Bruckner; it contained articles published shortly after the Regensburg Bruckner Festival. Most of these essays follow the same formula, highlighting Bruckner as the son of a schoolteacher and a schoolteacher himself, a vocation that put him in the good company of Franz Schubert and Max Reger. As an educator, Bruckner was racially pure, and his connection with the Upper Austrian soil spanned generations.[25]

[22] *Goebbels Reden 1932–1939*, pp. 284f.
[23] Ibid., 282.
[24] "Blood and Soil" (*Blut und Boden*) was one of the most fundamental propaganda formulas of the Reich whereby a healthy state is based upon the foundation of a unified *Volk*, a racial unity created by two factors: common blood and a common, indigenous soil. Under this formula the peasantry, as "blood source" to the German people, was elevated to an unprecedented lofty status, since the peasants' connection with the soil, plowed for the common good, was the most direct. Among other things, *Blut und Boden*

would justify German expansion to the south and east, which would begin with the "reclaiming" of Austria. A cogent discussion of *Blut und Boden* appears in the *Encyclopedia of the Third Reich*, ed. Christian Zentner and Friedemann Bedürftig, trans. Amy Hackett (New York: Macmillan, 1991), I, p. 92.
[25] "The South (i.e. Austrian) and North Germans exemplify the same German characteristics. If, then, as with Loewe, the blue or light colored eyes and the dark blond hair of the Master are mentioned as prominent characteristics, then – from these superficial characteristics – a path is shown

The victim of Jewish criticism

The second part of Goebbels's speech, the image of Bruckner as a victim of vicious Viennese criticism, served broader cultural ends. Lashing out at Hanslick and others allowed Goebbels to address a recently formulated ideological tenet, namely the intolerability of music criticism (or, more generally, art criticism). In fall 1936 the propaganda minister made a public proclamation against *Kunstkritik*, a decree widely circulated in journals on music, art, and film. Art criticism would be appropriate only along ideological grounds; otherwise art commentary (*Kunstbetrachtung*) would be the only permissible form of journalism. Goebbels acknowledges Bruckner with regard to the formation of this new decree: "If the public practice of *Kunstbetrachtung* has been restricted by law to official channels in the *new* Germany, then we believe we have also resolved a debt of gratitude to [Bruckner] who has struggled in solitude, tortured up to his death by his tormentors."[26]

The anti-Semitic flavor of these remarks, though less resonant today, was not lost on his audience: such remarks were fully in line with National Socialist ideology condemning Jews as unproductive, even parasitic. Hanslick and Kalbeck could not compose, they could only write about, and possibly destroy, the honest, creative artists who did. And if Goebbels's speech is vague about the connection between Bruckner, criticism, and international Jewry, Fritz Skorzeny leaves nothing to the imagination: "As Bruckner began his artistic career, international Jewry – in the guise of European Liberalism – had already taken up the fight against the German spirit, which in the arts had begun to stir."[27] This ugly stereotype of the Jew as carpet-bagger appeared in sharpest profile shortly thereafter in the propaganda film, *Der ewige Jude* (The Eternal Jew [Fritz Hippler, 1941]), a project personally supervised by Goebbels. The film juxtaposes carefully crafted shots of muscular Aryan workers toiling in factories with thin, bearded ghetto Jews haggling over merchandise no doubt wrought by the sweat of the Aryan brow.

Bruckner and *Gottgläubigkeit*

The propaganda minister, however, saved the most important element of Bruckner revisionism for last – a clever biographical sleight of hand

---

into the inner world of Bruckner. Indeed, it is a path by which all who share the same blood as Bruckner may travel." See Reinhold Zimmermann, "Anton Bruckner, der große Lehrermusiker," *Der Deutsche Erzieher*, 12 June 1937, 370.

[26] *Goebbels Reden 1932–1939*, p. 284.
[27] Fritz Skorzeny, "Anton Bruckner im Lichte deutscher Auferstehung," *Die Musik* 30 (1938), 311.

whereby Bruckner, after becoming acquainted with the work of Wagner, "retreats" from the role of church musician and "out of him emerges the distinctive symphonist."[28] After Bruckner's engagement with the realm of Wagner, he is elevated to the absolute symphonic sphere, a realm beyond liturgical obligation: "Here his creative genius frees itself of all ties to the church . . . He is filled with the victorious intoxication of form-giving, and a boundless feeling of freedom roars through his soul." Intentionally ignored, of course, were later sacred works such as the Te Deum and the 150th Psalm, an omission unchallenged both by German music scholars and by critics no doubt practicing *Musikbetrachtung*.

That Bruckner was a devout Roman Catholic, or even a Christian, is omitted entirely from the Regensburg address. His religious faith is described simply as "God-believing" (*Gottgläubig*), a Nazi political construction with unmistakable pagan overtones. To understand the context of *Gottgläubigkeit* we need to focus briefly on church-related events from 1933 to 1936. For 1936 not only marked a Bruckner anniversary and a ban on art criticism but also signaled a significant souring of relations between the National Socialists and the Catholic Church, exemplified by the July 1936 papal encyclical *Mit brennender Sorge* (With Burning Concern) and the establishment of the term *Gottgläubig* as an official alternative religious confession only four months later.

The relationship between the Nazis and the church is a vast, complex topic further complicated by Hitler's personal desire publicly to avoid the problem; even *Mein Kampf* skirts the issue. But Hitler's anticlerical beliefs were no secret to those in the inner circle, and the subject of religion came up now and again during the Führer's table talks. Herrmann Rauschning reports Hitler's private remark that "German Christianity is a distortion . . . one is either a German or a Christian. You cannot be both . . . We need free men who feel and know God in themselves."[29] Implicit in this statement is the perception that a belief in a doubtful hereafter is not only futile but a sign of weakness. This antagonism toward organized religion, particularly Christianity, was rooted in the view that ancient Greece served as an important model for modern Germany, a conviction held by German artists and intellectuals of the mid to late nineteenth century, particularly Nietzsche and Wagner.

Hitler chose appeasement as his initial strategy with regard to organized religion, and he succeeded early on with the Protestants who, after the downfall of the Kaiser, were without political direction. For these

[28] *Goebbels Reden 1932–1939*, p. 282.
[29] Guenter Lewy, *The Catholic Church and Nazi Germany* (New York: MacGraw-Hill, 1964), p. 26. Though three decades old, Lewy's study remains a major contribution to the field. See also the lengthy entry "Church Struggle" by Friedemann Bedürftig in the *Encyclopedia of the Third Reich*, I, pp. 140–44.

German Protestants anti-Semitism was no real obstacle. Nor did it largely disturb the Catholic Church for whom it was the Nazi's putative "social-ist" orientation that presented a more serious roadblock to formal rela-tions. The Vatican, moreover, perceived Bolshevism as a far graver international threat than fascism, as exemplified by their Lateran Treaty with Mussolini of 1929, which served as a model for Hitler's *Reichsconcordat* of 1933.

After the German November Revolution the Holy See tried and failed to ratify a formal treaty with the Weimar Republic, but they were able to succeed with Hitler, who saw much to gain. This national agreement of 1933 clarified a number of issues for Rome: financial subsidies to the church, legal status for the clergy, and a Nazi pledge to interfere neither with the work of the Catholic Church nor with its direct link to the Vatican. But a high price would be paid, for the church would have to stay out of national politics at every level. Moreover, it soon became clear that the Nazis would not stay out of Catholic affairs. They mounted a skillful strategy of unofficial intimidation whereby sermons were monitored, priests were harassed, and, of course, a propaganda effort designed to undermine the authority of the Catholic Church was launched by Nazi youth organizations.

By 1936 ties between Germany and the Vatican became irreparably frayed; the culmination was *Mit brennender Sorge*, a papal document that criticized Nazi anti-Semitism, anti-Christian political indoctrination in youth organizations, the erosion of civil liberties, and the deification of the Führer. The National Socialists immediately realized that their church policy, especially with regard to the Vatican, had failed. There was no choice but to recognize Nazism (or, more specifically, German-nationalist identity) as a religion itself and to make *Gottgläubig* an official term, a term proper to the "species-appropriate piety of the German nature."[30] This non-Christian, if not pagan, designation thus allowed those who had left the church to consider themselves still religious, yet it also insured that Jews who left their faith could not be included. The importance of retaining one's spirituality outside of the church was essential given that opposition to Bolshevism (materialistic and athe-istic) was an immutable component of Nazi dogma.

In short, the Third Reich made official something that it had believed all along: that the National Socialist "revolution" was as much spiritual as it was political.[31] German art became a holy art, and music its most sacred

[30] See "God-Believing," in the *Encyclopedia of the Third Reich*, I, p. 348.
[31] See Hans Müller, "Der pseudoreligiöse Charakter der nationalsozialistischen Weltanschauung," *Geschichte in Wissenschaft und Unterricht* 12 (1961), 337–42. Müller cites a revealing "confession of faith" taken by German youth: "I believe in the German mother who gave me birth. I believe in the German peasant who breaks the sod for his

manifestation. The view of music as a sacred art was hardly a Nazi construct; the notion prevailed throughout late nineteenth-century Germany and was held by composers and philosophers alike. Major voices of the Weimar era may have called this philosophy into question, but music as a *heilige Kunst* was soon resurrected in the 1930s with a disturbing political spin. The 1937 Regensburg ceremony placed Bruckner as a god in the holy temple of Valhalla. His music would be the sacred language and Nazism the mystical religion. The link between the Sunday-morning Bruckner ceremony and the Reich's new religious strategy was made concrete by a mass rally that very afternoon. Speaking to some 200,000 people gathered in Regensburg, Hitler – with heated pre-*Anschluss* rhetoric – used the term *Gottgläubigkeit* in public for the first time:

> I will never allow anyone to ever again tear this *Volk* asunder, to reduce it to
> a heap of warring religious camps . . . Generation after generation of our
> *Volk* will march on thus in our history, with this banner always in mind, this
> banner that places us under an obligation to our *Volk*, its honor, its freedom,
> and our community . . . We, therefore, go our way into the future with the
> deepest belief in God [*Gottgläubigkeit*]. Would all [that] we have achieved
> been possible had Providence not helped us?[32]

The pious Bruckner would be the messenger of that "divine Providence." His symphonies, especially in those spiritual slow movements that surpassed even Schubert's "heavenly lengths," were deemed a religious experience, and only those who shared the same blood and soil could fully comprehend the message.[33] Nowhere is this phenomenon better exemplified than in the Viennese *Dunkelkonzerte* of the early 1940s, in which the darkened Wiener Konzerthaus was transformed into a sacred space where listening to Bruckner became tantamount to attending church.[34]

people. I believe in the German worker who performs work for his people. I believe in the dead who gave their lives for their people. For my God is my people. I believe in Germany!" (pp. 337–38). It is reproduced in translation in Gilmer W. Blackburn, *Education in the Third Reich: Race and History in Nazi Textbooks* (Albany: State University of New York Press, 1985), pp. 76–77.

[32] Max Domarus, ed., *Hitler: Speeches and Proclamations 1932–1945: The Chronicle of a Dictatorship*, trans. Mary Fran Gilbert (Wauconda, Ill.: Bolchazy-Carducci, 1990), II, p. 903.

[33] A German review of non-Aryan Eugene Ormandy's interpretation of Bruckner's Fifth Symphony in Linz (1937) dismissed the performance in two sentences: "His art of conducting, which focuses on superficiality, is naturally foreign to Bruckner's Aryan form of art. Technically the 'Fifth' was realized with great verve, but inwardly he glossed over Bruckner's greatness." See Paul Günzel, "Kunst und Kultur im Bruckner-Land," *Zeitschrift für Musik* 104 (1937), 1024.

[34] For a discussion of these *Dunkelkonzerte* see Friedrich C. Heller, "Von der Arbeiterkultur zur Theatersperre," in *Das Wiener Konzerthaus*, ed. Friedrich C. Heller and Peter Revers (Vienna: Wiener Konzerthausgesellschaft, 1983), pp. 101ff. It is perhaps futile to find one specific model for the "dark-concert"; beyond the obvious Bayreuth–*Parsifal* parallel one should remember the force of darkness for various Nazi ceremonies, where focused light cut through the night: evening bookburnings, torch processions, nighttime political rallies with a spotlight on the Führer, and the like.

Other composers might be featured on the program, but the highlight was always a symphony by Bruckner.[35] A facsimile of one such program (see plate 4.2) suggests these strong religious overtones: before intermission (in a partially darkened hall) Mozart's *Regina coeli*, after intermission (in a fully darkened hall) Bruckner's Ninth, the only symphony that Bruckner dedicated to God himself.[36] But the composer would have to be separated from Christianity in order for the National Socialists to make him "God's messenger"; Bruckner the church composer had to be ignored. No doubt in synchrony with Regensburg, a host of articles appeared in 1937 attempting to downplay Bruckner's Catholicism. Peter Raabe stressed Bruckner's "deafness" to the material world: "Blessed are the pure of heart," he declared, "for they shall see God!"[37] Raabe described a symphonist who "talks to God," yet who writes church music of little importance.[38] This paradox cannot be appreciated outside the context of *Gottgläubigkeit.*

Werner Korte acknowledged Bruckner's Catholic roots, citing them as a reason for Hanslick's vehement criticism, but rejected the notion of Bruckner as a "martyr of the Catholic idea" or the perception of his music as an "apology for Christianity."[39] Reinhold Zimmermann got to the real issue, namely that "Catholic" and "Aryan" are contradictory terms: "It would be fundamentally wrong to view Bruckner solely or even primarily as a Catholic. Rather, [it is] the racially oriented consideration of his life and works [that] claims incontestable prerogative in the assessment of Bruckner's personality and achievement."[40] Zimmermann's notion is reminiscent of Hitler's private comment to Herrmann Rauschning that one is either German or Christian.

At face value, Goebbels's Regensburg speech commemorated a solemn, ceremonial moment, with obvious connections to the ultimate annexation of Austria, but as we have seen, his strategy served far wider purposes, fueling a domestic propaganda mechanism for years to come. Hitler's well-documented plans for St. Florian in the 1940s further

[35] The first *Dunkelkonzert* (17 November 1939) offered the Prelude to *Parsifal*, an organ work by Reger, and Bruckner's Seventh Symphony.
[36] These concerts by the Vienna Symphony were all under the direction of Hans Weisbach. The concert featured in plate 4.2 celebrated the fortieth anniversary of the founding of the Vienna Symphony.
[37] Peter Raabe, "Anton Bruckner," *Zeitschrift für Musik*, 104 (1937), 742.
[38] Ibid., 743–44.
[39] Werner Korte, "Anton Bruckners Musik," *Der Deutsche Erzieher*, 12 June 1937, 213–16.

Walter Schilling likewise uses Hanslick as a foil to downplay Bruckner's Catholicism: "Bruckner's music smacks neither of the Jesuit [*jesuitisch*] nor of the heretical as the poor scribes Hanslick and Dömpke have complained . . . [it] is religious in the broadest sense; it is not a manifestation of a religious formula or dogma, [rather] it is solemn [*weihevoll*] and elevated as [is] any true art." Schilling, "Bruckner-Erlebnis," *Zeitschrift für Musik* 104 (1937), 1325.
[40] Zimmermann, "Anton Bruckner, der große Lehrermusiker," 369.

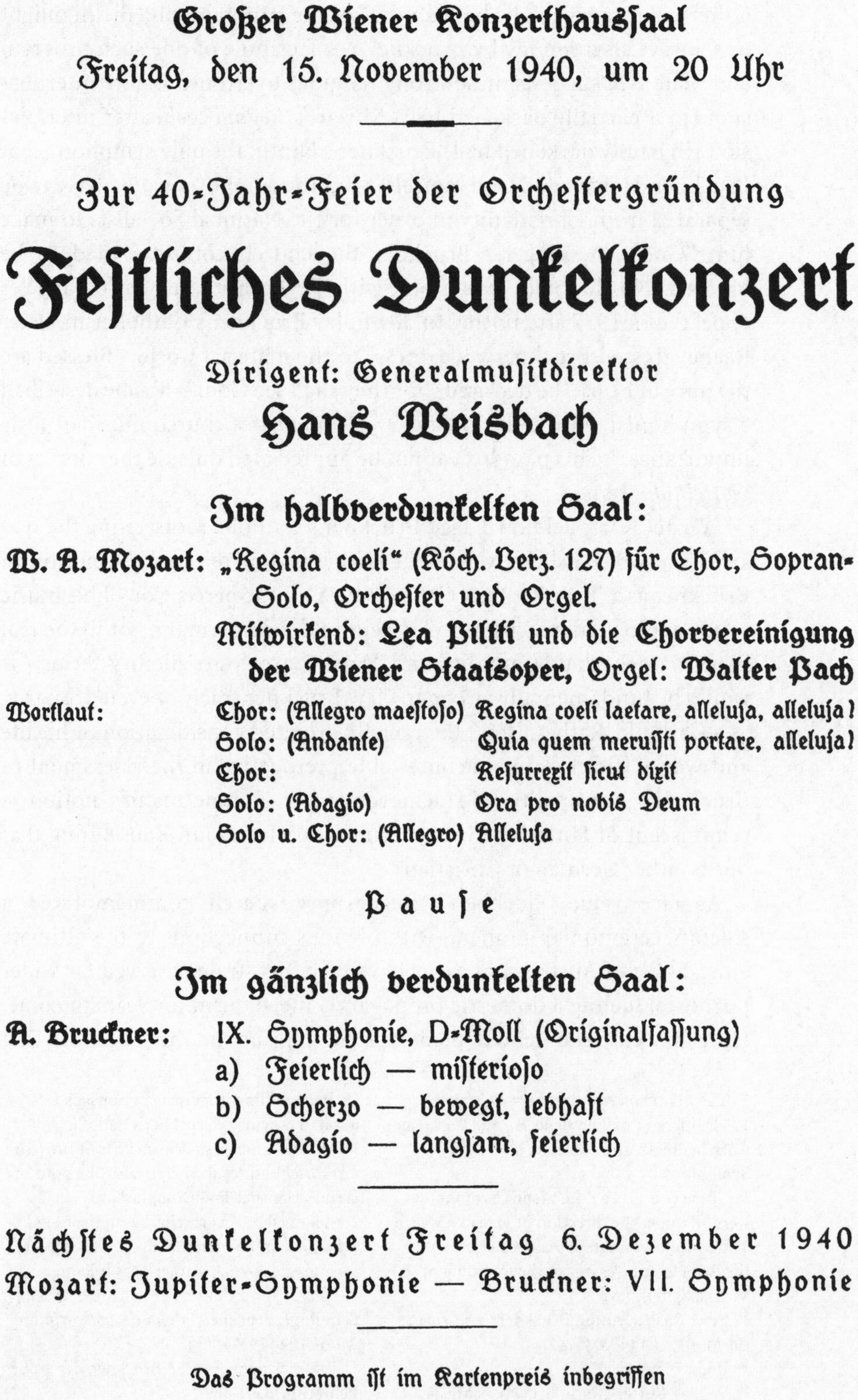

Großer Wiener Konzerthaussaal
Freitag, den 15. November 1940, um 20 Uhr

Zur 40-Jahr-Feier der Orchestergründung
Festliches Dunkelkonzert
Dirigent: Generalmusikdirektor
Hans Weisbach

Im halbverdunkelten Saal:

W. A. Mozart: „Regina coeli" (Köch. Verz. 127) für Chor, Sopran-
Solo, Orchester und Orgel.
Mitwirkend: **Lea Piltti** und die **Chorvereinigung
der Wiener Staatsoper**, Orgel: Walter Pach

Wortlaut:
Chor: (Allegro maestoso)	Regina coeli laetare, alleluja, alleluja!
Solo: (Andante)	Quia quem meruisti portare, alleluja!
Chor:	Resurrexit sicut dixit
Solo: (Adagio)	Ora pro nobis Deum
Solo u. Chor: (Allegro)	Alleluja

Pause

Im gänzlich verdunkelten Saal:

A. Bruckner: IX. Symphonie, D-Moll (Originalfassung)
a) Feierlich — misterioso
b) Scherzo — bewegt, lebhaft
c) Adagio — langsam, feierlich

Nächstes Dunkelkonzert Freitag 6. Dezember 1940
Mozart: Jupiter-Symphonie — Bruckner: VII. Symphonie

Das Programm ist im Kartenpreis inbegriffen

Plate 4.2   *Dunkelkonzert* program (Vienna, 1940)

illustrate how Bruckner remained a Nazi cultural icon throughout the war. Though the Bruckner-Stiftung was never fully realized, a Linzer Reichs-Bruckner-Orchester and Bruckner-Chor were established in conjunction with German radio in 1942, and they continued to perform, both in public concerts and on the air, until spring 1945.[41]

After the war

What were the postwar consequences, if any, of the Nazi appropriation of Bruckner's music? Or is this properly a misappropriation? One could conceivably argue that music, especially if untexted and non-programmatic, resists misappropriation, regardless of its time. But music was merely one strand in a complex network of biographical revisionism wherein Bruckner's life was rewritten in order to sustain racial policies, to validate an attack on *Kunstkritik*, and to create a religious icon for a political mythology. Whether or not contemporary German audiences believed the Nazi propaganda, whether or not they sensed their common soil upon hearing a rustic Scherzo, communed with God during an Adagio, or even perceived Teutonic heroism in a fugal Finale is another large, complex issue yet to be sorted out.

Whatever the case, immediate postwar domestic consequences of the Nazi Bruckner campaign seem to have been short-lived. True, the Reichs-Bruckner-Orchester was renamed the Philharmonica Broadcasting Orchestra in May 1945, during Allied occupation. But it regained its "Bruckner" designation (as the Bruckner Philharmonica Orchestra) just a month later without raising eyebrows. This admittedly small, isolated event sheds light on postwar Bruckner reception in general; unlike Wagner, Bruckner remained generally untainted by the immediate Nazi past. His works continued to thrive in Austrian and German repertoires without external opposition, and his music was never boycotted in Israel.

Yet Bruckner reception beyond the Axis orbit was not monolithic: for much of Europe, especially occupied Europe, Bruckner's music would inevitably recall German occupation, especially throughout the late 1940s and 1950s.[42] In postwar America Bruckner's music did not resonate in quite the same way; his music was largely unknown to concert audiences, no doubt equally ignorant of any Nazi cultural campaign. Indeed, the late forties saw something of a Bruckner renaissance in the

[41] Kreczi, *Das Bruckner Stift St. Florian*, pp. 147–314.
[42] One Danish conductor remarked: "[Bruckner's music] represented everything about Germany we hate, the marching boots, the concentration camps"; Landon, "The Baffling Case," 47f.

United States when, in 1948, the Bruckner Society of America relaunched its journal, *Chord and Discord*. The journal ran, albeit with gaps in publication, through 1969, and by then Bruckner performances were no longer novelties. Eugen Jochum, and later on Bernard Haitink, Daniel Barenboim, Herbert von Karajan, Klaus Tennstedt, and others would undertake ambitious Bruckner recording projects. More recently, with the advent of compact discs, projects have included such rarities as the original versions of the Second, Third, Fourth, and Eighth Symphonies.

Articles on Bruckner continued to appear in German and Austrian journals immediately after the war, though not nearly as many as had appeared during the heyday of the Nazi campaign. Postwar studies took on a more positivistic tone; references to race and soil gave way to editorial issues and analytical problems. German scholars felt unobliged to apologize for Bruckner the man, given the fact that he was neither an ardent German nationalist nor anti-Semitic. But neither did they nor their editors feel compelled to repudiate fabrications concerning Bruckner, race, and religion in Nazi-era issues of those very journals. The National Socialist problem remained largely unaddressed, a policy ultimately in dialogue with the broader *Nullpunkt* strategy of rebuilding rather than reflecting. But this code of silence has itself extended well beyond the postwar, as is exemplified by Leopold Nowak's Bruckner bibliography for the *New Grove*. The abundant ideological, propagandistic articles of the Nazi period are excluded from his list of sources. Those relatively few Nazi-vintage writings that managed to make the list are mostly ones devoid of any overt political content (a catalogue, published letters, memoirs, and the like).

The year after the end of the Second World War marked the fiftieth anniversary of Bruckner's death, an event celebrated by a meeting of the International Bruckner Society in Linz. There, on 27 July 1946, Max Auer, president of the reorganized society, gave an address noteworthy for its silence about the previous dozen years. His speech opens with the lines: "We have gathered here to pay tribute to Anton Bruckner on the fiftieth anniversary of his death. But we do not observe his death in mourning, rather we celebrate life and resurrection! And with joy we unite in the call: The king is dead, long live the king! And Bruckner is a king! A king of absolute music."[43] Though unmentioned, the apparitions of Hitler and Wagner haunt Auer's words. On the surface Auer celebrates Bruckner's death ("the king is dead"), and he looks to a new era of Bruckner research and reception. But beneath that surface lurk other ghosts: another king

---

[43] The speech is reprinted in Auer's *Anton Bruckner. Sein Leben und Werk*, 5th ed. (Vienna: Amalthea, 1947), p. 519.

has died, and, in the wake of the Führer's death, Bruckner the *Austrian* composer has been resurrected from the ashes of Nazi propaganda; the "king of absolute music" has been freed from the fetters of his musico-political association with Richard Wagner.

How different Auer's unrecorded remarks must have been in 1937, as he awarded the Bruckner medal to the Führer in Regensburg. Might they have echoed comments he published only a year earlier? Then, in a preface to the final volume of the Göllerich–Auer biography, he mounted a thinly veiled attack against Weimar-era "materialism," when "artistic Bolshevism was carried out to extremes," and where Bruckner's "God-consecrated art" served as a guide (*Führer*) to a better world – the world of 1936.[44] A decade later, Auer's Linz address stressed both Bruckner's Austrian roots and his international appeal, assertions that admittedly contradicted Nazi doctrine; but did this later speech successfully offset Auer's own earlier remarks? Is it enough that he vaguely alluded to a new era, saying nothing about the old? Clearly not, but as someone trying to launch a reformulated Bruckner society, to encourage more per-formances, and to win over larger audiences, who would want to reopen old wounds?

It could be argued that Bruckner and German politics were never dis-cussed in *Chord and Discord* either before, during, or after the war years. Of course, in the United States Bruckner was not a domestic political issue. He was marginalized not because of National Socialist activities but because his compositional style was alien to the Brahmsian paradigm of logic, balance, and economy so prevalent in the American academy at that time. His music may be better represented in current concert reper-toires and record catalogues, but the man and his work still remain at the fringe of the American musicological discourse, albeit a discourse in transition. Indeed, this present volume on Bruckner suggests just such a shift in direction. And though important issues (editorial, historical, cul-tural, and analytical) are discussed here for the first time or in fresh con-texts, it is equally clear that much remains to be explored with respect to how our present image of Bruckner has been consciously or uncon-sciously affected by the Nazi appropriation of the composer. Could one argue, for example, that important postwar Bruckner interpretations (exemplified by slow tempi and lush harmonies) have unwittingly carried over this phenomenon of Bruckner as Nazi religious icon to the contemporary symphony hall or recording studio? Can we edit or analyze Bruckner today ignoring the fact that such words as "authentic-ity," "purity," and "organicism" were encoded with distinct political

[44] Göllerich–Auer IV/4, pp. 61f.

meanings in Nazi-era Bruckner discourse? Admittedly, such questions suggest broader issues well beyond the scope of this essay, yet they must ultimately be addressed, for Bruckner research cannot move forward without confronting its past, especially the dark chapter of Bruckner reception during the Third Reich.

5 "Return to the pure sources": the ideology and text-critical legacy of the first Bruckner *Gesamtausgabe*

Benjamin Marcus Korstvedt

The first modern critical edition of the works of Anton Bruckner was published between 1930 and 1944 under the direction of Robert Haas.[1] Although it was never completed, the *Gesamtausgabe* revolutionized the text-critical reception of Bruckner's works.[2] The new edition included revised texts of eight of Bruckner's nine numbered symphonies; these were intended to replace – not supplement – all previous editions.[3] Seven of Bruckner's symphonies had appeared in print during his lifetime; these editions had been accepted as authoritative by his contemporaries as well as by performers and scholars in the decades following his death.[4] Their successful replacement required a body of criticism that denied their historical and text-critical validity. In its most influential formulation, the line of argument held that the first editions had been tainted by external influences and did not accurately reflect Bruckner's intentions, and thus new scores based on the composer's autograph manuscripts were needed.

During the 1930s this position was propounded, discussed, and ultimately legitimized in the German-language musical press. Although many of the arguments in favor of the *Gesamtausgabe* are tenuous, their validity was widely accepted at the time. Many critics and scholars saw

---

[1] The original *Anton Bruckner Sämtliche Werke. Kritische Gesamtausgabe* was published by the Musikwissenschaftlicher Verlag, Vienna, which was founded for this purpose. After 1938 the publishing apparatus was moved to Leipzig and then Wiesbaden. For a survey of the history of the *Gesamtausgabe* see Leopold Nowak, "Die Anton Bruckner Gesamtausgabe. Ihre Geschichte und Schicksal," in *Bruckner Jahrbuch* 1983/84, pp. 33–67.

[2] The *Gesamtausgabe* also made available a number of unpublished early works, including the Requiem in D minor, the *Missa Solemnis* in B♭ minor, the *Vier Orchesterstücke* and the "Linz" version of the First Symphony.

[3] The only numbered symphony not included in the first *Gesamtausgabe* was the Third. By 1945 Robert Haas had nearly completed an edition of the 1873 version.

[4] By the time of Bruckner's death in 1896 all of Bruckner's numbered symphonies had been published except the Sixth and the Ninth. The String Quintet, the three Linz masses, the Te Deum, Psalm 150 and many smaller choral pieces had also been published. Alexander Weinmann, "Anton Bruckner und seine Verleger," in *Bruckner-Studien. Leopold Nowak zum 60. Geburtstag*, ed. Franz Grasberger (Vienna: Musikwissenschaftlicher Verlag, 1964), pp. 121–38.

the new edition as the disclosure, after decades of obscurity, of the "real Bruckner." As Franz Moissl wrote in 1936, the *Gesamtausgabe* was "a liberation of the true symphonic will of the master."[5] By the end of the 1930s the Haas edition was widely accepted as definitive and had effectively ousted all earlier publications of the works it included.

This dismissal of the first printed editions has proven to be very durable; in large measure, it continues to shape – and, I contend, constrain unacceptably – current understanding of Bruckner's music. Despite its lasting influence, Haas's *Gesamtausgabe* has been subject to critical scrutiny. The most important stemmed from Leopold Nowak, who succeeded Haas as both director of the Music Collection of the Austrian National Library and general editor of the Bruckner edition.[6] Nowak not only picked up where Haas had left off, producing many new critical scores, he also revised and republished all the volumes Haas had done, rectifying some of the more dubious editorial decisions.[7] One facet of Haas's *Gesamtausgabe* escaped Nowak's reevaluation. During the last half century, the belief that the early printed editions of the composer's works are "inauthentic" has become a virtual article of faith of Bruckner reception.[8] Indeed, there is a consensus that the so-called "Bruckner Case" is closed: as Deryck Cooke wrote in the 1970s, "the first editions . . . have been utterly discredited."[9] At least to this extent, the basic canonical lines drawn by the first Bruckner *Gesamtausgabe* still define the textual province of Bruckner reception.

The assertion that the first editions do not reflect the composer's wishes is problematic on historical grounds. Bruckner never attempted

[5] *Brucknerblätter* 1 (1936), quoted in Alfred Orel, "Original und Bearbeitung bei Anton Bruckner," *Deutsche Musikkultur* 1 (1936/37), 201.

[6] Nowak became general editor of the *Gesamtausgabe* in 1946. Before his death in 1991 he produced editions of most of the versions of Bruckner's works. (The project is ongoing.)

[7] Nowak, "Bruckner Gesamtausgabe," 40–45. Nowak's was a distinct enterprise; he was careful to distinguish between the "alte" and "neue" *Gesamtausgabe*. His editions are based on his own recension; for practical reasons, he reused, with the necessary corrections, plates from the Haas editions of the First, Second, Fourth (1878/80), Fifth, Sixth, Seventh, Eighth (1890), and Ninth Symphonies. In the Second, Seventh, and Eighth Symphonies Haas conflated sources to create texts that he imagined Bruckner would or should have written under the best of all possible circumstances. Nowak pointed out that these

editions do not merit their label "Originalfassungen" but are better seen as hypothetical "Idealfassungen." Nowak, "Bruckner Gesamtausgabe," 40. Today Nowak's scores have replaced Haas's as the accepted, authoritative editions.

[8] One of the few articles to consider the historical importance of the early editions is Constantin Floros, "Historische Phasen der Bruckner-Interpretation," in *Bruckner-Symposion Bericht 1982. Bruckner-Interpretation*, ed. Othmar Wessely (Linz: Linzer Veranstaltungsgesellschaft, 1983), pp. 93–102. Floros explored the value of these editions as reflections of changes in Bruckner performance practice.

[9] Deryck Cooke, "Anton Bruckner," in *The New Grove Dictionary of Music and Musicians*, ed. Stanley Sadie (London: Macmillan, 1980), III, p. 360; "The Bruckner Problem Simplified," in *Vindication: Essays about Romantic Music* (Cambridge University Press, 1982), pp. 43–71.

to suppress, criticize, or renounce them. He attended performances based on most of these scores and, on several occasions, expressed his satisfaction with the concerts.[10] Furthermore, there is clear textual evidence testifying to the authority of several of the early prints. The *Stichvorlagen* for the first editions of the Second, Third, Fourth, and Seventh Symphonies, as well as the String Quintet, survive with extensive entries in Bruckner's hand.[11]

During the 1930s and 40s several scholars were aware of these facts. Perhaps the most important was Alfred Orel, who had been an original member of the editorial staff of the *Gesamtausgabe*.[12] In 1936 he criticized the new edition for what he saw as its unjustified rejection of previous editions, particularly those that had been published with Bruckner's apparent consent and approval.[13] Orel was joined by two European expatriates writing for English-language publications, Egon Wellesz and Werner Wolff.[14] Wellesz, in particular, questioned the credibility of the notion that the printed editions did not represent Bruckner's intentions. He suggested (quite rightly, I believe) that, far from being falsifications, the early editions embody a different, later phase of the creative process,

---

[10] Examples can be found in Bruckner's letter to Hermann Levi dated 27 February 1888 (Franz Gräflinger, *Anton Bruckner. Leben und Schaffen* [Berlin: Hesse, 1927], pp. 340–41); his letter to Felix Weingartner dated 27 January 1891 and his letter to Siegfried Ochs dated 3 February 1892 (Auer, *Bruckner gesammelte Briefe*, pp. 237–38 and 255–56).

[11] The first edition of the Seventh Symphony (Vienna: Gutmann, 1885) was apparently engraved directly from Bruckner's autograph. The *Stichvorlage* of the second edition of the Third Symphony (Vienna: Rättig, 1890) consisted of a mixture of pages from the first printed edition (which had been published by Rättig in 1878) and pages newly copied by Franz Schalk. The entire document, now Wn Mus. Hs. 6081, was thoroughly revised by the composer. The *Stichvorlagen* of the first editions of the Fourth Symphony (Vienna: Gutmann, 1889) and Quintet (Vienna: Gutmann, 1884) are copy scores with extensive additions and annotations in Bruckner's hand. The former is now in private possession; a complete set of photographs is in Wst M.H. 9098/c. Benjamin Korstvedt, "The First Edition of Anton Bruckner's Fourth Symphony: Authorship, Production and Reception" (Ph.D. diss., University of Pennsylvania, 1995); and "The First Published Edition of Anton Bruckner's Fourth Symphony: Collaboration and Authenticity,"

19th Century Music 20 (1996), 3–26. On the Quintet see Nowak, *Sämtliche Werke B*, XIII/2, "Vorwort."

[12] Orel prepared the edition of the Ninth Symphony that was published in the *Gesamtausgabe* in 1934, and his name was listed along with Robert Haas's on the title pages of the four other volumes that appeared before 1936.

[13] Orel agreed with the position of the *Gesamtausgabe* that "for the posthumously published editions [i.e. the first editions of the Sixth and Ninth Symphonies] Bruckner's manuscripts are doubtless the only correct textual basis." "Original und Bearbeitung bei Anton Bruckner," 221. Contrary to Haas, Orel did not admit any such blanket conclusion about the editions published during the composer's lifetime: such decisions, he wrote, "can only be addressed case-by-case, rather than on a general basis." Ibid., 222.

[14] Egon Wellesz, "Anton Bruckner and the Process of Musical Creativity," *The Musical Quarterly* 24 (1938), 265–90 and Werner Wolff, *Anton Bruckner: Rustic Genius* (New York: Dutton, 1942), pp. 261–70. Another criticism, more political, of the editorial approach of the *Gesamtausgabe* can be found in Emil Armbruster, *Erstdruckfassung oder "Originalfassung"? Ein Beitrag zur Brucknerfrage am fünfzigsten Todestag des Meister* (Leipzig: Jost, 1946).

one that was more responsive to practical considerations. Both Wellesz and Orel struck upon the central issue: there is no conclusive evidence that Bruckner considered the early printed scores inauthentic.

The editors of the *Gesamtausgabe* also realized that the dismissal of the first editions was not defensible purely on the basis of textual evidence. To justify their position they combined biographical and psychological interpretation in support of an idealist theory of textuality.[15] All professions of objectivity notwithstanding, ideology as much as scholarship shaped the preparation, reception, and legitimization of the new edition. By the late 1930s the *Gesamtausgabe* had been overtly politicized by the Nazi Government and had come to hold an esteemed place in the official culture industry.[16] The process crystallized with Joseph Goebbels's speech at the 1937 Regensburg Bruckner Festival, when he declared that, since Bruckner's symphonies were a precious national legacy, the Bruckner Society would henceforth receive an annual contribution to support the editing of the "original versions." Goebbels not only offered financial support to the *Gesamtausgabe*, he granted it Hitler's *imprimatur*.

> The Führer and his government consider it a cultural debt of honor to do all that is within their power to permit the whole German people to share [Bruckner's] blessed heritage and, by means of a large-scale promotion of Bruckner-cultivation, assist its effects to penetrate not only deeply, but broadly. On these grounds, they have decided to make a substantial annual contribution to the International Bruckner Society for the editing of the original versions of his symphonies until the complete works of the master are produced in the form he envisioned.[17]

This chapter will demonstrate that this frank politicizing played a formative role in developing the crucial notion that all earlier editions of Bruckner's symphonies were "inauthentic" and needed to be replaced by "original" texts. The editorial policies of the new edition, often riddled with historiographic contradictions, cannot be understood without reference to the ideological context of Austro–German musicology and Bruckner reception of the 1930s and 1940s.

---

[15] The Bruckner *Gesamtausgabe* was not unique; many critical editions prepared in this century have had broadly similar text-critical agendas. On the conceptual premises of modern Urtext editing and the role of text-critical paradigms in shaping the *Gesamtausgabe*, see Korstvedt, "Bruckner's Fourth Symphony," pp. 186–208.

[16] Geoffrey Sharp recognized this as early as 1942; he wrote, "the present *régime* in Germany has made a political gambit of the

Critical Edition." "Anton Bruckner: Simpleton or Mystic?" *Music Review* 3 (1942), 46–54.

[17] Quoted in Paul Ehlers, "Das Regensburger Bruckner-Erlebnis," *Zeitschrift für Musik* 104 (1937), 747. John Michael Cooper's English translation of this address is appended to Bryan Gilliam, "The Annexation of Anton Bruckner: Nazi Revisionism and the Politics of Appropriation," *The Musical Quarterly* 78 (1994), 605–09.

The ideological context of the *Gesamtausgabe*

It is no secret that the 1930s witnessed the darkest chapter in the history of Bruckner reception. The persona of Anton Bruckner and his music figured importantly in the cultural pantheon of National Socialism.[18] Many of the facts are familiar. Bruckner's music was routinely featured at mass rallies and in radio broadcasts. The Nazi government supported Bruckner festivals, including the notorious 1937 Regensburg Festival at which Adolf Hitler received the medal of honor of the International Bruckner Society. Propagandizing about Bruckner was prevalent: Joseph Goebbels described Bruckner as a symbol of "the spiritual and psychic community of destiny, insoluble even to this day, that unites the entire German people."[19] The Nazi appropriation of Bruckner was thorough even by the standards of its time and place. As Mathias Hansen wrote:

> No other musician, not even Wagner or Richard Strauss, indeed no other
> great artist of the past became so unconditionally and totally occupied by
> fascist ideology as did Bruckner.[20]

The glorification of Bruckner was reflected in both musical and critical practice. His music was widely performed and scholarly activity devoted to the composer increased markedly, particularly in 1935 and 1936 with the outbreak of the "Bruckner-Streit," as the debate over the *Gesamtausgabe* became public.[21] Scores of articles on Bruckner and his music also appeared in the non-specialist press. During this era, critical writing about Bruckner resonated loudly with many of the cultural tendencies that underlay National Socialism. Two paradigmatic manifestations were the prevalence of blatantly ideological representations of

[18] Peter Gülke, "Der Schwerige Jubilar: Zu Anton Bruckners 150. Geburtstag," *Musik und Gesellschaft* 24 (1974), 547–50; Mathias Hansen, "Die faschistische Bruckner-Rezeption und ihre Quellen," *Beiträge zur Musikwissenschaft* 28 (1986), 53–61 and *Anton Bruckner* (Leipzig: Reclam, 1987), pp. 19–41; Christa Brüstle, "Bruckner's 'Original' Fifth Symphony: Aspects of its Reception and Use (1933–1945)," unpublished paper read at "Perspectives on Anton Bruckner," Connecticut College, 23 February 1994; as well as my "Bruckner's Fourth Symphony" and "Anton Bruckner in the Third Reich and After (An Essay on Ideology and Bruckner Reception)," *The Musical Quarterly* 80 (1996), 132–60. Bryan Gilliam and Stephen McClatchie discuss aspects of this topic in their chapters in the present volume.

[19] Quoted in Ehlers, "Das Regensburger Bruckner-Erlebnis," 747.

[20] Hansen, "Faschistische Bruckner-Rezeption," 53.

[21] For example, after comprising a mere 10 percent of the repertory in the Vienna Philharmonic during the early and middle 1930s, Bruckner's music formed an average of 22 percent in 1941–45. The total fell to between 12 and 13 percent in the late 1940s and 1950s. His place in the repertory of the Vienna Symphony underwent a similar, if less extreme, upswing after the *Anschluss*. Desmond Mark, *Zur Bestandaufnahme des Wiener Orchesterrepertoires* (Vienna: Universal, 1979), pp. 32, 40, and 50. Also during the 1920s the *Zeitschrift für Musik*, for example, published fewer than a dozen articles on Bruckner. After 1932 the number rose sharply and peaked with a total of twenty-one contributions on Bruckner in 1936.

Bruckner as an Aryan hero and the identification of Bruckner's music with a mythical, lost spirituality. These critical themes were often allied with the highly charged metaphor of cultural rebirth. In 1936, for example, Max Auer argued that Bruckner's music offered a remedy to the modern corruptions that threatened German culture. He suggested that, as "the guide to a beautiful, spiritual world" and a "return to the pure sources," Bruckner's music offered potential salvation from the pressing dangers of "crass materialism" and "artistic Bolshevism."[22] An even more overtly political view can be seen in Fritz Skorzeny's article "Anton Bruckner im Lichte deutscher Auferstehung."[23] Skorzeny allied the increased popularity of Bruckner's music with the imagined "resurrection" of the German spirit effected by National Socialism. He claimed these phenomena were two sides of one coin: the source of the new "understanding" and "love" of Bruckner's music was the rebirth of the German *Volksgeist*:

> It was reserved for our age, to experience for the first time, with the deepest emotion, the break of dawn light, the great "Awake, the day is nigh." In this light the miracle of Anton Bruckner is fulfilled.[24]

Völkisch critical strategies were not confined to the margins of the critical discourse about Bruckner. A broad spectrum of the musicological discussion of Bruckner was infused with rhetoric of this sort. Consider, for example, the "Einleitung" of Robert Haas's influential biography:

> Anton Bruckner's artistic appearance presents a tightly bound essential unity of life and work of such keenly marked and extraordinary mental attitude, that its significance reaches far beyond purely musical concerns. In the age of machines and materialism it contains the full primordial power of German mysticism and allows its soulful fervor and ardor [*ihre seelentiefe Inbrunst and Glut*] to shine forth . . .[25]

---

[22] Auer's striking rhetoric merits lengthy quotation:

> For four years destruction was visited upon Europe [i.e. the First World War] . . . Out of deepest need the people called out for guidance. False leaders brought nations and peoples to the edge of the precipice in the following decades. It became apparent that without spiritual renewal, recuperation was not possible. A yearning for elevation out of the misery caused by the crass materialism of the preceding century grew ever greater . . . Artistic Bolshevism was carried to extremes. Against all this there was but one remedy: a return to the pure sources! What art was purer than that born of the deep religiosity of Bach, Beethoven and Bruckner. Especially Bruckner's God-consecrated art now found a fertile soil, at last it was rightly understood. For many thousands it was the guide [*Führer*] to a beautiful, spiritual world and thereby the foundations of a healthy and strong Bruckner movement were laid which is only now, after the World War, succeeding with elemental power. (Göllerich–Auer, IV/4, pp. 61–62.)

[23] *Die Musik* 30 (1938), 310–13.

[24] Ibid., 311.

[25] Robert Haas, *Anton Bruckner* (Potsdam: Athenaion, 1934), p. 1.

Following comments on Bruckner's profoundly German nature and comparisons with such icons of the German anti-modernist right as Meister Eckhardt, Jacob Böhm, and Rainer Maria Rilke, Haas closed his essay:

> This [Bruckner's] Weltanschauung is fully and thoroughly grounded in the German essence, its musical setting allows the German soul to stream forth unclouded; every cosmopolitan refinement and every admixture of foreign blood [jeder weltbürgerliche Schliff und jede fremde Blutmischung] is absent, as by a law of nature. Even the formative experience of Catholicism left no traces. Hence the Germans' impetuous, drunken love for this master is as understandable as is the reserve of other nations.[26]

In hindsight, the ideological biases of such critical positions are so clearly bound up with the culture of Nazism that today no responsible person would lend them any real credence.[27]

The origins of the Bruckner Gesamtausgabe

The roots of the controversy over the authenticity of the early printed editions extend back to the 1920s, when scholars began to suspect that the available editions might be unreliable. The issue was raised for the first time in 1919 in an article entitled "Wichtige Aufgaben der Musikwissenschaft gegenüber Anton Bruckner" by Georg Göhler, a German conductor and scholar.[28] He argued that the published scores of Bruckner's symphonies were so poorly prepared that they made performance unnecessarily difficult; a new critical edition was needed.[29] His perspective was that of a performer, rather than a scholar or philologist; his call for an edition that reflected "what Bruckner himself had originally written" was not based on evidence drawn from Bruckner's manuscripts. Rather, Göhler argued that inconsistencies in certain published editions (such as prevalent errors in the orchestral parts of the Sixth Symphony and discrepancies between the published orchestral score and piano score of the same symphony) were indicative of sloppy work by Bruckner's publishers (Verlagsschlamperei). He felt that an edition based on Bruckner's manuscript texts would allow conductors discretion about what to alter in performance.[30]

[26] Ibid., 6.
[27] Facets of the legacy of German Bruckner reception in the 1930s and 1940s, including most of Haas's study, have proven to be of more lasting value. Several books of continuing importance were published including the third and fourth volumes (Linz and Vienna years) of the Göllerich–Auer biography, as well as Robert Haas's study of the composer.

[28] Georg Göhler, "Wichtige Aufgaben der Musikwissenschaft gegenüber Anton Bruckner," Zeitschrift für Musikwissenschaft 1 (1919), 293–95.
[29] Göhler proposed 1927 for the publication of this new edition since Bruckner's works were under copyright until that date.
[30] Ibid., 294.

Alfred Orel published a reply that emphasized scholarly rather than practical concerns.[31] He rejected Göhler's permissive attitude towards textual license in performance and was at pains to distinguish between practical and "scholarly-critical" (*wissenschaftlich-kritisch*) editions. A critical edition of Bruckner's work, Orel argued, must be based on Bruckner's manuscripts. He invoked the authority of Guido Adler, who had studied under Bruckner at the Vienna Conservatory, to support his claim that there were significant discrepancies between the printed versions and autograph manuscripts of Bruckner's symphonies.[32]

Despite the articles by Orel and Göhler, editorial problems were not widely discussed in the abundant scholarly writing about Bruckner that appeared during the first half of the 1920s.[33] It was not until 1927 with the founding of the International Bruckner Society that these issues began to dominate. The original by-laws of the organization reflect the positions of both Göhler and Orel: they state that the central goals of the organization included "the preparation of a complete critical edition of Anton Bruckner's musical works" and "the publication of error-free practical editions [*fehlerfreier praktischer Ausgaben*]."[34]

The text-critical argument of the *Gesamtausgabe*

In practice, the *Gesamtausgabe* project assumed a dimension which could not have been foreseen in 1927, let alone 1919 when Göhler first called for a new edition. Total rejection of the early prints required an extensive campaign to establish the superiority of manuscript sources. One of the most important strategies was to invoke the authority of Bruckner's will. Bruckner bequeathed many of his autograph manuscripts to the Court Library in Vienna (now the Austrian National Library).[35] These were the

[31] Alfred Orel, "Bruckner-Ausgaben (Eine Erwiderung)," *Zeitschrift für Musikwissenschaft* 1 (1919), 422–24.

[32] Orel wrote that Adler had given a proseminar, "Erklären und Bestimmen von Kunstwerke" at the Musikhistorisches Institut der Wiener Universität. As part of this seminar, Orel gave a presentation on the textual problems of Bruckner's symphonies, enumerating "every single discrepancy" ("jede einzelne Diskrepanz") between Bruckner manuscripts and the printed editions. Ibid., 422.

[33] One of the few scholars to address the issue was Karl Grunsky, "Bruckner-Not: Eine Beitrag zur Neuherausgabe der Bruckner-

Partituren," *Neue Musik-Zeitung* 46 (1925), 213–14. In his *Bruckner* (Berlin: Hesse, 1925), Ernst Kurth addressed editorial problems only once, p. 603.

[34] The 1927 charter of the International Bruckner Society is quoted in Cornelius van Zwol, "Wie original ist eine Originalfassung?" *Bruckner Jahrbuch 1980*, p. 61.

[35] The text of this document has been widely reproduced. Two recent sources are Manfred Wagner, *Bruckner. Eine Monographie* (Mainz: Schott, 1983), pp. 300–01; and Rolf Keller, "Die letzwilligen Verfügungen Anton Bruckners," *Bruckner Jahrbuch 1982–83*, pp. 98–99. See also Elisabeth Maier's chapter in the present volume.

primary sources for the *Gesamtausgabe*. The first promotional pamphlet (1933) observed that Bruckner's will bound the National Library not only physically to preserve the manuscripts, but also to "ensure the accuracy of these texts by promoting worthy publications."[36] Claims that editors were "duty-bound" by the will to publish *only* manuscript versions of his works became a frequent refrain in the "Bruckner-Streit" of the 1930s.[37] In point of fact, the text of Bruckner's will does not state, or even suggest, that the bequeathed manuscripts are the only valid sources of his works.

Often the claim that the *Gesamtausgabe* fulfilled the dictates of Bruckner's will was allied with the notion that the composer believed his "original versions" (i.e. his manuscript versions) to be valid only for "later times" ("spätere Zeiten"). The will contains no such reference to posterity. Bruckner once used the phrase "spätere Zeiten" himself in quite a different connection. Writing to Felix Weingartner in 1891, he requested that the conductor cut the Finale of the Eighth Symphony, since "it would be much too long and is valid only for *spätere Zeiten* and indeed [only] for a circle of friends and cognoscenti."[38] Although this statement indicates that Bruckner harbored a belief that his works were destined for the future, its value as an argument against the first edition of the Eighth Symphony is uncertain. It is possible, in fact, that the manuscript Weingartner had in his possession was actually the *Stichvorlage* of the first edition.[39] If this were true, Bruckner, perhaps ironically in light of later interpretations of this letter, must have believed that the allegedly bowdlerized text of 1892 – and not the "Originalfassung" – was meant for later generations. The theme that Bruckner's music was intended for a later age was a mainstay of *völkisch* Bruckner criticism and resonated with aspects of Nazi cosmology.[40]

[36] The pamphlet is reproduced in Nowak, "Die Bruckner Gesamtausgabe," 53.

[37] Robert Haas, "Die neue Brucknerbewegung," *Zeitschrift für Musik* 103 (1936), 1185 and *Sämtliche Werke* A, II, "Einführung"; and Oskar Lang, "Noch einmal 'Der Ur-Bruckner,'" *Allgemeine Musikzeitung* 63 (1936), 279. This notion continued to be repeated after the war: Franz Grasberger, "Anton Bruckners Arbeitsweise," *Bruckner-Studien*, 33–34; Erwin Doernberg, *The Life and Symphonies of Anton Bruckner* (London: Barrie & Rockcliff, 1960), pp. 118–19 and Deryck Cooke, "Anton Bruckner," *The New Grove*, III, p. 30.

[38] "Bitte sehr, das Finale so wie es angezeigt ist, fest zu kürzen; denn es wäre viel zu lange und gilt nur für spätere Zeiten und zwar für einen Kreis von Freunden und Kennern," letter

dated 27 January 1891. Auer, *Bruckner gesammelte Briefe*, p. 237. Weingartner's performance was canceled when he was engaged in Berlin later in 1891.

[39] Bruckner did not normally send out autograph manuscripts for use in performance. In a subsequent letter to Weingartner (17 March 1891, ibid., p. 241) he requested that the conductor not physically alter the score or parts, since it was his "innermost wish" ("innigsten Bitten") that they be published unaltered, suggesting that the manuscript in question was intended as the *Stichvorlage*. After publishing the Seventh Symphony in 1885, Bruckner did not use autograph manuscripts as *Stichvorlagen*.

[40] Hans Weisbach explicitly allied the publication of the symphonies in their "ursprüngliche Gestalt" with Bruckner's

As a historical justification of the *Gesamtausgabe* it bears little weight.[41]

Despite appeals to the authority of Bruckner's will, the fact that most of these editions appeared in Bruckner's lifetime, and that he attended several performances of them, posed a difficult problem for supporters of the new edition. It was downplayed by situating it in largely fictitious biographical narrative. The story is familiar: Bruckner was a naive and simple soul, ill-suited to worldly affairs and, as such, was manipulated, duped, and even coerced by his young associates, especially Franz and Joseph Schalk and Ferdinand Löwe. They adapted and arranged Bruckner's symphonies to suit both contemporary fashion and practical expedience and then, so the story goes, imposed these revisions on the composer.[42]

Often the plot was given a psychological twist: Bruckner's self-confidence was so deeply shaken by his lack of public success, and particularly by Hermann Levi's rejection of the Eighth Symphony in October 1887, that he was rendered even more vulnerable to manipulation by opportunistic schemers. Editions of six of Bruckner's symphonies appeared between the crisis of October 1887 and the composer's death in 1896.[43] These publications were particularly suspect, since they were prepared at a time when Bruckner was supposedly unusually susceptible to untoward influence.[44]

The motivations of Bruckner's young associates were variously interpreted. Often they were considered well-meaning, if misguided, attempts to promote Bruckner's music by making it more palatable to popular taste. Other interpretations were less charitable: in a lecture, Robert Haas went so far as to claim, without demonstrable evidence, that Bruckner was under the sway of "sanctions" threatened by the Schalks and Löwe.[45] And, although he later claimed to have been misunderstood, several who attended the lecture heard Haas suggest that the shock Bruckner experi-

---

"prophetically foreseen 'later times.'" "Erfahrungen und Erkenntnisse," Internationale Bruckner-Gesellschaft, *Anton Bruckner. Wissenschaftliche und künstlerische Betrachtungen zu den Originalfassungen* (Vienna: n.p., 1937), p. 42.
[41] The phrase "für spätere Zeiten" has been invoked for this purpose more recently. See Nowak, ed., *Bruckner Sämtliche Werke B*, IV/2, "Vorwort" and Friedrich Blume, "Anton Bruckner," in *Die Musik in Geschichte und Gegenwart* (Kassel: Bärenreiter, 1952), II, cols. 358 and 378.
[42] The *locus classicus* of this narrative is Max Auer, "Der Streit um den 'echten' Bruckner im Licht biographischer Tatsachen," *Zeitschrift für*

Musik 103 (1936), 538–45 and 1191–96.
[43] The First (1893), Second (1892), Fourth (1889), Fifth (1896), and Eighth (1892) Symphonies and the second edition of the Third (1890).
[44] Haas, ed., *Bruckner Sämtliche Werke A*, IV/1, Vorlagenbericht, II–III.
[45] Haas made this claim in a private lecture that preceded the Viennese premiere of his edition of the Fifth Symphony on 15 March 1936. Paul Stefan reported that Haas claimed that "in the last years of his life, Bruckner was under the threat of sanctions [*Sanktionsdrohungen*] to alter his early works or to allow them to be altered." "Um Bruckner," *Die Stunde*, 15 March 1936, 4.

enced upon seeing the first printed edition of his Fifth Symphony in 1895 contributed to his death in the following year.[46]

Whatever their specific details, such psycho-biographical explanations served two purposes. They distanced the first editions from Bruckner's "real intentions" and provided the new editors with a moral imperative. The first prints were not the product of "inner, artistic reasoning," but the result of the influence of men who were unsympathetic to Bruckner's "robust, austere and organ-like instrumentation."[47] Publication of the "original" versions of Bruckner's symphonies was thus seen as more than the rectification of textual mistakes or sloppy editing: it was the correction of an injustice that had been visited upon one of the greatest and noblest of all "German" artists.

Ideology and the legitimation of the *Gesamtausgabe*

Historical and biographical arguments were only part of the discourse that legitimized the *Gesamtausgabe*. A large body of secondary criticism grew up in support of its editorial claims. This literature depended on a complex set of ideological and aesthetic assumptions. Some of the notions are, although questionable by present critical standards, morally unobjectionable: an idealist view that artworks transcend the material facts of their production; a notion of authorship as the free play of genius; and a belief that the basic goal of editing should be to produce a hypothetical Urtext. One set of premises was not so innocent: the pursuit of imagined textual purity was often couched in terms of one of the main cultural psychoses of National Socialism, the obsession with racial purity.

The Nazi preoccupation with race affected the editing of Bruckner's music in two ways. On one level, by representing (literally re-presenting) the untainted "German" texts, the *Gesamtausgabe* manifested a desire to free Bruckner's works from the specter of an imagined history of Jewish influence.[48] In his postwar critique of the *Gesamtausgabe*, Emil

[46] Max Morold, "Die wahre Bruckner?" *Zeitschrift für Musik* 103 (1936), 536–57 and Victor Junk, "Zur Urfassung von Bruckners fünfter Symphonie. Eine Erklärung," *Zeitschrift für Musik* 103 (1936), 546. Haas responded that he did not actually make this statement but had "related the experience with the Eighth and the events around the publication of the Fourth to the nervous crisis [*Nervenkrise*] of 1890." "Die neue Bruckner-Bewegung," 1184.

[47] Auer, "Die biographischen Tatsachen," 10.

[48] Even the debates about the *Gesamtausgabe* were see by some in racial terms. In declaring victory by the "neue Bruckner-Bewegung" (i.e. the supporters of the new *Gesamtausgabe*) in the battle over the Bruckner symphonies, Auer referred to "the veritable witchhunt against the 'real' Bruckner, that the Jewish Viennese press, above all, could not do enough to support." "Furtwängler setzt den Schlußpunkt zum Streit um die Fassungen bei Bruckner," *Zeitschrift für Musik* 106 (1939), 81.

Armbruster pointed out that anti-Semitism was a formative premise of
the edition.

> The defamation of Löwe and Schalk as "Jews and allies of Jews" [*Juden und
> Judengenossen*] had a determining influence on the position of the
> government of the Reich: Bruckner in Jewish hands, sultry eroticism
> dragged into nordic, *Übermensch* heroism [*nordisch-übermenschlichen
> Heroismus*] – this musical miscegenation must be put to an end once and for
> all![49]

The involvement of Löwe and the Schalk brothers was, at times, discussed
– and dismissed – in racial terms.[50] Max Auer, for instance, cast asper-
sions on the first prints as reflecting the unacceptable influence of "overly
refined city-dwellers [*überkultivierte Städter*]," a coded term for Jews.
Between the lines of Auer's argument lay the claim that such individuals
were incapable of understanding the essence of Bruckner, who was
"deeply rooted in the healthy earth of his Upper Austrian home."[51]

One function of the *Gesamtausgabe* was to remove Bruckner's scores
from the purview of the Viennese publishing house Universal-Edition. In
the decade after its founding in 1900, this firm had acquired the copy-
rights to all of Bruckner's symphonies and most of his large choral
works.[52] Since Universal-Edition had long been a target for reactionary
critics who identified it with such taboos as modernism, atonality,
Bolshevism, and Judaism, it is not surprising that the Nazis would have
been eager to dissociate Bruckner from the firm.[53] Nor should it be for-
gotten that, with the *Anschluss* and subsequent relocation of the
Musikwissenchaftlicher Verlag from Vienna to Leipzig in 1938, the Third

[49] *Erstdruckfassung oder "Originalfassung?"*
p. 2.

[50] Although Löwe was of Jewish descent, he
was not always identified as such. He is listed
as a "Halbjude" in *Lexikon der Juden in der
Musik*, ed. Theophil Stengel and Herbert
Gerigk (Berlin: Hahnefeld, 1941), p. 164. In
some Nazi-era books on Bruckner in which
the names of Jews were marked with asterisks,
Löwe's name was *not* so marked. See, for
example, Fritz Oeser, *Die Klangstruktur der
Bruckner-Symphonie. Eine Studie zur Frage der
Originalfassungen* (Leipzig:
Musikwissenchaftliche Verlag, 1939), p. 33,
and Peter Raabe, *Wege zu Bruckner*
(Regensburg: Bosse, 1944), p. 239. (I am
indebted to Brian Robison of Cornell
University for his help with the information in
the *Lexikon*.) Although the Schalks were
Gentiles, they were often mistaken for Jews,
both during their lives and posthumously.
Göllerich–Auer, IV/1, p. 570, and Ernst

Decsey, *Hugo Wolf* (Berlin: Schuster & Loeffler,
1906), pp. 3, 4, pointedly identified the Schalk
family as "Christian." As Thomas Leibnitz
pointed out, the Schalks' physical appearance,
which was easily caricatured with anti-Semitic
stereotypes, may have helped perpetuate the
supposition that they were Jewish. *Die Brüder
Schalk und Anton Bruckner* (Tutzing: Hans
Schneider, 1988), pp. 30–31.

[51] Auer, "Die biographischen Tatsachen," 10.

[52] See Herbert Vogg, *1876–1976. 100 Jahre
Musikverlag Doblinger* (Vienna: Doblinger,
1976), p. 25, and Alexander Weinmann,
"Bruckner und seine Verleger," p. 126.

[53] Douglas Jarman, "Vienna after the Empire,"
in *Modern Times: From World War I to the
Present*, ed. Robert Morgan (Englewood Cliffs,
N.J.: Prentice Hall, 1994), pp. 70–71 and 77;
Joel Sachs, "Some Aspects of Musical Politics
in Pre-Nazi Germany," *Perspectives on New
Music* 9 (1970), 78–79; Christa Brüstle,
"Bruckner's 'Original' Fifth Symphony."

Reich was able to claim the royalties that accrued from the performance of Bruckner's music.

At a deeper ideological level – one that is perhaps part of the cultural unconscious, but no less important – the desire to remove all "foreign" traces from the texts of Bruckner's compositions and to present pure, metaphysically authentic versions resonated with the myth of racial purity. This notion echoes disturbingly in an essay from 1937 by Rolf Pergler on the relative merits of the early printed editions and the Gesamtausgabe.[54] Here the metaphor of purity is transposed from a sociological to a textual plane. Pergler claimed that Bruckner's works were governed by the truth of the "Brucknerian formal principle [*das Brucknersche Gestaltungsprinzip*]"; accordingly, textual contaminations or, as he called them, "foreign bodies [*Fremdkörper*]," could be identified by their lack of harmony with the overall form and eliminated.[55] In Pergler's formulation textual accretions were analogous to the threat to the German people by the presence of non-Aryan blood.[56] Today, Pergler's desire to "eliminate" "foreign bodies" cannot fail to invoke chilling images.

Another tactic was to explain the intrinsic "authenticity" of the newly available "original versions" on the basis of stylistic criteria.[57] Although such studies were not overtly politicized, they were not free of ideological bias. The ideals of objective research were anathema to the principles of National Socialism.[58] Like much of the scholarship produced in the Third Reich, they were marred by circular logic: premises were based on conclusions and vice versa. Such scholarship was often couched in what Adorno later called "the jargon of authenticity."[59] This rhetorical approach, which was allied with reactionary anti-modernism, appealed to the mythology of the sacredness of the genuine, the rooted or, in Heidegger's words, "the splendor of the simple."[60] "Its language," Adorno wrote, "is a trademark of societalized chosenness, noble and homey at once."[61] Rhetoric replaced

[54] Rolf Pergler, "Der Durchbruch des stilbildenden Prinzips in den Originalfassungen der Symphonien von Anton Bruckners," in *Anton Bruckner. Wissenschaftliche und künstlerische Betrachtungen zu den Originalfassungen*, pp. 18–30.

[55] Ibid., 19.

[56] It is worth recalling Haas's comment that Bruckner's music was inherently free from "every admixture of foreign blood," *Anton Bruckner*, p. 6.

[57] A number of studies of this sort appeared in the 1930s. The longest and best-known of them is Oeser, *Die Klangstruktur der Bruckner-Symphonie*. See also Lang, "Noch einmal 'der Ur-Bruckner'"; Alfred Lorenz, "Zur

Instrumentation von Anton Bruckners Symphonien," *Zeitschrift für Musik* 103 (1936), 1318–25; Pergler, "Der Durchbruch des stilbildenden Prinzips"; and Frank Wohlfahrt, "Der Ur-Bruckner," *Deutsche Musikkultur* 2 (1937/38), 144–51.

[58] See George Mosse, "Science and National Socialism," *Nazi Culture: Intellectual, Cultural and Social Life in the Third Reich* (New York: Grosset & Dunlap, 1966), pp. 197–234.

[59] Theodor W. Adorno, *The Jargon of Authenticity*, trans. Knut Tarnowski and Frederic Will (Evanston, Ill.: Northwestern University Press, 1973).

[60] Ibid., 50.

[61] Ibid., 5.

critical argument. Dense tangles of prose substituted for intellectual depth.

Fritz Oeser, for example, opens his book, *Die Klangstruktur der Bruckner Symphonie*, with two opaque sections, "On the Situation of Bruckner Interpretation" and "On the Concept of Structure." He argued that the investigation of the originality and authenticity of Bruckner's works needed to be reframed by moving away from objective empiricism and historiography toward a sort of existential phenomenology.

> All questions concerning the human nature of [the works'] creator, his fate in time and surroundings and his historical position must remain "bracketed" for the purposes of analysis and the *Werkgestalt* must be regarded as a (provisionally) unique case offering information about Bruckner's personal style.[62]

Oeser's odd alliance between phenomenological and historical comprehension betrays a vicious hermeneutic circularity. He argued that the "simply 'given' of the musical work" is "perceptible to the senses," but, "it receives its fullness of sense and meaning from the spiritual 'background,' which is, in turn, secreted in the manifest sounding object [*im klingenden Realgebilde*] and is accessible only through this manifest object."[63] Since Oeser's concept of structure encompassed not only formal criteria but also the "spiritual basis" of the artwork, he was able to posit that engagement with the phenomenal reality of a composition could lead to understanding of its historical dimensions. "Art observation" alone (without recourse to the compositional history of the piece or its *Wirkungsgeschichte*) could ascertain the "content" of an artwork.[64]

[62] Oeser, *Die Klangstruktur*, pp. 11–12. This work struck a responsive chord with the editors of the *Gesamtausgabe*. It was Oeser's Ph.D. dissertation, "Die Klangstruktur und ihre Aufgabe in Bruckners Symphonik" (University of Leipzig, 1939), before it was published by the Musikwissenschaftlicher Verlag. During this period Oeser also assisted Robert Haas with the preparation of his editions of the Eighth Symphony (published in 1939) and the Mass in E minor (published in 1940). In 1941 the Musikwissenschaftlicher Verlag published Oeser's edition of Dvorak's Eighth Symphony. After the war, Oeser prepared the first modern edition of the 1878 Version of the Third Symphony, *Anton Bruckner 3. Symphonie in D-Moll, 2. Fassung von 1878. Mit Einführung und den Hauptvarianten der Endfassung* (Wiesbaden: Brucknerverlag, 1950). More recently, Oeser has prepared controversial editions of Bizet's *Carmen* (Kassel: Alkor, 1964) and Offenbach's

Tales of Hoffmann (Kassel: Alkor, 1977). For a sustained critique of the former, see Winton Dean, "The True *Carmen*?", *Musical Times* 106 (1965), 846–55; revised in Dean, *Essays on Opera* (Oxford University Press, 1990), pp. 281–300.
[63] Oeser, *Die Klangstruktur*, p. 13.
[64] Ibid., 12. Oeser's vocabulary echoed official Nazi positions. In 1936 Joseph Goebbels banned "Kunstkritik" as a nefarious product of "the age of Jewish infiltration of art" and incompatible with National Socialism. "Kunstkritik gesetzlich verankert," *Völkischer Beobachter*, 27 November 1936; reprinted in Joseph Wulf, *Die bildenden Künste im dritten Reich* (Gütersloh: Mohn, 1963), pp. 119–20. In the place of "criticism" Goebbels called for "art reporting" and "art observation." He was heeded by writers on music. See, for example, Wilhelm Zentner, "Musikbetrachtung statt Musikkritik," *Zeitschrift für Musik* 104 (1937), 260–61; and Wilhelm Matthes, "Aufgabenkreis

From this anti-historicist position, Oeser was able to claim that the "questionable authenticity" of the first editions could better be ascertained by means of "an examination against the criteria" of Bruckner's earlier manuscript versions than through historical research or textual criticism.[65] Of course, such an approach could lead only to the reinscription of *a priori* aesthetic and historical premises. Oeser's analyses do, in fact, reaffirm his assumption that the process of "concealing and painting-over the Brucknerian original and its recent discovery by later generations" is "a necessary and meaningful working of a historical and transhistorical justice."[66]

Oeser's discussion of the significance of Bruckner's manner of writing for brass instruments provides a good example of his confused mixture of aesthetic observation, essentialist hermeneutics, and appeals to existential authenticity. Bruckner's characteristic use of brass instruments, Oeser suggested, derived from the techniques of choral music and therefore embodied the essence of choral music-making, specifically "communal being" rather than "subjective experience." The authenticity of the *Gesamtausgabe* editions, Oeser believed, was evident in such passages: in the modern editions, the writing for the brass was more faithful to the inherent "choral soul" of the music than it was in earlier editions.[67] For Oeser, authenticity was more a metaphysical quality than a philological determination. It was, to borrow Adorno's phrase, "a mythically-imposed fate" to be divined through aesthetic experience.[68]

The *Gesamtausgabe* triumphant

The claim that the first editions were inauthentic became a shibboleth of official German Bruckner reception. As Emil Armbruster pointed out, after Goebbels's speech in 1937, the "debate was suddenly silenced when the Nazi government dictatorially called it off with the public declaration" of support for the Bruckner Society and the *Gesamtausgabe*. From this point on "the 'Kritische Gesamtausgabe' was sacrosanct and the 'neue Bruckner-Bewegung' was the winner of the feud."[69] It is instructive to

der Kritik und Kunstbetrachtung," *Zeitschrift für Musik* 104 (1937), 273–80. Oeser followed both the letter and the spirit of Goebbels's ban. As Rolf Geissler argued, critical writing about art threatened totalitarian fascism by exposing the social and historical contingencies of all assertions of truth. Oeser's critical strategy constructed the "authenticity" (read: truth) of Bruckner's music as free from social and historical condition. Rolf Geissler, *Dekadenz und Heroismus. Zeitroman und*

völkisch-nationalsozialistische Literaturkritik, Schriftenreihe der Vierteljahrsheft für Zeitgeschichte 9 (Stuttgart: Deutsche Verlags-Anstalt, 1964), pp. 22–24.
[65] Oeser, *Die Klangstruktur der Bruckner-Symphonie*, p. 11.
[66] Ibid., 10.
[67] Ibid., 53.
[68] Adorno, *Jargon of Authenticity*, p. 127.
[69] Armbruster, *Erstdruckfassung oder "Originalfassung"?*, pp. 1–2.

consider the more skeptical reception accorded the *Gesamtausgabe* outside of Nazi Germany. In Vienna, performances of the new editions of several symphonies (the First, Fourth, Fifth, Sixth, Ninth, and the Adagio of the Seventh) at the Seventh International Bruckner Festival in October 1936 prompted considerable unfavorable response. One outside observer commented on "the rather strange attitude of the Vienna critics. Though otherwise accessible [sic] to new ideas, these writers could not control their anger at the success of the original editions."[70] Many of the most trenchant critiques of Haas's editorial policy (i.e. those of Wellesz and Armbruster) issued from outside of the Third Reich.[71] One interesting dissenting view came from Donald Francis Tovey. In an essay written before the new critical edition had been published he singled out for particular praise musical elements found only in the first edition of the Fourth Symphony.[72] Tovey did not change his opinion after he became acquainted with the *Gesamtausgabe*. In 1939 he wrote:

> Today the pious restoration of Bruckner's original form and scoring is acclaimed as the restoration of things that were beyond the spiritual grasp of the age ... If these changes had been made after Bruckner's death or against his will, there would be a strong case for returning to his original versions; but, apart from their intrinsic merits, they were all accepted and published by him as expressing his final intentions. And it is to these that piety is due.[73]

Some German and Austrian scholars did directly criticize aspects of the *Gesamtausgabe*; such public opposition was not well received. The journal of the International Bruckner Society, the *Bruckner-Blätter*, was not willing to publish views that were unsympathetic to the *Gesamtausgabe*. Max Morold (a Viennese musicologist who had been privately labeled an "enemy of the Bruckner-mission" by Max Auer) criticized the journal for declining to print critical discussion about the new edition. To Morold this refusal was an abdication of scholarly responsibility, particularly since the scholarly community, and even the membership of the Bruckner Society itself, was of a divided opinion.[74] At least two writers who were ambivalent about the *Gesamtausgabe* – Friedrich Klose and Friedrich Herzfeld – felt compelled to employ the

[70] G. E. Arnold, "The Bruckner Festival at Vienna," *Musical Times* (December 1936), 1136.

[71] After the war, several German and Austrian scholars were critical of both the ideology and the textual criticism of the *Gesamtausgabe*, most notably, Emil Armbruster, *Erstdruckfassung oder "Originalfassung"?* and Wilhelm Oerley, "Von Bruckners eigener Hand. Revision der Revision," *Der Turm* 2 (1946), 138–42.

[72] "Bruckner: Romantic Symphony in E Flat Major, No. 4," *Essays in Musical Analysis*, 6 vols. (London: Oxford University Press, 1935–39), II: *Symphonies (II), Variations and Orchestral Polyphony*, pp. 69–79.

[73] "Retrospect and Corrigenda," *Essays in Musical Analysis*, VI: *Miscellaneous Notes, Glossary and Index*, p. 144.

[74] Unpublished letter in the Austrian National Library (Wn F18 Schalk 358/3/7).

terminology of religious apostasy. Herzfeld wondered if it was already considered "blasphemy" to raise reasonable arguments against the text-critical claims of the *Gesamtausgabe*.[75] Klose wrote that, even "at the danger of excommunication," he preferred the first edition of the Ninth Symphony to the new one.[76]

Perhaps the most important victim of this doctrinaire climate was Alfred Orel. At just the time he must have been formulating the dissent he articulated in "Original und Bearbeitung bei Anton Bruckner," his name ceased to appear in publications associated with the *Gesamtausgabe*, and his direct involvement with the project ended. As Franz Grasberger has suggested, Orel may well have been removed from his editorial position precisely because of his refusal to take a position against the first editions.[77] By stifling the *sine qua non* of rigorous scholarship – open debate about evidence and its interpretation – orthodoxy compromised the entire project.[78]

Conclusion

Despite many advances in text criticism of Bruckner's music in the postwar era – including, above all, those of Leopold Nowak – one shadow from the 1930s remains. As a rule, scholars and performers continue to accept as fact the central premise of the *Gesamtausgabe* that autograph manuscripts alone represent the "real" Bruckner and that these are the only texts that matter. As we have seen, the historical justification for this position is tenuous. In the case of some works, the notion that Bruckner was not involved in the publication process is incorrect.[79] For example, although the *Stichvorlage* of the Fourth Symphony was not an autograph manuscript, the composer played a major role in its preparation.[80]

[75] Friedrich Herzfeld, response to Oskar Lang's "Noch einmal 'der Ur-Bruckner,'" *Allgemeine Musikzeitung* 63 (1936), 481.
[76] Friedrich Klose, response to Alfred Orel, "Original und Bearbeitung bei Anton Bruckner," *Deutsche Musikkultur* 1 (1936/37), 223. Although Klose's statement reflects the climate of Bruckner reception, a certain irony in his preference for the first edition of the Ninth Symphony should be noted. It was edited by Ferdinand Löwe and published in 1903, seven years after Bruckner's death; it cannot be claimed to represent Bruckner's intentions.
[77] Franz Grasberger, "Einleitung," *Bruckner Symposion 1980. Die Fassungen*, ed. Franz Grasberger (Linz: Linzer

Veranstaltungsgesellschaft, 1981), p. 12.
[78] As Edward Said wrote, "The one thing intellectuals *cannot* do without is the full intellectual process itself. Into it goes historically informed research as well as the presentation of a coherent and carefully argued line that has taken account of alternatives." "The Politics of Knowledge," *Raritan* 11 (1991), 20.
[79] See note 9 above. In addition to the aforementioned *Stichvorlagen* for the Third, Fourth, and Seventh Symphonies and the Quintet, Bruckner's correspondence documents his involvement in the publication of his symphonies.
[80] See note 11 above.

Almost every page contains his handwriting. Bruckner's personal calendar refers to his work on this score and, in at least two letters, he accepted responsibility for the new version.[81] On 15 May 1888, he signed a contract with Gutmann authorizing its publication.[82]

In the past decade the theoretical basis for editing texts has been subject to considerable reexamination.[83] In particular, idealist models of authorship and textuality and the pursuit of a metaphysically pure and authentic Urtext have been criticized as conceptually naive and historically inappropriate. More recent – and, I believe, more theoretically cogent – critical models of textuality compel us to regard the authorship and production of texts in their historical and cultural complexity. From this perspective, Urtext editing is unacceptably compromised by its premises: its final textual product hides as much as it reveals. As Jerome McGann observed:

> The chief difficulties emerge when textual criticism has the effect of desocializing our historical view of the literary work. When we make decisions about the condition and significance of various texts on the simple criterion of the author's (final) intention we foster serious misconceptions about the nature of literary production. Too many relevant aspects of the literary work are de-emphasized, or even abstracted from the critical view altogether, when we operate on such a principle.[84]

Accepting the creation and production of published musical texts as social phenomena renders untenable any categorical assertion that Bruckner's intentions can be represented only by private, manuscript sources. Bruckner did collaborate with other people (copyists, engravers,

---

[81] Benjamin Korstvedt, "Bruckner's Fourth Symphony," pp. 297–310 and 318–28; and "First published Edition," 7–16.

[82] See Alexander Weinmann, "Anton Bruckner und seine Verleger," pp. 128–29.

[83] This process crystallized with Jerome McGann, *A Critique of Modern Textual Criticism* (University of Chicago Press, 1983), who further advanced his argument in *The Textual Condition* (Princeton University Press, 1991). Many other scholars have taken up the challenges offered by McGann's *Critique*. Philip Cohen and David H. Jackson, "Notes on Emerging Paradigms in Editorial Theory," *Devils and Angels: Textual Editing and Literary Theory*, ed. Philip Cohen (Charlottesville: University Press of Virginia, 1991), pp. 103–23; Paul Eggert, "Textual Product or Textual Process: Procedures and Assumptions of Critical Editing," *Devils and Angels*, ed. Cohen, pp. 57–77; Peter Shillingsburg, "An Inquiry into the Social Status of Texts and

Modes of Textual Criticism," *Studies in Bibliography* 42 (1989), 55–79; Jack Stillinger, "Multiple Authorship and the Question of Authority," *Text* 5 (1991), 285–86; and John Sutherland, "Publishing History: A Hole at the Centre of Literary Sociology," *Critical Inquiry* 14 (1988), 574–89. This discussion of the theory and methodology of textual criticism has not yet entered the mainstream of musicological thought. Among the musicologists to have addressed it are Philip Brett, "Text, Context and the Early Music Editor," in *Authenticity and Early Music*, ed. Nicholas Kenyon (Oxford University Press, 1988), pp. 84–114; James Grier, *The Critical Editing of Music: History, Method, and Practice* (Cambridge University Press, 1996), pp. 16–19; and James Hepokoski, "Overriding the Autograph Score: The Problem of Textual Authority in Verdi's *Falstaff*," *Studi Verdiani* (1992), 14–51.

[84] McGann, *Critique*, p. 121.

editors, proof-readers, friends, advisors) when he published his scores, but simply to reject these texts in search of a "pure, original" text is to go too far, too quickly. That scholars have, for more than half a century, been willing to do so reflects the continued influence of the text-critical ideology of the first Bruckner *Gesamtausgabe*. The dismissal of the first editions has, in effect, become an inherited dogma; in the process, it has assumed an undeserved mantle of truth and thus escaped critical skepticism.

It is not the objective of this study to advocate a wholesale abandonment of modern critical editions of Bruckner's music. Rather it is to remind scholars and performers that the composer's autograph manuscripts are *not* the *only* valid or historically important sources.[85] The early printed editions deserve to be studied. Their merits as authentic Bruckner must be re-assessed, and their potential as evidence about areas that are only imperfectly understood, including Bruckner's role in the publication of his symphonies and his evolving approach to revision and contemporary performance practice needs to be considered. We cannot hope to understand Bruckner's music in all of its historical and aesthetic complexity until we have studied these texts.

[85] This perception is starting to change. William Carragan, who is preparing a new critical edition of the Second Symphony, considers the first edition of this symphony (published by Doblinger in 1892) to be, in many ways, the soundest score yet published.

6 Bruckner and the Bayreuthians; or, *Das Geheimnis der Form bei Anton Bruckner*

Stephen McClatchie

It is often useful in studying the reception of Wagner's works to make a distinction between Wagnerians for whom the music dramas and the body of theory surrounding them were the sole area of concern, and those for whom the Master's cultural and political writings were no less central than the artistic products. For the latter – believers in the mission of Bayreuth, or "Bayreuthians," as Houston Stewart Chamberlain called them – to be a true Wagnerian was to follow the increasingly *völkisch*-nationalistic, arch-conservative ideology of the Bayreuth inner circle. Their inspiration was a body of anti-Semitic and racist prose from Wagner's last years: the so-called *Regenerationslehre*. Germany's defeat in the First World War only hardened the resolve of the Bayreuthians and their belief in their mission; Bayreuth now served as a symbol, perhaps only for a few, of the remnants of German greatness. This symbolism was assiduously cultivated by Adolf Hitler and the young National Socialist party in the early 1920s, culminating in 1923 with the publication of Houston Stewart Chamberlain's famous letter of support for Hitler.[1]

The primary organ for this movement was the periodical founded by Wagner himself: the *Bayreuther Blätter*, edited for its entire run (1878–1938) by Hans von Wolzogen.[2] The *Bayreuther Blätter* was the arbiter of opinion for Bayreuthians not just in matters of music, aesthetics, and culture in general, but also of religion, philosophy, and even politics.[3] A detailed study of its contents would chronicle the inter-

---

[1] For the text of this letter, see Geoffrey G. Field, *Evangelist of Race: The Germanic Vision of Houston Stewart Chamberlain* (New York: Columbia University Press, 1981), pp. 436–37 and chapter 10, "Bayreuth and Nazism." On the relationship between Bayreuth and the Nazi regime see Bernt H. Wessling, ed., *Bayreuth im Dritten Reich. Richard Wagners politische Erben. Eine Dokumentation* (Weinheim and Basle: Beltz, 1983) and Ernst Hanisch, "The Political Influence and Appropriation of Wagner," in *Wagner Handbook*, ed. Ulrich Müller and Peter Wapnewski, trans. and ed. John Deathridge (Cambridge, Mass.: Harvard University Press, 1992), pp. 186–201.

[2] Winfried Schüler, *Der Bayreuther Kreis von seiner Entstehung bis zum Ausgang der Wilhelminischen Ära. Wagnerkult und Kulturreform im Geiste völkischer Weltanschauung* (Münster: Aschendorff, 1971), p. 86. Schüler refers to Wolzogen as "the" Bayreuthian.

[3] Margaret Notley, "Bruckner and Viennese Wagnerism," pp. 54–71 in this volume.

section of aesthetics and culture with politics in late nineteenth- and early twentieth-century Germany, and their disastrous merger during the Nazi regime.[4] Without a doubt, the Bayreuth circle was a primary source of the National Socialist concept of *Kulturpolitik*.

As the composer perhaps most closely associated with Wagner and the Wagnerian camp in the aesthetic debates of the day, Anton Bruckner occupies a prominent position in the journal – especially in the reviews.[5] The index of the journal for the years 1928–32 lists more reviews of works by or about Bruckner than any other composer, including Beethoven. Publication of the *Gesamtausgabe* in particular was eagerly followed. Contributors to the journal included Alfred Lorenz, Karl Grunsky, Hans Alfred Grunsky (Karl's son), Max Morold, and Otto Baensch. With the exception of Baensch, they all published on Bruckner as well as Wagner, and all were concerned with issues of musical form. In many ways, Lorenz served as the catalyst: in his analyses Wagner and Bruckner meet, and political and musical-analytical ideologies are fused. The intersection of music and politics in Germany in the 1920s and 1930s is particularly evident in his work and that of the two Grunskys, who were very indebted to him. This paper opens with a brief description of Lorenz's method of musical analysis and its socio-political implications in the 1920s and 30s. It then considers the manner in which all three authors applied it specifically to Anton Bruckner .

I

The basis of Lorenz's method of formal analysis is the division of works into periods defined by tonality; these periods are internally articulated into one of several recurring formal types: strophic, rondo, *Bogen* (m–n–m), or Bar (m–m–n).[6] The method is rooted in the Schopenhauerian aesthetic position that the essence of music is understood as expression; music is a direct outpouring of a composer's will, and its sole aim is to awaken in the listener an empathetic response to, or copy of, the composer's will.[7] Such an aesthetic position, discussed, for example, in Friedrich von Hausegger's *Die Musik als Ausdruck,*

[4] Peter Viereck has termed this "metapolitics." *Metapolitics: The Roots of the Nazi Mind* (New York: Capricorn Books, 1961), pp. 3–5 and 106–25.

[5] One also finds memorial tributes and other celebratory mentions, for example, Karl Rutkowski, "Ein Gedenkwort zu Anton Bruckners dreißigjährigem Todestage (1 Okt. 1926)," *Bayreuther Blätter* 49 (1926), 191–92.

[6] Alfred Lorenz, *Das Geheimnis der Form bei*

Richard Wagner, 4 vols. (Berlin: Max Hesse, 1924–33; repr. Tutzing: Hans Schneider, 1966). Lorenz may have selected the lower-case letters "m" and "n" to describe formal structures in order to avoid possible confusion with key areas.

[7] Stephen McClatchie, "The Magic Wand of the Wagnerians: *Musik als Ausdruck*," *Canadian University Music Review* 13 (1993), 71–92.

results in emphasis on the production and reception of works of art. A piece of music is a communicative channel between composer and audience and is grasped instinctively and instantaneously by a properly attuned listener. This notion of subjective understanding is indebted to concepts borrowed from Gestalt psychology. In Lorenz's analysis, the periods into which works are divided are examples of instinctively perceived wholes.[8]

Although Wagner's works were Lorenz's primary analytical interest, he applied his method to other composers. For example, concerning Mozart's operatic Finales, Lorenz writes:

> Do not take it amiss that I apply to Mozart expressions which arose in relation to Wagner . . . This is not a case of forcing Wagnerian principles onto eighteenth-century composers (a damnable, entirely unhistorical enterprise which has produced many false conclusions), but rather of recognizing the *eternal laws of form*, to which Wagner, too, had to submit.[9]

Elsewhere Lorenz employs stronger terms:

> I discovered that all music is based on only a few formal types . . . which may be discovered in all sizes from the most extensive pieces of music to the shortest themes, and which, in their similar psychological effectiveness, provide the work with the same rhythmic momentum that is communicated to the listener and thereby awakens his enthusiasm.[10] . . . All of these formal types . . . are found in all classical, pre-classical, and post-classical music, and even in primitive and exotic music. Therefore they form the basis for a new typology of musical forms, understood [even] as it is created.[11]

Lorenzian formal analysis was very influential in Germany during the 1920s and 30s, and was applied to music by composers ranging from Schütz, Bach, and Beethoven to Liszt, Richard Strauss, Humperdinck, and Bruckner.[12] The studies vary in their fidelity to Lorenz's method; all

[8] For a detailed evaluation of Lorenz's aesthetics and ideology, see Stephen McClatchie, "Alfred Lorenz as Theorist and Analyst" (Ph.D. diss., The University of Western Ontario, 1994).

[9] Alfred Lorenz, "Das Finale in Mozarts Meisteropern," *Die Musik* 19 (1927), 622n.

[10] Alfred Lorenz, "Wege zur Erkenntnis von Richard Wagners Kunstwerk," *Bayreuther Blätter* 56 (1933), 113.

[11] Lorenz, *Geheimnis der Form*, III, pp. 187–88.

[12] Otto Baensch, *Aufbau und Sinn des Chorfinales in Beethovens neunter Symphonie* (Berlin & Leipzig: Gruyter, 1930); "Der Aufbau des 2. Satzes in Beethovens IX. Symphonie," *Bayreuther Festspielführer* (1925), 238–46; Joachim Bergfeld, "Die Formal Structur der Symphonischen Dichtungen Franz Liszts" (Inaugural Dissertation, Berlin 1931; Eisenach: Philipp Kühner, 1931); Josef Braunstein, *Beethovens Leonore-Ouvertüren. Eine historisch-stilkritische Untersuchung* (Leipzig: Breitkopf und Härtel, 1927); Hans Alfred Grunsky, "Der erste Satz von Bruckners Neunter. Ein Bild höchster Formvollendung," *Die Musik* 18 (1925), 21–34; 104–12; H. Kuhlmann, "Stil und Form in der Musik von Humperdincks Oper 'Hänsel und Gretel'" (Ph.D. diss., University of Marburg, 1930);

refer to *Bogen* and Bar forms, and most employ a similar method of presentation: formal charts with measure numbers.[13] Robert Haas's 1934 book on Bruckner, for example, employs Lorenzian formal analysis without charts and in a less systematic manner than other writers.[14]

Lorenz and many of his followers have something else in common: arch-conservative, nationalistic political leanings characteristic of the Bayreuthians. These often translated into support for National Socialism. The personal files of Lorenz and the Grunskys in the Berlin Document Center reveal that all three were party members, and the publications of Morold and Baensch, among others, betray strong party sympathies.[15] Articles in the *Bayreuther Blätter* from the 1930s frequently contain such charged phrases as "das Leben Bruckners dem Volk nahe zu bringen."[16] It can be demonstrated, moreover, that Lorenz's method of formal analysis parallels aspects of National Socialist thinking. The similarities, at first implicit, became more evident through the 1930s to the point that one wonders if some scholars were attracted to Lorenz's method precisely because it was easily assimilated into the National Socialist view.

The hierarchical nature of Lorenz's musical analyses suggests an analogy with the interlocking levels of party and national organization. For example, the *Stollen* and *Abgesang* of a large Bar form may themselves be in Bar form consisting of smaller Bars which further subdivide, and so on. The Nazi party and Germany as a whole after 1933 were organized in a similar hierarchical fashion into *Gaue, Kreise, Ortsgruppen*, and *Zellen*. Lorenz's emphasis on wholes rather than parts – indeed the devaluation of parts separate from wholes – is analogous to the Nazi emphasis on party ties and collectivity of the *Volk* at the expense of individualism and individual relationships such as those to family or church. His anti-intellectual emphasis on experience over rational thought echoes a similar

Wilhelm Luetger, "Bachs Motette 'Jesu meine Freude,'" *Musik und Kirche* 4 (1932), 97–113; Walter Maisch, "Puccinis musikalische Formgebung untersucht an der Oper 'La Bohème'" (Ph.D. diss., University of Erlangen, Neustadt an der Aisch: P. C. W. Schmidt'sche Buchdr., 1934); Heinz Röttger, "Das Formproblem bei Richard Strauss, gezeigt an der Oper 'Die Frau ohne Schatten' mit Einschluß von 'Guntram' und 'Intermezzo'" (Ph.D. diss., Munich, 1937; Berlin: Junker und Dünnhaupt, 1937); Willy Schuh, *Formprobleme bei Heinrich Schütz* (Leipzig: Breitkopf und Härtel, 1928; reprint, Niedeln, Liechtenstein: Kraus Reprint, 1976); Edmund Wachten, "Der einheitliche Grundzug der Straußschen Formgestaltung," *Zeitschrift für Musikwissenschaft* 16 (1934), 257–74. Many composers on the list are on the Wagnerian side of the aesthetic fence and, like Wagner, have been accused, at times, of "formlessness." With the exception of Karl and Hans Alfred Grunsky, I make no claims about the political/ideological positions of the scholars listed here.

[13] Lorenz mentions other similar studies which have not been available to me; many of these appear to have been doctoral dissertations under his supervision in Munich. *Geheimnis der Form*, IV, p. 193.

[14] Robert Haas, *Bruckner* (Potsdam: Akademische Verlagsgesellschaft Athenaion, 1934).

[15] I wish to thank Dr. David Marwell, director of the Berlin Document Center, for providing me with copies of files.

[16] Karl Grunsky, "Pfade und Wege," *Bayreuther Blätter* 59 (1936), 50.

National Socialist sentiment.[17] The evocation of an idealized German past by his focus on Bar form partakes of the same spirit as the Nazis' almost self-consciously archaic "Blut und Boden" mythologizing of that same past. Finally, Lorenz's and his followers' choice of music to analyze can be seen as a type of musical imperialism; there is no *Das Geheimnis der Form bei Gabriel Fauré*. Demonstrating the logical coherence of German music through analysis and linking it with German tradition reinforces its validity and stamps it with an *echt deutsch* imprimatur.

II

Although Lorenz offered lectures on Bruckner and his symphonies at Munich University, he did not publish any of the analyses associated with them. With one exception, his articles about Bruckner are part of a body of work indebted to his father Ottokar's research on genealogy and its potential as an historical tool.[18] Following his father's cyclic biological-genealogical model, he divided Bruckner's life into eight nine-year *Lebenswellen* of alternating productive and infertile artistic periods.[19] His position is clearly that of a Bayreuthian:

> It is thus no belittlement of Bruckner whatsoever if one recognizes what everyone with clear vision sees: that he matured greatly in the second half of his life. The *genius* was naturally always there, for it is a product of his ancestry, his race, and not of his surroundings and their influence (the creative force of the world is simply the will living in [all] organisms). However, the gift of genius must often be awakened by external impetus . . . Wagner was, and remains, the rouser of Bruckner's sublime genius.[20]

[17] This point is developed more fully in my dissertation.

[18] Lorenz taught two courses about Bruckner at Munich University: "Anton Bruckner" (Winter 1930–31, Summer 1933) and "Anton Bruckners Symphonien" (Winter 1928–29, Winter 1937–38, Summer 1939). I have been unable to trace any Lorenzian *Nachlass*. Ottokar Lorenz sought to replace the traditional historical structure based on periodization with one that employed genealogy. He proposed that the most natural structural element was the biological interval of the generation. Each century is comprised of three generations, and three centuries (3 × 3 generations) together form a cycle in which particular ideas are conceived, reach maturity, and decline. All history, argued Lorenz, follows this biological-genealogical model. The

consequence of such an approach is that attention is focused entirely on matters of genealogy and race to the exclusion of external factors such as environment; the political implications are obvious. Alfred Lorenz first adopted his father's *Generationslehre* in a 1928 history of music entitled *Abendländische Musikgeschichte im Rhythmus der Generationen. Eine Anregung* (Berlin: Max Hesse, 1928).

[19] Alfred Lorenz, "Die Wellenlinie in Bruckners Schaffenskraft," *Kirchenmusikalisches Jahrbuch* 25 (1930), 122–27; "Auf und ab in Bruckners Schaffenskraft," *Der Auftakt* 13 (1933), 128–31.

[20] Alfred Lorenz, "Zur Instrumentation von Anton Bruckners Symphonien," *Zeitschrift für Musik* 103 (1936), 1325.

Lorenz evinces no hesitation in linking Bruckner with Wagner; his published writings on Bruckner all date from the early 1930s, by which time the two had been clearly linked in the minds of the political right.

Studies by Karl Grunsky, a Stuttgart journalist who wrote extensively on musical matters, are ubiquitous in the publications of the Bayreuth circle. A regular contributor to both the *Bayreuther Festspielführer* and the *Bayreuther Blätter*, Grunsky was one of Lorenz's earliest and most enthusiastic proponents.[21] In addition to arrangements of Bruckner's symphonies for two pianos, he wrote three books about the composer. The first, from 1908, sees Bruckner in typically romantic terms as an unworldly genius, full of naive faith. Bruckner, to his credit, learned from Wagner, but had a sufficiently original nature to be able to keep these Wagnerian impressions in check: the line separating Wagner from Bruckner is in fact a cleft, not to be bridged even by friendship.[22]

Grunsky's 1922 study begins a shift in perception.[23] The two composers are closer together. Now Grunsky observes that, in Bruckner's works, the tools are often Wagnerian, but the end result is not. In a discussion of why Bruckner's music is not formless, he argues that one ought to value formal innovation in Bruckner symphonies just as one values formal innovation in Wagnerian music drama.[24] More important, in the wake of Germany's defeat in the First World War, Bruckner is presented in nationalistic terms. His is a soul rooted directly in God and in the *Volk*; the God invoked in a Brucknerian Adagio is that of the medieval German mystics, not necessarily that of the church.[25] Grunsky also compares Bruckner's symphonies with gothic cathedrals, arguing that the gothic

[21] The earliest published account of Lorenz's work is that of Karl Grunsky, "Die Formfrage bei Richard Wagner," *Die Musik* 15 (1923), 436–40.

[22] Karl Grunsky, *Anton Bruckners Symphonien* (Berlin: Schlesinger, 1908).

[23] Karl Grunsky, *Anton Bruckner* (Stuttgart: J. Engelhorns Nachf., 1922).

[24] In "Bruckner als Künder einer neuen Zeit," *Die Musik* 24 (1932), 333, Grunsky suggests that it is completely erroneous to separate Bruckner's symphonies from music drama.

[25] The mystic mentioned by Grunsky, Meister Eckhart (ca. 1260–1327/38), argued that there was a distinction between *Deus* (God), as found in the three persons of the Trinity, and *Deitas* (Godhead), which is the Ground of an indescribable God. He makes the same distinction between the faculties of the soul, such as memory, and the Ground of the soul, which he refers to as the *Fünklein* of the soul. He brackets off the discursive and imaginative activities that normally characterize conscious life and asserts that one may attain unity with the Godhead; the truly spiritual person reaches beyond God to the Godhead. For Eckhart the experience of mysticism is not describable in terms of thoughts or images. His assertion that the divine can be found within each individual soul was regarded as heretical by church authorities. The appeal of Eckhart's thought to National Socialists was its anticipation of the idealistic opposition of essence and appearance, and its obvious anticlericism. Hans Alfred Grunsky, *Seele und Staat. Die psychologischen Grundlagen des nationalsozialistischen Siegs über den bürgerlichen und bolschewistischen Menschen* (Berlin: Junker & Dünnhaupt, 1935), pp. 46–47, 75.

style reached its peak in Germany as in no other land. Nationalism turns vaguely threatening when resistance to Bruckner is made into a manifestation of decadence: "in the manner of struggle against Bruckner we see a sign of decay in the air long before the war."[26]

The alleged devaluation of Bruckner as a symptom of Germany's decline is more explicit in Grunsky's *Kampf um deutsche Musik!* (1933).[27] Here Beethoven, Wagner, and Bruckner, unproblematically linked together, are regarded as the culmination of German music, which, in Schopenhauerian terms, provides the listener direct access to the will. Grunsky traces the deterioration of German music in both the rise of modern music (derided as spiritual masturbation and depicted in sexually threatening terms) and in the waning reputation of Wagner. Throughout the book, "modern" and "Jewish" are linked in opposition to "German," and Grunsky argues that these "non-Germans" are incapable of understanding Bruckner:

> [These] others face the immense waves of intensification [*Steigerungswogen*] of Bruckner's music with puzzlement because their souls do not vibrate continually along with them, whereas for us the reverberation is so great that it continually sets new representations into motion.[28]

By 1936, political ideology has replaced musical nuance in Grunsky's work. Gone completely is his earlier concern to differentiate between Bruckner and Wagner. To see Bruckner as influenced only by Wagner's orchestral magic (and thus to devalue the music dramas as mere theater music) is impossible: "Bruckner's life is inseparably connected with Wagner . . . [T]hrough music, Bruckner felt himself to be internally bound with Wagner."[29] According to Grunsky, Bruckner heard Wagner's works as absolute music; he was concerned with their pure form, not just their unfolding action or *Klang*. In other words, he heard them just like Alfred Lorenz, but *avant la lettre*:

> Now, if Bruckner recognized the characteristic value of Wagnerian music from the beginning, this is proof that even at that time he heard almost in a Lorenzian manner [*lorenzisch*], and that he had an equal understanding of the secret of Wagner's musical form.[30]

Grunsky suggests that Bruckner instinctively grasped Wagnerian form and was completely convinced of the worth, value, and logical consistency of the music dramas. For Grunsky the Wagnerian *Klang* did not obscure but rather revealed form and logic; the same was true in Bruckner's symphonies. Anti-Wagnerian opinion in the new Bruckner

[26] Ibid., 113.
[27] Karl Grunsky, *Kampf um deutsche Musik!* (Stuttgart: Erhard Walther, 1933).
[28] Ibid., 10.
[29] Karl Grunsky, *Fragen der Bruckner-Auffassung* (Stuttgart: Heyder, 1936), p. 13.
[30] Ibid., 14.

movement contradicted the facts – should Bruckner be ashamed to have followed in the steps of the Bayreuth master? On the contrary, according to Grunsky, Bruckner was truest to himself when he held with Wagner.[31]

Grunsky, like Lorenz, allowed his National Socialist sentiments to infiltrate his scholarly work and was not averse to using his party connections for personal gain.[32] In a letter to the Reichsschrifttumskammer dated 10 May 1943, he requested permission to publish a new monograph on Bruckner outside of Germany, as his usual printer was at the front. According to the letter, the new work connected Bruckner with present-day concerns, undoubtedly political. Grunsky regarded it as his best work, containing the "experience of a lifetime." His death three months later must have prevented the book's appearance.[33]

The work of Grunsky's son, Hans Alfred, provides an even more interesting example of the juxtaposition of Wagner, Lorenzian analysis, Bruckner, and National Socialism. A philosopher, not a musicologist, he was professor at Munich University from 1935 to 1944 (Ordinarius from 1937) and concurrently held a research position with the Reichsinstitut für Geschichte des neuen Deutschlands. He was also associated with Alfred Rosenberg's ideological bureau, the NS-Kulturgemeinde. The younger Grunsky's major preoccupation during the 1930s and 40s was with National-Socialist philosophy: its history, clarification, and – not incidentally – its promulgation.[34]

During the 1920s Hans Alfred Grunsky was a student of Lorenz's and, like his father, an enthusiastic proponent of the latter's work.[35] Virtually all of his articles about music refer to Lorenz's type of dynamic formal analysis. Many of the parallels with National Socialism latent in Lorenz's writings are more evident; in fact, Grunsky is the only contemporary of Lorenz who makes the connection between Nazism and Lorenzian analysis explicit. In an article entitled "Form und Erlebnis," Grunsky writes:

> The most wonderful [thing] about this new science of form is that it corresponds completely to the ideal that the most recent academic works demand: it is not lifeless, but is intimately entwined with art, with life, and with the *Volk* . . . [Lorenz's] work . . . finds its true niche in the *Volk* . . . for it leads from the recognition of form [*Formerkennen*] to the experience of form [*Formerleben*].[36]

[31] Ibid., 20.
[32] Karl Grunsky (Pg. 420 233) joined the NSDAP sometime between July 1930, when his son Hans Alfred joined (Pg. 264 685), and November 1931, when Alfred Lorenz joined (Pg. 724 866). Pg. is the frequently encountered abbreviation for "Parteigenosse," party member. Lorenz's Nazi connections are explored in my dissertation, pp. 31–47.
[33] BDC Karl Grunsky file.
[34] Helmut Heiber, *Walter Frank und sein*

Reichsinstitut für Geschichte des neuen Deutschlands (Stuttgart: Deutsche Verlags-Anstalt, 1966), pp. 483–92.
[35] In 1943, he published a memorial to Lorenz entitled "Einer der uns fehlt: dem Gedanken von Alfred Lorenz," in *Neue Wagner-Forschungen. Erste Folge*, ed. Otto Strobel (Karlsruhe: G. Braun, 1943), pp. 35–42.
[36] Hans Alfred Grunsky, "Form und Erlebnis," *Bayreuther Festspielführer* (1934), 170.

In the 1920s, he undertook research, supported by the Notgemeinschaft der deutschen Wissenschaft, on the form of Bruckner's symphonies. The resulting work, *Formenwelt und Sinngefüge der Bruckner-Symphonien*, never appeared in print, as a result of the collapse of its publisher in the early 1930s.[37]

A 1925 article, published in two parts in *Die Musik*, provides a Lorenzian analysis of the first movement of Bruckner's Ninth Symphony.[38] The movement is presented as a two-part strophic form with a coda. Each *Hauptstrophe* is a *Bogen* form articulated into smaller formal types. The break between the strophes occurs between what is usually seen as the exposition and development (see the chart on p. 119). Grunsky does not invoke the traditional sonata formal paradigm, but rather heeds Lorenz's call to come up with an entirely new understanding based on the latter's own formal categories.[39]

The article opens with an explanation of Lorenz's method. Here Grunsky makes two important points. He suggests that Lorenz overlooked one formal type – the reversed Bar form, or *Gegenbar* (m–n–n: *Aufgesang, Gegenstollen, Gegenstollen*) – and he describes an *Urform* Bar from which all other forms develop.[40] Even more than Lorenz, Grunsky emphasizes the Germanic origins of the form, not only in the songs of the *Meistersinger*, but also in the constructs of such disparate philosophers as Jakob Böhme and Georg Wilhelm Friedrich Hegel: the thesis–antithesis–synthesis model.

> Therefore, I regard the thesis–antithesis–synthesis form as the original form [*Urform*] (logically, naturally not historically) of all musical events; as the common root from which all other forms spring, provided that they appear in their most profound organic significance . . . The original form is also by no means to be understood in the sense of something primitive. On the contrary: in it, the highest development is most mightily expressed; in it the synthesis resulting from the intensified fusion [*steigernden Vereinigung*] of opposites into a new, higher unity is most clearly, tautly, and actively represented . . . Bar and *Bogen* forms are simply two particular shapings which spring from the root of the original form.[41]

[37] Curiously this work is included in Nowak's bibliography of Bruckner in the *New Grove Dictionary of Music and Musicians*, where it is listed as published in 1931. Nowak also mentions another work, of which I have been able to find no trace: *Das Formproblem in Anton Bruckners Symphonien* (1929). A letter of 5 May 1933 (BDC) from Grunsky to the Kultusministerium states that the *Formenwelt* work was unpublished, and Lorenz refers to it in *Geheimnis der Form*, IV, p. 193 as unpublished.

[38] Hans Alfred Grunsky, "Bruckners Neunter."

[39] Alfred Lorenz, "Worauf beruht die bekannte Wirkung der Durchführung im 1. Eroicasatze?," *Neues Beethoven-Jahrbuch* 1 (1924), pp. 159–83.

[40] In subsequent volumes of *Das Geheimnis der Form*, Lorenz does employ the formal type, Gegenbar, and invariably credits Grunsky for its discovery.

[41] Hans Alfred Grunsky, "Bruckner's Neunter," 23–24. According to Grunsky, in the traditional Lorenzian Bar (m–m–n) the

Hans Alfred Grunsky's Analysis of the First Movement of Bruckner's Ninth Symphony (simplified)

I. Hauptstrophe (mm. 1–226) [Bogen]
   A   Großer Hauptsatz (mm. 1–96) [Reprisenbar]*
      Stollen I (mm. 1–18)
      Stollen II (mm. 19–26)
      Abgesang (mm. 27–96)
         Steigerung (mm. 27–62)
         Höhepunkt (mm. 63–76)
         Reaktion (mm. 77–96)
   B   Großer Mittelsatz (mm. 97–166) [2 strophes + coda]
      Strophe I (mm. 97–130)
      Strophe II (mm. 131–52)
      Coda (mm. 153–66)
   A   Großer Hauptsatz (mm. 167–226) [Reprisenbar]*
      Stollen I (mm. 167–78)
      Stollen II (mm. 179–90)
      Abgesang (mm. 191–226)
         Steigerung (mm. 191–214)
         Entsteigerung (mm. 215–26)

II. Hauptstrophe (mm. 227–516) [Bogen]
   A   Großer Hauptsatz (mm. 227–420) [potentiated Reprisenbar]*
      Groß-Stollen I (mm. 227–64)
      Gegen-Groß-Stollen II (mm. 265–302)
      Groß-Abgesang (mm. 303–32)
         Steigerung (mm. 303–32)
         Höhepunkt (mm. 333–400)
         Reaktion (mm. 401–20)
   B   Großer Mittelsatz (mm. 421–58) [single strophe]
   A   Großer Hauptsatz (mm. 459–516) [Reprisenbar]*
      Stollen I (mm. 459–66)
      Stollen II (mm. 467–78)
      Abgesang (mm. 479–92)
         Steigerung (mm. 479–92)
         Höhepunkt (mm. 492–504)
         Reaktion (mm. 505–16)

Coda (mm. 517–67)

---

* These forms are not fully perceptible in this simplification.

In 1934 Grunsky published a similar Lorenzian primer under the title of "Neues zur Formenlehre" proposing the addition of four *Mischformen*.[42] These are derived from combinations of Bars and *Bogen*, as shown below, and are Grunsky's Germanized permutations of binary form:[43]

Hans Alfred Grunsky's Mischformen
Bar + Bogen=Reprisenbar (m–m–n–m)
Bogen + Gegenbar=Echobogen (m–n–m–m)
Bar + Gegenbar=Echobar (m–m–n–n)
Gegenbar + Bar=Doppelbar (m–n–n–m or m–n–n–o)
Bogen + Bogen=4–teilige Bogenreihe (m–n–n–m)

Lorenzian analysis and National Socialist concerns continued to intersect in Grunsky's life. In a letter of 5 May 1933 to the Kultusministerium, he attempted to exploit his Nazi ties to obtain a position at Munich University, proposing the foundation of a chair in National Socialist philosophy.[44] Although the letter deals primarily with philosophical issues, Grunsky not only proposes a series of lectures on "Richard Wagner's works as the source of a Germanic world-view," but also links Bruckner and National Socialist ideology in a quite direct manner:

> National Socialism as the source and subject of philosophical consciousness: that may appear bizarre to liberal dabblers in philosophy [*liberalistischen Bücherphilosophen*]. All further thoughts can only be a necessary consequence of that sentence: that true philosophy is always, and always will be created out of life. However, not only the destiny of peoples or individuals, but also *myths, fairy-tales, poems*, and *artworks* of all types can become the subject of philosophical contemplation and interpretation; often deeper metaphysical content lurks in these last … In this sense, over many years, with the support of the Notgemeinschaft der deutschen Wissenschaft, I have developed an entirely new aesthetic theory of form and rhythm and applied it to Anton Bruckner's symphonic works at the same time.

Grunsky saw an obvious connection between Lorenzian formal analysis and National Socialism and regarded his work on Bruckner as appropriate for the times.

A final illustration of the interpenetration of art and politics in

polarity between the *Stollen* is lessened, and the *Abgesang* is regarded as an intensification rather than a synthesis; in the *Bogen* form, the antithesis is found in the middle of the form, and the synthesis is more passive and closer to the original thesis than in the *Urform*. The deviation from Lorenz can be attributed to Grunsky's nationalistic preoccupations.

[42] Hans Alfred Grunsky, "Neues zur Formenlehre," *Zeitschrift für Musikwissenschaft* 16 (1934), 35–42.
[43] Robert Haas occasionally does the same thing in his Bruckner book, once even referring to *Barbogenform* (A A′ B A′); see Haas, *Bruckner*, p. 111.
[44] BDC Hans Alfred Grunsky file.

Grunsky's work is found in a lecture delivered in Munich in 1938 on "Jacob Böhme as the Creator of a Teutonic Philosophy of the Will." He claims to find in Böhme the "formal world and intellectual structure" of a Bruckner symphony.[45] While Grunsky's comment is surely intended only as an illustrative analogy – albeit one "of deepest significance to our race" – it is striking that Grunsky should light on Bruckner. As an adherent of the expressive aesthetic, Grunsky regarded all music as the direct expression of the will of the composer; music is will. There is an important slippage in meaning inherent in the evocation of "will" by the National Socialists, however, whereby the central concept of Schopenhauerian philosophy is coarsened and celebrated as an instinctive and brutal will to power.

The case of Hans Alfred Grunsky is particularly clear. Considered in conjunction with the writings of his father, Karl, and his teacher, Alfred Lorenz, his work on Bruckner offers a compelling example of the difficulty of separating the aesthetic from the political during the 1920s and 30s. Recent developments in literary theory have suggested that works of interpretation or criticism are no less subjective or "artistic" than the objects of interpretation themselves. Often unconscious subjectivity surfaces as ideology in the sense described by Louis Althusser.[46] There is a connection between musical aesthetics and political myth-making, whether in terms of a focus on Germanizing musical terminology (deriving all form from the Bar form, for example), or through emphasis on the power of will. The intersection of National Socialist ideology, Lorenzian formal analysis, and Bruckner, while perhaps only coincidental, is all the more significant because it is not unique.[47] While Bruckner played an important role in National-Socialist *Kulturpolitik*, the figure of Richard Wagner is ever present. It is with Wagner and his Bayreuth followers that we must begin if we are to take up the challenge of trying to separate the intertwining threads of aesthetics, philosophy, and politics in fascist Germany.

---

[45] Hans Alfred Grunsky, *Jakob Böhme als Schöpfer einer germanischen Philosophie des Willens* (Hamburg: Hanseatische Verlagsanstalt, 1940), p. 5; see also Heiber, *Walter Frank*, p. 487.
[46] See Louis Althusser, "Ideology and Ideological State Apparatuses," in *Essays on Ideology* (London: Verso, 1984), pp. 1–60, and

Terry Eagleton, *Ideology: an Introduction* (London and New York: Verso, 1991).
[47] A similar paper could be written about Liszt or Strauss, since the music of both composers was also coopted by the Nazi propaganda machine, studied by scholars implicated in the regime, and analyzed according to Lorenz's methodology.

7 Josef Schalk and the theory of harmony at the end of the nineteenth century

Robert W. Wason

As the source of inauthentic passages in Bruckner's music, Josef Schalk (1857–1900) is one of the more controversial Bruckner students.[1] However, to the music theorist and historian of music theory he is also an interesting mind who attempted to confront important music-theoretical questions of his day through creative extension and modification of the theory Bruckner had taught him. His series of articles published in 1888–90, "Das Gesetz der Tonalität," borrows its banner headline from Fétis and Helmholtz, who had promulgated *tonalité* in French and German-speaking realms.[2] The articles seek to develop the theory of harmony that Schalk received from Bruckner (who in turn had received it from Sechter) into an analytical system capable of accounting for Wagner's innovations in the realm of chromatic harmony. Almost certainly he was inspired to undertake this project by Karl Mayrberger's analysis of *Tristan*, which Bruckner is said to have known and which, likewise, was based upon Sechter's theory of harmony.[3] Schalk proposed modifications that are interesting in their own right. They also adumbrate features of more radical revisions of Viennese harmonic theory proposed a few years later by Schenker and Schoenberg, as I have shown in an earlier study.[4] Ten years after the publication of "Das Gesetz der Tonalität" Schalk returned to his theoretical project, developing it further in work that remained unpublished. An investigation of its main themes forms the core of the present study.

Schalk's final investigations provide a link between the last stage of Sechter/Bruckner theory and the theories of harmony of the next genera-

---

[1] For a recent documentary study on this aspect of Schalk's activities, see Thomas Leibnitz, *Die Brüder Schalk und Anton Bruckner* (Tutzing: Hans Schneider, 1988); "Ein Wagnerianer zwischen Anton Bruckner und Hugo Wolf", *Bruckner-Jahrbuch* (1980), pp. 119–28.

[2] *Bayreuther Blätter* 11 (1888), 192–97, 381–81; 12 (1889), 191–98; 13 (1890), 65–70.

[3] "Die Harmonik Richard Wagners an den Leitmotiv aus 'Tristan und Isolde' erläutert," *Bayreuther Blätter* 4 (1881), 169–80; also published separately (Bayreuth: 1882).

[4] Heinrich Schenker, *Harmonielehre* (Vienna: Universal, 1906); Arnold Schoenberg, *Harmonielehre* (Vienna: Universal, 1911); and Robert W. Wason, *Viennese Harmonic Theory from Albrechtsberger to Schenker and Schoenberg* (Ann Arbor: UMI Research Press, 1985; Rochester, N.Y.: University of Rochester Press, 1995), pp. 102–11.

tion, for whom nineteenth-century views were distinctly passé. Moreover, in addressing chromaticism as its central topic, this unpublished work offers a perspective on a phenomenon that is fundamental to compositional technique in the later nineteenth century. Sechter's theory of harmony was diatonically based in the most conservative sense; his remarks on chromaticism were few and mainly cautionary. Surviving notes from Bruckner's university harmony classes also give short shrift to chromaticism and, though some chromatic voice-leading exercises probably connected with Bruckner's Conservatory teaching survive, these are, characteristically, unencumbered by any explanatory text.[5] Among the partisans of Sechter and Bruckner, Schalk was the only one known to have confronted the vexing questions of chromaticism.

It must be remembered that Schalk's final music-theoretical effort survives only in a working draft, and that his notion of "chromaticism" – and very likely that of his teacher – is very different from present-day points of view. From a modern perspective it is, in many respects, problematic. Still, present-day analysts of Bruckner's music would do well to ponder the views of one of his most devoted students – views held quite possibly by the composer himself. At the very least Schalk helps us understand why certain chromatic techniques that seem to cry out for explanation were virtually unexplored by nineteenth-century theorists.

The Schalk material in question survives in a miscellany catalogued by the Music Collection of the Austrian National Library as an "Aufsatz über die Chromatik."[6] In fact, at just under 6,800 words, it is a loose, untitled assemblage of observations on apparently diverse music-theoretical matters – a music-theoretic "diary," most of which was written in the late summer of 1898.[7] The organization is erratic; redundancies occur frequently; and, at points, the narrative becomes a series of tenuously related epigrams.[8] Certainly Schalk would have refined and reorganized his ideas considerably, had they been published. This article will follow the chronological sequence of ideas in Schalk's "diary" only occasionally.[9]

[5] Wason, *Viennese Harmonic Theory*, pp. 81–83.
[6] Wn Fonds, F18 Schalk 410. See Leibnitz, *Die Brüder Schalk*, pp. 325f., which includes a catalogue of the Schalk *Nachlass*, though not in sufficient detail that it mentions the individual items by name. I should like to thank Professor Alfred Mann for invaluable advice in preparing the transcript of Schalk's essay.
[7] Dates occur at five locations in the manuscript. After the opening date of "4. Aug. 1898" at the top of the (untitled) first page, new topics on p. 2 are preceded by "6." and "9." [August], respectively, perhaps indicating

a slow start to the work. Schalk seems to have interrupted the writing on p. 17; halfway down the page the centered heading "Zur Chromatik" is found, dated "24. Aug. 98". Most of the essay was probably written in August 1898 or very soon thereafter, because the last date, "13./VI. 99.", appears near the top of the last full page of the manuscript. Schalk died on 7 November 1900.
[8] See Wason, *Viennese Harmonic Theory*, p. 111.
[9] The departures from Schalk's order will be evident from the page numbers in the Wn source (arabic numerals in parentheses) after all direct quotations or summaries.

While the "Aufsatz über die Chromatik" is more an *Entwurf* or perhaps a *Versuch* than an "*Aufsatz*," I shall take the liberty of referring to it as "the essay." Chromaticism *is* the general theme that ties its remarks together. Schalk's notion of "Chromaticism" differs from that of the contemporary American music theorist, who concentrates on the interaction among processes intrinsic to the seven-note diatonic system – rendered for the sake of practicality by one of the twelve-note subsets of the twelve pitch classes of equal temperament in either its "major" or "minor" permutation – and those processes intrinsic to the universal set of twelve pitch classes itself.[10] Schalk's understanding of chromaticism, retraceable to the Greeks, develops the metaphor of "color" in all of its musical ramifications. The essay's opening entry begins with a definition of chromaticism: "the use of the half-step interstices that are foreign to the natural, diatonic scale" – the "seven plus five" notion of chromaticism that Mitchell decries. There is already much here that portends later developments, both usual and unusual, but we shall let it sit and resonate, as Schalk does.

An exposition of the main theme of the "Gesetz der Tonalität" articles follows.[11] The notions of chromaticism and modulation, Schalk complains, have not been clearly distinguished from one another, a complaint that rings true before Schenker's formulation of *Tonikalisierung*:

> By modulation we mean change of tonic ... the succession of modulations in a musical passage – even one of the largest proportions – is controlled by the Law of Tonality. A very few exceptions in the area of dramatic music and isolated unsuccessful experiments only confirm the rule. (1)

Chromaticism is likewise subject to the "Law of Tonality" according to Schalk. But while diatonic modulation announces the new tonic, chromaticism, though also dependent upon the tonic operative in a given context, often loosens and occasionally suspends the sense of tonality entirely. In new music, which often dwells on what he calls the *Vermittlungsformen* of chromaticism – most prominently, the diminished seventh chord – the sense of tonality is completely lost for some

[10] See William Mitchell, "The Study of Chromaticism," *Journal of Music Theory* 6/1 (1962), 2–31; this view reaches a more developed form in Gregory Michael Proctor, "Technical Bases of Nineteenth-Century Chromatic Tonality: A Study in Chromaticism" (Ph.D. diss., Princeton, 1978). Mitchell remarks at the beginning of his article that "it has been necessary ... to remove from the forefront ... the assumption of long standing that chromaticism consists of 'seven tones plus five tones.'" It is not by accident, after all, that this view of chromaticism arose contemporaneously with the development of more strictly twelve-tone theory; indeed serial theory, "atonal theory," and important components of Proctor's "nineteenth-century chromatic tonality" all spring from the seminal ideas of Milton Babbitt. These might be present embryonically in the work of a few earlier theorists, but they are largely new and original.

[11] Schalk demonstrates how Wagner achieves tonal unity in passages that involve chromaticism and modulation; see Wason, *Viennese Harmonic Theory*, pp. 106–110.

listeners. All of this is consistent with our present-day view of late nineteenth-century chromaticism; we are only disappointed that Schalk stops here. In the brief paragraph that ends this entry, Schalk sketches a historical-developmental theory of chromaticism in three stages:

> In the first, chromaticism is limited to melodic chromatic tones, unsupported chordally; in the second, chordal tones are altered chromatically as well: in particular, minor thirds become major, and perfect fifths become diminished; in the third, the use of chromaticism is extended even to the fundamentals of chords, though this is often more apparent than real. (1)

Those familiar with Sechter's system of harmony will recognize Schalk's attempt to update it: Sechter subjugated chromaticism to diatonic rule by maintaining that *all* chromatically altered tones occur above a fundamental bass that remains diatonic and unalterable. As a characterization of eighteenth- and early nineteenth-century practice, the idea is serviceable, though insufficient.[12] Sechter had little use for the mixing of major and minor modes, and Schalk likewise maintains that the relative – and not the parallel – major–minor relationship is always the true explanation of minor's dependency upon major (19). Schalk's refusal to countenance modal mixture is in line with the views of Sechter and Bruckner. His admission of occasional chromatic fundamental progression (with the hastily added disclaimer that it is more often "apparent than real") goes beyond Sechter (and Bruckner or Mayrberger, for that matter), and is presumably an attempt to come to terms with the music of his own day.[13]

The essay continues with a very brief – and surprising – entry, dated 6 August. Here Schalk maintains that a chromatic motive possesses a

---

[12] Sechter's structural support of chromaticism amounts to a cycle of fifths subposed beneath "apparent" chromatic alteration. Thus "diminished seventh chords" are, in reality, "incomplete dominant ninth chords," and *chromaticism in general* is explained only through alteration of dominant-functioning chords – in today's harmony-book parlance, "secondary dominants" and their alterations. Simon Sechter, *Die Grundsätze der musikalischen Komposition*, 3 vols. (Leipzig: Breitkopf und Härtel, 1853–54), I, p. 120. The explanation stems from Rameau.

[13] Though Schalk does not mention the dialectical implications of this theory, one cannot help noticing that the melodic chromaticism of the first period is apparently combined with the chordal support of the second to create the "chromatic fundamental basses" of the third. A typically nineteenth-century "evolutionary" view, the theory can also be seen as a recasting, in fundamental-bass language, of the three stages of Fetis's *tonalité moderne*: 1. *ordre transitonique* (characterized by the dominant seventh chord and by modulation, but basically diatonic; chromaticism receives no chordal support); 2. *ordre pluritonique* (characterized by chromatic and enharmonic modulation; chromaticism clearly achieves chordal support); and 3. *ordre omnitonique* (as in Schalk's theory, the logically and historically necessary – but as yet not fully extant – third stage; for Fétis, the "universalité des relations tonales"). See Renate Groth, *Die französische Kompositionslehre des 19. Jahrhunderts* (Wiesbaden: Steiner, 1983), p. 61.

specific "expressive character" that is lost if the motive is transposed. He cites the second appearance of the "Desire Motive" from *Tristan und Isolde* (B–C–C♯–D), curiously neglecting to mention that this second appearance is a transposition of the first(!) Upon transposing it down a step (to A–B♭–B♮–C), Schalk claims that the note B♭ must be "forced" to continue to B, while the C makes the move to C♯ with "greater ease." Regardless of how convincing we find this particular example, *Tristan* certainly bears out Schalk's main point when one considers the various appearances of the "Tristan Chord" in its original pitch-class form, respelled, reinterpreted and made to behave very differently throughout. Schalk qualifies his position slightly:

> Through accompanying chords the same expressive character may be forced upon a transposition, as is often necessary during the course of a piece. However, the original invention [of the motive] occurs completely in the tonality that corresponds to it. (2)

Later, Schalk elaborates:

> All too little attention is paid to the fact that, with the choice of key resulting from the invention of the primary musical idea, the composer also chooses a locus for the flight of his creative phantasy, and not just a point on the circle of keys. (5f.)

And still later we read, underlined for emphasis:

> the more meaningful the spiritual content of a work, the more respectful it is of its absolute pitch level – its tonality. (10)

"Das Gesetz der Tonalität" has broad ramifications indeed.

In the next entry, dated 9 August, Schalk begins to develop a theory of leading tones. Such an approach to the problem of chromaticism is consistent with a general tendency in turn-of-the-century music theory to regard the leading tone in "chromatic harmony" as analogous to the fifth in "diatonic harmony" – i.e. as the model interval of musical motion.[14] First, he sets down the notions of ascending and descending leading tones, as opposed to tones that are capable of being at rest. He then lists the six possible "transformations" of one into the other, placing them in two categories: the transformation of tones of rest into leading tones and vice versa, and the transformation of the two types of leading tones into each other (fig. 7.1).

Schalk begins the entry dated 28 August by attempting to put these abstract transformations into practice. He starts to develop real-time

---

[14] See, for example, the *Harmonielehre* by Rudolf Louis and Ludwig Thuille (Stuttgart: Klett, 1906).

System   I.   (a) ascending leading tones   (b) descending leading tones
                      (♯ type)   (♭ type)

         II.   (a) tones capable of being at rest

         III. (a) transformation of tones at rest into ascending LTs.
               (b)   "   "   "   "   "   "   descending " .
               (c)   "   " ascending LTs " tones at rest.
               (d)   "   " descending LTs"   "   " " .

         IV.   (a) Transformation of ascending LTs into descending LTs.
               (b)   "   " descending "   " ascending LTs.

Fig. 7.1

Ex. 7.1   Beethoven, String Quartet in B♭ Major, Op. 130, first movement, mm. 50–55

Gesetze. The first reads "every chromatic degree may be reached melodically and made independent, or capable of being at rest, through rhythmic preference (accented beat, longer duration)" (12). Among other
examples, Schalk cites the Beethoven String Quartet, Op. 130; his pitch
letter-name description makes it clear that he has the passage in ex. 7.1
(first movement, mm. 51–53) in mind: the D♭ of m. 53 is transformed
through accent and duration from a leading tone to a tone of rest.

The development of melodic-chromatic "rules" breaks off, but
towards the end of the essay, Schalk begins to develop rules to account for
apparent licenses in dissonance treatment in new music. First:

If passing tones are doubled at the unison or octave, it is sufficient if one
progresses strictly by step; the other is thereby set free and may move by skip
[see ex. 7.2a]. Similarly, the resolution of a dissonance may be represented by
another voice [*Auflösung durch Stimmvertretung*]: if passing tones in
contrary motion heading to an octave demand a chromatic tone, one of the
voices usually changes course and leaps in order to avoid the doubling [see
ex. 7.2b]. (21)

Anyone searching for a comprehensive set of such rules describing late
nineteenth-century practice will look in vain for them in Schalk's essay,

Ex. 7.2a

Ex. 7.2b

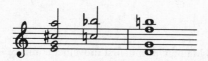

which seldom refers to real musical examples. Cyril Hynais, Schalk's colleague and fellow Bruckner student, adds a few additional rules in a series of tantalizing articles published in 1901.[15]

Schalk continues to develop his theory of leading tones with a description of their historical genesis and their location in the modern key system: diatonic scale-degree seven offers the model of the ascending leading tone, scale-degree four the model of the descending leading tone. "The combination of both represents the most complete expression of the key on the smallest scale." Of course, the statement might have been written by Rameau, for the idea goes back to his "major and minor dissonances" and *dominante-tonique*. Since it is unlikely that Schalk was acquainted with Rameau's work (Sechter knew Rameau only through Kirnberger and Marpurg's translation of d'Alembert), Schalk probably got the idea from some intermediary source.

The fact that scale-degree four may function as subdominant as well as leading tone to three makes it less "energetic" than scale-degree seven, a tendency that is even more pronounced in minor, according to Schalk (5). There, the increased prominence of the subdominant, coupled with scale-degree four's whole-step relationship to three, means that scale-degree four "prefers to assert itself as subdominant." Looking for a more appropriate descending leading tone in minor, Schalk first finds scale-degree flat six; the combination of flat six and seven forms the boundaries of the diminished seventh chord, the "characteristic dominant chord" in minor (6). He then proposes a more suitable candidate for the role of archetypal descending leading tone: flat two, which he designates the "true *minor leading tone*, since it leads [in descent] to the tonic, just as the *major leading tone* does in ascent" (7).

Exx. 7.3a and b demonstrate the importance of the Neapolitan to

[15] See Wason, *Viennese Harmonic Theory,* pp. 100–02, especially the discussion of the "ascending seventh."

Ex. 7.3a

Ex. 7.3b

Schalk.[16] Schalk's notes read: "the understanding of chromaticism is fur-
thered through the knowledge of the Neapolitan sixth (scale-degree four
with suspension of the flatted thirteenth)." As ex. 7.3b shows, Schalk
reads the fundamental of the Neapolitan as scale-degree four (as Sechter
and Bruckner had); it also shows that he had no problem with the stepwise fundamental progression that results when the Neapolitan moves
directly to V; Sechter always interpolated another pre-dominant fundamental between to avoid the step.[17]

Schalk continues to explore the topic of leading tones by developing
the analogy with diatonic fifths. He ties the two leading-tone motions to
the circle of fifths:

> The ascending step is the symbol of the sharp keys, the descending step the
> symbol of the flat keys. Just as the dominant exceeds the subdominant in

[16] Examples 7.3a, 7.3b, and accompanying text
are taken from Wn Fonds, F18 Schalk 409,
cataloged as *Übungsheft (Harmonielehre); mit
handschriftlichen Notizen*. Though this source
dates from a much earlier point, Schalk's
interpretation of the Neapolitan chord
remained essentially the same in the
Übungsheft, the "Gesetz der Tonalität"
articles, and the essay on chromaticism.
[17] Wason, *Viennese Harmonic Theory*, p. 56.

importance and independence, the sharp keys are likewise superior to the
flat keys (4).

The two leading tones are the chromatic manifestations of the most
fundamental musical forces, which Schalk goes on to describe with vivid
visual metaphors. The sharps "press upwards, towards light," while the
flats "strive towards the depths, into darkness"(4). Though the language
is quaint, this is not an idiosyncratic vestige of outmoded ideas; a much
more influential contemporary, Hugo Riemann, provided exactly the
same explanation fifteen years later in one of his last essays, on the
"mental image" of tones:

> Tonal motion is valued as an *upward and downward motion* in space and, at
> the same time, as an *alteration in strength of light*. Higher is at once brighter,
> lower at once darker."[18]

For both Riemann and Schalk, the diatonic scale is at the center of
motion up and down, or of the visual spectrum from bright to dark – to
use both metaphors.[19] To understand Schalk's version of musical "color,"
we must realize that it is to be applied to the color*less* diatonic scale. For
Schalk, there is only one diatonic scale: the pure, *unaltered* letter names
or "Stammtöne." This *Urskala* represents a fixed and neutral mid-point in
tonal space, from which the remaining pitches emanate, their positions
anchored by the *Stammtöne*. Schalk's "expressive characteristics" are likewise fixed, and the "Law of Tonality" itself is, at the level of the individual
work, a recreation of this ontology of the tonal system.

All pitches other than the unaltered letter names are, therefore, in
some sense, "chromatic." They never relinquish that characteristic,
though they may find themselves in a locally diatonic context. The
Stammtöne never lose their identity either; though they may be forced to
serve as leading tones, they prefer to be tones at rest. Thus, the ascending
leading tone is "forced" in flat keys because, in most cases, it is a
Stammton. The reverse is also true: the descending leading tones are
"forced" in sharp keys (4). The problem is more pronounced with the

---

[18] Robert W. Wason and Elizabeth West
Marvin, "Riemann's 'Ideen zu einer Lehre von
den Tonvorstellungen': An Annotated
Translation," *Journal of Music Theory* 36/1
(Spring, 1992), 93.
[19] Hermann Stephani, *Der Charakter der
Tonarten* (Regensburg: Gustav Bosse, 1923)
finds Adolf Bernhard Marx to be the
originator of the idea that C is the center of
motion in tonal space. Marx proposed
designating "the sequence of upward
alterations with '+', downward alterations

with '−', and the middle tone C with '0.'
This succession of tones – or rather the
major keys that take them as tonics –
contains a *polar opposition* of keys that move
step by step into the heights and the depths,
its 'point of indifference' in the middle." A. B.
Marx, *Gluck und die Oper* (Berlin, O. Janke,
1863), quoted in Stephani, p. 56. See also
Rita Steblin, *A History of Key Characteristics
in the Eighteenth and Early Nineteenth
Centuries* (Ann Arbor: UMI Research Press,
1983), pp. 4 and 185.

names of keys, especially in the flat direction, which "bear the relativism of their origins, yet are used as primary tonics" (15). It is this "absolute" character of the diatonic letter names that causes the natural sign to be used in our notational system for "correction" to pure letter names. In Schalk's transformational terms, the same sign signifies the transformation of a leading tone into a tone at rest *and* a tone at rest into a leading tone. At one point Schalk complains about this confusion (9), apparently unaware that his absolutist notion of diatonicism undercuts his relativist notion of leading-tone transformations. Indeed, this tension is at the heart of his essay, and may well be one of the reasons that it never reached completion.

The further along the circle of fifths away from C, the more "chromatic tones" a key contains, and the more "chromatic" it becomes. Schalk goes on to propose the "color-equivalents" shown in fig. 7.2. Once again, he is not alone. Schalk calls C major the "white" key; Hermann Stephani refers to it as the key "without shading or coloring."[20] In Schalk's estimation the exact assignment of colors is of less importance than the "contrast" – perhaps not precisely definable – that exists between the keys.

> It must not be overlooked that the brightening or darkening tonal direction is a product of the succession of keys and is to be understood thoroughly in a relative sense. (8)

Schalk cites the first act of *Siegfried* as an example in which the affective contrasts resulting from *progression* of keys are crucial:

> It begins in the dark key of Bb minor and rises bit by bit to a sunny and jubilant D major . . . The entrance of the sharp keys is especially striking and particularly satisfying after the extended use of the flat keys. (13)

One wonders if the associative use of tonality of which Robert Bailey has spoken has its origins in the character of keys.[21]

Of course, the tonal system did not always operate this way. According to Schalk, before the generation of the upper and lower reaches of the tonal system, the absolute tone-spatial location of the pure letter-name pitches was unimportant. However:

[20] Stephani, *Charakter*, pp. 99–100; Rita Steblin, *Key Characteristics*, p. 4. It is not easy to find agreement between various instances of synaesthesia in their assignments of color to pitch or key; see the *MGG* article by Albert Wellek, s.v. "Farbenhören."

[21] Robert Bailey, "The Structure of the *Ring* and Its Evolution," *19th Century Music* 1/1 (July, 1977), 48–61; see especially pp. 51–55, on "associative tonality." Wagner is a particularly interesting case in this regard, since, as Stephani points out (pp. 10–11), he had dismissed the "individuality of the keys" as "imaginary" and a "chimera." Stephani and Schalk are not alone in finding evidence for such key-characters in Wagner's music, despite his denial.

Fig. 7.2

(white)	C major	colorless, simple, secure (innocent, tendency towards G)
	G "	friendly, gay, childlike, idyllic (Haydn)
yellow	D "	grander, warm, youthful-masculine (Mozart)
red	A "	(radiantly) joyous, brilliant

(green)	E "	somewhat darker than the previous
	B "	
	F♯ "	

a minor	purple, violet
e minor	(grey) Mendelssohn
b	
f♯	increasing excitement
c♯ minor	(moonlight)
g♯/d♯	almost venomously green

C♯ major can hardly be regarded as an independent tonality. With regard to color, [it] does not produce any intensification of the previous tonalities because it is too easily confused enharmonically with D♭, through which we are transported into completely different softer, more toned-down and shadowy regions. The connection of sharps and flat in the circle of fifths (and thus the meeting of opposite colors) involves another problem (the polarity of light?)

F major	dreamy, gently earnest (At the beginning of the "Pastoral Symphony" Beethoven gives us a peaceful country scene as Haydn represented it so frequently. His more serious temperament transforms the Haydn G major into a Beethoven F major)

(brown)	B♭ "	versatile
(blue)	E♭ "	shadowy, almost sombre, masculine seriousness

	A♭ "	solemn, softly reconciled
	D♭ "	elevated
	G♭ "	spiritually gloomy

With the use of chromatic tones began the doctrine of the "colorless scale", which (in modern parlance) presents a generalized C major at any arbitrarily chosen pitch-level. But it was also through chromaticism that the ear learned to distinguish somewhat later the various sonic characteristics of the diatonic scales and chords according to their absolute pitch height. Despite this, modern theory completely ignores these characteristics and treats each key according to the same laws as C major, as a transposition. (10)

This theory worked as long as one moved only according to the circle of fifths, in which the individual key-characteristics experience merely the slightest change moving in one direction or the other. But the use of third relations already causes problems. Is the modulation from C to E really the same as the modulation from A♭ to C? According to this account, yes – but the effect of the sound is almost the opposite. (15)

Instead of boiling down all keys to replications of a single diatonic scale, a true theory of chromaticism must start by

Fig. 7.3

I = c(1)	N = e(5)	R = g♯/a♭(9)
K = c♯/d♭(2)	O = f(6)	S = a(10)
L = d(3)	P = f♯/g♭(7)	T = a♯/b♭(11)
M = d♯/e♭(4)	Q = g(8)	U = b(12)

investigating the essential differences between the major and minor
keys, and not treating them simply as transposable patterns. The many
undeniable difficulties that appear to emerge thereby should not be a
deterrent ... on the contrary, the new problems should be an incentive to
enliven music theory through essential connections to the areas of aesthetics
and psychology – to make fruitful a field which has long been notoriously
arid. (10)

And why has this not been done already? The culprit is easy to find,
though Schalk was powerless against it:

To view the twelve modern keys as completely equivalent and independent is
a general error that results from temperament. (7)

The proponents of temperament are only drawing logical consequences
when they throw out our notational system, which makes the chromatic
tones dependent upon the diatonic ones, and invent new names
corresponding to 12 equally spaced tonal degrees. In that case, they should
dispense with the traditional names, and begin with the letter I for C, in
order to retain alphabetical order, or use 12 numbers (included here as well),
although the numbers bring with them the instinctive desire to set 1 to
tonic, which would conflict with every tonality other than C [fig. 7.3]. (14)

Among the "proponents of tempered tuning" to whom Schalk refers is
surely the Viennese H. J. Vincent, who proposed a mod-12 integer notation.[22] Vincent's and Schalk's are the first of many attempts at a twelve-
tone notation (later efforts by Busoni and Schoenberg are better
known).[23] Schalk does not accept equal temperament and the consequent
reform of the notation system as a "fait accompli"; to fix every point on
the pitch continuum would rob music of its life force:

It is precisely the countless fine gradations of pitch level that enliven the
dead tonal material – that produce the living character of a tonal
progression ... In our heavily burdened system of notation, we must

[22] H. J. Vincent, "Ist unsere Musiktheorie
wirklich eine Theorie?" (Vienna, n.d.
[probably 1890]). See Robert W. Wason,
"Progressive Harmonic Theory in the Mid-
Nineteenth Century," *Journal of Musicological
Research* 8 (1988), 55–90.
[23] Ferruccio Busoni, *Versuch einer*

organischen Klaviernotenschrift (Leipzig:
1910); Arnold Schoenberg, "Eine neue
Zwölfton-Schrift," *Anbruch* (January, 1925);
reprinted in *Style and Idea* (Berkeley and Los
Angeles: University of California Press, 1984)
as "A New Twelve-Tone Notation,"
pp. 354–62.

recognize a symbolic history of the art of musical composition worthy of respect. The system shows us clearly how tonal formations starting from the simplest, natural ones were built up and developed to the greatest diversity and complexity, [though] music theory has almost completely ignored this extraordinary instructional aid. (14–15)

Schalk's notion of "chromaticism" was, as remarked at the outset of this chapter, the traditional "seven plus five." In his uncompromising presentation, however, it becomes clear that this traditional notion is not simply a theory imposed upon the tonal material, but arises from a profoundly diatonic understanding of the tonal material itself. A century before Schalk wrote his essay, Vogler had attempted to reverse priorities by viewing the chromatic scale as the universal set from which each diatonic key was extracted ("seven out of twelve"), so it is not as though the opposing view was unknown, even in Vienna.[24] But "seven out of twelve" necessarily brought with it temperament – not as a practical approximation to an ideal maintained in some realm (even if only mental), but as a complete and sufficient description of the tonal material. Schalk refuses to accept this, polemicizing at every opportunity against "das temperierte System."[25] He constantly invokes just ratios to explain points he wishes to make in harmony and voice-leading, but in the end, we are left wondering whether this is all theory, or whether it has some relationship to musical practice. Further, why is Schalk such an ardent supporter of the "characters of the keys"? And how do they fit with his ideas on tuning?

Of course, there may be no relationship to practice; we may be dealing here with pure theory. The historian of theory is intimately familiar with divisions of the monochord, invocations of the *corps sonore*, etc., most of which amount to just intonation, and which often function as epistemological props to support music-theoretical systems.[26] Zarlino's preference

[24] Wason, *Viennese Harmonic Theory*, p. 15.
[25] Schalk never calls it "gleichschwebende Temperatur." Still, the "proponents of temperament" who would "invent new names corresponding to 12 equally spaced tonal degrees" are obviously proponents of *equal* temperament. Further contextual evidence supporting the conclusion that Schalk's "temperiertes System" means "equal temperament" will be presented below.
[26] Pythagorean intonation serves as the initial epistemological prop until just intonation supplants it during the Renaissance. The latter's history in the West may be traced to Didymus's tuning of the tetrachord, which is preserved by Ptolemy in the second century AD. The Pythagorean tuning of the tetrachord, attributed to Eratosthenes (3rd century B.C.), consists of two 9:8 whole tones, and a "leimma" (256:243 – the "remainder" from the 4:3 fourth that bounds the tetrachord). Didymus (1st c. A.D.?) introduced the distinction between the "major" and "minor" whole tone (9:8 and 10:9), which, together, produce the 5:4 major third; this, in effect, adds a "syntonic comma" (81:80 – the difference between the two forms of the whole tone, and thus between the Pythagorean and "pure" major thirds) to the "half step," which becomes 16:15; an advantage, in Didymus's view, is that all ratios are the favored "super-particular" (n+1:n). Didymus's tuning of the tetrachord E–F–G–A (16:15, 10:9, 9:8) ultimately becomes the basis of just intonation. Ptolemy takes essentially the same tetrachord, though he reverses the order of whole steps (16:15, 9:8, 10:9), for his "tense (syntonic) diatonic."

for this tuning caused him to reorient Glareanus's twelve modes and place the Ionian first – perhaps the coronation of Schalk's *Urskala* – though his recommendation that such tuning be used in practice met with strong criticism.[27] Just intonation continued as the basis of Rameau's theoretical system, although he was to favor first an irregular temperament, and ultimately equal temperament in practice.[28] Further, the two most important harmonic systems in German-speaking lands in the nineteenth century – the systems of Hauptmann and Sechter – assume just intonation, though both theorists recognized the inevitability of temperament in practice.[29] Ultimately, Riemann attempted a dialectical rapprochement with temperament by formulating his notion of "enharmonic identification," claiming that while our minds conceive of intervals according to just ratios, we are able to resolve discrepancies between our conceptions and tempered intervals from the outer world.[30] For Riemann, just intonation represented more than an epistemological connection with "nature"; it became a psychological law of musical perception. But still, it had little to do with the composition or performance of music.

However, it was during Schalk's career that just intonation moved as close to practice as it ever has. Helmholtz took up the cause in the middle of the nineteenth century, inspiring many attempts to build just-tuned keyboard instruments. Perhaps the most complex of these, consisting of "a twenty-six-note keyboard in just intonation, capable of mechanical transposition of any of twelve semitones, thus giving a total of 312 notes, with,

[27] Zarlino's preference for the so-called "harmonic mean" as a way of dividing intervals leads him to prefer the C–C octave. He divides that octave in the manner that stretches back to antiquity – harmonically and arithmetically (C–F–G–C). But then he divides each fifth harmonically (C–E–G/F–A–C), and the further harmonic division of each of these (lower) major thirds places the larger whole step lowest, yielding a hexachordal tuning of C/D (9:8) D/E (10:9) E/F (16:15) F/G (9:8) G/A (10:9). Finally, the harmonic division of the pure minor third A/C (6:5) yields A/B (9:8), B/C (16:15). Though not all divisions are harmonic, Zarlino argues that they "are all somehow a consequence of divisions that are harmonic. The results . . . cannot be obtained except in the C-octave." Zarlino, *On the Modes*, tr. Vared Cohen and ed. Claude V. Palisca (New Haven and London: Yale University Press, 1978), Introduction (by Palisca), pp. xvi–xix.

Critics of Zarlino quickly recognized that just intonation was impossible to realize in the practice of *a capella* vocal music. Giovanni Benedetti's examples show that the various sizes of melodic whole and half steps (which

must necessarily result if the vertical consonances are tuned according to just ratios) lead to inevitable rising and falling of overall pitch level. See Claude Palisca, *Humanism in Italian Renaissance Musical Thought* (New Haven and London: Yale University Press, 1985), Chapter 10 ("The Ancient *Musica Speculativa* and Renaissance Musical Science"), in particular, pp. 244–65.

[28] Thomas Christensen, *Rameau and Musical Thought in the Enlightenment* (Cambridge University Press, 1993), pp. 201f.

[29] This tuning of the diatonic scale yields "pure" major triads on I, IV and V and thus came to be a favorite of many theorists of harmony. The most serious deficiency of just intonation is the "II chord" that results: of the seven white notes, four are tuned as pure (3:2) fifths from C (F–C–G–D), while the remaining three are tuned as pure fifths from E (A–E–B), which itself is a pure third (5:4) above C. This means that the fifth D–A (which is "doubly generated") is a full syntonic comma (21.5 cents) smaller than pure.

[30] See Wason and Marvin, "Riemann's 'Ideen,'" 76–77, 99–100, 109–10.

however, much repetition," was one built by Shohé Tanaka, a student of Helmholtz.[31] This is probably the instrument upon which Bruckner heard the "Prelude" from *Lohengrin*.[32] Could this be the ideal state that Schalk had in mind? It hardly seems likely, for even if such instruments had become practical enough to catch the attention of musicians rather than scientists, the transposition of just intonation to all twelve tones would have created the situation that Schalk warned against: treating all keys as replications of C major. Instead of all keys being "out of tune" by precisely the same amount – as they are in equal temperament – they would be precise replications of a just-tuned C major (complete with a correction of the defective "II" chord!). Moreover, the enharmonic puns which are essential to the music of Schalk's mentor, Bruckner, make temperament a necessity.[33]

However, equal temperament is not the only way to construct a tonal environment in which such puns can be realized: between the polar opposites of just intonation and equal temperament lies an infinite number of possible *nonequal* temperaments that are also "circulating" and "unrestrictive" – that is, that contain closed circles of fifths, and allow notes tuned as sharps to be used as flats and vice versa. (The so-called "noncirculating" and "restrictive" tuning systems – all just tunings and meantone temperaments – do not provide such an environment.[34]) Such "well-temperaments" – known technically as "irregular," since their constituent fifths are not all of the same size – were in common use

[31] J. Murray Barbour, "Just Intonation Confuted," *Music and Letters* 19 (1938), 57.
[32] Friedrich Eckstein, *Erinnerungen an Anton Bruckner* (Vienna: Universal Edition, 1923), p. 38.
[33] See Timothy L. Jackson, "Schubert as 'John the Baptist to Wagner-Jesus': Large-scale Enharmonicism in Bruckner and his Models," *Bruckner-Jahrbuch 1992* (1995), p. 73.

Eckstein and Bruckner listened to Tanaka play enharmonic progressions on his just-tuned keyboard: ". . . we had the unique pleasure of having performed for us in reality, through clearly hearable tonal steps and changes of keys [on the instrument], what normally would be ideal modulations [*Umdeutungen*] negotiated only in the mind" (Eckstein, *Erinnerungen*, p. 39). It is easy to envision Bruckner and his student reveling in what must have seemed a "slow-motion," didactic analysis of enharmonic passages, which, in art music, are elliptical, requiring a leap in the musical thought process. But as Jackson points out, temperament is a necessity for such passages to have their proper musical effect; the enharmonically "equivalent" tones must really be the same. The ellipsis, the pun

on the same sounding pitch, and subsequent change of direction are crucial to the aesthetic reactions we associate with such passages.
[34] In standard "quarter-comma" mean-tone, each fifth is reduced in size by one quarter of the syntonic comma (about 5.5 cents, as opposed to the 2-cent reduction of fifths in equal temperament), so that four fifths (minus two octaves) add up to a just (5:4) third. Further, this "equal tempering" of the fifths divides the major thirds into whole steps of equal size (the "geometric mean" of the 5:4 major third, as opposed to the 10:9 and 9:8 whole steps of just intonation). In this temperament, eight of the major thirds are less than six cents wide of just (equal tempered major thirds are 14 cents wider than just), but the remaining four "major thirds" (really diminished fourths) B/Eb, F#/Bb, C#/F, G#/C are 33–36 cents wider than just, and thus essentially unusable. Moreover, this much tempering of the fifths means that the "circle" of fifths is broken – at the so-called "wolf fifth" (really a diminished sixth), which may be between 56 and 24 cents wide of pure, depending upon the "shade" of mean-tone (the wolf-fifth is 36 cents wide in quarter-comma meantone).

throughout the seventeenth and eighteenth centuries.[35] Indeed, a recent study has shown that they were still in broad usage in the nineteenth century; moreover, that study claims that though the *theory* of equal temperament may have had its proponents from early on (Vincenzo Galilei and Mersenne were among them), the technical requirements for the tuning of true equal temperament on relatively rapidly decaying keyboards (harpsichords and pianos) were not in place until 1917.[36] Many of the hundred-odd temperaments that the study demonstrates, while allowing at least occasional use of all major and minor keys, are characterized by pronounced differences in tuning in the various keys – especially those at the extremes of the circle of fifths. Particularly in the keys of B♭ minor and E♭ minor, the "minor thirds ... are more minor ... and the major thirds ... more major in the old tuning systems," so that the expressive difference between the two is more pronounced than in other minor keys.[37] Certainly this state of affairs provides a convincing explanation for the "characters of the keys," at least as they existed in keyboard music.[38]

The larger musical ramifications of such tunings bear investigation as well. The parallels that have been noted between Chopin's C major etude, Op. 10 and the C major Prelude from Bach's *Well-Tempered Clavier* Book I, to cite two of many possible examples, are more than structural; they preserve expressive characteristics appropriate to their particular keys as well. Although temperament required the adjustment of certain features of the idealized, just C major, that abstract ontology of the tonal system that both

[35] See Mark Lindley's survey in *New Grove*, s.v. "Temperament" (XVIII, 660–74, especially 667–69).

[36] Owen Jorgensen, *Tuning, containing the Perfection of Eighteenth-Century Tuning, the Lost Art of Nineteenth-Century Temperament, and the Science of Equal Temperament* (East Lansing: Michigan State University Press, 1991). Jorgensen has amassed an impressive amount of material on keyboard tuning (by tuners) from the early eighteenth century into the early twentieth. As piano tuners know, equally tempered fourths and fifths are close enough to pure that they beat very slowly and must constantly be checked by listening to quickly beating thirds and sixths. Until relatively recently, tuners simply did not know this. In fact, they did not even count beats until relatively recently, and they continued to believe that thirds and sixths beat too fast to count until 1917. (pp. 4–7).

Alexander Ellis, Helmholtz's translator and a scientist and acoustician of great accomplishment himself, corroborates this thesis in the appendix on tuning added to his translation of *Tonempfindungen* in 1885: he checked eight keyboard instruments – pianos,

organs and harmoniums – with his scientific instruments, and found deviations from equal temperament in all eight. Hermann von Helmholtz, *On the Sensations of Tone* (New York: Dover, 1954), pp. 484–85; see Jorgenson, *Tuning*, p. 1.

[37] Jorgensen, *Tuning*, p. 582. The major thirds in these keys are the "diminished fourths" of mean-tone temperament (cf. footnote 34). Many "well-temperaments" may be thought of as being derived from meantone, and thus they retain perceptible differences in the tunings of these "thirds," while at the same time narrowing them so that they are usable.

[38] All of the metaphors used to describe the keys – whether of affect, color or direction in tonal "space" – point to one conclusion: that the keys actually sounded different from one another to the writers of those descriptions. It is difficult to accept that such differences can be accounted for by eighteenth- and early nineteenth-century explanations cataloged as "physiological" or "psychological" by Rita Steblin. Rather, her category of "physical" explanations seems more plausible. See Steblin, *A History of Key Characteristics*, p. 10.

Schalk and Riemann present is not irrelevant to a well-tempered pitch-world: such tunings attempted to preserve the pure "white-note" thirds, while gradually introducing more tempering of thirds as one moved around the circle of fifths. The notion of a chromatic pitch spectrum anchored to a fixed diatonic beginning point may even have implications for our understanding of pitch perception: recent psychological studies show that test subjects with absolute pitch are significantly more secure with pitch identification of white notes; even subjects with relative pitch scored better with white notes.[39]

Presuming that Schalk heard such well-temperaments on a daily basis goes a long way toward explaining just why he might have proposed such a theory of "chromaticism." Schalk, however, seems not to have understood the subtleties of temperament at all, and perhaps this is one reason why he was unable to develop his ideas further. Mixed in with his polemic against equal temperament is the oft-encountered notion that Bach's *Well-Tempered Clavier* marks the "invention of tempered tuning" (8), and "equal temperament" is clearly meant here. Perhaps the most convincing evidence that by "temperament" Schalk understood *only* the possibility of equal temperament is his second-to-last sentence, dated 13 June 1899, which reads: "how is it that on instruments with fixed tunings the sound characteristics of the keys are not lost, but rather emerge more sharply than they do in the orchestra? (25)" Schalk, the pianist, may have been told that his piano was tuned in equal temperament, but apparently it was not!

Schalk's claim that the "sounding together of various instruments, no matter how superbly tuned and played, is always subjected to minimal deviations in intonation that arise through the striving toward ideal pitch by many individuals" (25) certainly contains much truth, though it smacks strongly of Helmholtz.[40] Given our ignorance of intonation in large

[39] Annie H. Takeuchi and Stewart H. Hulse, "Absolute-Pitch Judgments of Black- and White-Key Pitches," *Music Perception* 9/1 (Fall, 1991), 27–46. "Subjects compared the pitch of an auditory tone with a visually presented pitch name and responded Same or Different. The absolute-pitch possessors responded significantly more slowly to black-key auditory pitches, and to black-key visual pitch names, than to white-key pitches and pitch names." (from the abstract) The accuracy of identification of pitches for both the absolute-pitch group and the relative-pitch group was also greater for white notes. See the chart on p. 33.

[40] Considering the strong influence of Helmholtz and Riemann, that "ideal pitch" would very likely be "just" in Schalk's view. Barbour ("Just Intonation Confuted") confronts the notion that musicians intone

just intervals "naturally" in practice. He finds that the nearly ubiquitous use of vibrato by singers and string players makes the intonation of just intervals by small vocal and string ensembles a near impossibility, and he cites one empirical study which concludes that "singers in the physical sense are never on pitch, [though] in another sense, the perceptual, they are heard on pitch" (p. 55). String players are taught, Barbour says, "to stop a sharped note higher than the enharmonically equivalent flatted note – a characteristic of the Pythagorean tuning and the exact opposite of just intonation." Although the string player "displays all sorts of irregularities of pitch, he approaches the Pythagorean tuning of pure fifths and very sharp thirds." The natural horn and trumpet "necessarily used just intonation, except as any wind player is able to modify his pitch

ensembles, it is difficult to say much about the extent to which the "characters of the keys" are realized in chamber music and the orchestra, though they may well be. Presumably Schalk believed that he heard them there, given his skeptical attitude toward keyboard instruments, and this brings us to the inevitable question: what implications does this discussion of tuning have for our analytical understanding of Bruckner's music? In any investigation of this question, one certainly would want to start by knowing the tuning of the organs that Bruckner played.[41] The problem here is somewhat more complicated, for the slow decay of organ tone allows time to count beats, and thus, by Jorgensen's reasoning, one *could* tune truly equal temperament. Yet preliminary, informal research indicates that many turn-of-the-century organs were tuned in non-equal temperaments.[42] Thus, it is likely that Bruckner played in tunings that preserved the character of the keys. If this is so, these idiosyncrasies would have become a part of his tonal imagination and very likely been transferred to his instrumental composition as well. The problems of ensemble tuning notwithstanding, does this not point to essential differences in Bruckner's conception of the various keys, to an association of particular keys with "appropriate" thematic material, etc., and thus to a much more complicated situation than our equally tempered notion of "chromatic harmony" admits?

The present study can only broach these questions – not answer them. But analysts of Bruckner's music would do well to stay abreast of the search for answers, for the humble process of transposition that Schalk so disliked has become the very foundation of the music theory and analysis of our era. In turn, it is important to remember that equal temperament, in its neutral, positionally unassertive division of pitch space, provides the physical performance conditions that make transposition a viable experiential phenomenon. To assert the reality, on a continuing and observable basis, of non-equal temperaments, would have radical consequences indeed for our practice of musical analysis.

somewhat . . . ," but "Helmholtz's statement that 'brass instruments naturally play in just intonation and can only be forced to the tempered system by being blown out of tune' could not possibly be applied to modern instruments having a complete chromatic scale" (p. 56).

Barbour's primary goal was to discredit the notion that musicians, regardless of the instruments they play, naturally think in just intervals, and certainly he shows that things are not that simple. What we need now are studies to find out just how musicians from various backgrounds *do* think of intervals, and how ensemble intonation works.

[41] The present state of ignorance in this matter is epitomized by Rudolf Quoika's *Die Orgelwelt um Anton Bruckner* (Ludwigsburg: Walcker, 1966), which gives thorough descriptions of the construction and registration of organs Bruckner was known to have played, but contains no information whatsoever on their tuning. Likewise, one looks in vain for help in the *New Grove* article s.v. "Organ."

[42] David Higgs, Chair of the Organ Department at the Eastman School of Music, reports that some turn-of-the-century French organs were not in equal temperament. In reacting to this paper, William Carragan noted the presence of non-equal temperaments in turn-of-the-century Austrian organs as well.

8 The Finale of Bruckner's Seventh Symphony and the tragic reversed sonata form

Timothy L. Jackson

[Sonata form] gives German music the world-wide validity which it can never lose.   *Wilhelm Furtwängler*

In Otto Böhler's famous "shadow-pictures" of Brahms's and Bruckner's "reception in heaven," amid the general festivity, the recently deceased artists are greeted by colleagues and predecessors, friends and enemies (plates 8.1–2). In Heaven-Parnassus the animosities of earth are renounced as Bruckner is greeted by Liszt and Wagner (plate 8.1), Brahms is welcomed by Bruckner, and Mendelssohn and Wagner stand amicably side by side at the organ (plate 8.2). Böhler's designs do more than depict *post mortem* collegiality; they suggest that these composers belong together as joint creators of a single great Masterwork encompassing all individual productions: the living tradition of German music. Since Bruckner synthesized classical with "New German" influences, the semantic content of his music may be decoded with reference to both classical and avant-garde traditions. Bruckner's art is firmly rooted in the classical tradition; Haydn, Mozart, Beethoven, Schubert, Cherubini, and even Brahms profoundly influenced him; only later did he become acquainted with Berlioz, Liszt, and Wagner. Accepting Böhler's premise that each composer builds upon his predecessors' achievements, the present study interprets the Finale of Bruckner's Seventh Symphony (1883) in the larger context of a classical genre of "tragic" reversed sonata form.

In late eighteenth- and nineteenth-century German sonata forms, parallelism between the order of groups in reprise and exposition is normative. Reversed sonata forms are uncommon in this tradition after about 1770; thus, the reversed recapitulation may be an architectural and tonal "deformation" of "textbook" sonata form. The "spatial" organization of normative sonata form is displayed in fig. 8.1a.[1] The

---

[1] I am indebted to discussions of form in the writings of Felix Salzer, Saul Novack, Carl   Schachter, and James Hepokoski.

Plate 8.1   Otto Böhler: *Bruckner's Arrival in Heaven*

groups in the exposition occupy "exposition space," the corresponding groups in the recapitulation are assigned to "recapitulation space," and the introduction, development, and coda each occupy their own respective spaces. Reversed sonata form (fig. 8.1b–d) alters the order of groups in the recapitulation. In a two-group reprise, the second initiates recapitulation space (fig. 8.1b). The coda and recapitulation spaces may be elided, if the recapitulation of the first group material doubles as the coda. When the exposition comprises three groups, the reversed recapitulation may take the form third group, second group, and first group (fig. 8.1c). A variant places the recapitulated introduction before the reversed groups (fig. 8.1d). Fig. 8.1e shows another variant: the development begins but is interrupted by the recapitulation of the second group; it then continues, leading to a coda, which also functions as the recapitulation of the first group. In this case, the recapitulation is elided with both the development and coda spaces. Two different types of partially reversed recapitulation are identified in figs. 8.1f–g. In the first, the normative order of the groups is preserved in the reprise;

Plate 8.2   Otto Böhler: *Brahms's Arrival in Heaven*

the sonata design is "reversed" by placing the first group's opening music *after* the second group, where it begins the coda (fig. 8.1f). Another type of partially reversed sonata form occurs when the groups are reversed and the first group's initial theme is the climax of the development (fig. 8.1g).[2]

When it occurs in a small but significant repertoire from the late eighteenth and nineteenth centuries, the reversed recapitulation may

[2] For a detailed discussion of Tchaikovsky's use of this form in the *Tempest Overture* and the first movement of the Fourth Symphony, see Timothy L. Jackson, "Aspects of Sexuality and Structure in the Later Symphonies of Tchaikovsky," *Music Analysis* 14 (1995), 3–29.

have tragic, programmatic implications.[3] This "tragic" deformation is both formal and tonal. In his discussion of tragedy in the *Poetics*, Aristotle defines *peripety* – an essential component of tragic plots – as:

> a shift of what is being undertaken to the opposite . . . in accordance with probability or necessity . . . as for example in the *Oedipus* the man who has come, thinking that he will reassure Oedipus, that is, relieve him of his fear with respect to his mother, [but] by revealing who he once was, brings about the opposite.[4]

In the best tragic plots, this shift comes about not "thanks to wickedness but because of some mistake of great weight and consequence."[5] Peripety occurs in the tragic reversed sonata when the recapitulation opens with the second or third group, the recapitulated material being recomposed so that the tonic due at the beginning of the recapitulation is either suppressed or devalued. In the compositions to be discussed, Aristotle's "mistake of great weight and consequence" corresponds both to the "incorrect" disposition of the recapitulation with the second or third group first and to the fundamental harmonic "mistake" whereby the tonic associated with the second or third group is either displaced or revealed to be an "apparent" tonic.[6]

However conjectural interpreting a formal-tonal event in programmatic-rhetorical terms may be, it is a time-honored theoretical practice. The frame of reference for virtually all discussions of form in the seventeenth through early nineteenth centuries was still Greek dramatic and linguistic rhetorical theory. Throughout this period, strictly instrumental music, no less than texted music, was considered to convey an underlying poetic, philosophical, or religious message. For example, Giuseppe Carpani, an early biographer of Haydn, states that "a musical composition is an oration that is made with figurative sounds instead of

[3] Charles Rosen (*Sonata Forms*, rev. ed. [New York: Norton, 1988], p. 286) takes note of the reversed recapitulation only in passing, without mentioning its possible tragic significance. For a bibliography of studies of sonata form to 1978, see James Webster, "Schubert's Sonata Form and Brahms's First Maturity," *19th-Century Music* 2 (1978), 19, note 1. Several articles devoted to the recapitulation may be mentioned: Eugene K. Wolf, "The Recapitulations in Haydn's London Symphonies," *The Musical Quarterly* 52 (1966), 71–89; Roger Kamien, "Aspects of the Recapitulation in Beethoven Piano Sonatas," *The Music Forum* 4 (New York:

Columbia University Press, 1976), pp. 195–235.
[4] Aristotle, *Poetics*, trans. Gerald F. Else (Ann Arbor: The University of Michigan Press, 1970), pp. 35–36.
[5] Ibid., 38–39.
[6] For recent discussions of "real" and "apparent" harmonies, see Eric Wen, "Illusory Cadences and Apparent Tonics: The Effect of Motivic Enlargement upon Phrase Structure," *Trends in Schenkerian Research*, ed. Allen Cadwallader (New York: Schirmer, 1990), pp. 133–44; Timothy L. Jackson, "Current Issues in Schenkerian Analysis," *The Musical Quarterly* 76 (1992), 242–63.

(a) Normative sonata form

(Introduction)	First group Second group	Development	First group Second group	(Coda)
Intro. space	Exposition space	Development space	Recapitulation space	Coda space

Beethoven – Op. 59/3 (1803)
Schubert – *Quartettsatz* (1820, publ. 1870)
Berlioz – *Symphonie fantastique* (1828, publ. 1845)
Liszt – *Les Préludes* (1848)

(b) Reversed recapitulation (two groups)

(Introduction)	First group Second group	Development	Second group First group	(Coda)
Intro. space	Exposition space	Development space	Recapitulation space	Coda space

Brahms – Cello Sonata, Op. 38/3 (1866)
  – *Tragic Overture*, Op. 81 (1881)
  – Violin Sonata, Op. 108/4 (1889)
Schoenberg – Second String Quartet, Op. 10/1 (1907)
Sibelius – Fourth Symphony, Op. 63/4 (1909)
Schoenberg – Third String Quartet, Op. 30/1 (1927)

Second group Recap. First group = Coda	
Recapitulation space	
Coda space	

(Recapitulation and coda spaces elided)

Haydn – Symphony No. 44/4 (1771)
Mozart – *Idomeneo*, Quartet (1781)

Second group First group	Introduction
Recapitulation space	Coda space

Brahms – *Schicksalslied*, Op. 54 (1868)

(c) Reversed recapitulation (three groups)

First group Second group Third group	Development	Third group Second group First group Coda
Exposition space	Development space	Recapitulation space Coda space

Wagner – *Tannhäuser Overture* (1845)
Bruckner – Seventh Symphony/4 (1883)

(d) Reversed recapitulation (variant)

Introduction First group Second group	Development	Introduction Second group First group Coda
Intro. space	Exposition space	Development space	Recapitulation space Coda space

Mahler – Sixth Symphony/4 (1904)

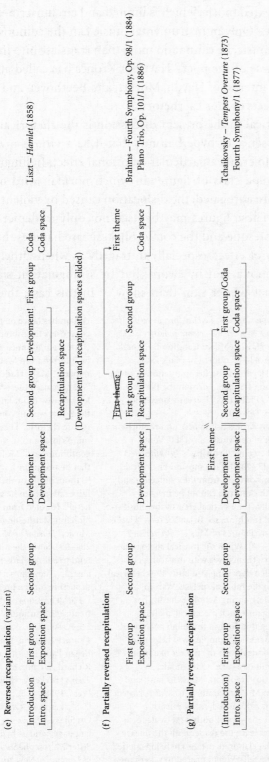

Fig. 8.1 Normative, reversed, and partially reversed sonata forms

words."[7] For Carpani, instrumental music is a *higher* form of rhetoric than texted music, which is limited and circumscribed by the specifics of its text: "Only in instrumental music can the composer be an Orator; in vocal music, he cannot do more than translate into musical language the discourse of the poet." Hartmut Krones has called attention to the profound interest of Haydn, Mozart, and Beethoven and their generation in all aspects of musical rhetoric.[8]

Critical to the present discussion is the rhetorical figure *hyperbaton*. The essence of hyperbaton is that it be a *vitium*, a violation of normal usage to create a particular emotional effect. In linguistic theory, hyperbaton is a class of figures in which normal word order and semantic logic are abrogated, the dislocation caused by violent or disordered feelings.[9] These figures may be used not only to depict the tragic but also the grotesque and the comic. Shakespeare handles them with an infinite variety of effect, especially in tragedy as when Othello plans to murder Desdemona, not by sword, but by strangulation since he "would not mar that whiter skin than snow."[10] In this case, the dislocation of the

[7] Giuseppe Carpani, *Le Haydine, ovvero lettere su la vita e le opere del celebre maestro Giuseppe Haydn* (Milan: Candido Buccinelli, 1812), pp. 43–44, quoted in Mark Evan Bonds, "Haydn's False Recapitulations and the Perception of Sonata Form in the Eighteenth Century" (Ph.D. diss., Harvard University, 1988), pp. 158–59.

[8] Hartmut Krones, "Rhetorik und rhetorische Symbolik in der Musik um 1800. Vom Weiterleben eines Prinzips," *Musiktheorie* 3 (1988), 117–40. But the musical-rhetorical discussions of form from the eighteenth and nineteenth centuries cannot be invoked uncritically (for a critical view of the musical-rhetorical tradition, see Brian Vickers, "Figures of Rhetoric/Figures of Music?" *Rhetorica* 2 [1984], 1–44). When the musical rhetoricians do concern themselves with musical specifics, all too often they simply identify the rhetorical figures on the musical surface. Warren Kirkendale, quoting Arnold Schmitz, has warned against such piecemeal analysis, cautioning that "only a thorough analysis of the entire musical complex will help: one should not deal with the figures like fruit plucked out of a cake" (Kirkendale, "'Circulatio'-Tradition, 'Maria lactans,' and Josquin as Musical Orator," *Acta Musicologica* 56 [1984], 70). Indeed, many musical-rhetorical analyses of both large-scale form and figures leave the reader with the uneasy feeling that elaborate means are being applied to describe self-evident procedures. Perhaps a

certain hesitance on the part of Baroque composers to embrace the specifics of contemporary musical-rhetorical analysis can be inferred from Mattheson's rather pointed remark: "Many readers will say to themselves, 'We have used these figures and things for so long now without knowing anything about them that we can continue in this way and ignore rhetoric.' These persons seem even more ridiculous to me than the bourgeois gentilhomme of Molière, who did not know that he was using a pronoun when he said, 'I, thou, or he,' or that he was using the imperative when he said to his servant, 'Come here!'" (quoted from Hans Lenneberg, "Johann Mattheson on Affect and Rhetoric in Music," *Journal of Music Theory* 2 [1958], 204–05). Since the musical-rhetorical treatises tend to address larger formal issues in the abstract, they can serve only as a point of a departure for the present discussion.

[9] For definitions of this figure from rhetorical treatises of Antiquity and the Renaissance, see Lee A. Sonnino, *A Handbook to Sixteenth-Century Rhetoric* (London: Routledge and Kegan Paul, 1968), pp. 179–80. See also Richard A. Lanham, *A Handlist of Rhetorical Terms* (Berkeley: University of California Press, 1968), p. 56.

[10] Shakespeare, *Othello*, Act 5, scene 2, line 3. On Shakespeare's use of the "vices of language," and of hyperbaton in particular, see Sister M. Joseph, *Shakespeare's Use of the Arts of Language* (New York, 1947), pp. 54–56.

hyperbaton both depicts Othello's jealous rage and foreshadows its tragic consequences. By violating the formal-tonal order of normative sonata form, the tragic reversed recapitulation is a large-scale hyperbaton. Indeed, the Baroque musical rhetorician Johann Adolph Scheibe identifies hyperbaton as "the removal of . . . [a] musical idea from the expected order."[11]

In employing the term "deformation" in connection with the tragic reversed sonata form, I draw upon recent work of James Hepokoski, who defines sonata deformation as "a strikingly non-normative individual structure, one that contravenes some of the most central defining traditions, or default gestures, of a genre while explicitly retaining others." The point of reference is "the normative practice, or set of reified defaults, urged by the *Formenlehre* traditions, for better or worse a fundamental frame of reference for the institution of Germanic art music at least from the time of A. B. Marx on."[12]

The tragic reversed sonata form with the connotation "deformation" has a different pedigree and significance from the symmetrical sonata form.[13] Many early classical sonatas (ca. 1740–80) incorporate the reversed recapitulation as a stable, symmetrical formation. In these pieces, the reversed recapitulation occurs as a chiasmus-like formation. These symmetrical sonata forms are not deformations; the tonic at the beginning of their recapitulations is usually real rather than displaced or apparent. Examples of the symmetrical recapitulation can be found in the symphonies of Johann Stamitz (ca. 1740–50), although this formal disposition is less common in Stamitz's music than generally believed.[14] Some twelve works by Haydn feature symmetrical recapitulations. Mark Evan Bonds remarks that "this procedure is largely abandoned after 1770," observing that "it is all the more striking that Mozart abandons the procedure [of the reversed recapitulation] so suddenly and at almost

[11] George Buelow, "Rhetoric and Music," in the *New Grove Dictionary of Music and Musicians*, ed. Stanley Sadie (London: Macmillan, 1980), p. 794.
[12] James Hepokoski, "Fiery-Pulsed Libertine or Domestic Hero? Strauss's *Don Juan* Revisited," in *Richard Strauss: New Perspectives on the Composer and His Work*, ed. Bryan Gilliam (Durham, N.C.: Duke University Press, 1992), p. 143; *Sibelius: Symphony No. 5* (Cambridge University Press, 1993), pp. 6–7.
[13] I prefer to identify this early classical reversed recapitulation as "symmetrical sonata form," thereby eliminating the term "reversed" with its connotation of "deformation." The reversed recapitulation is also essentially

different from palindrome, in which the musical materials themselves are retrograded. For recent discussion of palindrome in Schubert and Berg see Brian Newbould, "A Schubert Palindrome," *19th-Century Music* 15 (1992), 207–14; Barbara Dalen, "'Freundschaft, Liebe, und Welt': The Secret Program of the Chamber Concerto," *The Berg Companion*, ed. Douglas Jarman (Boston: Northeastern University Press, 1989), pp. 141–80.
[14] See Eugene K. Wolf, *The Symphonies of Johann Stamitz: A Study in the Formation of the Classic Style* (Utrecht/Antwerp: Bohn, Scheltema and Holkema; the Hague/Boston: Nijhoff, 1981).

precisely the same time as Haydn."[15] The symmetrical recapitulations of the first movements of Mozart's Piano Sonata, K. 311 (1777) and Violin Sonata, K. 306 (1778) show that Mozart had not jettisoned the earlier formal practice entirely. Both were composed during the composer's trip to Mannheim and Paris and perhaps exhibit local influences. French composers had a penchant for symmetrical sonata form well into the first part of the nineteenth century. Cherubini employs it in his overture to *Anacréon* (1803), as does Berlioz in *Harold in Italy* (1834) and the Overture to *Benvenuto Cellini* (1838). Perhaps influenced by French models, Wagner employs three-group symmetrical sonata form in the Overture to *Tannhäuser* (1845).

In a small number of reversed sonata forms in the German tradition post ca. 1770, the reversed recapitulation combined with the displaced tonic has programmatic significance, representing tragic peripety wraught by capricious and unkind Fate. Late eighteenth-century instances include: the Finale of Haydn's Symphony No. 44 in E minor (1771, subtitled, possibly authentically, the "Trauersymphonie"), the great Quartet from Act III of Mozart's *Idomeneo* (1781), and the Overture to Cherubini's *Médée* (1797).[16] Once the normative procedures of sonata form had been codified in the *Formenlehre* of the mid nineteenth century, composers and theorists working in the second half of the century attached special significance to deviations. The reversed sonata form of the Andante from Beethoven's Third "Rasumovsky" Quartet (1803) (which may have served Schubert as a model for his *Quartettsatz* of 1820), prompted A. B. Marx to describe it as "seltsam fremd."[17] Schubert's *Quartettsatz* may have provided both Brahms and Bruckner with a formal model for tragic works in reversed sonata form; these include, by Brahms, the Finales of the first Cello Sonata in E minor, Op. 38 (1866) and the Third Violin Sonata in D minor, Op. 108 (1889), the *Schicksalslied*, Op. 54 (1868–71), and the *Tragic Overture*, Op. 81 (1881); and by Bruckner, the Finale of the Seventh Symphony (1883).[18] By 1883, Bruckner may have studied the above-mentioned works by Haydn, Cherubini, Beethoven, and Schubert, and possibly Brahms's

[15] See Bonds, "Haydn's False Recapitulations," pp. 287 and 301–2. The interested reader may wish to examine these works (listed by Bonds), which include the symphonies 21/II (1764), 31/I (1765), 59/IV (1766–68), 44/IV (ca. 1770), 87/IV (1785) and the string quartets Op. 1/1/III (1755–59), Op. 2/6/V (1755–59), Op. 50/3/I (1787), Op. 71/2 (1793).
[16] Cherubini was trained in Italy and later resided and worked in France; his musical language is so close to that of late Haydn and Mozart, and middle-period Beethoven that he may be included in the present discussion of the German classical tradition.
[17] Quoted by Joseph Kerman, *The Beethoven Quartets* (New York: Knopf, 1967), p. 149.
[18] Brahms owned the manuscript of Schubert's *Quartettsatz* and urged its publication in 1870.

Schicksalslied and *Tragic Overture.*[19] The Seventh Symphony was the piece that catapulted Bruckner to world fame; well into the early part of this century, it was Bruckner's best-known symphony. Perhaps the tragic Finales of Mahler's Sixth Symphony (1904) and Sibelius's Fourth Symphony (1909), and the first movements of Schoenberg's first two string quartets (1907 and 1927) were influenced by the Finale of Bruckner's Seventh, if not by the earlier, classical works discussed in this article.

The genre of the tragic reversed sonata form is the antithesis of the "dark-to-light" or "strife-to-victory" model. In the narrative plots of pieces examined below, the cruel blows of destiny are never overcome as they are, for example, in Beethoven's Fifth and Ninth Symphonies, Schumann's Second Symphony, and Tchaikovsky's Fifth Symphony;[20] there is no rescue, no *deus ex machina*, no song of rejoicing. Only the Finale of Bruckner's Seventh Symphony is an exception to this principle; in a typically Brucknerian synthesis of opposites, the composer grafts a triumphant coda – usually associated with the "darkness-to-light" narrative model – onto the main body of a tragic reversed sonata form. Semantic analysis suggests that Bruckner forms a hybrid of antithetical genres to signify both the catastrophic impact of Wagner's death and the triumph of his immortal music. The Finale is both a late nineteenth-century *déploration sur la mort de Wagner* and a valedictory panegyric.

Technical aspects of design–structure correlation

David Beach has explained the essential distinction, first made by Felix Salzer, between "design" and "structure," a distinction which will be assumed throughout the present discussion.[21] As is well known, Schenker's pioneering discussion of the structures underlying sonata design in *Free Composition* does not constitute an exhaustive inventory of the structural or design possibilities of sonata form, a deficiency which

[19] Bruckner had probably studied the scores of the first two Brahms symphonies (published in 1877–78), and the *Tragic Overture* (published in 1881). His late critique of Brahms reported by August Stradal, "Erinnerungen aus Bruckners letzter Zeit," *Zeitschrift für Musik* 99 (1932), 973, reveals that he knew both the Schumann and Brahms symphonies.

[20] See Anthony Newcomb, "Once More 'Between Absolute and Program Music': Schumann's Second Symphony," *19th-Century Music* 7 (1984), 233–50. Joseph C. Kraus, "Tonal Plan and Narrative Plot in Tchaikovsky's Symphony No. 5 in E Minor," *Music Theory Spectrum* 13 (1991), 21–47.

[21] David Beach, "Schubert's Experiments with Sonata Form: Formal-Tonal Design versus Underlying Structure," *Music Theory Spectrum* (1993), 1–18. In view of the centrality of the frequently complex, *contrapuntal* design-structure correlation in sonata form, it is surprising how little has appeared on this subject.

Oster sought to remedy in his notes and addendum.[22] Schenker remarks cryptically that "even a reordering of the original sequence of the material is possible in the recapitulation, since the fundamental line and the bass arpeggiation ultimately restore the balance."[23]

More recently, a number of analysts have begun to fill in some of the gaps in Schenker and Oster's account of sonata form. Beach, for example, has studied subdominant recapitulations in Schubert. Sonatas with subdominant recapitulations and sonatas with reversed recapitulations may be generically related in so far as both avoid an expected structural tonic at the beginning of the recapitulation and replace interruption with an undivided *Urlinie*. Carl Schachter's analysis of the ♭III recapitulation in the Finale of Schubert's Ninth Symphony also sheds light on the problem of Schubert's non-tonic recapitulations.[24] More generally, Jack Adrian's detailed studies of sonata form systematically explore some of the territory already mapped out by Schenker and Oster.[25] Building on Oster's addendum, Adrian defines the ternary sonata form as one in which the structural tonic supporting the *Kopfton* returns twice in the course of the movement: at the beginning of the development and again at the onset of the recapitulation. Ternary sonatas contain *three* rather than the customary two "structural downbeats," as defined by Robert Morgan.[26] According to Adrian, this repertoire includes the first movements of Brahms's Violin Sonata in G Major, Op. 78 (1878–79), Piano Trio in C Major, Op. 87 (1880), Fourth Symphony, Op. 98 (1884–85), and Clarinet Sonata, Op. 120, No. 2 (1894). The first movement of Brahms's Fourth Symphony is in fact a special case; here, the structural tonic supporting the primary tone does not appear at the real beginning of the recapitulation (m. 259) but is instead reserved for the onset of the coda (m. 394) in the partially reversed sonata form, as will be explained below.[27]

The sonata forms under consideration in this chapter are character-

[22] Heinrich Schenker, *Der freie Satz. Neue musikalische Theorien und Phantasien* (Vienna: Universal Edition, 1935), trans. Ernst Oster, *Free Composition* (New York: Longman, 1979), pp. 133–40.

[23] Ibid., 138.

[24] Carl Schachter, "Mozart's Last and Beethoven's First: Echoes of K. 551 in the First Movement of Opus 21," *Mozart Studies*, ed. Cliff Eisen (Oxford: Clarendon Press, 1991), pp. 250–51. For a quite different reading, which obscures the structural significance of the motion to III♯3 in the recapitulation, see Webster, "Schubert's Sonata Form," 33.

[25] Jack Adrian, "The Ternary-Sonata Form," *Journal of Music Theory* 34 (1990), 57–80; and "The Function of the Apparent Tonic at the

Beginning of Development Sections," *Intégrale* 5 (1990), 1–53.

[26] Robert Morgan, "The Delayed Structural Downbeat and its Effect on the Tonal and Rhythmic Structure of Sonata Form" (Ph.D. diss., Princeton University, 1969).

[27] In fairness to Oster, it should be pointed out that it is Adrian, not Oster, who claims a tonic return at the beginning of the recapitulation in the first movement of the Fourth Symphony. In addition, Adrian overlooks the ternary sonata form of the slow movement of Bruckner's Sixth Symphony (1879–81). Interestingly, Brahms and Bruckner independently explored the ternary sonata form at roughly the same time (1878–81).

ized not only by a reversal in the order of groups in the recapitulation, but also by tonal displacement of the tonic normally associated with the beginning of the recapitulation. In the tragic program, the cruel hand of Destiny upsets the sonata design and destroys or distorts the expected harmonic-tonal structure. In some examples of tragic reversed sonata form, reversing the order of groups in the recapitulation involves displacing the recapitulated second group's tonic by a more background chord, sometimes by a prolonged dominant extending out of the development. The *definitive* return of the tonic (with its associated structural downbeat) does not coincide with the return of the second group, but rather is saved for the culminating recapitulation of the first group.[28]

The background tonal structures in tragic reversed sonata forms are quite different from the interruption structures underlying sonata form presented by Schenker in *Free Composition*. With the most common type of late eighteenth-century reversed sonata form, the primary tone is not regained at the beginning of the recapitulation. Instead, the upper voice is undivided as $V/\hat{2}$, prolonged through the development *and* the recapitulation of the second group, resolves to $I/\hat{1}$ over the recapitulation of the first group. Because $I/\hat{1}$ (which coincides with the return of the first group) completes the large-scale structural descent in the upper voice, the recapitulation of the first group may simultaneously function as a coda. In normative sonata structure, interruption coincides with the break in the musical discourse between the end of the development and the onset of the recapitulation. In reversed sonata form, however, recapitulation of the second and first groups constitutes a design-structural unit; instead of an interruption between the end of the recapitulated second and first groups, $V/\hat{2}$ resolves to $I/\hat{1}$ within an undivided structure. In Schenker's sonata model, the return to the structural tonic supporting the primary tone at the beginning of the recapitulation signifies a tonal return deep in the middleground. The idea of a second chance in the deep middleground is foreign to tragic reversed sonata form. In the tragic context, the undivided upper voice and continuously unfolding harmonic-contrapuntal process parallel the inexorable unraveling of tragic destiny.[29]

If some interpreters have misread the design of works in reversed

[28] This chapter and Morgan's above-cited dissertation are related. Morgan is primarily concerned with non-reversed sonata designs in which the return of the structural tonic with its associated structural downbeat is delayed. This study probes the delay of the structural downbeat resulting from the postponed recapitulation of the first group in the reversed sonata form.

[29] This connotation is context dependent, not intrinsic to reversed sonata form. One would be hard pressed to consider as "tragic" the first movement of Schubert's "Trout" Quintet, which also has an undivided *Urlinie* (see Beach, "Schubert's Experiments with Sonata Form").

sonata form, this may be, in part, because the form has not been recognized as a legitimate genre. Tovey regards instances of reversed sonata design in Cherubini as evidence of a "deficient sense of form," observing rhetorically and yet paradoxically that "Cherubini had a very good sense of form; he was profoundly moved by Haydn and Mozart, nor did Beethoven fail to influence him more than he liked to admit to himself. But his treatment of the Viennese forms results only by a precarious series of flukes in anything that can be judged by the same criteria."[30] Furthermore, the relationship between reversed sonata design and undivided tonal structure is frequently complex and can easily provoke confusing, even contradictory analyses. Too often, the source of ambiguity is to be imputed to the analyst rather than the composer. For example, contrary to Daniel Coren's assertion of *"ambiguity* [my emphasis] in Schubert's recapitulations," the relationship between design and tonal structure in Schubert is complex but *unambiguous*.[31] Arnold Schoenberg's remarks quoted below concerning the form of the first movement of his Second String Quartet show just how difficult it can be, even for the composer himself, to clearly explain the complex, potentially confusing relationship between reversed sonata design and tonal structure. Leopold Nowak, in his 1956 study of the Finale of Bruckner's Seventh Symphony, was the first to identify the reversed sonata design – previous and even subsequent analysts have been baffled by the form.[32] For example, Bruckner's contemporaries Hermann Levi and Hugo Wolf found this Finale "incomprehensible," although they eventually came to appreciate it as "der schönste" and "der grossartigste." Robert Simpson, writing in 1963 (*after* Nowak's article had appeared), still sidesteps the formal issue, observing only that "it [the Finale] is unique in form and difficult to describe."[33] The analysis of works which may have served as models attempts to place Bruckner's use of the reversed recapitulation in a larger historical context. We shall begin by exploring the technical aspects of the reversed recapitulation and then consider its various tragic-programmatic significances.

[30] Donald Francis Tovey, "Berlioz, *Harold in Italy*," in *Essays in Musical Analysis*, 6 vols. (Oxford University Press, 1935–39, repr. 1989), *Symphonies and Other Orchestral Works*, p. 173.

[31] Daniel Coren, "Ambiguity in Schubert's Recapitulations," *The Musical Quarterly 60* (1974), 568–82.

[32] Leopold Nowak, "Das Finale von Bruckners VII. Symphonie," *Über Anton Bruckner. Gesammelte Aufsätze* (Vienna: Doblingers), pp. 30–33. The interpretation of the design presented here agrees with analyses by Nowak and Theodor Wünschmann, *Anton Bruckners Weg als Symphoniker* (Steinfeld: Salvator Verlag, 1976), pp. 135–37.

[33] Robert Simpson, "The Seventh Symphony of Anton Bruckner: An Analysis," *Chord and Discord*, 2 (1963), 65.

The second group over dominant prolongation

The most common way of composing the second group's recapitulation in the reversed sonata form is to continue dominant prolongation through the return of the second group. In the Finale of Haydn's Symphony No. 44, the recomposed bridge section (mm. 112–37) leads directly into the recapitulation of the second group (ex. 8.1a). As shown in the graph, dominant prolongation extends through the second group's recapitulation, the definitive tonic arrival being saved for the recapitulation of the first group, which doubles as a coda. Strong V–I cadences in the second group are undermined; for example, the expected tonic in m. 151 is reinterpreted as a V of IV. The chromatic voice-exchange in the development is then recomposed (m. 158) leading into an extension of the dominant, which prepares the definitive tonic return (m. 175). The large-scale $\hat{5}$–$\hat{6}$–$\hat{5}$ neighbor note "x," which spans the exposition, development, and recapitulation of the first group, constitutes an enlargement of the motive presented by the subject (exx. 8.1a–b).

The Quartet from Mozart's *Idomeneo* provides a more elaborate example. Its formal–textual correlation is consistent with the reversed design shown in ex. 8.2. *Terzetti* 3–5 (*Serena il ciglio irato* etc.) are set by the second group in the exposition (mm. 34–67) and recapitulation (mm. 92–153), while *terzetti* 1–2 (*Andrò ramingo e solo* etc.) are initially set by the first group and bridge in the exposition (mm. 1–33) and, when the text is repeated, by the development (mm. 67–91). The truncated recapitulation of the first group (mm. 153–end) returns to the first line of the opening *terzetto*.[34]

Although the second group in a major mode sonata is usually in the dominant, ex. 8.2 shows that the expected dominant in the Quartet's second group is displaced to the beginning of the development by a descending arpeggiation of the dominant minor, F–D♭–B♭. The B♭ minor of mm. 39–55 is an apparent dominant inserted into this over-arching arpeggiation. The dominant attained at the beginning of the development is prolonged through the recapitulation of the second group and definitively resolves to the tonic only in the recapitulation of the first group at the end. As the graph illustrates, two huge prolongations of an apparent tonic are inserted into the large-scale motion from B♭ (V) to C♭ major (♭VI) and back to B♭. Although the initial tonic minor prolonged in mm. 97–129 is greatly extended by a drawn-out prolongation of its dominant (mm. 101–18), this tonic is an apparent I♭3, caught within the

---

[34] Daniel Heartz, "The Great Quartet in Mozart's *Idomeneo*," *The Music Forum V* (New York: Columbia University Press, 1980), p. 239, misreads the formal design of the Quartet and its large-scale harmonic structure. Following the repetition of the text beginning in m. 67, he oversimplifies matters by dividing the design into two parts, mm. 1–67 and 67–end.

Ex. 8.1 Haydn, Symphony No. 44 ("Trauersymphonie"), Finale

a) Middleground

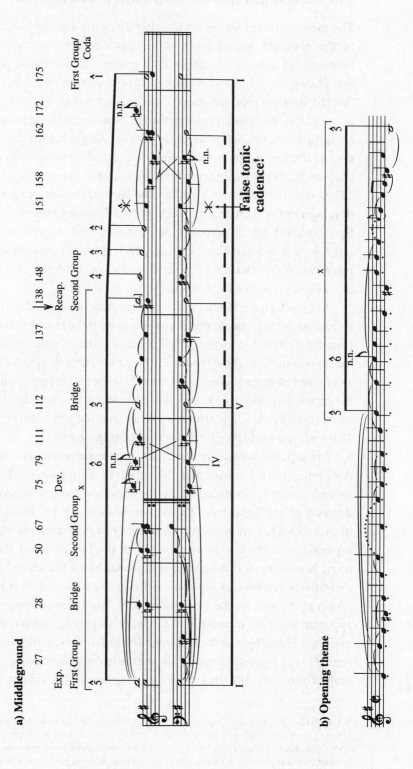

b) Opening theme

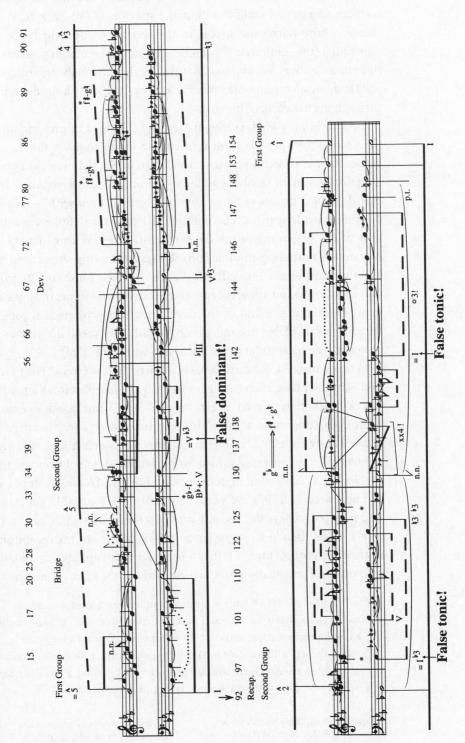

Ex. 8.2   Mozart, *Idomeneo*, Act III, Quartet, Middleground

underlying motion from V to ♭VI. The tonic major in mm. 142–47 is similarly an apparent I caught within the motion of ♭VI back to V. These massive, false harmonic spaces in the second group, which appear to contradict the underlying harmonic logic, may embody Idomeneo's dilemma: either he violates natural order through infanticide, or political-social-moral order (which, as king, he is duty bound to uphold) through the breaking of his vow.

In Cherubini's *Médée* Overture (ex. 8.3), instead of prolonging III in the second group, as is typical of minor-mode sonatas, the composer poises the entire second group on V/III. In m. 96, the music suggests the E♭ major dominant resolving to the A♭ major tonic; however, the A♭ major chord (m. 96) proves to be an apparent tonic caught within continuing dominant prolongation. The withheld III chord is definitively achieved only at the beginning of the development, where it immediately disintegrates in unfolding modulations. By recapitulating the second group exactly transposed from V/III to V/I, the F major tonic (m. 205=m. 96) also functions as an apparent rather than structural tonic; thus, the dominant reached at the end of the development is prolonged through the recapitulation of the second group, definitively resolving to the tonic only with the recapitulation of the first group (mm. 276ff.).

Writing in 1874, Edward Bellasis reports that a certain "Herr Greiner told Schindler that 'at an eating house near the Josephstadt, Vienna, there was a clock that played overtures and airs from good operas, and Beethoven (possessor of the full score [of *Médée*]) was wont to place himself quite close to it, that he might hear his favorite piece, the overture to *Médée*.'"[35] The reversed sonata form of the Andante of Beethoven's Op. 59, No. 3 may have been directly modeled on the *Médée* overture (which had appeared in 1797, five years before Op. 59, No. 3). In the A minor Andante (ex. 8.4a), the second group returns first in A major (mm. 100–13) and then in E♭ major (mm. 119–29), prior to the recapitulation of the first group (mm. 141ff.). Joseph Kerman, apparently unfamiliar with reversed sonata design, equivocates about the form of the Andante:

> Classification of this Andante as a movement in sonata form makes little sense, even though it incorporates a section rather like – yet curiously unlike – a development section, and even though it manages what sounds like a "second theme" with passable sonata-form normality . . . To speak of such a movement as a sonata form with irregularities is like calling a dog irregular when it grows long whiskers, washes its face, and miaows.[36]

[35] Edward Bellasis, *Cherubini: Memorials Illustrative of his Life and Work* (London, 1912; repr. New York: Da capo press, 1971), pp. 64–65.
[36] Joseph Kerman, *The Beethoven Quartets*, p. 150. For a critique of Kerman's naive "analysis" of the development, see William Mitchell's 1967 review, *The Musical Quarterly* 53 (1967), 425.

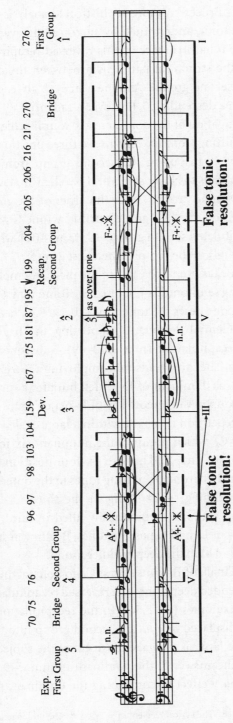

Ex. 8.3 Cherubini, *Médée*, Overture, Middleground

Common-sense analysis interprets the tonic (A) major of the second group's recapitulation (mm. 100–13) as a structural tonic as understood by Robert Bruce.[37] A more sophisticated analysis explains A major as an apparent tonic undermined by surrounding events. In order to understand the tonal structure of this reversed recapitulation, it is helpful to observe the structural parallelism between the opening themes of the first and second groups. As shown in ex. 8.4b–c, each group presents an *Anstieg* to a descending $\hat{3}$–line over a cadential V^{6-5}_{4-3}. In the second group, the prolongation of the dominant six-four is achieved in a rather unusual way by shifting from six-four to six-three position prior to the cadential resolution. Transposing the second group from C major to A major (ex. 8.4d) leads to closer structural parallelism – with mixture – between first and second groups. Since the order of the groups is reversed in the recapitulation, the first group's primary tone C ($\hat{3}$, m. 1) is displaced by the recapitulated second group's C♯ (♯$\hat{3}$, m. 102), which then collapses as if it were D♭ (♭$\hat{4}$) to the recapitulated first group's C ($\hat{3}$, m. 141, exx. 8.4a and d). This idea is prepared early in the piece by emphatic statements of the descending semitone D♭–C (mm. 25–30 and mm. 60–63).

At first one hears the tonic (m. 110, ex. 8.4a) as a definitive resolution of the cadential dominant supporting the beginning of the second group's recapitulation (mm. 100–09). Subsequent events subvert this resolution. The short transition employing a 5–6 exchange (mm. 113–15) leads to B♭ as dominant of E♭, which initiates a surprise repetition of the second group in the remote key of E♭ major (mm. 116–29, ♭V of A). This E♭ major repetition is caught within a large-scale voice-exchange involving E and C♯, which prolongs the dominant six-four by shifting it from six-four to six-three and back to six-four position.[38] The E♭ major repetition produces chromatic passing tones in the outer voices: E♭ in the upper voice functioning as D♯ filling in the third C♯–E, and E♭ in the bass descending within a chromatically filled-in third, E–E♭–D–C♯. Through the duality of D♯ and E♭ passing tones, Beethoven suggests an augmented seventh (E♭–D♯) in the deep middleground.

In the Finale of Brahms's First Cello Sonata, the dominant prolongation is extended deeper into the reversed recapitulation than in any of the previous examples (ex. 8.5a). In the recapitulation, the definitive tonic return is displaced *beyond* the second group into the middle of the first group. The latter is a fugal exposition of the subject in the tonic at mm. 1–4 with the answer in the dominant in mm. 5–9. Brahms achieves the extraordinary effect of continuing the dominant prolongation through

[37] Robert Bruce, "The Lyrical Element in Schubert's Instrumental Forms," *The Music Review* 30 (1969), 134.

[38] The prolongational strategy is established in the second group (mm. 40–42, ex. 8.4c).

Ex. 8.4   Beethoven, String Quartet, Op. 59, No. 3, Andante

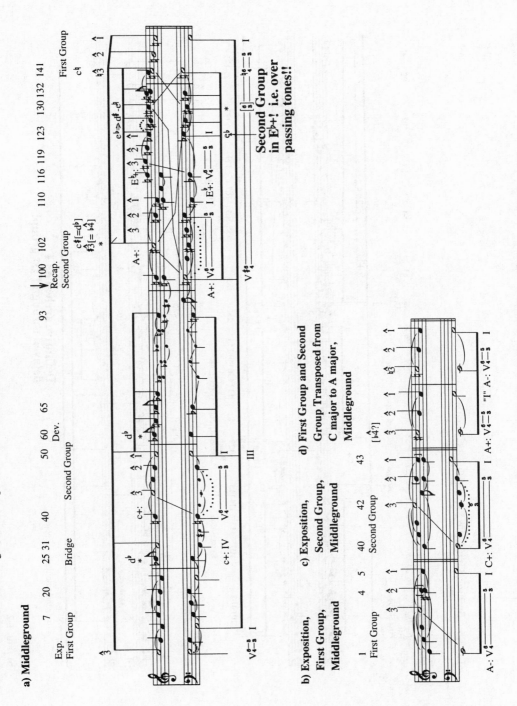

Ex. 8.5 Brahms, First Cello Sonata, Op. 38, Finale

a) Middleground

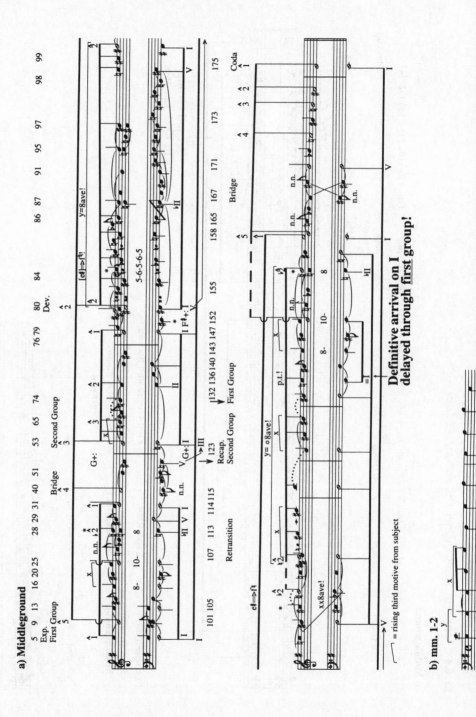

b) mm. 1-2

recapitulation of the *first* group (mm. 132ff.) by an astonishingly simple device: he omits the initial four-measure tonic statement of the subject. The recapitulation begins with the answer on the dominant. Although Brahms restates, in mm. 132–58, the contents of mm. 5–31 virtually unchanged, these measures are tonally revalued in the larger context. Whereas in the exposition, the tonic at mm. 1–4, 9–12, 16–19, and 25 is structural, in the recapitulation it is caught within continuing dominant prolongation; its function in the later context is to support a passing tone E in the upper voice (m. 136) on its way up to F (m. 158).

The middleground of this work grows out of two essential motivic ideas contained in the fugue subject: the ascending third, motive "x"; and the octave leap, motive "y" (ex. 8.5b). Enlargements of "x," sometimes filled in chromatically, are indicated with brackets in ex. 8.5a. The middleground voice-leading of the development grows organically out of "y," which is first stated as F♯–F♯ (mm. 80–99) and then distorted as a diminished octave F♯–F♮ ($\hat{2}$–♭$\hat{2}$, mm. 107–55). This second, distorted enlargement of the octave motive, filled in by enlargements of the rising third motive, spans the retransition, the return of the second group, and at least half of the return of the tonally revalued first group.

In the *Schicksalslied* (ex. 8.6a), Brahms modifies reversed sonata form by omitting the first group from the recapitulation. Implicit in reversed sonata form is the idea of circularity or return to point of origin. In tragic situations, circularity becomes metaphorical for entrapment or flight without escape. The above-cited Quartet from Mozart's *Idomeneo*, for example, concludes with Idamante's opening cry of despair. Indeed, all of the characters in the Quartet find themselves caught on a treadmill of tragic destiny, since a solution to the conundrum has not yet presented itself. Although Brahms sacrifices the recapitulation of the first group in the *Schicksalslied*, the idea of circularity implied by the reversed sonata design is intensified there by redeployment of the introduction as a coda.[39]

Two recent analyses of the *Schicksalslied* by Alan Luhring and John Daverio concur in their interpretation of the design as a "double sonata form."[40] Both analysts regard the setting of the first two stanzas (mm. 29–96) as a sonata in E♭ linked by a transition to the setting of the third stanza, a second sonata in C minor. In this interpretation, the first sonata

[39] Schubert in "Am Meer" from *Schwanengesang* similarly reuses the introduction as coda to represent tragic circularity.

[40] See Alan Luhring, "Dialectical Thought in Nineteenth-Century Music as Exhibited in Brahms's Setting of Hölderlin's 'Schicksalslied,'" *Choral Journal* 25 (1985), 5–13 and John Daverio, "The *Wechsel der Töne* in Brahms's Schicksalslied," *Journal of the American Musicological Society* 46 (1993), 84–113. While Daverio's article is the more wide-ranging, his conclusions about the work's form and meaning are remarkably similar to Luhring's.

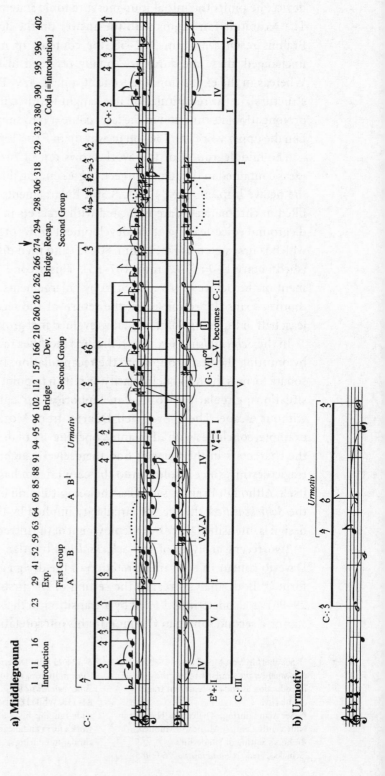

Ex. 8.6   Brahms, *Schicksalslied*, Op. 54

a) Middleground

b) Urmotiv

Ex. 8.6 *Schicksalslied*

c) Exposition, Second Group (mm. 112-165), Middleground

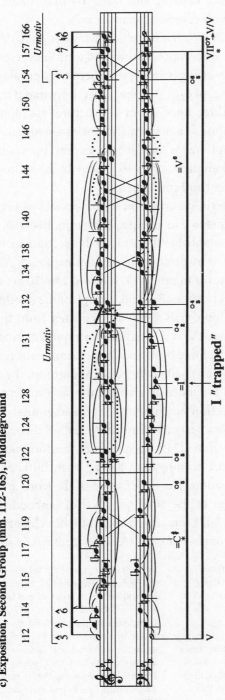

d) Development (mm. 166-266), Middleground

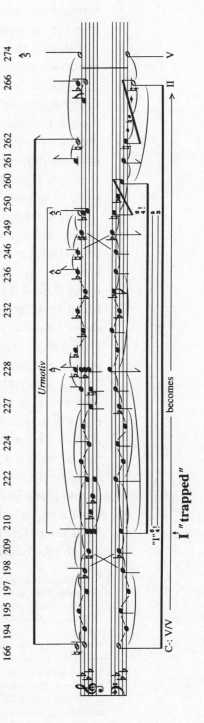

lacks a development section, the motion to the dominant in m. 64 substituting instead for the development. Ex. 8.6a proposes an alternative formal-tonal analysis where Luhring and Daverio's first sonata constitutes the *first group* of a single reversed sonata form.

This first group (mm. 29–96) is a strophic binary design AB/AB′. The poem's initial two stanzas are composed of six and nine lines respectively. The strophic design of the setting parallels the poem's design, as A and A′ set the first four and six lines of each strophe respectively, and B and B′ set the remaining two and three lines. From a structural standpoint, the dominant in m. 64 functions as a divider, and not as a structural dominant supporting interruption, as one might expect in a sonata or sonatina. This dividing dominant serves to articulate the setting of the two strophes into antecedent and consequent.

Both Luhring and Daverio describe the second sonata as being in C minor, reading a move from I to V in its exposition (mm. 104–79). Ex. 8.6c shows that Brahms never establishes the tonic in this section; instead, the key of C minor is suggested by prolonging its dominant, G.[41] As shown in exx. 8.6c–d the tonic chords in mm. 113, 128, and 210–50 are trapped within middleground progressions. Ex. 8.6d, a graph of the development, shows how the C minor tonic tries vainly to free itself from the unrelenting grasp of the prolonged V of V. This tonic entrapment grows out of the earlier subversion of the tonic by the prolonged dominant (ex. 8.6c). Lacking a modulation and a tonally defined second group, the passage encompassing mm. 104–179 does not constitute a complete sonata exposition. Instead, this section functions as the second group within the over-arching reversed sonata design. As shown in ex. 8.6a, the recapitulation of the second group (mm. 274ff.) begins over the dominant of the ultimate C tonic, dominant prolongation having been initiated by the second group in the exposition. The upper voice of the work as a whole constitutes an enlargement of the *Urmotiv*, which is embedded in the storm theme (ex. 8.6b): B♭, $\hat{5}$ of E♭ major, is drawn into the orbit of C minor as $\hat{7}$, and then collapses through A♭ ($\hat{6}$) to G ($\hat{5}$, compare exx. 8.6a and b).[42]

[41] Techniques of suggesting key without prolonging its tonic are explored in Carl Schachter, "Analysis by Key: Another Look at Modulation," *Music Analysis* 6 (1987), 295–304.

[42] Programmatically, mankind tries to reverse this fall in mm. 298–332 by converting "fallen" F♭ (♭$\hat{4}$) into "redeemed" E (♮$\hat{3}$, ex. 8.6a), but is pulled back into the mire with D♯ (♯$\hat{2}$) falling as E♭ ($\hat{3}$), through D♭ (♭$\hat{2}$) to C ($\hat{1}$). For the religious significance of enharmonic transformation, see Timothy L. Jackson, "The Enharmonics of Faith," *Bruckner Jahrbuch*

1987–88 (1990), pp. 4–20; "Schubert as 'John the Baptist to Wagner-Jesus': Large-scale Enharmonicism in Bruckner and his Models," *Bruckner-Jahrbuch 1991–93* (1995), pp. 63–64; "Bruckner's Rhythm: Syncopated Hyperrhythm and Diachronic Transformation in the Second Symphony," *Bruckner-Symposion Bericht. Anton Bruckner – Persönlichkeit und Werk, 1992* (Graz: Akademische Druck- und Verlagsanstalt, 1995), p. 97, and the analysis of Bruckner's *Vexilla regis*, "Bruckner's Metrical Numbers," *Nineteenth-Century Music* 14 (1990), 121–22.

The second group over a passing tone

The unusual form of Schubert's *Quartettsatz* has provoked conflicting analyses.[43] However, its reversed sonata design is clear, as shown in ex. 8.7a.[44] The brief but intense first group (mm. 1–26) leads directly into an extended second group composed of three distinct thematic ideas: a lyrical first theme (mm. 27–60), a violent second theme (mm. 61–76) followed by a brief transition (mm. 77–90), leading to a lyrical third, closing theme (mm. 93–140).[45] The development spans mm. 141–94. The reversed recapitulation preserves the established sequence of the three thematic areas within the second group, while modifying the material tonally: the first theme returns at mm. 195–228, the second theme at mm. 229–40, the transition at mm. 241–56, and the third theme at mm. 257–304. The coda then takes care of the recapitulation of the first group at mm. 305–end. As we have seen, it is not uncommon, in reversed sonata designs, for the recapitulation of the first group to simultaneously function as the coda. In the *Quartettsatz*, as in the above-cited Haydn and Mozart examples, the coda doubles as the recapitulation of the first group.

The structural tonic is attained (m. 257 in ex. 8.7a), sixty-two measures after the onset of the design recapitulation. The middleground of the *Quartettsatz* constitutes a massive enlargement of the opening *Aussensatz*, c–d–e♭–e–f–f♯–g in the upper voice supported by a descending tetrachord, the *lamento* bass C–B♭–A♭–G (exx. 8.7a–b).[46] The B♭ over

[43] James Webster claims that Schubert's *Quartettsatz* "is not in sonata form" ("Schubert's Sonata Form," 26). Coren vacillates in his interpretation of the *Quartettsatz's* design. He comes frustratingly close to identifying reversed sonata form, observing that "it is possible, when one looks back over the movement, to understand everything from the return of the secondary theme at measure 195 to the end as a recapitulation with the primary material displaced to the closing bars" (Coren, "Ambiguity," 576). However, he discounts the possibility that the opening may function both as a coda and recapitulation of the first group, asserting that the music of mm. 305–end is "not left-over recapitulatory material." In the end, Coren rejects the reversed recapitulation as "working on paper" but going "against the psychological effect of the piece." Instead, he hears the development continuing *through* the return of the secondary theme, with the precise beginning of the recapitulation remaining "ambiguous."

[44] Bruce in his 1969 article had already

identified the reversed recapitulation in the *Quartettsatz*, although he believed the work to contradict the sonata style in its larger tonal organization. The subdivision of the second group into three sections was observed by Jack Westrup, *Schubert Chamber Music, BBC Music Guides* (Seattle: University of Washington Press, 1969), p. 29.

[45] Unlike Bruce, I do not regard mm. 93–140 as a third group. Whether one reads a two- or three-group exposition does not affect a reading of the tonal structure. If mm. 93–140 constitute a third group, then the recapitulation exhibits the irregular order, second group, third group, followed by first group. I find it more elegant to view mm. 93–140 as part of the second group so that the recapitulation is simply reversed – i.e. the second group follows the first.

[46] The *topos* in this piece, as in so many other tragic works by Schubert, is confrontation with death in the midst of life, the soul's mournful reaction to mortality represented by the *lamento* bass or descending tetrachord. On this point, see Timothy L. Jackson, "Schubert's

Ex. 8.7 Schubert, *Quartettsatz*

a) Middleground

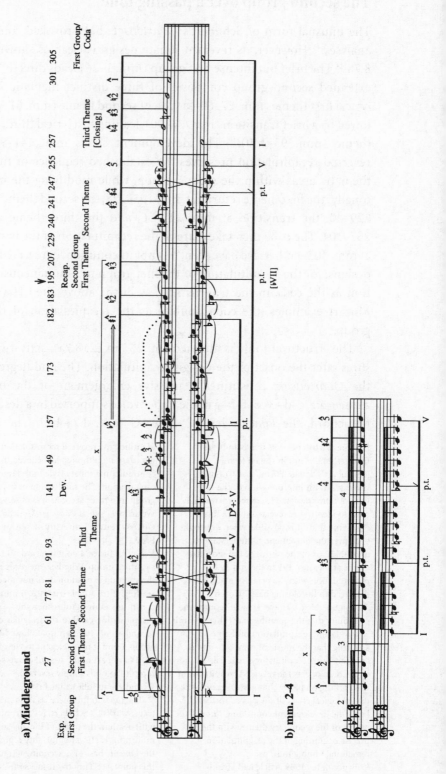

b) mm. 2-4

which the second group returns (m. 195) is revealed to be a passing tone within the descending tetrachord. [47]

The second group over submediant prolongation

Schubert's bold and imaginative projection of the reversed recapitulation over ♭VII could have deeply impressed Brahms, who owned the manuscript of the *Quartettsatz* and urged its publication in 1870. The complex relationships between design and tonal structure in Schubert's sonata forms may well have inspired Brahms's own imaginative design–structure counterpoints. The Finale of Brahms's Third Violin Sonata provides a further remarkable example of reversed sonata form; in this case the second group is recapitulated over VI.

If analysts have debated whether to describe this Finale as a sonata or rondo, their differences may be ascribed to the movement's especially complex design–structure correlation. In an unpublished analysis, Schenker described the form as a seven-part rondo "after the Mozartian model," as follows: "A1– (mm. 1–38, in D minor) B1– (mm. 39–112, in A minor) A2– (mm. 114–29, in D minor) C1– (mm. 130–71, moving from G minor through B♭ minor, C♯ minor to F minor) A3– (mm. 172–217, F minor to D major) B2– (mm. 218–92, D minor) A4 (coda, mm. 293–end, D minor)."[48] In an analysis published in the early thirties, Edwin Evans offers both a rondo interpretation similar to Schenker's and a sonata

Revisions of *Der Jüngling und der Tod* D 545a-b and *Meeres Stille* D 216a-b," *The Musical Quarterly* 75 (1991), 348; Erdmute Schwarmath, *Musikalischer Bau und Sprachvertonung in Schuberts Liedern* (Tutzing: Hans Schneider, 1969), pp. 105–18; Ellen Rosand, "The Descending Tetrachord: An Emblem of Lament," *The Musical Quarterly* 65 (1979), 346–69.

[47] The first theme of the second group, beginning in A♭ major (VI) in m. 27, does not occur over a structural harmony or *Stufe* occupying its own harmonic-durational space. Rather, as shown in the analytical sketch, A♭ is caught within a prolongation of the initial tonic, which moves to V of V in m. 91. A chromaticized voice exchange (involving C♯, E♭, and E) leads from I (m. 1) to V of V (m. 81). As shown in ex. 8.7a, the voice exchange creates a chromatic line in both outer voices, C (m. 1)–C♯ (m. 81)–D (m. 91). This chromatic line (labeled "x") is then recomposed through the development, as D♭

(m. 157) is enharmonically converted into C♯ (m. 182). The bass from the opening through the beginning of the recapitulation is organized in unfolded thirds, the ascending third C (m. 1)–E♭ (m. 182) answered by the descending third D (m. 183)–B♭ (m. 195).

I have benefited from David Beach's bass graph of the *Quartettsatz* in "Harmony and Linear Progression in Schubert's Music," *Journal of Music Theory* 38 (1994), 13–17. Beach, like Webster, hears G prolonged through mm. 77–93. As is apparent from my graph and accompanying remarks, I attach greater significance than Beach to the linear progression C–C♯–D (my motive "x") in the exposition, which I hear recomposed through the development in the manner described above.

[48] Heinrich Schenker, unpublished analysis of Brahms's Third Violin Sonata, Ernst Oster Collection in the New York Public Library, folder 34, 279–82. This undated analysis is probably quite early, before 1923.

analysis in which the recapitulation of the first group begins in m. 172.[49] Evans was uncomfortable with his own sonata analysis, especially with locating the return in m. 172, remarking that "the slight reference to first subject at the return (or third rondo section as the case may be) is a feature almost amounting to omission of the theme." Perhaps a more compelling, rondo interpretation would assimilate Schenker's and Evans's second return (mm. 172–213) within a larger C (mm. 130–217) to yield a *six*-part rondo form: ABACBA.

Is the return of the opening material in mm. 114–29 the first return in a rondo or a reminiscence, which initiates a sonata development? Designating the first group A, the second group B, and the development C, it becomes clear that the five-part reversed sonata form ABCBA is related, at least outwardly, to the six-part rondo form ABACBA. Furthermore, if the composer makes reference to the opening (A) at the beginning of the development – a common procedure in sonata forms – reversed sonata form can easily become confused with rondo. Arno Mitschka identifies the Violin Sonata's Finale as being in sonata form without commenting on the order of the groups in the recapitulation.[50] Michael Musgrave asserts that "the form is not a rondo, but rather another special type of sonata form in which the first subject reappears as though a rondo after exposition, to lead to development after which the second subject is recalled with the rest of the original material."[51]

Different concepts underlie the reversed sonata and rondo forms. In sonata form (with both regular and reversed recapitulations), the exposition is characterized by polarity between groups, which are distinguished by key, thematic content, and general mood. Exposition and recapitulation counterbalance one another, the boundaries and materials of each group generally being preserved in the recapitulation, even if order is reversed and certain modifications are made to accommodate tonal structure. In rondo form, the returns of A serve as goals of tonal action, separated by recurrences of B and C, which function as intervening episodes. If the opening material (A) returns at the beginning of the development in a sonata, it serves as a point of departure for the development (C) rather than as a goal. A further distinction between the two forms concerns the subsequent treatment of the second group in the sonata and the first episode in the rondo. Essential to the sonata idea is that the recapitulation of the second group be rigorously modeled on the

[49] Edwin Evans, *Handbook to the Chamber and Orchestral Music of Johannes Brahms: Complete Guide for Student, Concert-goer and Pianist* (London: William Reeves, 1935), pp. 241–42.

[50] Arno Mitschka, *Der Sonatensatz in den Werken von Johannes Brahms* (Gütersloh, 1961), p. 280.

[51] Michael Musgrave, *The Music of Brahms* (London: Routledge and Kegan Paul, 1985), p. 192.

second group in the exposition, preserving its polarity with the first group. In the rondo, on the other hand, the recurrence of B material is potentially freer in its recapitulation.

It is informative to compare the first return in the Finale of Brahms's Violin Concerto – a genuine six-part rondo form (ABACBA+coda) – with the reminiscence of the opening at the beginning of the development in the Violin Sonata's Finale. In the concerto-rondo, the first return (mm. 93ff.) is a clearly marked goal. It occurs in the tonic and retains the theme's character, basic shape and harmonic structure. If the Finale of the Violin Sonata were in rondo form, one might expect the auxiliary cadence of mm. 1–21 to be brought back in full. Instead, the return is truncated so that only mm. 1–16 return as mm. 114–29, perched entirely on an apparent dominant.[52] The usual practice in rondo is to preserve the incipit of the theme and vary the continuation. But the incipit in mm. 114–17 differs from mm. 1–4, further weakening the rondo effect.

In my view, the Violin Sonata's Finale is a reversed sonata form rather than a rondo, the first group being recapitulated in mm. 293–330 *after* the second group in mm. 216–292 (ex. 8.8a). True to the sonata principle, Brahms recapitulates the second group exactly. This group (mm. 37–113) is subdivided as a small ternary form – A at mm. 37–76, B at mm. 77–103, A′ at mm. 104–13 (ex. 8.8b) – and is recapitulated note for note at mm. 216–92. The first group (mm. 1–30) is a small binary form composed of two sections supported by an auxiliary V–I cadence: A (mm. 1–16) on the dominant, and B (mm. 17–30) on the tonic. This small form is recapitulated *after* the second group, with A at mm. 293–310 and B at mm. 311–30. The bridge from the exposition (mm. 31–36), which prepares the return of the second group in mm. 210–15, is attached to the retransition at mm. 194–209. The modified return of the opening (mm. 114–29) may be interpreted plausibly as a reminiscence initiating the development. The form of development (mm. 114–93) is as follows: varied reminiscence of the opening (part 1, mm. 114–29), fantasy on material from the first and second groups (part 2, mm. 130–71), and contrapuntal development of first group material (part 3, mm. 172–93).

The analytical sketches further show the complex and unusual interrelationship between reversed sonata form and undivided tonal structure. Major junctures in design do not invariably coincide with harmonic points of arrival. For example, the first group and its recapitulation provide a clear instance of harmonic–structural overlap. The design of the

---

[52] Harmonically, this putative V chord (mm. 118–29) is not stabilized further (ex. 8.8a–b); instead, as shown in the graphs, it is a back- relating sonority dependent on the F major triad of mm. 40ff. as its upper third.

Ex. 8.8a Brahms, Third Violin Sonata, Op. 108, Finale

a) First Middleground

Ex. 8.8b Brahms, Third Violin Sonata, Finale

b) Second Middleground

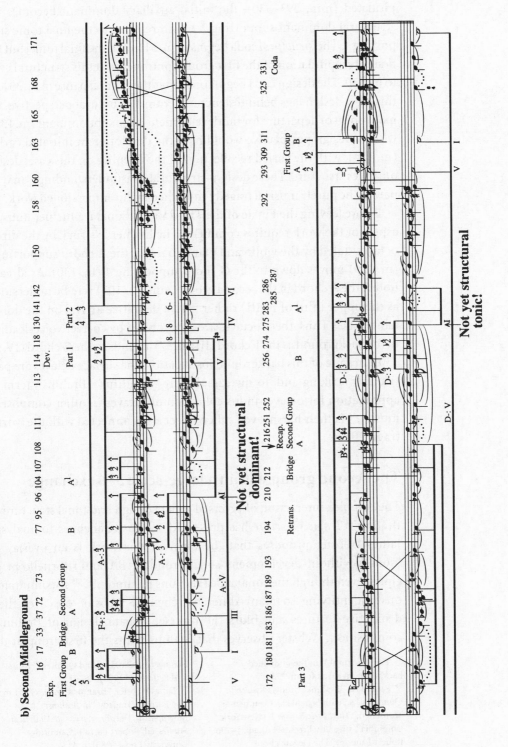

first group (mm. 1–30) straddles a V–I cadence. When this group is recapitulated (mm. 293–330), the initial auxiliary dominant becomes the structural dominant supporting $\hat{2}$, which resolves to the final tonic supporting $\hat{1}$. The *structural* coda begins in m. 311 with the final tonic, but the *design* recapitulation of the first group continues past this structural coda to m. 330. The design coda begins only after the general pause in m. 331. In this case, design lags behind structure. From a structural perspective, the main point of departure for the development is the subdominant (m. 130), while a design perspective would have the development initiated earlier (m. 114), with the varied recollection of the opening. In this case, design outpaces structure. These design–structural "misunderstandings" may be part of the purely musical tragedy embodied in this impassioned work.

Before leaving the Finale of the Third Violin Sonata, a further unusual aspect of the work requires comment. The listener is struck by the direct octaves stated by the violin and piano (bass) as the A chord supporting $\hat{5}$ (m. 129) moves down to the G chord supporting $\hat{4}$ (m. 130). As already noted, the A chord in the second group (mm. 92–107) is to be understood as the upper third of F (III) rather than a definitive arrival on the dominant of D.[53] Thus, these octaves are ameliorated by correct voice-leading in the background as the F chord (III, m. 37) ascends to the G chord (IV, m. 130). In spite of this background justification, the surface octaves are particularly striking and, to my ears, hardly "beautiful" (Brahms's term of approbation for octaves in his collection of octaves in other composers' music).[54] Is their harsh, even sullen affect also connected with the work's tragic effect?

The second group within a large-scale 5–6 exchange

The complex interaction of reversed sonata design and tonal structure in Brahms's *Tragic Overture* has presented serious challenges to analysis. James Webster proposes that the form of this work is an overlay of "sonata-without-development, sonata-rondo, *ABA*, and ritornello principles, even though the sonata idea remains paramount."[55] By simultaneously identifying so many different schemes, Webster obscures their distinctive features and blurs the reversed sonata design of Brahms's composition. Webster observes that Brahms omits the first group at the

[53] The structural V in the undivided background is saved for m. 293.
[54] Paul Mast, "Brahms's Study, *Octaven u. Quinten u. A.*, with Schenker's Commentary Translated," *The Music Forum V* (New York: Columbia University Press, 1980), pp. 1–196; Robert Laudon, "The Debate about Consecutive Fifths: A Context for Brahms's

Manuscript 'Oktaven und Quinten,'" *Music and Letters* 73 (1992), 48–61.
[55] James Webster, "Brahms's *Tragic Overture*: The Form of Tragedy," in *Brahms: Biographical, Documentary, and Analytical Studies*, ed. Robert Pascall (Cambridge University Press, 1983), p. 111.

beginning of the recapitulation (mm. 300ff.) without recognizing Brahms's broader design strategy. The recapitulation of the first group is not left out; rather, a recapitulatory apotheosis of its initial section – in which mm. 367–402 transform mm. 1–20 – is placed *after* the recapitulation of the second group (mm. 300–66, ex. 8.9c).[56] The rather complex reversed sonata form may be outlined as follows:

Section 1: Exposition (mm. 1–184)

    First group (mm. 1–65)

        Part 1 (mm. 1–20)

        Part 2 (mm. 21–65)

    Bridge (mm. 66–105)

    Second group (mm. 106–84)

        Part 1 (mm. 106–25)

        Part 2 (mm. 126–41)

        Part 3 (mm. 142–184)

        Bridge to development (mm. 185–207, based on introduction)

Section 2: Development (mm. 208–63)

    Bridge to recapitulation (mm. 264–99)

Section 3: Recapitulation of second group (mm. 300–66)

    Part 1 (mm. 300–19)

    Part 2 (mm. 320–35)

    Part 3 (mm. 336–66)

    Recapitulation of first group, part 1 (mm. 367–402)

    Coda (mm. 403–22)

    Conclusion (mm. 423–end)

Beethoven's *Coriolan Overture* may have served as a model for Brahms's *Tragic Overture*. In both overtures, the *major* tonic associated with the recapitulation of the second group is trapped within a large-scale 5–6 exchange (compare exx. 8.9a and c). The middlegrounds of the

---

[56] Webster mistakes this varied recapitulation of the first group for the onset of the coda, which he takes too soon at m. 379. Mitschka, like Webster, does not recognize that mm. 367–403 represent the recapitulation of the first group (Mitschka, *Der Sonatensatz*, p. 288). Thus Mitschka completely disregards the reversed sonata design and, like Webster, takes the coda too soon. He regards the coda as beginning in m. 367, even earlier than Webster. In my view, the coda spans mm. 404–22 and is unusual insofar as it constitutes an interpolation within the final descent $\hat{2}$–$\hat{1}$ rather than the customary elaboration of $\hat{1}$ (see the parentheses in ex. 8.9c). Like many earlier analysts, Webster believes that the *Tragic Overture* is in some kind of sonata form; Claudio Spies, on the other hand, claims that sonata form *per se* is a "fiction" and that, in the *Tragic Overture*, Brahms recapitulates segments of earlier material to "restore deluded confidence to believers in 'form,' and to appear to resolve ambiguity for sceptics" (Spies, "Form and the *Tragic Overture*: An Adjuration," in *Brahms: Biographical, Documentary, and Analytical Studies*, pp. 391–98). Against this proposition, one may cite Robert Pascall's conclusion that "one fact emerges from consideration of the forms of these movements – that Brahms was often a sophisticated and intricate formalist" (Pascall, "Some Special Uses of Sonata Form by Brahms," *Soundings* 4 [1974], 63).

Ex 8.9a–b   Beethoven, *Coriolan Overture*, Op. 62, Middlegrounds

a) First reading

b) Second, alternative reading

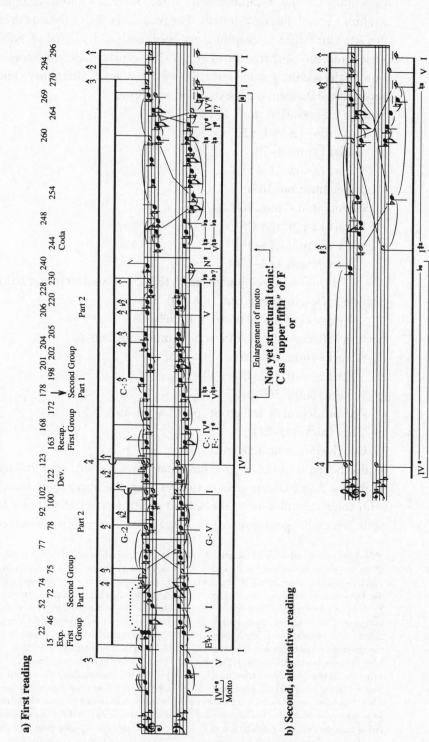

Structural duality represents Coriolan's indecision, his "two-mindedness".

Ex. 8.9c   Brahms, *Tragic Overture*, Op. 81

c) Middleground

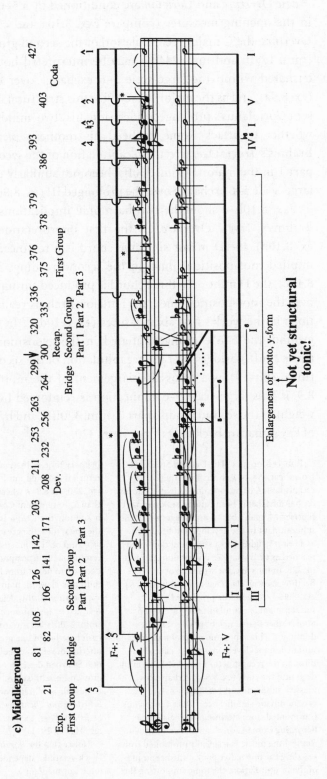

Tragic Overture and *Coriolan* are conditioned by a 5–6 motto presented in the opening measures (compare exx. 8.10a and c). In the *Coriolan Overture*, the C major recapitulation of the second group's lyrical part 1 (mm. 178ff. and mm. 244ff.) may be interpreted both as the V of IV, ensnared within the large-scale 5–6 exchange over the prolonged IV (ex. 8.9a), and as the major I (ex. 8.9b); this structural duality may represent Coriolanus's prolonged indecision, his "two-mindedness" regarding whether to attack Rome or heed his mother's plea to retreat.[57] In Brahms's *Tragic Overture*, the recapitulation of the second group's lyrical part 1 in the major I (mm. 300ff.) becomes similarly ensnared within a large-scale 5–6 exchange over the prolonged III (ex. 8.9c).

Exx. 8.10b–c show the two harmonic implications of the motto of Brahms's *Tragic Overture*. In the first interpretation (labeled "x" in ex. 8.10b), the D minor six-three chord is a re-voiced extension of an implied root-position tonic. In the second reading (labeled "y" in ex. 8.10c), the D minor six-three chord is produced through a 5–6 exchange over the root-position, mediant F major. Brahms realizes both implications in the work's first six measures (ex. 8.10d).[58] In the deep middleground, the 5–6 exchange initiated in the exposition's second group (mm. 106ff.) bridges over the recapitulation of the second group's part 1 (mm. 300–19) as a colossal enlargement of the motto's "y" form (ex. 8.9c). This large-scale 5–6 connection is reinforced by the tremendous weight of the second group's part 2 (mm. 320ff.), and by Brahms's change of key signature back to D minor in m. 320.

[57] Robert Morgan ("The Delayed Structural Downbeat," 64–69) asserts that "the recapitulation of the opening cadential chords . . . has mistakenly been called a subdominant reprise." Morgan's bass graph suggests that the subdominant in the development functions as a lower neighbor to a structural dominant reached as early as m. 72 and prolonged until m. 228. In my view, the structure of Beethoven's *Coriolan Overture* is different. As exx. 8.9a–b suggest, the prolonged subdominant is a fundamental harmony or *Stufe*, rather than a neighbor chord to the dominant. This subdominant prolongation initiated in the development may extend through the recapitulation (ex. 8.9b) and even deep into the coda (ex. 8.9a). Perhaps this massive subdominant prolongation has programmatic significance. Just as Coriolanus is prevented from attaining his goals – first becoming Roman consul and, later, destroying Rome – the music is tragically prohibited from reaching the normative goal at the beginning of the recapitulation: the tonic supporting the

primary tone, $\hat{5}$. Instead, the definitive tonic return is deferred until well into the coda (m. 270, ex. 8.9a), where it supports $\hat{3}$, rather than $\hat{5}$. To represent Coriolanus's prolonged hesitation, the *Urlinie* is picked up only late in the coda; thus, the greatly attenuated $\hat{4}$/IV acts as a kind of "*Urlinie* suspension" whereby the resolution $\hat{3}$/I is postponed – like Coriolanus's decision to desist from his course of revenge – until the "eleventh hour." Wagner's intuitive appreciation of this delayed resolution is revealed by his comment that in this passage (mm. 270ff.) "all inward storms and struggles rush together in one great resolution; the offering of self is sealed" ("alles Schwanken und Stürmen des Inneren drängt sich in einen grossen Entschluss zusammen; das Selbstopfer ist beschlossen"). Richard Wagner, *Sämtliche Schriften und Dichtungen. Volks-Ausgabe. Sechste Auflage*, 16 vols. (Leipzig: Breitkopf und Härtel, 1911), V, p. 175.

[58] Notice that the dominant in the motto is "back-relating," dependent on the preceding tonic $^6_3$ or mediant $^5_3$.

Ex. 8.10a   Beethoven, *Coriolan Overture*, mm. 1–15 Middleground
Ex. 8.10b–d Brahms, *Tragic Overture*, "x" and "y" forms of the *Urmotiv* implied by the motto in mm. 1–6

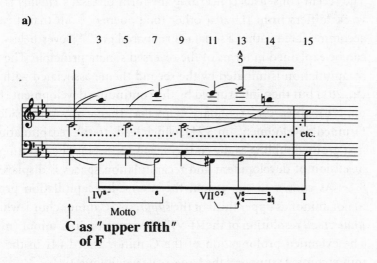

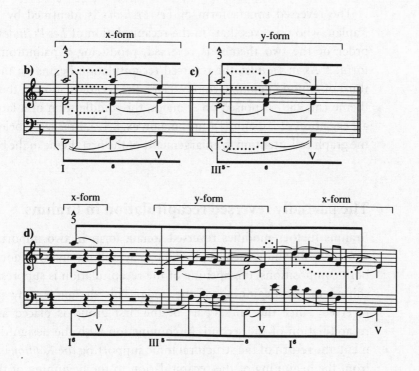

The second group over the upper third of a fundamental harmony

The recent consensus concerning the form of Liszt's *Hamlet* is that this work "differs from [Liszt's] other tone poems . . . in that it cannot be accommodated within a sonata-form paradigm."[59] Nevertheless, its form can be explained in terms of the reversed sonata principle. The reversed recapitulation is initiated by the second theme associated with Ophelia (m. 201) but then interrupted by the continuing development (begun in m. 176); thus, the secondary "Ophelia" theme is swept aside by the resumed development (m. 221), which leads to the recapitulation of the first group doubling as the coda (m. 343, ex. 8.11). The resulting overlap or elision of development and recapitulation spaces is displayed in fig. 8.1e. As shown in the graph, the reversed recapitulation prolongs E major-minor as upper third of the *suppressed* C minor chord, which is the *understood* resolution of the ♭II-VII^{07} progression in C minor (m. 150ff.). The extended prolongation of the C minor chord (♭II in the larger B minor context) supports the large-scale neighbor e♭ (♭$\hat{4}$).

The reversed sonata form of *Les Préludes* is identified by Richard Kaplan, who observes that "in the recapitulation of *Les Préludes* . . . the order of the two themes is reversed, producing a palindromic arch form."[60] As in *Hamlet*, the reversed recapitulation begins on the upper third of a fundamental harmony. Here, the recapitulation of the second theme (m. 260) is poised on A major, the middle term of a large-scale arpeggiation of F major (IV in C major, ex. 8.12). Brackets labeled "x" in the graph call attention to enlargements of the first theme in the bass.

The partially reversed recapitulation in Brahms

Brahms further modifies reversed sonata form in two important late works, the first movements of his Fourth Symphony and C minor Trio. In both compositions, the opening of the recapitulation is suppressed and shifted to the beginning of the coda. This design is only partially reversed, since the initial part of the first group is placed after the recapitulation of the second. In conjunction with the design displacement, the return of the structural tonic supporting the *Kopfton* is shifted from the beginning of the recapitulation to the beginning of the coda

[59] Linda Jean Popovic, "Harmonic and Formal Process in the Symphonic Poems of Franz Liszt" (Ph.D. diss., Yale University, 1993), p. 143. Richard Kaplan agrees ("Sonata Form in the Orchestral Works of Liszt: The Revolutionary Reconsidered," *19th-Century Music* 8 [1984], 144).

[60] Kaplan, "Sonata Form," 151.

(exx. 8.13a and 8.14a). The backgrounds of the first movements of the Fourth Symphony and the C minor Trio, like those of all other sonatas considered in this article, are undivided; neither composition employs interruption. In the Fourth Symphony (ex. 8.14a), the recapitulation begins (mm. 259ff.) over the submediant as upper fifth of the Neapolitan augmented sixth chord (mm. 373ff.) embellishing the tonic (mm. 394ff.), while in the Trio (ex. 8.13a), the recapitulation (mm. 126ff.) is supported by a dividing dominant. In both pieces, the structural action of the *Urlinie* descent is displaced to the design coda.[61]

The ascending triadic motive "x" (ex. 8.13b) presented at the outset of the first movement of the C minor Trio also underlies the first subject of the second group (ex. 8.13c). A motivic reason for Brahms's decapitating the first group's recapitulation may be clarified with reference to the middleground graph (ex. 8.13a). Detaching the structural tonic supporting the *Kopfton* $\hat{5}$ from the beginning of the recapitulation (m. 126) and shifting it to the coda (m. 192) allows the outer voices to project enlargements of "x" deep into the recapitulation.

In the first movement of the Fourth Symphony, the shadowy reference to the opening at mm. 246–58 does not constitute the definitive beginning of the recapitulation either structurally or motivically. Rather, the true beginning of the recapitulation is postponed until m. 259ff., when the music literally recapitulates mm. 5ff. in the exposition. Ex. 8.14a analyzes the illusory return at mm. 246–58 in the context of the movement as a whole. Specifically, the graph shows the structural tonic supporting $\hat{5}$, which one would expect at the beginning of the recapitulation, displaced to the beginning of the coda (mm. 394ff.). As in the C minor Trio, the beginning of the coda (mm. 394ff.) doubles as the structural–design recapitulation of the initial four measures of the first group.[62]

[61] Here, one detects the influence of Beethoven. See, for example, the preceeding analysis of the *Coriolan Overture*, in which the $\hat{5}$–$\hat{1}$ *Urlinie* descent is shown to continue out of the main body of the piece *through* the design coda. Thus, the general principle articulated by Schenker that codas prolong $\hat{1}$ after the structural action of the *Urlinie* requires qualification. See also Brahms's *Tragic Overture*, where the coda is interpolated between the resolution of $\hat{2}$ to $\hat{1}$.

[62] Analysts have interpreted the design of Brahms's Fourth Symphony's first movement in quite different ways. Most regard the development as beginning in m. 145 with a reminiscence of the opening twelve measures (mm. 145–56), a procedure evoking the tradition of the repeated exposition. Robert Pascall accounts for the truncated recapitulation of the first group (mm. 259ff.) by explaining the recall of the opening in mm. 145–56 as the beginning of the recapitulation, which is then interrupted by the development and recommences in mm. 259ff. He therefore interprets the design as a "sonata with displaced development" in which "the development has been moved into the recapitulation (or the recapitulation has been split into two unequal parts and the first of these has been displaced)" (Pascall, "Some Special Uses of Sonata Form by Brahms," 59). Surely, the reminiscence of the opening at the beginning of the development – a common procedure in classical sonata form – is related to the convention of repeating the exposition and should not be mistaken for the beginning of the recapitulation (Pascall's interpretation).

Ex. 8.11 Liszt, *Hamlet*

a) First middleground

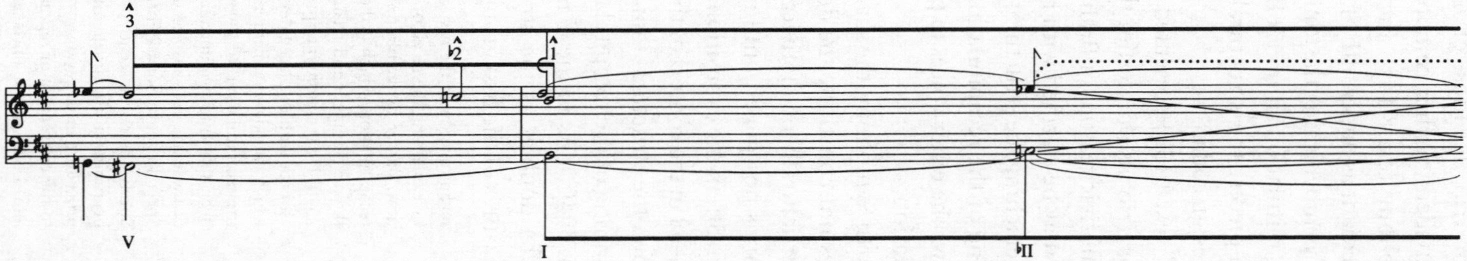

b) Second middleground

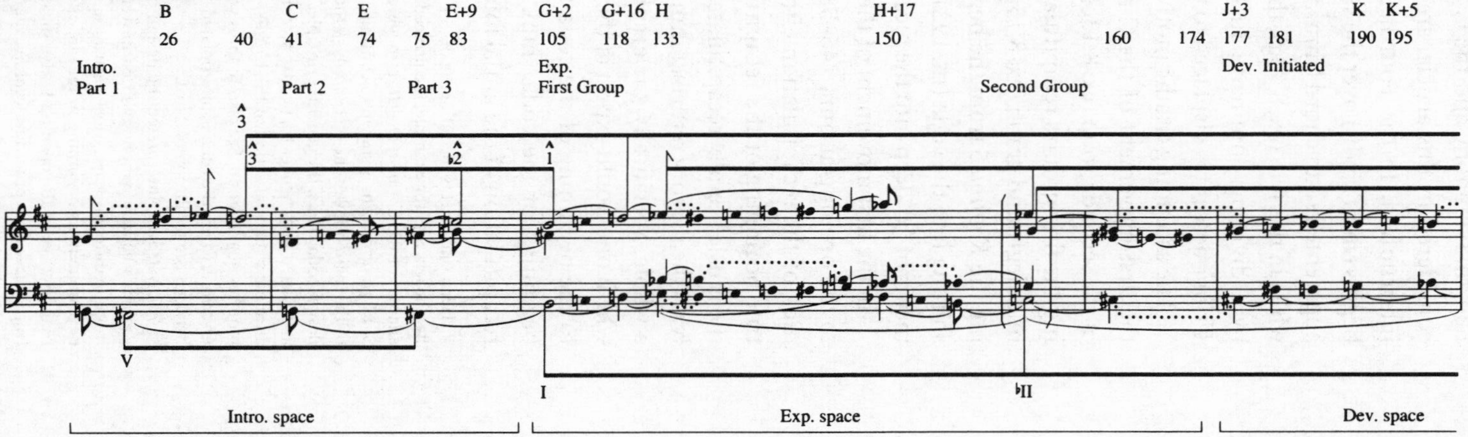

Intro.
Part 1

B
26

C
40

Part 2

E
74

E+9
75

Part 3

83

G+2
105

Exp.
First Group

G+16 H
118 133

H+17
150

Second Group

160

J+3
174 177

Dev. Initiated

181

K K+5
190 195

Intro. space

Exp. space

Dev. space

Ex. 8.11 continued

a) First middleground (cont.)

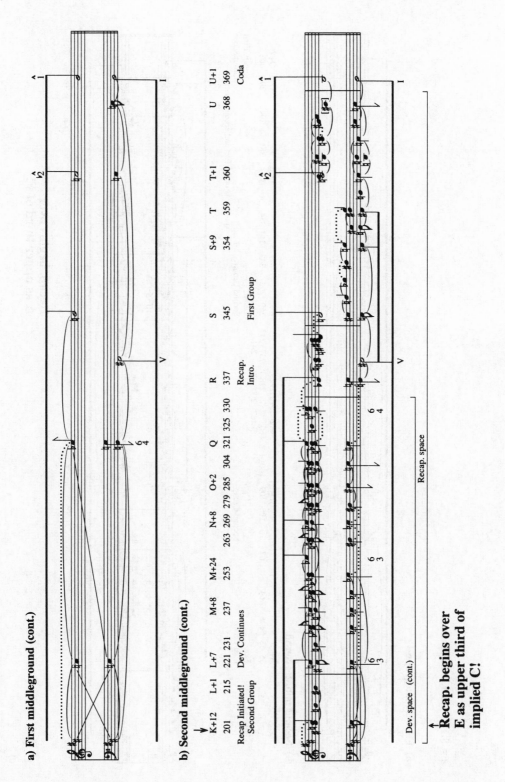

b) Second middleground (cont.)

Ex. 8.12 Liszt, *Les Préludes*

a) **First middleground**

5̂
4̂ 3̂
2̂ 1̂
I
V
I

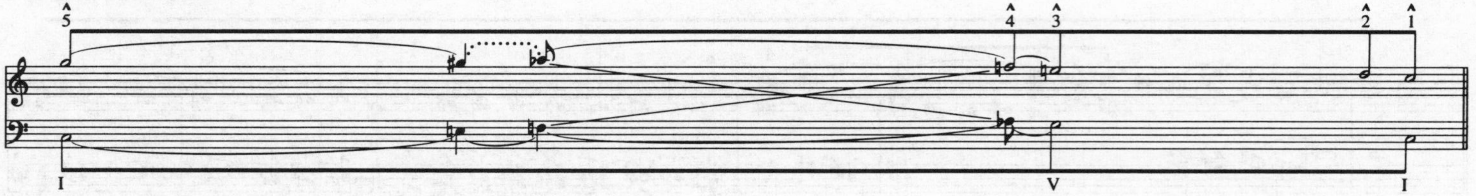

b) **Second middleground**

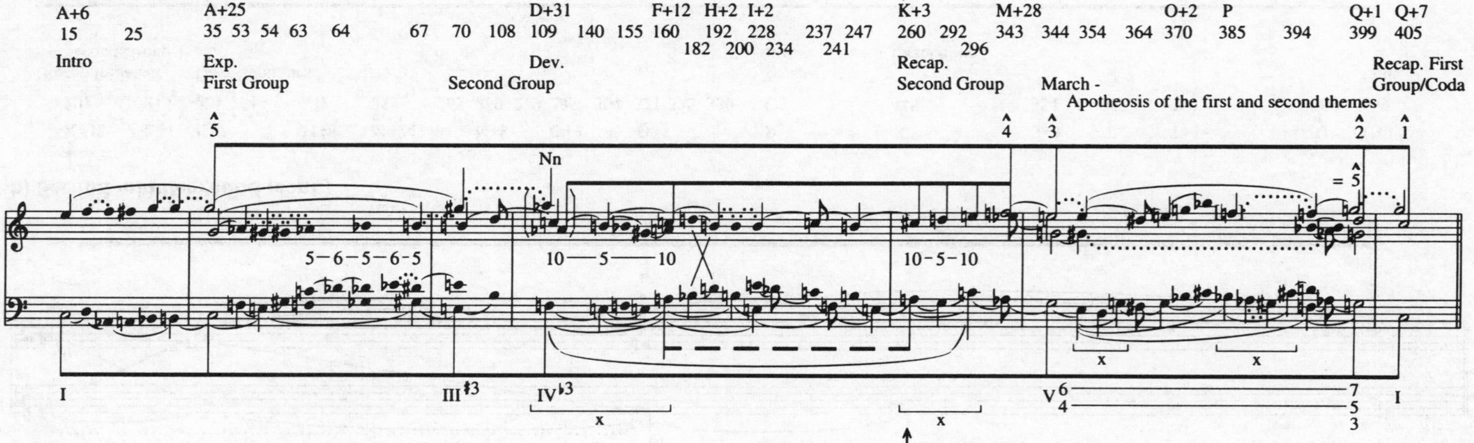

A+6 A+25 D+31 F+12 H+2 I+2 K+3 M+28 O+2 P Q+1 Q+7
15 25 35 53 54 63 64 67 70 108 109 140 155 160 192 228 237 247 260 292 343 344 354 364 370 385 394 399 405
182 200 234 241 296
Intro
Exp.
First Group
Second Group
Dev.
Recap.
Second Group
March -
Apotheosis of the first and second themes
Recap. First
Group/Coda
Nn
5–6–5–6–5
10—5—10
10-5-10
= 5̂
x
I
III♮3
IV♭3
V 6 4
7 5 3
I
Recap. begins over
A as upper third of F!

c)

Vn. 1
m. 1
pizz.
arco
x

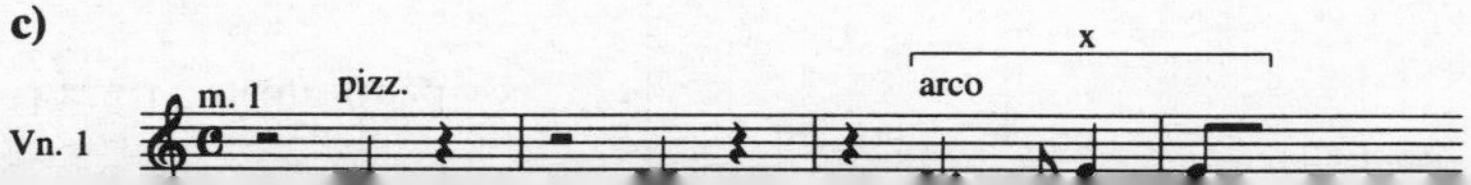

Ex. 8.13 Brahms, Trio, Op. 101, first movement

a) Middleground

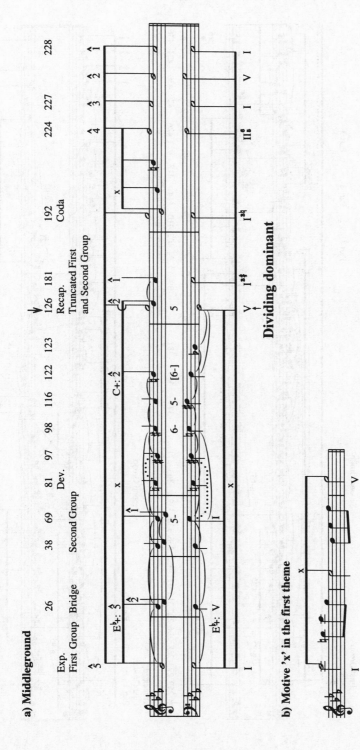

Dividing dominant

b) Motive 'x' in the first theme

c) Motive 'x' in the second theme

Ex. 8.14a Brahms, Fourth Symphony, Op. 98, first movement

a) Middleground

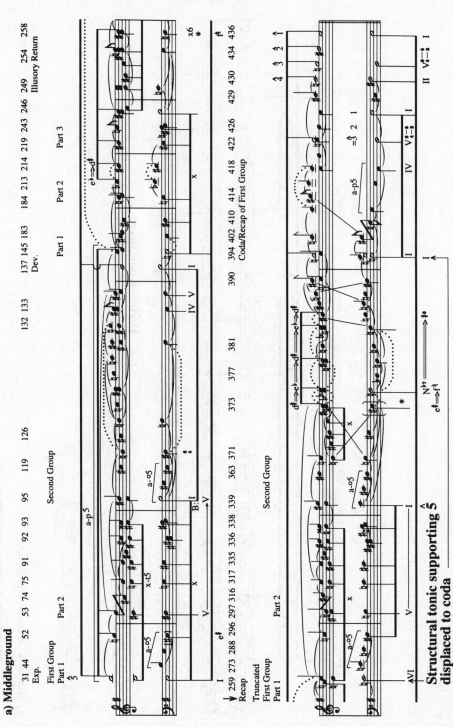

**Structural tonic supporting $\hat{5}$
displaced to coda**

* - The augmented sixth associates these points in the movement

Ex. 8.14b–e   Brahms, Fourth Symphony, first movement

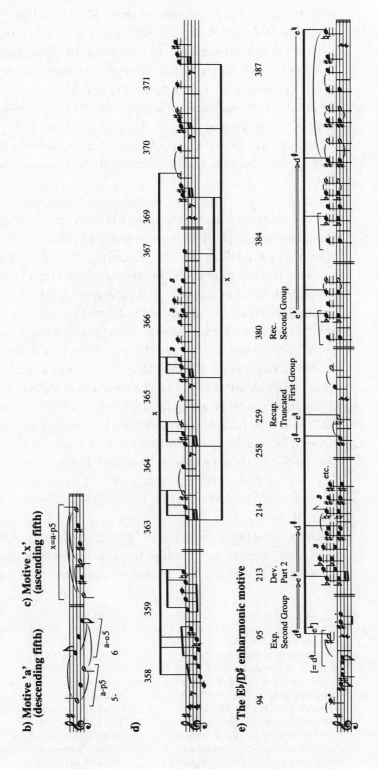

The end of the development (strings, m. 258) is motivically connected with the end of the recapitulation (mm. 373ff.) through the interval of the augmented sixth F–D♯ ($♭\hat{2}$–$♯\hat{7}$, see the asterisks in ex. 8.14a). The dominant prolonged through the second group in the exposition and the development is not a structural dominant supporting interruption, as in normative sonata form, but rather the upper fifth of the tonic, which then moves to the submediant as upper fifth of the Neapolitan. The main body of the movement is suspended over a colossal 5–6–5 exchange, as the tonic moves up to the Neapolitan in a contrapuntal neighbor motion, I–♭II–I. The harmonic I–II–V–I action of the *Ursatz* is reserved for the coda.

Exx. 8.14b–d call attention to significant foreground motives, which are connected with the middleground voice-leading shown in ex. 8.14a. Much has been made (by Schoenberg and by others) of the motivic significance of the falling third.[63] Certainly, chains of falling thirds are a motivic preoccupation of Brahms, especially in his late works.[64] But the motivic substance of this movement is derived primarily from the *fifth* – descending and ascending, perfect and diminished forms – which is *subdivided* into thirds (exx. 8.14b–d). The aforementioned 5–6–5 exchange in the background grows naturally out of the first theme, which comprises two descending fifths, perfect ("a–p5") and diminished ("a–05"), separated by a sixth (ex. 8.14b). The inversion of the initial fifth, filled in chromatically, forms a significant motive, labeled "x" on ex. 8.14c ("x"="a–p5i"). Brahms calls attention to the inversional relationship between "a" and "x" at the outset, as B–G–E ("a," m. 1) becomes E–G–B ("x," m. 5). Overlapping enlargements and diminutions of "x" are exhibited in ex. 8.14d, spanning both Tovey's "cloudy, mysterious" chords (mm. 358–62) and the fanfare motive (mm. 363–71) in the second group.[65]

Recognizing the unifying role of "x" in the first group of the exposition reveals the motivic relationship, through invariant statements of "x," between the first group, the development, and the recapitulation of the

[63] Schoenberg, "Brahms the Progressive," in *Style and Idea: Selected Writings of Arnold Schoenberg*, ed. Leonard Stein (Berkeley: University of California Press, 1984), p. 406; Walter Frisch, *Brahms and the Principle of Developing Variation* (Berkeley: University of California Press, 1984), p. 143; Louise Litterick, "Brahms the Indecisive: Notes on the First Movement of the Fourth Symphony," in *Brahms 2: Biographical, Documentary and Analytical Studies*, ed. Michael Musgrave

(Cambridge University Press, 1987), pp. 228–32.
[64] See, for example, the Finale of the D minor Violin Sonata, analyzed above, and the *Vier ernste Gesänge*, Op. 121, discussed by Arnold Whittall, "The *Vier ernste Gesänge* Op. 121: Enrichment and Uniformity," in *Brahms: Biographical, Documentary and Analytical Studies*, ed. Pascall, pp. 191–207.
[65] Tovey, *Symphonies and Other Orchestral Works*, pp. 221–22.

first group (ex. 8.14a).[66] Because "x" in the bass ("x–t0") and "x" transposed up a fifth ("x–t5") in the inner voice simultaneously span both parts of the exposition's first group (mm. 1–95), when the first group is transposed down a fifth in the recapitulation (mm. 259–339), "x" is held invariant at t0 in the inner voice. These invariant enlargements of "x" in the exposition and recapitulation are linked by the massive enlargement of "x" in the bass of the development (mm. 145–246). In a rough, unpublished graph, Schenker profiles "x" in the bass of the development.[67] Nevertheless, he fails to exploit this insight to explain the motivic connection, through "x," between the organization of the bass in the development and other parts of the piece.

The three-group reversed recapitulation in Bruckner

In the Finale of Bruckner's Seventh Symphony, the exposition is divided into three groups: first (mm. 1–34), second or *Gesangsthema* (mm. 35–92), and third, closing group (mm. 93–146, ex. 8.15a). The reversed recapitulation retrogrades the order: third (mm. 191–212), second (mm. 213–46), bridge (mm. 247–74), first group (mm. 275–314), and coda (mm. 315–end).

The first and second groups are in E major and G♯ major (enharmonically equivalent to A♭ major) respectively. In a major-mode sonata exposition, one expects the third group to be in B major, the bass completing a large-scale arpeggiation of the tonic triad, E–A♭–G♯–B (I–♭IV=III–V). Here, the third group and the development occur over A (IV), which delays the arrival of the expected structural dominant (ex. 8.15b). The putative structural dominant supporting the recapitulation of the third group is subsequently converted into a passing chord

---

[66] Regarding the exposition of the Fourth Symphony, some writers identify a three-group lay-out (or three-key exposition), while others delineate only two groups (or two-key exposition). The distinction between these competing interpretations depends upon the status of the music in mm. 53–94, specifically whether this music constitutes the second group of a three-group exposition (Tovey, *Symphonies and Other Orchestral Works*, p. 221) or an "intermediate motive" within a two-group exposition (Evans, *Handbook*, pp. 146–54). In my reading, simultaneous enlargements of "x" in the bass and "x" transposed up a fifth ("x"–t5) in the inner voice (ex. 8.14a) weld mm. 1–95 into a harmonic and formal unity. Thus, Tovey's

"second subject" (mm. 53–94) is subsumed within Evans's first group (mm. 1–94), the real second group commencing later in mm. 95ff. In my reading, design and tonal structure correlate so that the arrival of the V as upper fifth of the initial I coincides with the onset of the second group in m. 95. The F♯ major chord supporting Tovey's second subject – the V/V of mm. 53ff. – is subsumed within the ascending fifth in the bass ("x").

A final comment on ex. 8.14a: the top voice's enharmonic prevarication spans the movement. The upper voice queries whether C𝄪–D♯ is really D–E♭, the issue being decided in favor of the former interpretation just prior to the coda (m. 387).

[67] Oster Collection, folder 34, 210–14.

Ex. 8.15a Bruckner, Seventh Symphony, Finale

a) Middleground

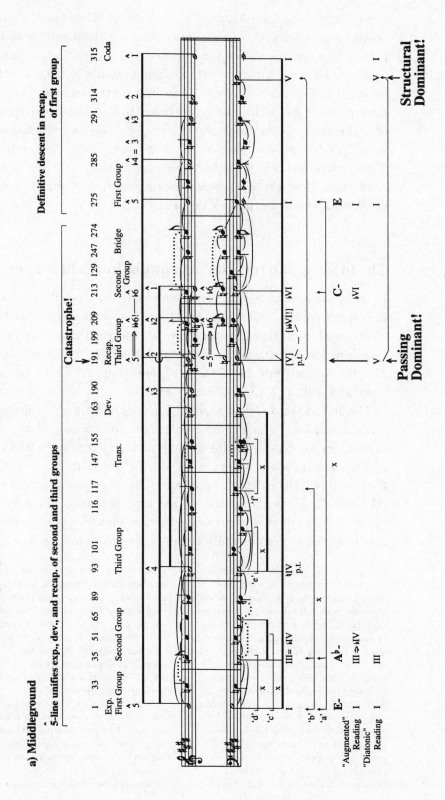

Ex. 8.15b–d Bruckner, Seventh Symphony, Finale

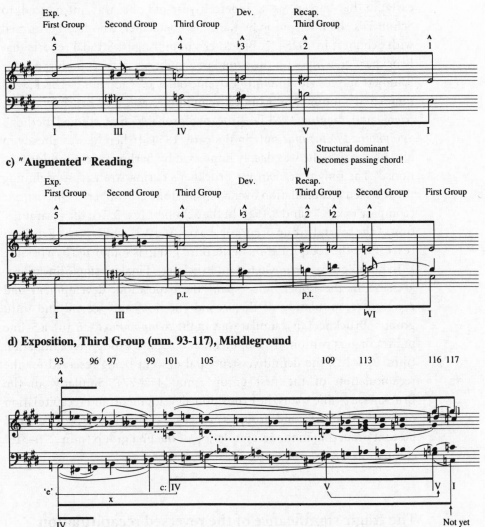

b) "Diatonic" Reading

c) "Augmented" Reading

d) Exposition, Third Group (mm. 93-117), Middleground

leading to C major (♭VI), which supports the recapitulation of the second group (ex. 8.15c). Thus, the unconventional "augmented" background projecting the augmented triad E–G♯=A♭–C (I–III=♭IV–♭VI) underlies the main body of the movement. The essential distinction between the two backgrounds is the absence of a structural dominant in the "augmented" background. The structural dominant, suppressed at the beginning of the recapitulation, is released just prior to the coda (see the arrow connecting mm. 191 and 314 in ex. 8.15a).

Aspects of structure and form in Bruckner's Finale may derive from Schubert's *Quartettsatz* and the first movement of Berlioz's *Symphonie Fantastique*. Bruckner encountered Schubert's songs and chamber music early in his career; as a nineteen-year-old, he was introduced to Schubert's chamber music by Karoline Eberstaller, who had performed with Schubert in 1825–27. Bruckner's pupil August Stradal reports that Bruckner "grew up with the sound of Schubert's music, and his love for Schubert stayed with him into extreme old age."[68] Johann Herbeck, who premiered a number of Schubert symphonies, was also Bruckner's close friend and mentor.[69] While Bruckner probably first studied Berlioz's *Symphonie Fantastique* only in the early 1860s (when he was already in his late thirties), he was deeply impressed by Berlioz's technical innovations.[70] The only precedent for Bruckner's daring strategy of beginning the reversed recapitulation over a passing tone is Schubert's *Quartettsatz* (compare exx. 8.7a and 8.15a). In the Schubert (ex. 8.7a), the recapitulation of the second group occurs over a passing ♭VII while, in the Bruckner (ex. 8.15a), the recapitulation of the third group is supported by a passing V. In both Berlioz's *Symphonie* and Bruckner's Finale, a single linear progression in the upper voice spans the exposition, development and reversed recapitulation of the second (Berlioz) and second and third groups (Bruckner) in a similar way. In the *Symphonie* (ex. 8.16), a $\hat{5}$–line unifies the exposition, development, and second group's recapitulation (mm. 72–412), the definitive structural descent being reserved for the recapitulation of the first group (mm. 412–77). Similarly, in the Bruckner, a $\hat{5}$–line spans the exposition, development, and recapitulation of the third and second groups (mm. 1–274), the definitive structural descent occurring in the recapitulation of the first group (mm. 275–315, compare exx. 8.15a and 8.16).

The tragic significance of the reversed recapitulation

Tracing the genre of reversed sonata form through two centuries exposes a complex network of overlapping, interpenetrating, and inherited significances. Almost certainly, composers did not deliberately set out to compose Aristotelian notions of tragedy or figures of ancient Greek linguistic rhetoric into their tragic works.[71] Rather, their thinking was subtly

[68] Stradal, "Erinnerungen," 972. Bruckner is reported to have improvised on Schubert songs at a concert in London in 1871.
[69] For a detailed discussion of Schubert's impact on Bruckner, see Jackson, "'Schubert as John the Baptist,'" 61–107.

[70] Bruckner was introduced to Berlioz's music by Ignaz Dorn, a violinist in the Linz Theater (Göllerich–Auer, III/1, p. 246).
[71] We do know that Brahms was deeply interested in the culture and thought of classical antiquity.

Ex. 8.16 Berlioz, *Symphonie Fantastique*

Definitive descent in recap. of first group

5-line unifies exp., dev., and recap. of second group

| 49 | 61 | 72 | 139 | 140 | 143 | 150 | 159 | 168 | 187 | 200 | 230 | 234 | 293 | 299 | 312 | 313 | 323 | 324 | 356 | 407 | 408 | 412 | 439 | 443 | 475 | 477 |

Intro.   Exp. First Group   Second Group   Dev.   Recap. Second Group   First Group   Coda

Not definitive arrival on I!

conditioned by ancient ideas of drama and expression handed down over centuries. As Brian Vickers observes:

> [Classical] rhetoric was a major concern of most writers at the formative period of their lives, when habits of reading and writing are picked up, seldom to be shaken off. We need to relive this culture in order to appreciate the importance of rhetoric . . . in hundreds of contexts of life then, and to habits of mind which have since disappeared."[72]

In the Quartet from Mozart's *Idomeneo*, the Overture to Cherubini's *Médée*, Liszt's *Hamlet*, and Brahms's *Schicksalslied* and *Tragic Overture*, the assertion of the "tragic" significance of the reversed recapitulation can be supported with reference to the plot or program. On his way back from the Trojan war, Idomeneo is rescued by promising Neptune to sacrifice the first person he meets upon his return, who turns out to be his own son Idamante. Mozart's deformational reversal of the recapitulation is motivated by Idomeneo's threatened violation of the natural bond between father and son with all its tragic consequences. In the overture to *Médée*, Cherubini also employs the reversed recapitulation to represent infanticide. The tragedy of Medea's transgression of natural order by the murder of her own children is paralleled by the violation of normative sonata form.[73] In Liszt's *Hamlet*, the reversed recapitulation is motivated, in part, by the unnatural crimes of fratricide and patricide. With regard to Ophelia, Liszt observes that "she collapses under her mission."[74] This collapse is represented by suppression of C minor, which should have been associated with Ophelia's theme, and by sweeping aside her theme at the beginning of the reversed recapitulation. Ophelia's attempt to initiate the recapitulation is overwhelmed by Hamlet's revenge in the resumed development, which enacts his murder of his uncle.

The incompleteness of the reversed sonata form in Brahms's *Schicksalslied* creates "broken" circularity in the domains of form and tonality: the expected recapitulation of the first group is suppressed, and the introduction returns as the coda in the "wrong" key of C major. Here, the tragedy of human destiny is expressed in striking formal and tonal discontinuities. Just as men, jealous of the gods, wish to share their blissful, immortal existence, the music desperately tries to return to its point

[72] Brian Vickers, "On the Practicalities of Renaissance Rhetoric," in *Rhetoric Revalued*, ed. Brian Vickers (Binghamton, N.Y.: Center for Medieval and Early Renaissance Studies, 1982), p. 133.

[73] Cherubini's unusual harmonic procedures in the second group are also programmatic: just as III (A♭ in the exposition) and the major I (F major in the recapitulation) are overwhelmed by prolonged dominants (V/III and V respectively), Medea's natural maternal instincts are completely annihilated by her insatiable lust for revenge.

[74] Humphrey Searle, *The Music of Franz Liszt* (London: William and Norgate, 1954; 2nd ed. New York: Dover Publications, 1966), p. 74.

of tonic origin, but without success. The road back to the E♭ major realm of the gods is blocked by omission of the expected recapitulation of the first group and by transposition of the introductory music from E♭ to C major. Man's futile attempts to close the broken circle only serve to drag him down, depicted by the *downward* transposition of the opening music.[75]

Webster's analytical graph of Brahms's *Tragic Overture* takes the D major of the second group's recapitulation as a fundamental harmony on the same structural plane as the D minor tonic.[76] He criticizes Brahms for a too literal recapitulation of the second group beginning in the tonic major (mm. 300–66) after the extended major tonic transition (mm. 264–99):

> The fact that a work in sonata style must ordinarily observe the "sonata principle," recapitulating material which originally appeared outside the tonic, does not compel a composer to repeat every paragraph literally. The "pathos" of the tonic major has already been exploited, and the addition of nuances . . . do not compensate for the redundancy or the loss of psychological cogency. It is a pity that Brahms did not take lessons in the free recapitulation of second groups from Haydn.[77]

Although the recapitulation of the second group is indeed a literal transposition, as shown in ex. 8.10e, the material is completely revalued in the larger context of the motion III–I6, the colossal enlargement of the opening motto. Surely, such revaluation in the face of invariance is a feat as remarkable as any transformation. Nor does the music lose "psychological cogency," as Webster claims; rather, Brahms's literalness is moti-

---

[75] Some have claimed that Brahms attempts to synthesize the antithetical worlds of the gods and men and thereby "go beyond" Hölderlin's poem. According to Luhring, "a new condition exists [in the coda] for both the blessed and mortals" (Luhring, "Dialectical Thought," 6). Daverio agrees, arguing that Brahms wishes to suggest "gods and mortals, contrary to the ultimate message of Hölderlin's poem, are interdependent, not antithetical terms" (Daverio, "The Wechsel der Töne," 108). As is well known, Brahms toyed with the idea of bringing back the first two lines of the poem in the coda (just as Mozart does at the end of the *Idomeneo* Quartet). Had he done so, he would have suggested that the gods could somehow inhabit or at least merge with the human scheme, thereby confirming the notion of synthesis. But in order to remain true to the poem's pessimistic, strikingly unresolved antithesis – and to his initial conception of the *Schicksalslied* – Brahms decisively rejected any such resolution.

[76] Webster, "Form of Tragedy," 100. Certainly, one has to be very careful about "reading away" tonics. In this case, the major tonic is to be understood as an apparent rather than a structural tonic for the tonal and motivic reasons presented above.

[77] Webster, "Form of Tragedy," 115. Webster also criticizes Mitschka for regarding the entire span, mm. 189–319 (including the development and recapitulation of the second group), as a middle section (ibid., 108). Mitschka goes more deeply than Webster into the work's tonal structure by taking cognizance, if only intuitively, of the large-scale connection between the F major of the second group in the exposition and the D minor $^6_3$ chord in part 2 of the second group in the recapitulation.

vated by his program; it is in the nature of tragedy that, try as one might to elude Destiny, it is inexorable and inescapable. Even as the music attempts a completely regular recapitulation of the second group, the enlarged motto asserts its hegemony, bending the literally recapitulated material to its will and revaluing it in its own image.

The "tragedy" expressed by deformational reversal of the recapitulation in "pure" instrumental music is admittedly of an abstract, undefined nature. For example, tragedy "in the abstract" is evoked by the reversed recapitulation and suppression of the expected tonic in the Finale of Haydn's "Trauersymphonie"; a similar effect is created by the reversed recapitulation and unexpected, retrospective undermining of the major tonic (m. 110) in the Andante of Beethoven's Op. 59, No. 3. The illusory, mirage-like return of the opening theme at the beginning of the recapitulation in the first movement of Brahms's Fourth Symphony sets up the tragic denouement in the coda.[78] As the music passes through once familiar territory (the recapitulation of the truncated first and second groups), landmarks now appear changed and foreign because of the tonal revaluation of the recapitulated material in the undivided structure. During the music's prolonged absence,[79] Fate has destroyed its "home" in the lyrical opening theme, which is now restated in anguished double forte stretto.[80]

Scholars have debated whether the Bruckner symphonies are "absolute" or program music. To be sure, the symphonies are effective as absolute music; nonetheless, many of them are infused with programmatic ideas. In 1894, Bruckner commented on the Adagio of his Seventh Symphony, remarking, "Yes, gentlemen, I really did write the Adagio about the Great One's [Wagner's] death. Partly in anticipation, partly as Trauermusik for the actual catastrophe."[81] Bruckner did not provide a program for the Seventh Symphony (as he did for the Fourth and Eighth Symphonies).[82] Allusions to Beethoven's Eroica, Wagner's Ring, and Liszt's Faust Symphony suggest that not just the Adagio, but the symphony as a whole refers programmatically to Wagner's final illness and death, and to the impact of his departure upon the world of music.

[78] Tovey hears, in mm. 246–58 of the Fourth Symphony, the prophecy of a catastrophe: "the great cloud figure . . . separates the first two steps of the theme, with all the majesty of the Norns prophesying the twilight of the gods" (Symphonies and Other Orchestral Works, p. 222).
[79] Attenuated by the partially reversed recapitulation.
[80] Mm. 394ff. in the Fourth Symphony (compare with mm. 208ff. in the Trio).

[81] "Ja meine Herren, das Adagio habe ich wirklich auf den Tod des Grossen geschrieben. Teils in Vorahnung, teils als Trauermusik nach der eingetretenen Katastrophe." Göllerich–Auer, IV/2, pp. 80–81.
[82] For detailed discussion of the programs of Bruckner's Fourth and Eighth Symphonies, see Constantin Floros, Brahms und Bruckner. Studien zur musikalischen Exegetik (Wiesbaden: Breitkopf und Härtel, 1980).

Bruckner may have modeled this larger program directly on Beethoven's *Eroica* Symphony, which he knew intimately.[83] In the *Eroica*, which is programmatically related to the *Prometheus Ballet* through the Piano Variations, Op. 35, the death of the hero (here Napoleon-as-Prometheus) is mourned in the slow movement (the *Marcia funebre*), and his apotheosis is celebrated in the Scherzo.[84] Perhaps the impulse to compose a symphony commemorating Wagner's heroic life and death came from the initial encounter in September 1873, when Wagner took the rather unusual step of showing his Viennese guest the plot for his grave behind his villa, Wahnfried.[85] Although Bruckner had completed both the first movement and the Scherzo in 1882 (in April and September respectively) – *before* Wagner's death on 13 February 1883 – the coda of the first movement, like the Adagio, "anticipates" the Master's death: the quotation of the *Schlafmotiv* from the end of *Die Walküre* in mm. 417–19 draws a parallel between Brünnhilde's magic sleep and Wagner's impending eternal sleep of death.[86] As in the *Eroica*, the hero's funeral cortege is portrayed in the Adagio; the joyful Scherzo and opening of the Finale represent his apotheosis.[87] In Bruckner's Finale, Wagner is honored as a Promethean Savior, as Christ-Faust, alchemist-discoverer of new modes of musical expression and "Master of all masters."[88] Synthesizing disparate narrative genres, the Finale projects a multifaceted program. The Wagnerians, bereft of their Master, lament his death as a disastrous setback (the "tragic" reversed recapitulation); simultaneously, the great masters of German music and their heavenly consorts (plates 8.1–2) rejoice in Wagner's arrival in Heaven-Parnassus, asserting the ultimate triumph of the Wagnerian legacy ("darkness-to-light" transfiguration in the coda).

Bearing these general considerations in mind, the structural analysis

[83] Bruckner's heavily annotated score of Beethoven's *Eroica* is in the Gesellschaft der Musikfreunde in Vienna. His detailed analytical notes on this work have been preserved in his calendar for 1873 (Leopold Nowak, "Metrische Studien von Anton Bruckner an Beethovens III. und IX. Symphonie," and "Anton Bruckners Eroica-Studien," *Gesammelte Aufsätze*, pp. 105–15 and pp. 257–65.

[84] Harry Goldschmidt proposes that the program of the inner movements of the *Eroica* is derived from the ballet (*Beethoven, Werkeinführungen* [Leipzig, 1975], pp. 29–33). In the *Marcia funebre*, Prometheus falls at the hand of Melpomene, the tragic Muse, while in the Scherzo, the hero is called to eternal life by Thalia, the laughing Muse of comedy and her companions Pan and the satyrs.

[85] Göllerich–Auer, IV/1, p. 240.

[86] Constantin Floros identifies the citation without explaining it in terms of the symphony's larger narrative ("Die Zitate in Bruckners Symphonik," *Bruckner Jahrbuch 1982–83*, p. 15).

[87] Timothy L. Jackson, comment on Steven Parkany's "Kurth's Bruckner and the *Adagio* of the Seventh Symphony," *Nineteenth-Century Music* 13 (1989), 75.

[88] Stradal reports that Bruckner "often compared Schubert with John the Baptist. All of Schubert's harmonic procedures showed that the promised one, Richard Wagner, would soon appear on the musical horizon" ("Erinnerungen," 972).

(ex. 8.15) may now be correlated with semantic issues. If the joyful transformation of the Symphony's opening theme in the Finale's first group represents Wagner's arrival celebrated in Heaven-Parnassus, the terrifying music of the third group unleashes a *terremoto* following his passing (the last movement of Haydn's *The Seven Last Words on the Cross* comes to mind); celestial rejoicing is tempered by the disastrous effects on earth. Recall that the diatonically conditioned listener expects the reversed recapitulation, which opens with the third group (mm. 191–212), to assert the expected structural dominant (due with the third group at the end of the exposition, completing a large-scale tonic arpeggiation E–A♭=G♯[89]–B). To represent the *terremoto* unleashed by Wagner's death, the order of the groups in the recapitulation is tragically reversed (peripetic hyperbaton) and the expected structural dominant, B, becomes an ascending passing chord leading to the lowered submediant, C. The catastrophic effect of Wagner's death is portrayed in the climactic m. 212 as the putative structural dominant B ($\hat{5}$) is converted – through a heart-stopping enharmonic transformation (pun intended!) – into its enharmonic equivalent C♭ (♭$\hat{6}$/♭VI); the passing tone B and the resolution tone C are enharmonically "frozen" in B=C♭. Only when the real structural dominant is attained just prior to the coda (mm. 299–314) does the music cadence diatonically in E major. Wagner's soul and music have finally overcome physical mortality and, although the Man has departed, the Message will echo and resonate triumphantly for all eternity (the coda's composed-out echo of all the main themes, mm. 315–end).

This program is reinforced by a mesh of subtle allusions to Wagner's *Ring* and Liszt's *Faust Symphony*.[90] Bruckner works a quotation of the "Valhalla" theme into the beginning of the second group (appropriately, the first entrance of the Wagner tubas in mm. 43–44). Simultaneously the chorale and the "walking" bass evoke the Pilgrims' Chorus from *Tannhäuser*. Thus, the second group's solemn processional music depicts the host of Wagner's earthly followers bearing their Master's body to eternal rest in the burial plot in Wahnfried (which Wagner had pointed out to Bruckner a decade earlier). The leitmotifs for "golden apples" and "twilight of the gods" at the beginning of the development (mm. 133ff. and 147ff.) may signify that Wagner, like the gods, is destined to enjoy eternal life, but that he, like them, must pass from this earth. The quota-

[89] The A♭ of the second group (mm. 35–92) represents both the lowered subdominant and the mediant. The displacement of IV by ♭IV, as in Bruckner's later E works (the motet *Vexilla regis* and the Adagio of the Ninth Symphony), may connote the Savior's death – here, perhaps also the crucifixion of "Wagner-Christ" on the Cross of the Viennese Brahmsian hegemony (Timothy L. Jackson, "Bruckner's Metrical Numbers," 130, note 68).

[90] Astonishingly, there seem to be no references to these quotations in the literature.

tion of the sword motive just prior to the triumphant recapitulation of the first group (mm. 271–74) intimates that a new Master – perhaps Bruckner himself – will lay claim to the sword Nothung in the present hour of "need" to continue the battle for the Wagnerians.

August Stradal reports that Bruckner knew the *Faust Symphony* intimately.[91] The structure of the first movement of the *Faust Symphony* is conditioned by the augmented triad A♭–C–E (labeled "x" in ex. 8.17).[92] The background of Bruckner's Finale is similarly premised upon "x" (ex. 8.15a). In ex. 8.17, bracket "a" shows that "x" determines the harmonic path from the introduction to the recapitulation, while bracket "b" calls attention to "x" simultaneously nested within the development; in ex. 8.15a, bracket "a" identifies an enlargement of "x," which spans the exposition through to the recapitulation of the first group. The definitive arrival on the flat submediant (C major) coincides with the recapitulation of the second group. Anticipatory motions to C major at the end of the first group and within the second and third groups project nested statements of "x," which are identified by brackets "b"–"d." Bracket "e" reveals a transposed statement of "x" (A–D♭–F) within the third group, which is shown in more detail in ex. 8.15d.

Bruckner deeply admired Wagner the harmonic innovator as a prototypical Faust figure discovering, in new harmonic resources, the tonal Philosopher's Stone alchemistically linking music with greater forces in the universe. As Constantin Floros observes, Liszt identified the augmented triad with "Faust's erudition, with his disposition to reflection

---

[91] In the early 1860s, Bruckner received a copy of the first edition of Liszt's *Faust Symphony* from his friend Ignaz Dorn (Göllerich–Auer, III/1, p. 246). Although Bruckner had studied the *Faust Symphony*, Stradal ("Erinnerungen," 973) states that he was unfamiliar with the symphonic tone poems, with the exception of *Tasso*.

[92] The middleground reading of Liszt's *Faust Symphony* provided in ex. 8.17 differs from one provided by Howard Cinnamon ("Tonic Arpeggiation and Successive Equal Third Relations as Elements of Tonal Evolution in the Music of Franz Liszt," *Music Theory Spectrum* 8 [1986], 12, Cinnamon's ex. 8.8). In my view, the top voice is better read from $\hat{5}$ rather than $\hat{3}$. Taking the upper voice from $\hat{3}$, as Cinnamon does, obscures the signal importance of the chromatic motive A♭–G (C–: $\hat{6}$–$\hat{5}$), which, in conjunction with its diatonic variant A–G (C–: $\sharp\hat{6}$–$\hat{5}$), dominates the movement. A particularly telling moment in this regard is the recomposition of the beginning of the first group in the

recapitulation (mm. 419ff.), where A♭ is emphatically led to G. Cinnamon's analysis also overlooks the motivic significance of Liszt's move to C in the bass in the development (m. 334); this C is the middle term of a descending arpeggiation of the augmented triad motive E–C–A♭ identified by bracket "b" in ex. 8.17. Robert Morgan's pioneering study of "Dissonant Prolongation: Theoretical and Compositional Precedents" (*Journal of Music Theory* 20 [1976], 49–91) 91, discusses Liszt's projection of the augmented triad in the *Faust Symphony* and the late piano music. See also R. Larry Todd, "The 'Unwelcome Guest' Regaled: Franz Liszt and the Augmented Triad," *Nineteenth-Century Music* 12 (1988), 93–115; Rey M. Longyear and Kate R. Covington, "Liszt, Mahler and a Remote Tonal Relationship in Sonata Form," in *Studien zur Instrumentalmusik. Lothar Hoffman-Erbrecht zum 60. Geburtstag*, ed. Anke Bingmann (Tutzing: Hans Schneider, 1988), pp. 457–65.

Ex. 8.17 Liszt, *Faust Symphony*, first movement, Middleground

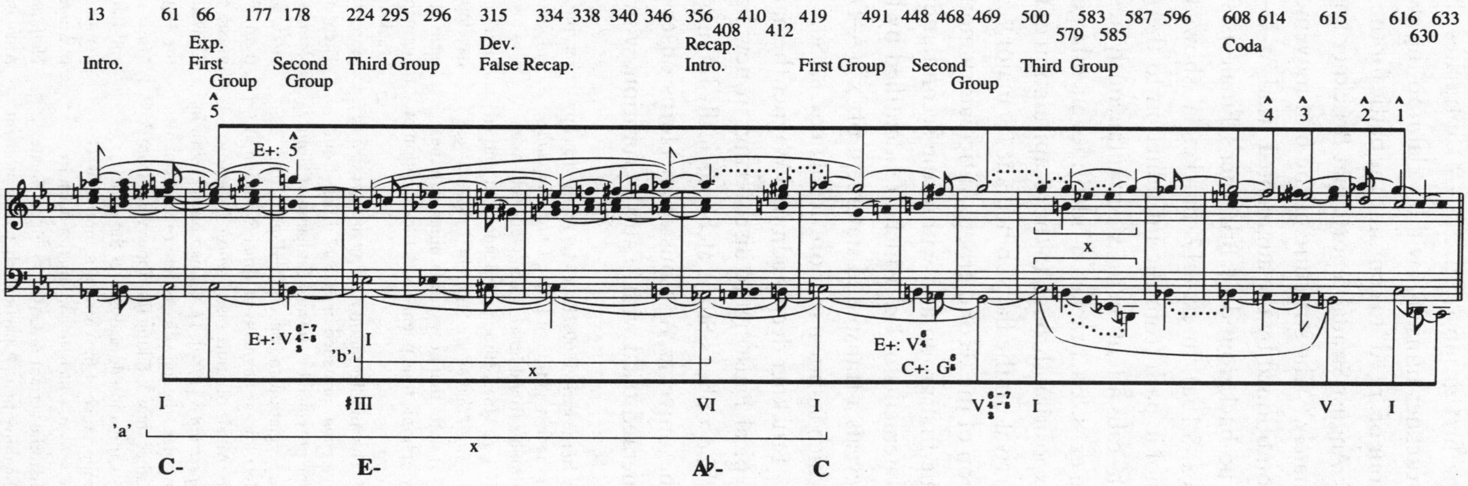

and speculation, his lust for knowledge, and with the brooding side of his personality."[93] Thus, it is entirely appropriate that the augmented triad which, in Liszt's *Faust Symphony*, represents Faust as thinker-experimenter and path-finder, should become an epigram for Wagner in Bruckner's valedictory Finale. Through this motivic association with Liszt's *Faust Symphony*, Bruckner bids a final farewell to "Wagner-as-Faust."

Nachklang: reception of the Seventh Symphony's Finale by Mahler, Sibelius, and Schoenberg

The "tragic" reversed recapitulation in Bruckner's Finale may have directly influenced leading composers of the next generation, especially Mahler, Sibelius, and Schoenberg. In a conversation with Alma, justifying the chorale in the Finale of his Fifth Symphony, Mahler acknowledged that Bruckner had served as a model.[94] The chorale in the Finale of Mahler's Sixth (first presented in mm. 49–97) also seems to be Bruckner-inspired: it introduces a typically Brucknerian octave-leap-plus-third motive, familiar from Bruckner's Fifth and Ninth Symphonies, the Finale of the String Quintet, and the Fugue from Psalm 150. Additionally, the counterpoint Mahler derives from this motive has a distinctly Brucknerian flavor.

These striking foreground allusions to Bruckner in the Finale of Mahler's Sixth Symphony suggest deeper, more far-reaching correlations: the reversed recapitulation may be modeled on the Finale of Bruckner's Seventh.[95] Although Mahler's recapitulation opens with the recomposed introduction (mm. 520–74, ex. 8.18a), the recapitulation proper is reversed, the second group (mm. 575–609) being recapitulated before the first group (mm. 642–772). As shown in the graph, the main body of the movement occurs over subdominant prolongation, while the tonic return is saved for the recapitulation of the first group. The reversed

[93] Constantin Floros, "Die Faust-Symphonie von Franz Liszt. Eine semantische Analyse," *Franz Liszt, Musik-Konzept 12* (1980), p. 64.
[94] See Constantin Floros, *Gustav Mahler: The Symphonies*, trans. Vernon Wicker (Portland: Amadeus Press, 1993), p. 159. It is obvious that Mahler disregarded his wife's admonition to avoid Brucknerian chorales in his Sixth Symphony!
[95] Bruckner's influence upon Mahler intensified over the course of Mahler's compositional career. During the period of personal contact, Bruckner's compositional influence upon Mahler is least evident. After the older composer's death in 1896, Mahler's music begins to assimilate characteristically Brucknerian gestures, motivic materials, techniques, formal patterns, genres, and modes of address. The dialogue with Bruckner in Mahler's later symphonies (especially in the Fifth, Sixth, Ninth, and Tenth Symphonies) is complex and multifaceted – like Mahler's personal relationship with the older composer.

Ex. 8.18   Mahler, Sixth Symphony, Finale

a) Middleground

b) mm. 7-11, Urmotiv

recapitulation is placed over a passing tone E♭: the B♭ major of the second group is not a structural, Neapolitan harmony, but rather the upper fifth of the E♭ chord (mm. 606–09), which is, in turn, a passing chord leading from the subdominant D to its upper third F. As the asterisks in exx. 8.18a–b indicate, the upper voice composes out a colossal enlargement of the opening violin motive, E♭–D–D♯–E. Here, as the Brucknerian model, the dislocation of the reversed recapitulation resonates with the devastating impact of the hero's death; it embodies malignant Destiny which, in Mahler's own words, "fells the hero like a tree."

Sibelius was present at a performance of Bruckner's Third Symphony in December 1890, and in a letter to his fiancée speaks "of the enormous impression it has made on me."[96] Scholars have heard echoes of Bruckner in Sibelius's *Kullervo* Symphony (1892) and *En Saga* (1893); perhaps the chorale in the Finale of Sibelius's Fourth Symphony is also modeled on Bruckner.[97] The second group's short, repetitive chorale phrases, initially presented by winds and brass (mm. 144ff.), are strongly reminiscent of Bruckner's chorales, especially in the Fifth Symphony.[98] As in the Schubert, Bruckner, and Mahler examples, the reversed recapitulation – here the recapitulation of the second group's chorale (m. 281) – takes place over a passing tone (ex. 8.19). The graph suggests that the large-scale bass arpeggiates the tonic triad A–C–E♭–D♯–E. The A, associated with the beginning of the recapitulation of the first group (mm. 318–37),

96 Erik Tawaststjerna, *Sibelius*, vol. I: *1865–1905*, trans. Robert Layton (Berkeley and Los Angeles: University of California Press, 1976), p. 77. Sibelius heard the successful world premiere of the third version of Bruckner's Third Symphony in the fourth Philharmonic concert conducted by Hans Richter. The program also included Beethoven's *Leonore Overture* No. 2, and Grädener's Violin Concerto. Karl Ekman claims that Sibelius told him: "I never met Anton Bruckner personally. But I was present at the original performance of his sextet. I was sitting quite close to him and had a good opportunity of observing him. A kindly little old man, who seemed rather lost in the world. He was short of stature, but disproportionately stout. The joking Viennese called him 'ein Rhinozeros mit Nachtigallenkehle (a rhinoceros with the throat of a nightingale)'" (Karl Ekman, *Jean Sibelius: His Life and Personality*, trans. by Edward Birse [New York: Knopf, 1938], p. 94). Since the first complete performance of Bruckner's *Quintet* took place in 1885, and Sibelius did not arrive in Vienna until *1890*,

this account must be confused.
97 Phillip Coad observes that "Hints of the Brucknerian 'chorale' are often to be found in the closing bars of Sibelius's largest works." "Bruckner and Sibelius" (Ph.D. diss., Cambridge University, 1985), p. 314. Tawaststjerna (*Sibelius*, vol. I, pp. 109–10) calls attention to the Brucknerian aspects of *Kullervo*. Veijo Murtomäki discusses the Brucknerian influence on *En Saga* ("The Problem of Narrativity in the Symphonic Poem *En Saga* by Jean Sibelius," in *Musical Signification. Essays in the Semiotic Theory and Analysis of Music*, ed. Eero Tarasti [Berlin and New York: Mouton de Gruyter, 1995], pp. 477–78). Teuvo Ryynänen suggests that the chorale in the Fourth Symphony's *Finale* is inspired by Bruckner ("Tematiikan ja muodon suhteesta Sibeliuksen sinfonioissa," M.Mus. diss. [Sibelius Academy, 1988]).
98 Sibelius heard Bruckner's Fifth Symphony in Berlin in 1911 and was "completely enraptured." Ekman, *Sibelius*, p. 193. Whether he had studied the score at an earlier date remains an open question.

Ex. 8.19 Sibelius, Fourth Symphony, Finale

a) Middleground

| B | C+10 | E+14 | F+6 | G+8 | H | H+1 | K | K+11 | L+16 | M | M+8 | M+10 | O | O+13 | P+6 | R+8 | R+13 | S+5 | S+11 | T+15 |
| 48 | 89 | 135 | 144 | 167 | 217 | 218 | 266 | 281 | 318 | 330 | 337 | 339 | 385 | 398 | 404 | 430 | 435 | 446 | 452 | 483 |

Exposition
First Group
Second Group
Development
Recapitulation
Second Group
First Group
Coda

"Apparent" tonic!

b) Bass enlargement of the primary tritone A-D♯

is an apparent tonic (=I) interpolated between C (III) and E♭ (♭V). Thus, the passing tone B supporting the second group's recapitulation fills in the third between C (III, m. 144) and the apparent tonic A (=I, m. 318).[99]

Erik Tawaststjerna has suggested that Sibelius's Fourth Symphony is autobiographical, reflecting the composer's preoccupation with death prompted by a bout of throat cancer.[100] While working on this symphony, Sibelius also considered setting Edgar Allan Poe's "The Raven," but instead incorporated some preliminary ideas for the song into the material associated with the chorale. Poe's Raven, a personification of eternal despair (the bird settles over the poet's door to depart "nevermore") broods over the whole symphony. "Eternal despair" at the inevitable dissolution of life is expressed metaphorically both through the reversed recapitulation and the slowly unfolding $\hat{5}$–line. Stretched out over vast spans of music, as the $\hat{5}$–line descends, entropy triumphs and the hero's life inexorably ebbs and dissipates back into chaos and nothingness. This representation of devolution seems to have terrified Sibelius himself, who remarked of it, "beyond that lies madness or chaos."[101]

In program notes for his Second Quartet, Schoenberg calls attention to the first movement's reversed sonata design, observing "the tendency (retraceable to Beethoven) of changing the order [of the groups] in the recapitulation."[102] Thus, according to Schoenberg, the reversed recapitulation begins with the second group in m. 107 (exx. 8.20b and d). He continues that "the recapitulation proper begins in F [in mm. 146ff.] and only gradually returns to F sharp [in mm. 202ff.]." The contradiction regarding the location of the recapitulation is more apparent than real, since Schoenberg subtly distinguishes between "recapitulation" and "recapitulation proper": the latter begins with the recapitulation of the first group in F major (mm. 146ff.), while the former is initiated in m. 107, not in m. 146, as a number of analysts have assumed.[103]

[99] For a detailed analysis of Sibelius's Fourth Symphony, see Timothy L. Jackson, "The *Meta-Ursatz*, Crystallization, and Entropy in the Music of Jean Sibelius," *Sibelius Studies*, ed. Timothy L. Jackson and Veijo Murtomäki, (Cambridge University Press), forthcoming.

[100] Erik Tawaststjerna, *Sibelius*, vol. II: *1904–1914*, trans. Robert Layton (Berkeley and Los Angeles: University of California Press, 1986), p. 199.

[101] Quoted from Veijo Murtomäki, *Symphonic Unity: The Development of Formal Thinking in the Symphonies of Sibelius,* Studia Musicologica Universitatis Helsingiensis (Helsinki, 1993), p. 87.

[102] Arnold Schoenberg, "An Introduction to My Four Quartets," in Ursula von Rauchhaupt, *Schoenberg, Berg, Webern: The String Quartets: A Documentary Study*, trans. Eugene Hartzel (Hamburg: Deutsche Grammophon Gesellschaft, 1971), p. 44. Presumably, the Beethoven reference is to the Andante of Op. 59, No. 3.

[103] Schoenberg probably distinguishes "the recapitulation proper" from "the recapitulation" for tonal reasons. The recapitulation of the second group (mm. 107ff.) is tonally unstable compared to the F major recapitulation of the first group (mm. 146ff.). Jan Maegaard (*Studien zur Entwicklung des dodekaphonen Satzes bei Arnold Schoenberg*, 2 vols. [Copenhagen:

Ex. 8.20a–d Schoenberg, Second String Quartet, first movement

a) Mm. 1-6

b) Middleground

c) Second group in the exposition, mm. 43-47

d) Second group in the recapitulation, mm. 107-11

The "collapse" of the F♯ minor to F major, presented in the first eleven measures (ex. 8.20a), is enlarged in the movement as a whole (ex. 8.20b). In the bass, F♯ ($\hat{1}$) "ascends" to enharmonically equivalent G♭ (♭$\hat{2}$) at the beginning of the development (m. 70); the initial bass descent F♯–E♯=F♮ ($\hat{1}$–♯$\hat{7}$=♭$\hat{1}$) helps to articulate the diminished second between F♯(I) and G♭

(♭♭II).[104] The tenth at the second group in the recapitulation (m. 107) inverts to the sixth at the second group in the exposition (m. 43, compare exx. 8.20b–d). Thus, the dominant in the exposition (V6, m. 43) is reconstrued as an "apparent" dominant C♯ major in the recapitulation (=V!, m. 107); revalued enharmonically as D♭ major, it now functions as the upper fifth of G♭ major (♭♭II, m. 145). G♭, in turn, becomes a Neapolitan augmented sixth resolving to F major (m. 146).

As in other examples of reversed sonata form presented in this study, the formal–tonal dislocation in Schoenberg's first movement may have tragic, even autobiographical significance. Schoenberg composed this quartet at a time of great emotional stress when he was temporarily estranged from his wife Mathilde (née Zemlinsky) during her brief but intense affair with the young painter Gerstl. Allen Lessem speculates that "an understanding of some significant aspects of the work would certainly reveal a 'programmatic' representation of the crisis which threatened in 1907–08."[105] While some have interpreted the second movement's quotation of the folk-song "Ach, du lieber Augustin, alles ist dahin" as referring to the demise of tonality, more probably this folk-song quotation also relates to a secret program connected with Schoenberg's marital crisis. Perhaps the "deception" of the "apparent" dominant (C♯ becoming D♭, the upper fifth of G♭) and the "fallen" tonic (F major) are programmatically associated with Mathilde's "betrayal" of the sanctity of marriage and her "fall" from grace.

While in the famous late essay "Brahms the Progressive" (1947) Schoenberg lionized Brahms, during the early twenties he also admired Bruckner.[106] If Bruckner was often held up as a simple-minded yet

---

note 103 (*cont.*)
Wilhelm Hansen, 1972), II, p. 37), Alan Lessem (*Music and Text in the Works of Arnold Schoenberg: The Critical Years, 1908–22* [Ann Arbor: UMI Press, 1979], p. 21), and Catherine Dale (*Tonality and Structure in Schoenberg's Second String Quartet, Op. 10* [New York: Garland, 1993], p. 100) do not identify the reversed sonata design.
[104] The development begins in m. 70, not in m. 90, as Dale asserts. Its onset is clearly marked by the striking design change in m. 70. The contrapuntal work with the descending fifth motive (the inversion of the first subject's ascending fifth) combined with other motivic fragments is, of course, typical for a development. Furthermore, the musical material of mm. 70ff. does not return later, leading one to conclude that this music belongs to the development rather than the exposition. The ghostly reference to the opening idea in mm. 90–97 constitutes a frustrated attempt to lead into a regular recapitulation of the first

group, instead of marking the beginning of the development (Dale's interpretation).
[105] Lessem, *Music and Text*, p. 21.
[106] Rudolph Reti cites Bruckner as an important model for Schoenberg's first-period works. In his opinion, early Schoenberg, like Bruckner, is harmonically adventurous and, at the same time – unlike Strauss, Reger, and Mahler – never abandons "traditional, indeed, conservative concepts." According to Reti, "a propensity for almost Wagnerian romanticism, of a slightly Viennese variety (perhaps derived from Bruckner), speaks from many parts of Schoenberg's early works . . . One has the feeling that in these works he [Schoenberg] clings more carefully, more rigidly, to the classical cadential concept than did his immediate forerunners" (Rudolph Reti, *Tonality, Atonality, Pantonality: A Study of Some Trends in Twentieth Century Music* [New York: Macmillan, 1958], p. 33).

inspired Parsifal-like composer – even by those (like Mahler) who were sympathetic to him – Schoenberg's unpublished notes in a biography of Bruckner published in 1922 reveal that he did not subscribe to this view.[107] Furthermore, by supervising an arrangement of Bruckner's Seventh Symphony for his Society of Private Performances – an organization dedicated to excellent, instructive concerts of avant-garde music – Schoenberg seems to have considered this work important for the modernist movement. The arrangement by pupils Hanns Eisler, Karl Rankl, and perhaps Erwin Stein prepared under Schoenberg's tutelage was one of the Society's most ambitious projects.[108]

Why *Bruckner*? Earlier, Schoenberg had relied primarily on his "ear," but by the early twenties he sought greater logical rigor in structuring his own and his pupils' work. Renouncing purely intuitive in favor of more calculated creativity, Schoenberg began to explore the twelve-tone row as a compositional matrix. In place of the "bells and whistles" of contemporary Wagnerian orchestrations, the Schoenberg circle's stripped-down, neo-classical arrangement of Bruckner's Seventh Symphony clearly highlights its remarkable formal-tonal structure. It may not be coincidental that, as the twelve-tone method gestated, Schoenberg became interested in Bruckner, a composer with a similar penchant for pre-compositional planning, for superimposing "prime" and "inverted" forms of themes, and for "retrograding" the order of the groups in the recapitulation.

Perhaps, then, the Finale of Bruckner's Seventh also served as a model for the first movement of Schoenberg's serial Third String Quartet,

---

[107] The book, by Richard Wetz (also a composer, who was heavily influenced by Bruckner), is in the Arnold Schoenberg Institute (Los Angeles). Schoenberg inserted a number of notes and underlined many words and passages as if questioning them. One crucial paragraph especially aroused Schoenberg's ire. Wetz dismisses the role of reason, calculation, and logic in composition in general and in Bruckner's music in particular. Wetz writes:

> The creative is not anchored in reason which works with concepts; it flows full of riddles and secrets out of the realm of the unconscious . . . To take the consciously understandable as a point of departure for creative technique must . . . lead to an unholy error concerning the nature of tonal art [underlining by Schoenberg].

In the margin, Schoenberg exclaimed: "Idiot!!" (Richard Wetz, *Anton Bruckner. Sein Leben und Schaffen* [Leipzig: Reclam, 1923], 28).
[108] With the exception of the Johann Strauss, whose waltzes were arranged to provide light relief from the usual heavy dose of contemporary music, Bruckner was the sole composer of his (entirely nineteenth-century) generation to be included on the program. For more on the Society, see Leonard Stein, "The Privataufführungen Revisited," in *Paul A. Pisk: Essays in His Honor*, ed. John Glowaki (Austin: University of Texas Press, 1966), pp. 203–08; Bryan R. Simms, "The Society for Private Musical Performances: Resources and Documents in Schoenberg's Legacy," *Journal of the Arnold Schoenberg Institute* 3 (1979), 127–50; Walter Szmolyan, "Die Konzerte des Wiener Schoenberg-Vereins," *Oesterreichische Musikzeitschrift* 36 (1981), 82–104. The Viennese Society folded before the Bruckner arrangement could be performed. Schoenberg later brought the score and parts to the United States (the manuscripts are now in the Arnold Schoenberg Institute). The first widely publicized public performance occurred in conjunction with the International Bruckner Conference at Connecticut College in February 1994.

Op. 30 (1927).[109] Here again, the reversed recapitulation may programmatically represent a catastrophe. Schoenberg recalls:

> As a little boy I was tormented by a picture of a scene of a fairytale, "Das
> Gespensterschiff" ("The Ghostship"), whose captain had been nailed
> through the head to the topmast by his rebellious crew. I am sure that this
> was not the "program" of the first movement of the Third String Quartet.
> But it might have been, subconsciously, a very gruesome premonition which
> caused me to write this work, because as often as I thought about this
> movement, that picture came to my mind.[110]

To summarize: an overview of the interaction between reversed sonata
design and structure reveals that the structural upper voice is usually
undivided rather than interrupted; the coda may either recompose the
Urlinie or present it for the first and only time. In the Haydn, Mozart, and
Cherubini examples, the Beethoven String Quartet, the Berlioz
Symphonie, and the Brahms Cello Sonata and *Schicksalslied* (exx. 8.1–6,
and 8.16), the recapitulation of the second group occurs over dominant
prolongation continuing out of the development. Furthermore, in the
Brahms Cello Sonata (ex. 8.5), the prolonged dominant continues
beyond the recapitulation of the second group well into the recapitulation of the *first* group. In the Finale of the Brahms Violin Sonata (ex. 8.8),
the submediant functions in an analogous way, the submediant prolongation initiated in the development continuing beneath the recapitulation of the second group. The other works considered prevent or
undermine a tonic recapitulation of the second group through contrapuntal 6–5 exchanges, arpeggiations, and passing motions. In the
Schubert, Bruckner, Mahler, and Sibelius examples, the reversed
recapitulation occurs over a passing tone (compare exx. 8.7, 8.15,
8.18–19). The recapitulated second group of Brahms's *Tragic Overture*
(ex. 8.9) begins over an apparent major tonic chord (D major), which is
trapped within a 5–6 exchange as III$_3^5$ (F major) is converted to minor I6
(D minor). The first movements of Brahms's Fourth Symphony and C
minor Trio (exx. 8.13–14) may be cited as examples of partially reversed
sonata form. In these works, the first and second groups are recapitulated
in the usual, non-reversed order. The recapitulation of the first group is
truncated to postpone the definitive return of the opening and structural
tonic supporting the primary tone until the beginning of the coda.

Taking the rhetorical and musical-rhetorical theory of earlier

[109] The reversed form may be delineated as
follows: first group (mm. 1–32), bridge
(mm. 33–61), second group (mm. 62–93),
development (mm. 94–173), recapitulation of
the second group (mm. 62–206), bridge
(mm. 207–34), recapitulation of the first
group (mm. 235–77), and coda (mm.
278–341).

[110] Schoenberg, "An Introduction to My Four
Quartets," 59.

centuries as its point of departure, this study has exposed the rhetoric of the "tragic" reversed recapitulation in a series of works extending from Haydn and Mozart to Brahms, Bruckner, Mahler, Sibelius, and Schoenberg. Within this genre, reversing the order of groups in the recapitulation generally entails displacing the background tonic normally expected at the beginning of the recapitulation. The genre's formal and tonal peripetic hyperbaton bespeaks a deep-structural compositional rhetoric, which supports and, in certain cases, even peripheralizes the tragic gestures of the foreground. Perhaps Tovey was intuitively aware of this all-encompassing background rhetoric when he wrote:

> The true tragedy, whether in pure music of the most "absolute" kind or in literature, might, then, be described as a grand design, compelling our assent, and containing elements which, while making a powerful appeal to our emotional sympathies, are placed, so to speak, *out of the centre of the design* [my emphasis], so that the true and inevitable working out of the design brings these emotions to a crisis as it crushes the objects of our sympathy, and leaves us, not miserable with impotent vexation, but strengthened by the conviction of its own supreme grandeur and truth.[111]

[111] Tovey, from the essay on the Brahms Piano Quartet in C minor, Op. 60 (*Essays in Musical Analysis: Chamber Music*, p. 204).

9 Some aspects of prolongation procedures in the Ninth Symphony (Scherzo and Adagio)

Edward Laufer

Readers of Schenker's *Harmony* will perhaps recall, with amusement, Schenker's quoting his (unnamed) harmony teacher explaining to his students, "That is the rule, gentlemen. Of course, *I* don't compose that way."[1] Schenker was appalled: what kind of attitude was that! If there were fundamental musical principles which had evolved from the nature of musical art, how could these arbitrarily be disregarded and mocked? In fact, perhaps Bruckner (for it was he) was *not* disregarding and scorning these musical laws which were taught for good reason; rather, he was intuitively obeying others which took precedence: laws whose existence may not have been apparent to his technical consciousness. That is, there were principles which Bruckner could readily enunciate to his pupils, just as surely as there were those which he, like any great composer, could only know by intuition. The latter he could not have conceptualized, and hence was unable and even unconcerned to explain them. He followed them nonetheless.

Musicians familiar with Schenker's analytical approach are well aware that certain technical procedures described by him are more typical of some composers than of others.[2] From this perspective, Bruckner's compositional procedures would often be considered to be not quite classical ones. Even apart from a *Schenkerian* view, they are frequently described as distinctive (i.e. individual) or defective, depending on one's attitude.

In an intriguing and informative article published in 1982, Hellmut Federhofer brought to light a host of hitherto unpublished observations by Schenker on Bruckner, with whom Schenker had studied harmony for two years (1887–89). These comments supplement and add weight to the critical remarks which Schenker himself published in *Der Tonwille* and

[1] H. Schenker, *Harmony*, trans. E. Mann-Borgese (University of Chicago Press, 1954), p. 177.
[2] It would make an interesting study to delineate, in some detail from a Schenkerian viewpoint, various composers' stylistic and technical preferences.

Kontrapunkt.[3] His stern criticism of Bruckner the symphonist, despite his high esteem for Bruckner the man, went so far as to deny him any *real compositional technique* and, especially, to deny him the gift of being able to create *organic large-scale prolongations*. Although he found *individual* moments to be grand and truly beautiful in themselves, they were just separate sections – they did not cohere. They were placed next to each other, somehow, without any organic connection. Here are a few of Schenker's remarks:

> The often really considerable beauty of individual moments does not compensate for the lack of the organic . . . All the beauties, melodic and harmonic, are of no avail: of compositional technique there is no trace, in Bruckner . . . Does Bruckner's invention not arouse your suspicions, in that it resides always only in pathos, or ecstasy, or the *Ländler*? . . . The moment of ecstasy would grant him [a few bars of music]; then, disaster would set in. What next? Each moment is an end unto itself . . .

> Take a work by Beethoven or Brahms. How difficult it is, often, even for the most musical ears, to trace the thematic connections: so concealed, so hidden behind the consciousness . . . With Bruckner all of this lies right on the surface . . . Nothing is avenged so much in art as technical defects. One day, things will go badly for Bruckner, because his technique is defective.

> I heard Bruckner improvising. He knew only one dimension – a space of about twenty bars, beginning each space with the tonic, and on the downbeat. This is comparable to the stodgy effect, in literature, of beginning each sentence squarely with the subject.[4]

[3] H. Schenker, *Der Tonwille*, 10 vols. (Leipzig: Tonwille-Flugblätterverlag, 1923), V, p. 46; and H. Schenker, *Kontrapunkt*, 2 vols. (Stuttgart and Berlin: J. G. Cotta'sche Buchhandlung Nachfolger, 1910), I, pp. 136–38. Schenker's comments were reprinted after his death by Oswald Jonas in "Heinrich Schenker. Über Anton Bruckner," *Der Dreiklang* 7 (1937), 166–76. This article includes three additional short essays on Bruckner dating from 1893 and 1896. From *Der Dreiklang*:

> Even for a composer like Bruckner, the art of prolongation . . . was no longer attainable. In many cases [Schenker cites a few spots in the Seventh and Ninth Symphonies] Bruckner's ear could not hear together as an entity the beginning and ending points of a motion. Both points remain without inner connection to one another, and all the pushing and shoving between both of them, however artfully carried out in detail, exhausts itself purely physically without

even intending to achieve any relationship, as, for example, by means of a third, fourth, fifth, sixth, or octave progression – which must be there if the motion is to make any sense at all . . . If [this kind of aimless mass] falls to the lot of even a Bruckner, who has after all bestowed upon us . . . such marvellous tonal images, then what really is to be said of the legion of others?"

From H. Schenker, *Counterpoint*, trans. John Rothgeb and Jürgen Thym, 2 vols. (New York: Schirmer, 1987), I, p. 99:

> Since [Bruckner's harmonies] are so disorderly and meandering – such an abuse of third-relations, ascending or descending, with most extensive chromatic alteration! – he obviously found it difficult to span a unified contrapuntal line over harmonies that are not really unified.

[4] Hellmut Federhofer, "Heinrich Schenkers Bruckner-Verständnis," *Archiv für Musikwissenschaft*, 34/3 (1982), 198–217.

It might be argued that some of Schenker's critical remarks date from a time *before* he had arrived at his mature analytical approach, i.e. *before* his mature understanding of organic, large-scale prolongations. But this is not the case: the criticisms continued relentlessly throughout Schenker's life. His attitude may, in part, have been colored by what he considered Bruckner's naive view and inadequate grasp of underlying theoretical principles (expressed in the quotation from *Harmony*) as well as by his dismay at Bruckner's improvisational "inability."[5] Schenker's reservations are, in fact, strangely at odds with Bruckner's widespread reputation as an improviser.

Even during his student years Schenker was striving for a "genuine connection between theory and the living work of art," a connection he found lacking in Bruckner's works.[6] In his view, Bruckner understood only the surface and the narrow, literal aspects of the rules of counterpoint, not their underlying psychological bases: "The freedom of creation and the rules of counterpoint were two separate matters," the latter dispensable whenever the muse beckoned. "How countless new musical progressions could result from the meaning of the rule and, however free these might seem to be, still reside within the rule, Bruckner could never understand..."[7]

Perhaps it was precisely this which Schenker, too, could not understand: how Bruckner's "free" way of composing could still reside within the *meaning* of the "rules," albeit in a manner neither the great symphonist nor the great theorist was aware of. Nonetheless, Schenker's observations are always revealing, in that they point unerringly to precisely those procedures which appear to stand apart from "classical" ones. No doubt, in this respect, they are revealing of Schenker as well. In their perspicacity Schenker's comments reveal something of the greatness (and limitations) of each, the intuitive composer and the searching musical thinker.

One of my objectives is to consider, from the perspective of Schenker's analytical approach, some of Bruckner's distinctive, individual procedures and to understand why they were problematic, as far as Schenker was concerned. In particular, I shall consider the question of organic, large-scale prolongations in the second and third movements of the Ninth Symphony and try to suggest certain typical Brucknerian procedures.

---

[5] I offer a further conjecture later, note 17.   [7] Ibid., 168.
[6] Jonas, "Schenker. Über Anton Bruckner," 166.

Scherzo

How is one to read the harmonically extraordinary opening of the Scherzo? Schenker, in *Harmony*, suggests a diminished seventh with an altered third (ex. 9.1).[8] According to his later theory, this would have been an inadequate explanation, for he would have shown that a *dissonance* cannot itself be *composed out* (that is, extended by means of *consonant* harmonies functioning as *passing* or *neighboring* chords). We must, therefore, understand an initial V-chord as being conceptually present (ex. 9.3) and elaborated as in ex. 9.4. From ex. 9.4 it is a short step to what Bruckner writes (ex. 9.5). The difficulties and the characteristic Brucknerian sonority result from the omission (elision) of the opening V-chord, with its bass A. Bruckner further obscures the V-meaning by passing over the e^2 subdivision (ex. 9.5) before m. 23 and by emphasizing motivically the passing notes e♭ and g♯ (which of course oppose e♮ and g♮ of a V^7). Eliding the e^2 gives rise to the two-note groups (ex. 9.6) which in turn become the motivic third d^1–e^1–f^1 (mm. 43–49), the point of arrival.

It is of no avail merely to describe technicalities: one must at least attempt to recognize the artistic or psychological motivations which called forth specific technical procedures. The movement opens with a measure rest. Quite apart from its rhythmic implications, the rest (like the initial harmonic elision) is emblematic of a programmatic idea of beginning from nowhere, from an indefinite horizon, in order to reach for a distinct, definite point of arrival – the three-note motive in mm. 43–49.

In what sense is the opening prolongation organic? Ex. 9.2 shows the underlying rising sixth-figure, strikingly worked in again and again. As shown in exx. 9.2, 9.5, and 9.6, the three-note motive (d^1–e^1–f^1, mm. 43–49), the e♮–e♭ figure, and the g♯–a figure all recur in revalued guises (cf. m. 89), marking the arrival of the V (mm. 89–114). These concealed middleground motives bespeak a sophisticated compositional technique. That the initial V, then the I (mm. 43–88), then the V (mm. 89–114) should all be rooted in the same underlying middleground motive (ex. 9.2) is not only a striking compositional feat, but one which we can perceive as leading organically from the "indistinct" opening (with the elided V) to the grand culmination (mm. 97ff.). Exx. 9.6 and 9.7 show the underlying middleground upon which ex. 9.2 is placed. Contrary to Schenker's assertions, Bruckner does unify large sections of music not only through prolongations, but through coherently developing middleground motives!

---

[8] Schenker, *Harmony*, p. 286.

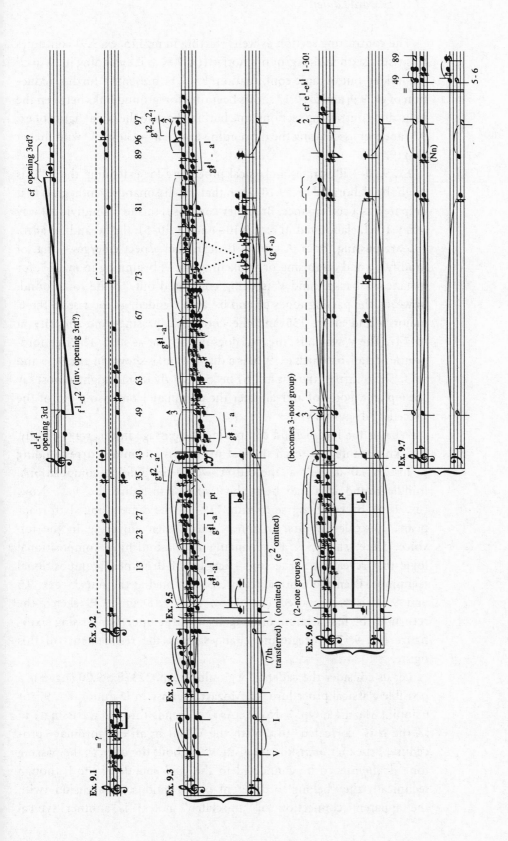

The contrasting section as well (starting in m. 115, ex. 9.9) continues this rising sixth middleground motive (ex. 9.8) as if extending it up to c♯^{2} – a hidden but organic continuation. Ex. 9.11 presents a further reduction of ex. 9.9; and ex. 9.12 shows beautiful foreground links between the main and contrasting sections, one harking back to the g♯^{1}–a^1 figure of ex. 9.5, another associating the descending fourth a^2–e^2 at m. 97 with that at m. 119.

Ex. 9.10–1 illustrates a classical procedure for extending the V. This might be elaborated (ex. 9.10–2) so that the dissonant seventh, g^2, is first prepared as a consonance. Bruckner composes this in his individual way (ex. 9.10–3, elaborated in exx. 9.10–4 and 9.10–5): the c♮^{2} and b♭^{1} at m. 135 are passing tones. A typical Brucknerian aspect emerges – that of modifying and disguising or weakening the V: beginning in m. 135, for instance, a background V is being composed out. In the foreground, however, the passing tones c♮^{2} and b♭^{1} are extended, giving rise to the C major sound at m. 135 and the chromatic passing-tone sonority at m. 147. The V, which is "meant," does not appear as such. The rich foreground detail, of which ex. 9.10 is a distillation, is shown in exx. 9.13 and 9.14. The return of the I at m. 161 becomes a vivid, one might almost say *triumphant*, point of arrival, after the chromatic composing-out of the preceding disguised V.

What is the idea behind composing the passage in this way? Clearly, Bruckner wanted to reach the I at m. 161 in a manner corresponding to his arrival at the I at the outset, where the guiding compositional middleground idea had been the rising sixth-figure (ex. 9.2). Now, (ex. 9.16), over the course of mm. 119–61, the same rising sixth reappears, concealed at first in inner voices, then emerging in the top voice. Here, surely, is a convincing and astonishing compositional logic that reveals the true sophistication of Bruckner's compositional technique. Even the motivic feature e♮–e♭, noted at the outset (exx. 9.5 and 9.6), is recomposed (ex. 9.15). Exx. 9.18 and 9.19 sketch the return of the first section, once again with the underlying rising sixth-figure (ex. 9.17): foreground changes mark the restatements of this figure.

Let us consider the cadence beginning at m. 223. Ex. 9.20 suggests a possible classical procedure (cf. Mozart, Fantasy in D minor, K. 397, or Chopin, Mazurka, Op. 7, No. 2). As ♭$\hat{2}$ descends through a passing $\hat{1}$ to ♯$\hat{7}$, the ♭$\hat{2}$ is "corrected" to ♮$\hat{2}$ with the V. But in an extraordinary procedure, Bruckner *omits* the requisite V. Without the due c♯^{2}, the passing tone d^2 *appears* to be connected to the *goal-note* d^2 of the I, though technically they belong to different prolongations. This elision (with the apparent connection of "unrelated" notes) is another typical

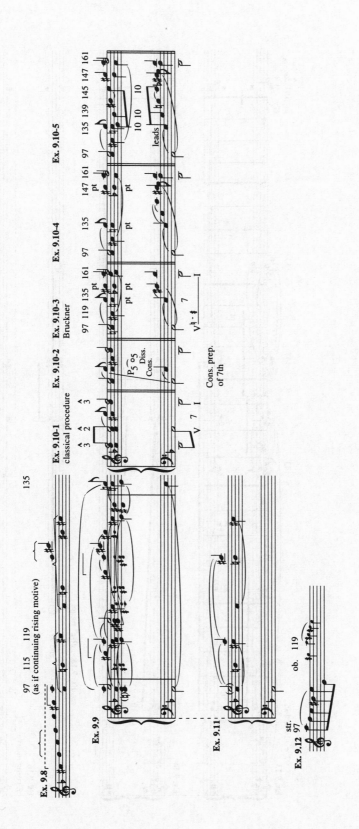

135

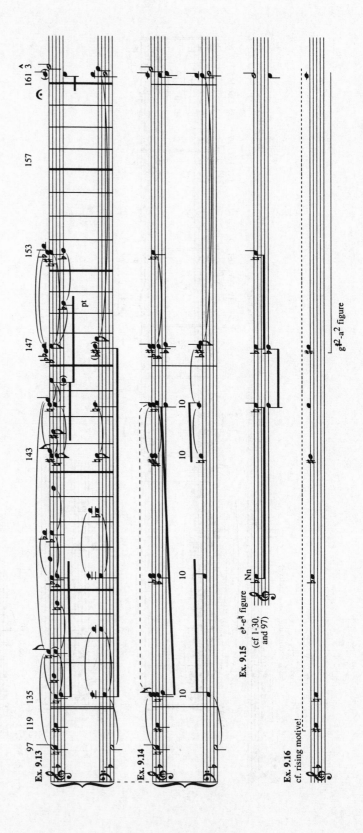

Ex. 9.13

Ex. 9.14

Ex. 9.15 e♭-e♮ figure
(cf 1-30, and 97)

Ex. 9.16
cf. rising motive!

g♯²-a² figure

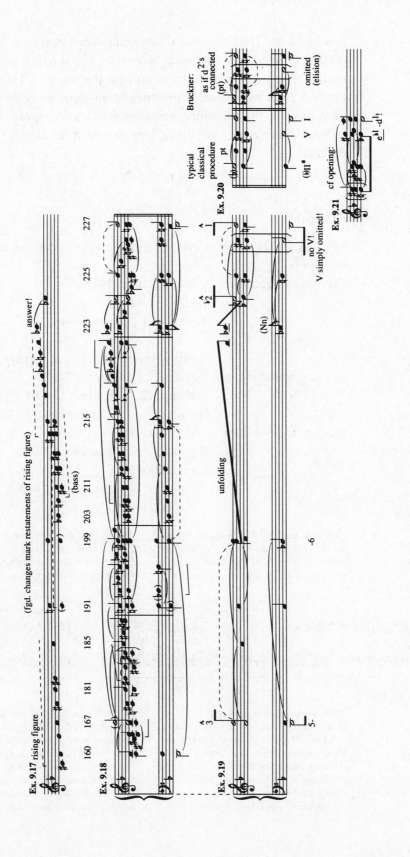

Ex. 9.17 rising figure

(fgd. changes mark restatements of rising figure)

answer!

160   167   181   185   191   199   203   211   215   223   225   227

(bass)

Ex. 9.18

Ex. 9.19

unfolding

(Nn)

no V!

V simply omitted!

typical
classical
procedure

Bruckner:
as if d 2's
connected

omitted
(elision)

Ex. 9.20

Ex. 9.21

cf opening:

-6

Brucknerism.[9] Here the underlying compositional reason for this procedure, in which the top voice moves eb^2–d^2, surely is related to the motivic e^1–eb^1–d^1 (ex. 9.21) from the opening (ex. 9.5). This figure now emerges from its concealed presence in an inner voice to the clearest expression in the top voice, revealing itself, so to speak, just for the cadence. Once again, the V has been modified or, in this case, simply evaded.

Adagio

My view of the sonata form of this movement may be described as follows:[10]

Expositional Section	1st subject, mm. 1–16
	Transition, 17–44
	2nd subject, 1st part, 45–46
	2nd part, 57–64
	Closing=modified return of 1st part, 65–76
Developmental section	1st part, cf. 1st subject, 77–128
	2nd part, cf. 2nd subject, 129–62
	Return of 1st subject motive, 163–72
Recapitulatory section	2nd subject, 173–85
	Crescendo to climax, 186–199–206
	Final section:
	2nd part of 1st subject, 207–18
	Coda, 219–43

[9] There are probably few *classical* instances of this sort of procedure (elision, with linking notes; here is one from Mozart's Piano Concerto, K. 491, II. Of the two examples shown below, that beginning at m. 24 is perhaps preferable because of the (understood) consonant harmonic support for the top-voice note f^2 in m. 30:

[10] The designations "expositional," "developmental," and "recapitulatory sections" rather than "exposition," "development," and "recapitulation," are more in keeping with Bruckner's own term "Abteilung." This reading of the form of the Adagio could be controversial on two counts: the "development" is indicated as beginning – unusually – on the tonic, and the "recapitulation" as opening with a highly *developmental* treatment of the second subject. As to the first point, there is a specific compositional reason for Bruckner's starting the development on I: this, as we shall see, has to do with the larger compositional intent to *begin anew* as if reaching back to the opening

The expositional section

Like the Scherzo, the Adagio also begins with an elision; in this case, an initial I-chord is only *conceptually* present, but not yet stated. The idea here (as in the Scherzo) is to express growth and cumulation: starting as if from a distant, almost indeterminate spot; gradually taking shape; and expanding. Reinforcing this poetic metaphor is, from a Schenkerian standpoint, the absence, at the outset, of the initial primary tone of the fundamental line. In fact, an important compositional idea ties in with this: that of only realizing the high g#^{3} (the $\hat{3}$ of the fundamental line) over the course of the movement. This notion – the long delay, and trying again and again before finally achieving the goal-note g#^{3} – is central to the poetic intent, and is present right from the outset, like a seed which will only later burst into bloom.

The opening bars are difficult to read because of what Schenker would call the *addition of a bass*: inner voices may be placed *below* the real bass. (Thus the A and G♯ indicated by whole notes in mm. 3–4, ex. 9.23, are inner voices, not the real bass.) Although the following period (mm. 8–17) might, at first glance, appear to substantiate Schenker's criticism and have no organic connection to the preceding measures, as shown in ex. 9.23 it constitutes a very freely composed restatement of the opening period. The bass is restated (mm. 7–13, e–c♯: cf. mm. 1–4, e–c♮–B); as is the rising top line (mm. 8–13, b^1–f♯^{2}: cf. mm. 4–6, b^1–f♯^{2}). The augmented sixth sonority of the voice exchange (mm. 1–4) recurs at m. 12 (asterisks in ex. 9.23; also shown in ex. 9.25), and the chromatic figures c♮^{2}–b^1 and a♯^{1} – b^1 from the opening motive (ex. 9.22) are subtly recomposed (circled in exx. 9.22–1 and 9.23). Ex. 9.22–2 shows the two motivic components. Ex. 9.22–1 illustrates that the ascent of mm. 3–7 and mm. 13–17 (another freely composed restatement) are melodic expressions of the opening motive in enlargements. Exx. 9.22–2 and 9.24 suggest how the top line (e^3–f♯^{3}–g♯^{3}) tries to recompose the ascending third-figure of the motive (marked by braces, exx. 9.22–2 and 9.23).

Ex. 9.27 indicates that the opening motive of the first subject also underlies the transition to the second subject, mm. 17–44 (ex. 9.28). The b^1 and b♭^{1} remain hidden in inner voices, and the descending figure (mm. 29–32) is filled in. In this way the descending line b♭^{1} – c♮^{1} (mm. 29–32) is "explained"; indeed, the hidden connection and compositional

in order to aim one more time for the climactic point of arrival (mm. 199–206). As to reversing the order of the subjects in the recapitulation, in this movement (as in a work such as Chopin's Sonata in B♭ Minor, Op. 35) a partial reason would be that the first subject had been worked so consistently in the development that its restatement could hardly have provided the necessary contrast for the beginning of the recapitulation. Moreover, the strong tonic return at m. 173 clearly indicates the beginning of a new section which corresponds tonally and, in a real sense, formally to the opening section.

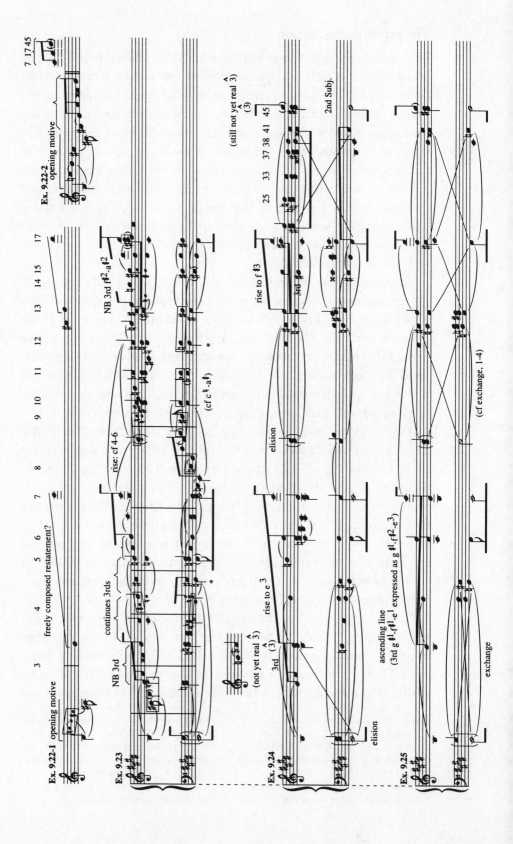

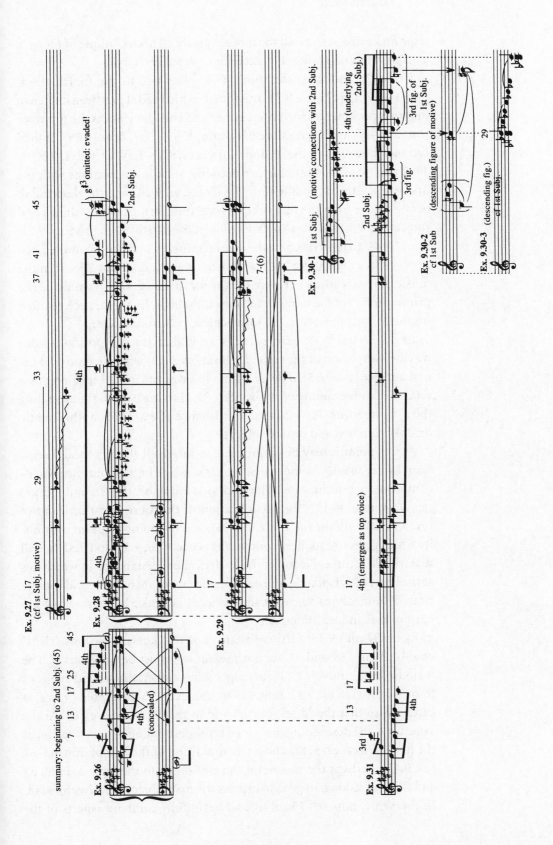

logic make this passage all the more beautiful! This technique of *filling in* a disjunct figure is quite characteristic of Bruckner's style.

Exx. 9.26 and 9.31: the third $g\sharp^1$–e^1 gives rise to the fourth $f\sharp^1$–$c\sharp^1$ mm. 13–17; at m. 17 (ex. 9.31) this fourth, which had at first been hidden in inner voices, emerges in various guises and enlargements as the top voice (mm. 17–41) and even as the bass, mm. 17–37 ($F\sharp$–$D\sharp$, ex. 9.29). It then *becomes* the fourth of the second subject (ex. 9.31–1, $f\natural^1$–$c\natural^1$)! Exx. 9.30–1, 30–2 and 30–3 illustrate further masterly motivic connections with the first subject: the ascending third-figure (cf. ex. 9.24) and the descending octave-figure from the first subject, both transformed within the second subject. Ex. 9.32 rewrites the expression of the fourth-figure from ex. 9.31, mm. 17–41, to illustrate how this figure is worked into the second subject, ex. 9.33. In ex. 9.33, the high $a\flat^2$ shown in m. 45 does not appear in the music. It is as if Bruckner were *aiming* for this note, which would be the primary tone $\hat{3}$ of the movement, but withholds it. Its appearance, so often promised and prepared, is not to be achieved until much later.

Exx. 9.34 and 9.35: here, perhaps, an underlying compositional idea was the association of the second subject (ex. 9.34) with the motive of the first subject (ex. 9.35). The $c\flat^2$ of m. 48 takes on special meaning as a reminder and revaluing of the $b\natural^1$ of m. 35. Harking back to the ascending third-figure of ex. 9.22–2 is the third-figure of ex. 9.36, another subtle link between first and second subjects!

At this point it may be appropriate to interrupt the technical discussion to reconsider some of Schenker's misgivings about Bruckner's compositional technique. The recomposition of the second period (ex. 9.23, mm. 8–17); the identification of the ascending third-motive (ex. 9.22–2) with the top line (ex. 9.25); and the point-to-point continuity which gives rise to the second subject (exx. 9.26, 9.31, and 9.32) are all remarkable technical features the analytical understanding of which lies at the heart of Schenker's approach. In the face of such subtle and sophisticated connections and transformations, Schenker's reservations are curious and, indeed, untenable.

Exx. 9.37 and 9.38: further instances of Brucknerian elisions. The C chords at mm. 69 and 73 are not present but must be understood. The melodic line, mm. 69–73, is no empty scale; rather, the second subject's fourth-figure (cf. ex. 9.32, mm. 45–46, and ex. 9.37, the dotted braces) is extended so that the "due" fourth c^2–g^1 in m. 69 becomes c^2–$e\natural^1$. At the same time, the descending line c^2–$e\natural^1$ is the descending-figure, filled in, of the first subject (ex. 9.40) and a recomposition of the line of mm. 62–64 (ex. 9.41). Perhaps the reason for the motion up to the high $a\flat^3$ in m. 62 and then back down to $g\flat^2$ is to express the first subject's motive, filled in. In this sense, mm. 69–73 subtly and beautifully combine aspects of the

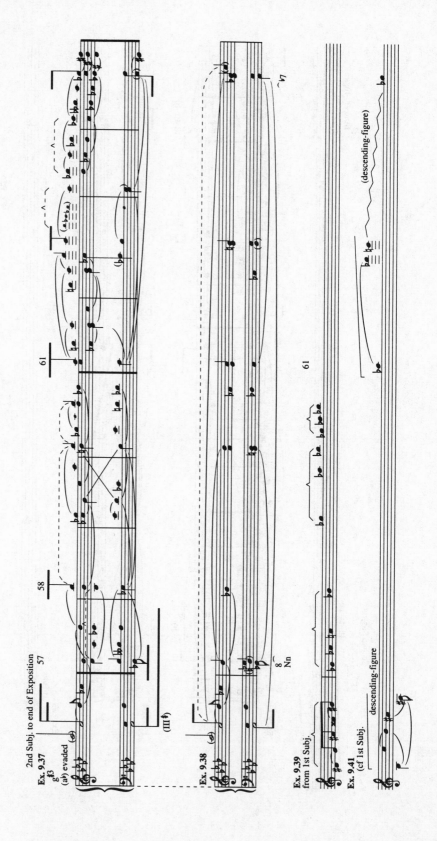

Ex. 9.37

2nd Subj. to end of Exposition

(a♭) evaded

57

58

61

(III♭)

Ex. 9.38

V7

Nn

Ex. 9.39
from 1st Subj.

61

Ex. 9.41
(cf 1st Subj.

descending-figure

(descending-figure)

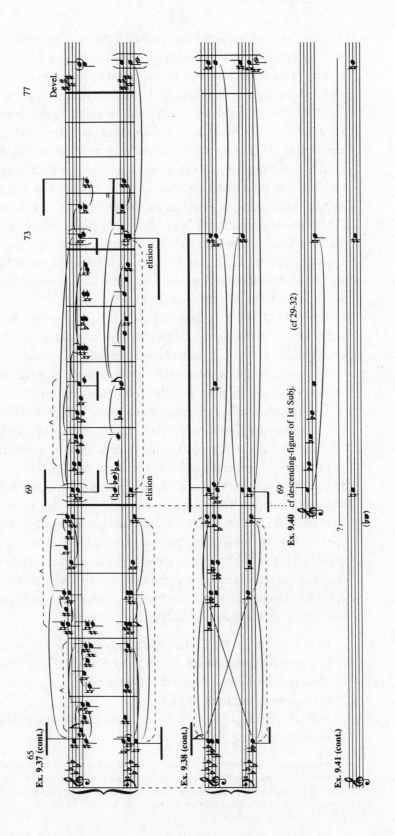

Ex. 9.37 (cont.)

Ex. 9.38 (cont.)

Ex. 9.40   cf descending-figure of 1st Subj.   (cf 29-32)

Ex. 9.41 (cont.)

65 (cont.)

69

73

77

Devel.

elision

elision

69

69

first *and* second subjects! Just possibly, the striking elisions in mm. 69 and 73 further draw attention to this relationship.

Ex. 9.44: a classical composer might have proceeded by extending an A♭ I chord through a chromaticised voice exchange to go to a II♮ chord. Ex. 9.45 shows Bruckner's very odd voice exchange. The point of a *chromaticised* voice exchange is that it leads decisively to the next chord, marking it as a goal. In ex. 9.45, Bruckner, most unusually, does not proceed to a new degree (as in ex. 9.44), but *returns* to the E major I chord in m. 77 as if to point out that since the main top line had not yet been able to reach the desired high g♯³ (as aimed for in m. 45, exx. 9.26, 9.42–1 and 9.43) it must start all over at m. 77 and try again. Schenker's criticism of starting "each time with a I-chord" is here not quite apt. Because the due high g♯³ had been evaded, in order to try for it again, from the *same* starting point, Bruckner *deliberately* and quite logically begins the development on the tonic. (In classical practice, this is rare.)[11]

Exx. 9.42–2 and 9.43 suggest how this goal note (g♯³) had been *poetically* hinted at, but not yet achieved, in terms of voice-leading; the high a♭³ at m. 60 is a passing tone and not a real point of arrival.

Ex. 9.46: a motivic explanation for the strange voice exchange is surely, once again, a vast expansion of the first subject's motive.

Ex. 9.47: the top line attempts to rise to the high g♯³, but falls short at g♯³ (m. 121). For the V-prolongation starting at m. 93, not only is the motive of the first subject applied to the voice-leading framework as a foreground motive (ex. 9.48; and in the bass, filled in, ex. 9.50–1), but also, as in ex. 9.50–2, the passage as a whole is placed upon a vast enlargement of the same motive! This is quite astonishing. At the high point (mm. 121–28), the last notes of this motive are triumphantly celebrated, so to speak, as if this were now the true arrival (circled notes, ex. 9.50–2). Strikingly, in ex. 9.53 the resolution of the neighbor notes is withheld: in this way, the elided resolution connects directly with the ensuing A♭ chord (m. 129) – a characteristic Brucknerian procedure – noted in ex. 9.30 as well. A few details should be noted:

> Ex. 9.47: from m. 93, the harmonic goals and subdivisions along the way are marked by abrupt changes in dynamics and orchestration. The elisions in mm. 115–19 have the effect of postponing and heightening the wonderful outburst at m. 121.
>
> Ex. 9.51: perhaps the fourth-figure of the second subject is also to be understood here.

[11] For classical development sections beginning on the tonic, see Ernst Oster's comments in his translation of Schenker's *Der Freie Satz* (New York: Longman, 1979), p. 140; and Jack Adrian, "Development Sections that Begin with the Tonic" (Ph.D. diss., Eastman School of Music, University of Rochester, Rochester, N.Y., 1987).

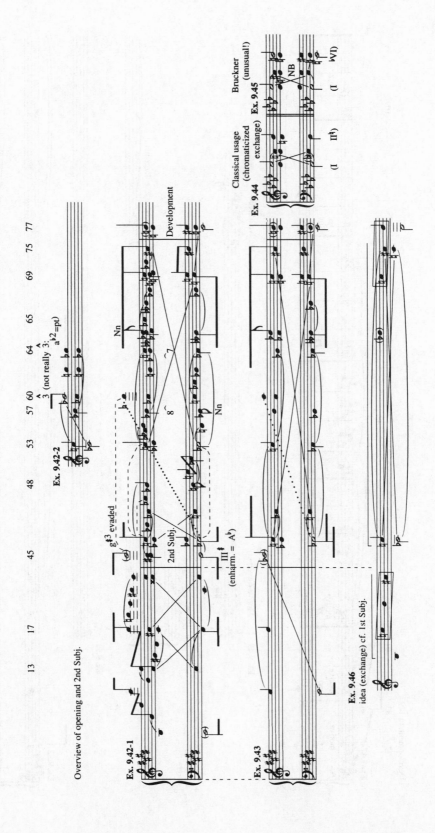

Overview of opening and 2nd Subj.

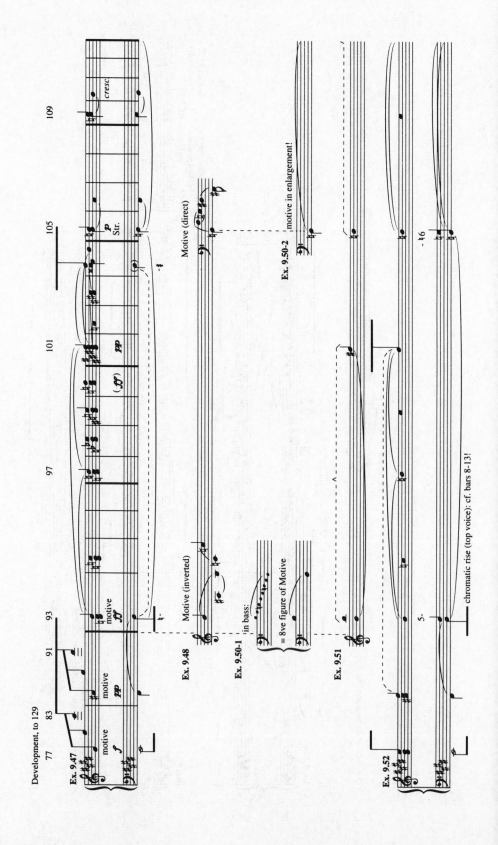

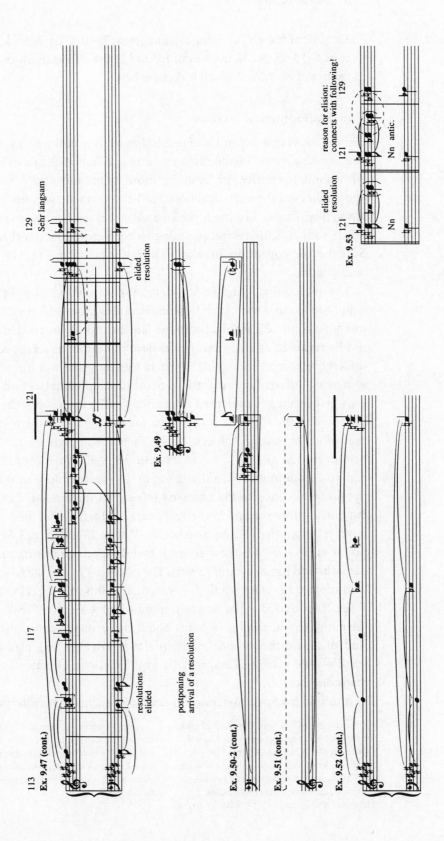

Ex. 9.52: although the rising top line (mm. 93–101) harks back to mm. 8–13 (ex. 9.23), from mm. 105 to 121 the *bass* leads, since it is the motive of ex. 9.50–2 which is decisive here.

The developmental section

Certain musicians' attitudes to musical analysis would wish to acknowledge *ambiguity* as a possible factor – i.e. to maintain that a passage might, with similar validity, be read in more than one way.[12] Schenker's approach, even the analytical notation he developed, does not allow for ambiguity. That is, in a *single* sketch a passage is read one way *or* another, not both.[13] It is, therefore, tempting to conjecture that another reason Schenker did not admire Bruckner's way of composing is that he found it ambiguous.

The difficulties I find in the development section may, of course, simply reflect my own analytical shortcomings; but just possibly there might be some real ambiguity in the larger musical design. This should not be regarded as a compositional flaw, but rather as an aspect of the underlying compositional idea itself. In this context, I will consider three somewhat different interpretations of the developmental section.

A first reading is presented in exx. 9.54–9.57. In ex. 9.54, the general idea behind the top part is the quest for the high $g\sharp^3$ (which had been evaded at the second subject, m. 45, then at the high $g\natural^3$, m. 121). At neither m. 138 nor m. 173 is it attained. Ex. 9.55 shows the V of m. 93 composed out to m. 163; although at m. 163 there *is* no V in the music, the problem concerns the necessity to read an *understood* V at m. 163. Supporting this reading is the reappearance there of the first subject's motive: this motive had appeared on the V at m. 93 and m. 105. Returning just at m. 163, it links these spots; it had disappeared during the quasi-parenthetical passage, mm. 129–63. The $g\natural^3$ of m. 121 and the $f\times^3$ of m. 167 lend support to such a reading. Contradicting this reading is the fact that V (ex. 9.55, m. 93) is not strongly emphasized. Can this V really govern the entire course of events? What about the strong G chord in m. 121? And, of course, the absence of an actual V-return at m. 163, plausible in a smaller-scale prolongation, may be problematic in an extended, chromatic one like this.

A second reading is suggested in exx. 9.59 and 9.60. This interpretation

[12] See, for example: Daniel Coren, "Ambiguity in Schubert's Recapitulations," *The Musical Quarterly* 60 (1974), 568–82; and Allen Cadwallader, "Foreground Motivic Ambiguity: Its Clarification at Middleground Levels in Selected Late Piano Pieces of Johannes Brahms," *Music Analysis* 7/1 (1988), 59–91.

[13] In problematic cases one can, of course, attempt alternative readings, but in different sketches. Moreover, the elisions discussed may indeed suggest a kind of *poetic* ambiguity, in that something is left out, to be supplied by the listener.

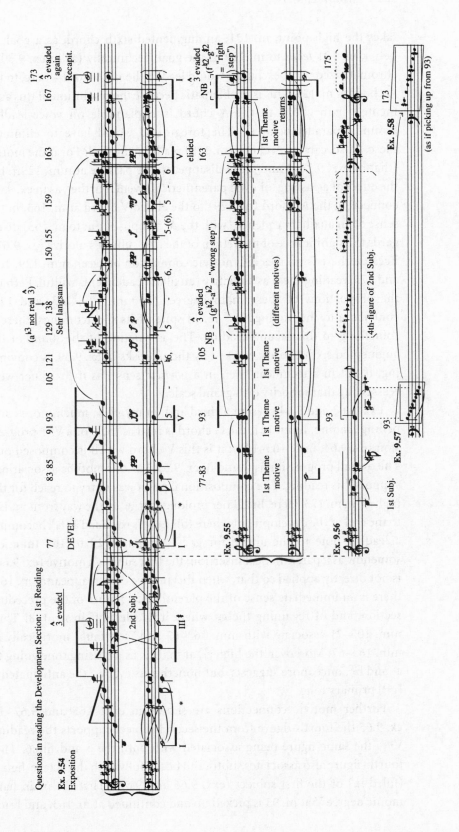

Questions in reading the Development Section: 1st Reading

Ex. 9.54
Exposition

DEVEL.

(a♭3 not real 3̂)

Sehr langsam

3̂ evaded

Recapit.

3̂ evaded again

elided

NB ⌐ (f♯2_g2)
= "right step"

NB ⌐⌐ (g♯1_a♭2 = "wrong step")

1st Theme motive returns

1st Theme motive (different motives)

1st Theme motive

1st Theme motive

Ex. 9.55

Ex. 9.56

Ex. 9.57

Ex. 9.58

1st Subj.

4th-figure of 2nd Subj.

(as if picking up from 93)

2nd Subj.

takes the high point, m. 121, an augmented sixth chord, as a goal; or better, m. 121 *leads* to m. 129 as the goal. Technically (as in ex. 9.60) a chromaticized voice exchange would lead to the *next* chord – here, to the A♭ chord in m. 129. This is problematic because the resolution of this augmented sixth chord to the A♭ chord is implausible on voice-leading grounds: parallel octaves. (The foreground would have to eliminate these.) Also, can the A♭ chord (m. 129) really be the goal? For if the motive (that of exx. 9.23–1 and 9.61) disappears, the passage at mm. 129ff. has the effect of a passing, or even parenthetical, event. Further, as in ex. 9.60, connecting the A♭ chord (m. 129) to the elided V chord at m. 163, in the sense of an auxiliary cadence (with the A♭ composed out to m. 163) disregards the significance of the return of the first subject's motive (ex. 9.61). Because there is no specific motivic connection between mm. 129, 163, and 173, reading these as an entity (auxiliary cadence) is willful. Perhaps the proportions of these main degrees (at mm. 129, 163, and 173) contribute to the "ambiguity." Yet in spite of its shortcomings, there is something to this second reading. The association of the *sound* of the augmented sixth chords, marked by the asterisks in ex. 9.59, is convincing, if not in a technical, then in a *poetical* sense, as if Bruckner were reasserting that sonority on a grand scale.

Exx. 9.62 and 9.64 present a third and, in my view, much more compelling reading. In m. 121, the G chord is read as the 6 of a V^{5-6} progression (ex. 9.64, mm. 105–121): it is this V chord which is composed out. The overall progression is found in ex. 9.63. Various motivic associations support this reading. The compositional point was to try to reach for the high $g\sharp^3$ in m. 173. Here, Bruckner prolongs the $g\natural^3$ all the way from m. 121 to the end of the development where this note is revalued as $f\texttimes^3$, becoming a leading note to the aimed-for $g\sharp^3$. Thus mm. 129 to 163 function somehow as a parenthetical insertion; the first subject's motive (ex. 9.66) is not directly applied so that, when this motive does reappear at m. 163, there is an immediate sense of the parenthetical nature of the preceding section, and of regaining the $g\natural^3$ where it had left off in m. 128! Thus mm. 105–21 associate with mm. 163–67 and "continue" motivically at mm. 163–67. Moreover, the high $a\flat^3$ at m. 129, as a passing tone going to a^2 and $b\flat^2$, once more suggests, but nonetheless evades, the anticipated 3 ($g\sharp^3$) primary tone.

Further motivic connections are shown in exx. 9.65 and 9.67. In ex. 9.65 the fourth-figure from the second subject supports the reading V^{5-6}, the same figure being associated with both the 5 and the 6. This fourth-figure also associates subtly and beautifully with the octave-figure (filled in) of the first subject (exx. 9.66 and 9.67). That the main harmonic degree V at m. 93 is picked up and continued at m. 163, and leads

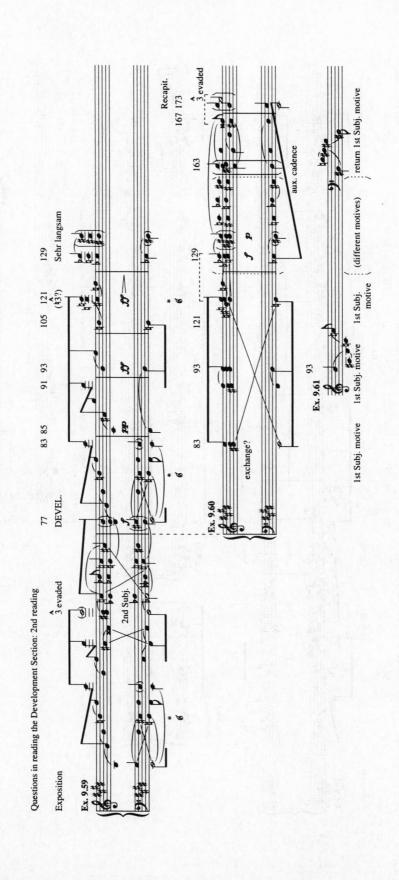

Questions in reading the Development Section: 2nd reading

Questions in reading the Development Section: 3rd Reading (preferred)

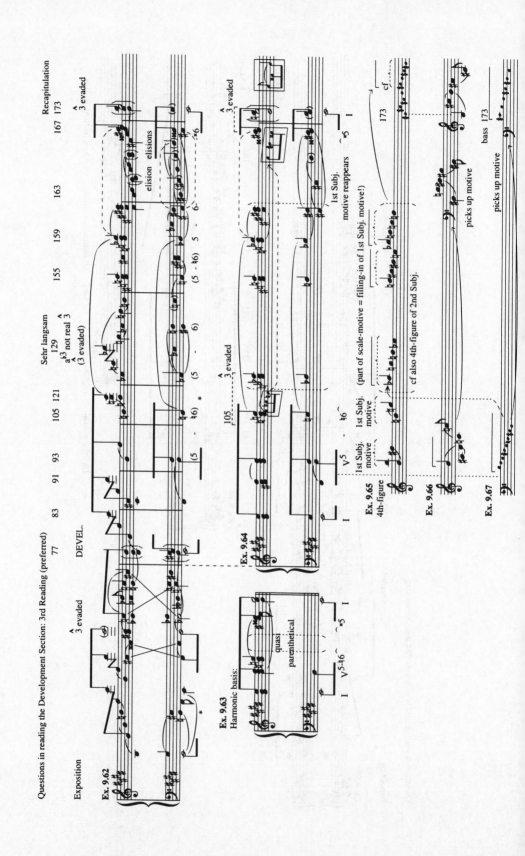

to I at m. 173, is wonderfully clarified by the return of this (filled in) figure at m. 173 (exx. 9.66 and 9.67). A guiding line for the entire course of the development section is the main top-voice ascending third $e^2–f\sharp^2–g\natural^2(=fx^2)–g\sharp^2$ (ex. 9.64), a vast enlargement of the third of the first subject (ex. 9.22–2), a simple, logical, and remarkable compositional idea!

Ex. 9.68 presents a summary of the developmental section.

Ex. 9.69 attempts to clarify Bruckner's curious harmonic progressions in mm. 129–55 and, in more detail, mm. 151–55. It is likely that such progressions would have been the kind of procedure which irritated Schenker because, in the foreground, they depart altogether from classical usage. But Bruckner's way of composing here is both logical and highly individual, as is illustrated by contrasting his procedure with a "classical" one. The parallel octaves and fifths of ex. 9.69–1 might have been broken up by a 5–6 motion (ex. 9.69–2), but Bruckner first writes a 5–7 motion (ex. 9.69–3). He expands this with an *elided* 6 (ex. 9.69–4, m. 151) which he goes on to compose out (the E major chord at m. 151)! Exx. 9.69–5 to 9.69–9 attempt to clarify the succession, step by step. Whereas a classical composer might have included a passing tone $d\natural^2$ (ex. 9.69–5), Bruckner writes a $d\sharp^2$ (ex. 9.69–6) which is given consonant support (ex. 9.69–7) and further elaborated as in exx. 9.69–8 and 9.69–9, with registral changes.[14] With its complex chromaticism, elision, and changes of register, the passage at mm. 129–55 represents a striking modification of classical usage. There is a good reason for the elision of the E chord in m. 151 (ex. 9.69–9): a *stated* E chord might have sounded too much like a premature return to the tonic, which is not due until the recapitulation at m. 173. In m. 151 an E chord is meant to function only as V of the A in m. 155. Even a stated V of A might have given too much emphasis to that A chord (m. 155), which is not a main goal.

Ex. 9.70: perhaps the most difficult section of the movement, in terms of understanding the voice leading. At m. 141 the music is the same as the opening (cf. ex. 9.23) where one must read a I chord (unstated, elided). Here the context has changed: it is now the *E♭ chord* (m. 139) which is being composed out. As in exx. 9.23 and 9.24, one difficulty results from *added bass* notes: at times, Bruckner places *inner* voices *below* the real bass or else we must *supply* a bass note where Bruckner has omitted it. Moreover, as in mm. 145–47, bass and top parts are not metrically aligned with one another. The voice leading is summarized in exx. 9.73 and 9.74. The oblique lines in exx. 9.70 and 9.74 call attention to the notes which

---

[14] Here we can see how the harmonic support for the third $e^2–d\sharp^2–c\sharp^2$, exx. 9.69–6 to 9.69–8, gives rise to the often-noted "bass motion by thirds": the latter procedure is not an end in itself, but the result of supporting a voice-leading motion in an upper part.

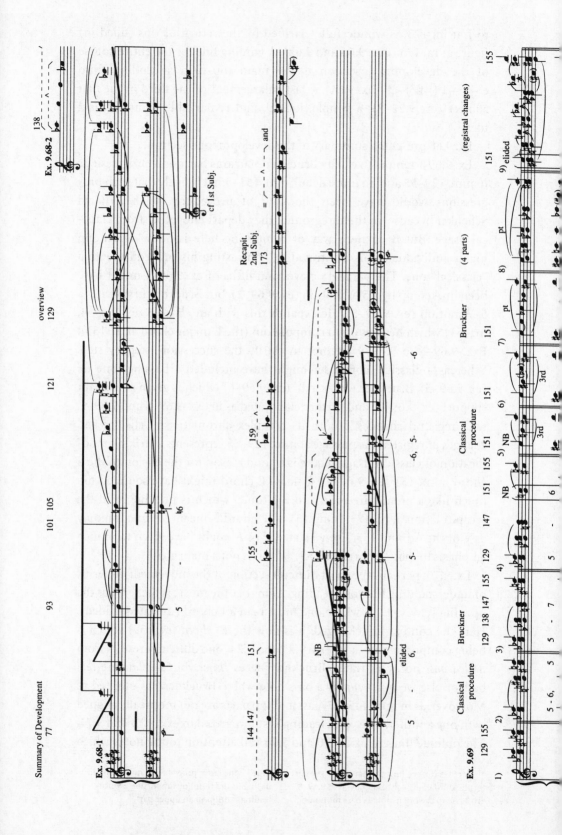

belong together. Perhaps the idea behind the foreground voice-leading difficulties (ex. 9.70) is a programmatic one: getting lost or going astray.[15]

Exx. 9.71 and 9.72: in various guises, and in enlargement, the four-note figure from the second subject is worked in.

The recapitulatory section

Ex. 9.75 sketches the recapitulation's drive to the climax at m. 199. Ex. 9.75–1 shows the main progression; ex. 9.75–2 an elaboration; and ex. 9.75–3 a further elaboration. Ex. 9.75–4 suggests the parallel octaves threatened by the outer voices; ex. 9.75–5 indicates that these are not really parallel octaves since, in the *middleground*, the motion is actually A to G♯ in the bass (ex. 9.75–6). Exx. 9.75–7 and 9.75–8 show more detail; ex. 9.75–9 is another way of expressing the same progression.

Remarkably, and with unswerving logic, Bruckner once again recomposes the ascending third-figure of the first subject (ex. 9.75–10; cf. exx. 9.22–2, 9.62, 9.63, and 9.68) in a vast enlargement, as the top voice, mm. 173–99. The motivic association with the first subject, though concealed, is now clinched; as in exx. 9.75–9 and 9.10, the restatements in the top line review and sum up this final, decisive ascent to the high g♯[3] ($\hat{3}$), m. 199. This is perhaps the reason for the top line's reasserting f♯[2] at m. 197 (asterisk), leading to the f×[2], which recalls the f×[1] of the first subject (cf. ex. 9.75–10).

Ex. 9.76 sketches this magnificent *crescendo* rise in foreground and middleground detail. As noted in the commentary to ex. 9.75, it is only in m. 199 that the primary tone $\hat{3}$ (g♯[3]), awaited throughout the movement, appears. The foreground "parallel octaves," just discussed, further mark this point. So does the grinding dissonance, created by applying to the III♯ chord (ex. 9.76, m. 199) an unresolved triple appoggiatura. (The understood resolution is given in the middleground reduction, ex. 9.78.) Where do these appoggiatura notes come from?

As in ex. 9.79, it is once again the opening motive, concealed and spread out in a vast enlargement, which stands behind the entire *crescendo* passage! Indeed, perhaps even *two* statements are present, emerging from their concealed beginnings to burst forth just at the climax (in ex. 9.79, one incomplete motivic statement is shown in whole-notes, the other in half-notes).[16] That the *crescendo* passage is placed

[15] It is as if, metaphorically speaking, the composer were ascending a high peak (the high g♯[3]) to look back over the difficulties and wrong turns of his life along the way up, and from that peak pausing to look forward into the face of eternity and the Everlasting. Perhaps such a notion is not foreign to the poetic idea of this movement. Such an interpretation, too, ties in with the idea of a parenthetical insertion, mm. 129–163 (ex. 9.64). In this way, a further delay is composed, to heighten the sense of having found the right path – the sense of eventual attainment.

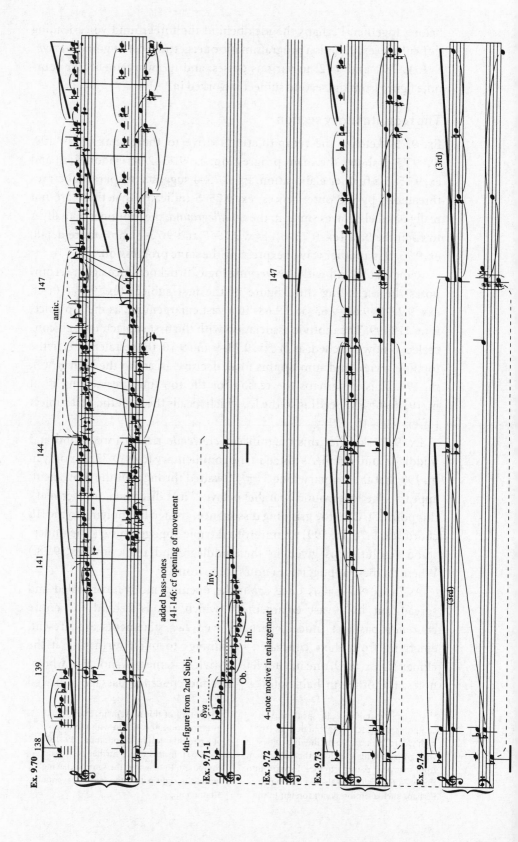

Ex. 9.70

138 139 141 144 147

antic.

added bass-notes
141-146: cf opening of movement

4th-figure from 2nd Subj.

Ex. 9.71-1

8va

Inv.

Ob. Hn.

4-note motive in enlargement

Ex. 9.72

147

Ex. 9.73

Ex. 9.74

(3rd)

(3rd)

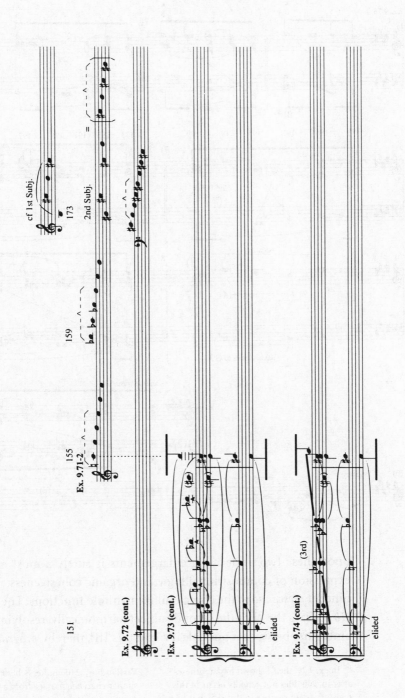

Recapitulation (Return 2nd Subj., bar 173) to High point (199-207)

Ex. 9.75

upon these two underlying enlargements is surely a most exhilarating expression of compositional logic and organic cohesiveness.[17] The magnificent *crescendo* to the climax fulfils manifold functions. The *goal-chord* III# realizes the A♭ of the second subject harmonically, resolving a lurking ambiguity between a possible ♭IV and this III#, thereby *programmatically*

[16] In ex. 9.79, the fx^2 shown in parentheses after m. 206 does not actually occur in this register: its appearance in this sketch is merely to "complete" the motive. The due fx only appears in m. 207, as an inner-voice g#^{1}.
[17] Federhofer, "Schenkers Bruckner-

Verständnis," 210, quotes Schenker on a similar *crescendo* passage from a different symphony:

Once, during a class, Bruckner called me over to the piano. "Listen, Mr. Schenker," he said, and played only one passage, which

resolving earlier conflicts and false steps. The already mentioned *top-voice ascent* realizes the motivic third (e^2–f$\natural^2$–g$\sharp^3$) of the first subject (cf. exx. 9.22–2 and 9.75) in yet another grand enlargement. This third attains, at last, the long-awaited and aimed-for *primary tone* g$\sharp^3$ ($\hat{3}$). Here, too, *the associative augmented sixth chord* sonority just before the climax (m. 198) harks back to the same sound at earlier occasions (cf. ex. 9.54, asterisks) as if now to indicate the goal to which that previous augmented sixth chord sonority had been destined. If one accepts that there might have been some *deliberate* ambiguity in the developmental section, the point would have been to express a sense of *searching* for the path which here is finally found, and which resolves the difficulties that occurred along the way. Indeed, what astonishing compositional mastery – to tie in all of these technical and programmatic aspects!

Ex. 9.80 proposes an alternative reading of this passage, based on a voice exchange, involving the characteristic augmented sixth chord. Exx. 9.81 and 9.82 provide an overview of the movement to this point.

The final section and coda

Ex. 9.84: by *eliding* the resolution of the multiple dissonances of m. 199 (exx. 9.76, 9.77, 9.78, 9.80–6, 9.83) Bruckner not only emphasizes the climactic point of arrival, he also connects the resolution with the ensuing harmony (compare the same procedure in exx. 9.20 and 9.53). The b$\sharp^1$ at m. 206 connects to the c$\natural^2$ (=b$\sharp^1$) at m. 207 (see NB, ex. 9.84; arrow in ex. 9.83). This c$\natural^2$ (with the inner voice a$\sharp$) is significant because it (and the a$\sharp$) associates with the c$\natural^2$ of the first subject, the characteristically altered tone, emphasized by the ninth leap. These notes, c$\natural$ and a$\sharp$, are worked into the ensuing passage (mm. 207–20, ex. 9.83).

As mentioned in the discussion of the formal design of the movement,

obviously represented a *crescendo.* "Do you think that's enough, or should I make it go on further?" He didn't let me hear what preceded or followed the *crescendo* passage. Later I was able to ascertain that it was a passage from the *Seventh Symphony*, on which he had been working at the time. But how could he ask about something like that? . . .
Schenker was appalled and incredulous. His attitude was, "How should *I* know, if *he* doesn't? And on what basis?" Of course Bruckner must have known perfectly well what he was about. Timothy Jackson, to whom I am indebted for many comments concerning this paper, conjectures (in a personal communication) that "Bruckner may have been playing with Schenker, and that the humor apparently escaped the young and rather serious student. Bruckner took other students like Hans Rott and Gustav Mahler much more seriously – probably because he thought (rightly) that they had more compositional talent than Schenker." Jackson wonders if "Schenker probably never forgave Bruckner for this 'slight': something of this comes through in the tone of Schenker's remarks." In my view, Schenker's lofty, high-minded devotion to his artistic ideals, as well as his admiration for Bruckner the man, would not have been compromised by any straightforward criticism from his erstwhile teacher. It is also possible that Bruckner, as pedagogue, was, in an odd way, challenging his pupil's compositional acumen.

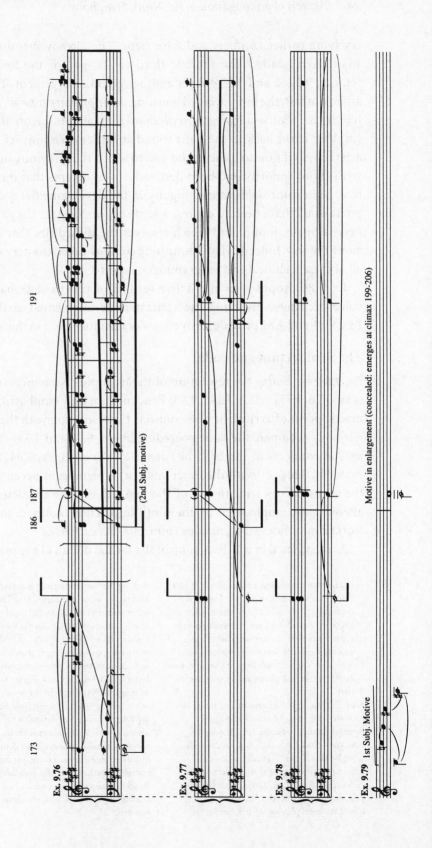

Ex. 9.76

Ex. 9.77

Ex. 9.78

Ex. 9.79 1st Subj. Motive

173

186 187

191

(2nd Subj. motive)

Motive in enlargement (concealed: emerges at climax 199-206)

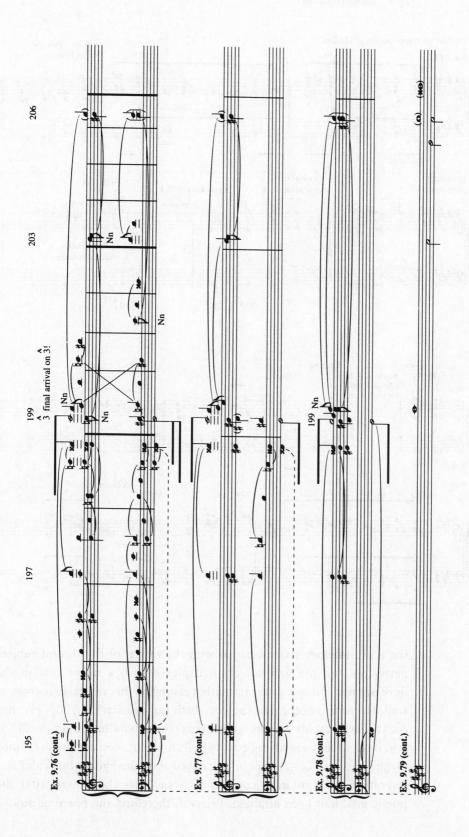

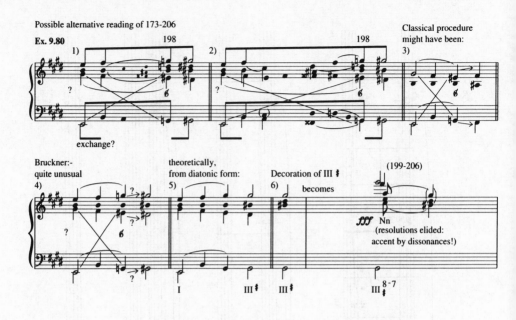

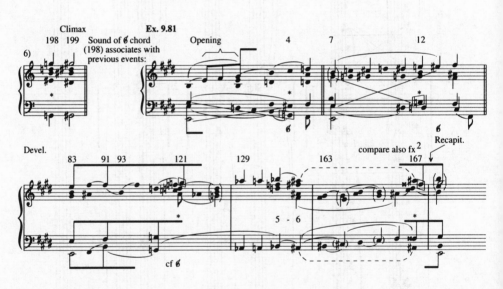

the recapitulatory section began with the return of the second subject partly because the first subject had played such a major role in the development. Now a programmatic reason for this reversal emerges as well. The return of the first subject which reappears at mm. 207–19, after the climax, presents only its second part (corresponding to mm. 9–17). It is as if the urgent, searching quality of its first part, depicted by the minor ninth b–c^2 (ex. 9.22–2) were now resolved and transfigured into calm and serenity. Such resolution could only occur after the climax, after the poetic goal had been attained. Perhaps, therefore, the opening motive

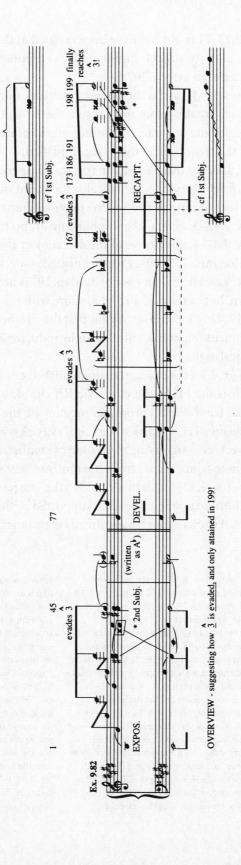

Ex. 9.82

EXPOS. DEVEL. RECAPIT.

OVERVIEW - suggesting how $\hat{3}$ is evaded, and only attained in 199!

(ex. 9.22–2) could not have been restated at the outset of the recapitulation, and its urgent minor-ninth component could not be directly
restated even at mm. 207ff.

Ex. 9.87–1: just as the opening motive's minor ninth-figure had been
followed by the rising third-figure, here too, the rise to the climax had
expressed the first part (the minor ninth) of the first motive (ex. 9.87–2).
Now the second part (the rising third-figure) is due: this appears, amaz-
ingly, as $c\natural^2$–e^2 (ex. 9.87–2). In this way the period from mm. 207 to 219 is
not an arbitrary or mechanical restatement of mm. 8–17, but a beautifully logical continuation of the previous climactic *crescendo* ascent.

Ex. 9.87–3: a coda-like summing up of this third-figure.

Ex. 9.87–4: the motive of the first subject also underlies the entire progression mm. 207–20 – a further organic aspect.

Ex. 9.86: the E major sonority at m. 207 is not to be taken as a real tonic
return, but as the 6 of a III$^{5–6}$ motion, with the real tonic arriving only at
m. 219. This 5–6 motion means that the III♯ chord is seamlessly fused into
the concluding tonic, without an introducing V, as would be requisite in
classical usage.[18]

In ex. 9.91, the characteristic anguished $c\natural^2$ of the first subject's motive,
which is the b♯^{1} of the climactic III♯ chord, is finally "corrected," so to
speak. The restless chromatic urgency of the $c\natural^2$ gives way here at the
conclusion (cf. circled notes and asterisks, ex. 9.90) to the diatonic,
"correct" $c\sharp^2$ – signifying resolution of conflict, and serenity. In m. 227 the
two-note falling figure from the motive (ex. 9.92–2) has become a rising
figure (ex. 9.92–1), further marking the "correction" of $c\natural^2$ to $c\sharp^2$. The final
$\hat{2}$ of the fundamental line is *not* supported by the V, as would be the case in
classical works – for reasons already mentioned.

---

[18] Compare other Brucknerian instances of
weakening or omitting the V, as: exx. 9.5, 9.10,
9.20, 9.37 mm. 73–77, 9.55, 9.60, 9.69–9. The
tonic just reappears at m. 219, without
dominant preparation; its union with the
III$^{5–6}$ brings about a sense of cohesiveness,
uninterruptedness, and ultimate serenity. If
the first subject, with its opening melodic leap,
its chromaticism, rhythmic irregularity,
harmonic complexity (cf. the different
readings, opening and exx. 9.70, 9.73, 9.74),
added bass notes, and elisions, represented
emotional agitation and an unsettled and
searching state – then the second subject, with
its greater harmonic stability and rhythmic
regularity, expressed a glimpse of the sought-
after serenity and noble tranquillity. In this
sense, the movement as a whole would
represent reaching for, and finally attaining,
that ideal, fraught with difficulties and
evasions all along the way. The final
realization, the achievement of serenity at the
conclusion, is absolute. Now, the harmonic
merging and stability is such that there is even
no supported descent, but only a maintained
I-chord. The line does not even *close* in the
high register, as if the high g♯^{3} of the climax
(m. 199) were left up there, on high, to sound
on into all eternity. Ex. 9.88, the *inversion* of
the second subject, perhaps has a
programmatic meaning. The inversion, in a
poetical sense, repudiates its previous *contrast*
with the first subject, and joins with it
(ex. 9.89) to signify the attainment of oneness
and tranquillity, where opposition and
contrast are no more.

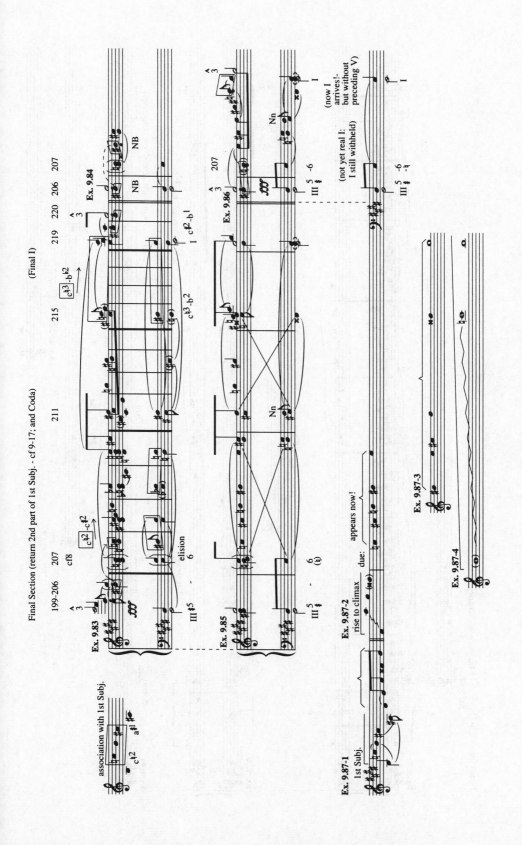

Final Section (return 2nd part of 1st Subj. - cf 9-17; and Coda)

(Final I)

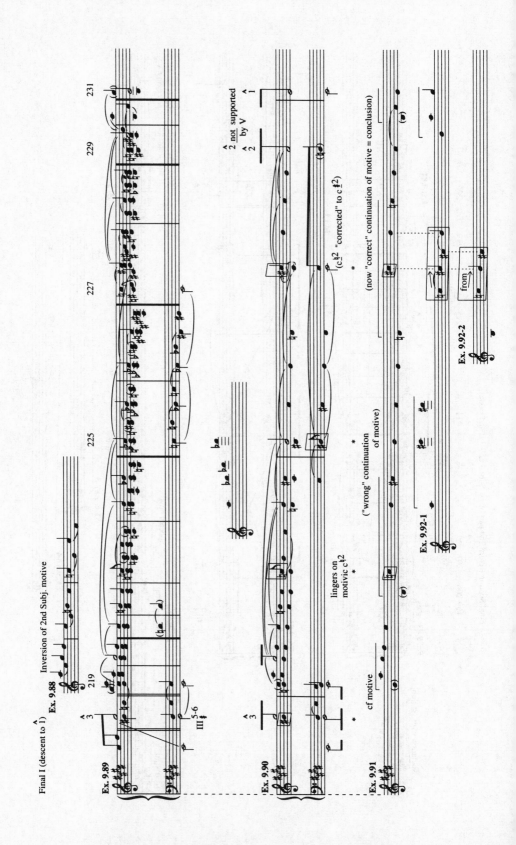

Final I (descent to $\hat{1}$)   Inversion of 2nd Subj. motive

Ex. 9.88

Ex. 9.89   219   225   227   229   231
$\hat{3}$
III$^{5-6}_{4}$

Ex. 9.90 $\hat{3}$ lingers on
motivic c♮2
*   *   * $\hat{2}$ not supported
by V
$\hat{2}$ $\hat{1}$

Ex. 9.91   cf motive   ("wrong" continuation
of motive)   [c♮2 "corrected" to c♯2]
*   (now "correct" continuation of motive = conclusion)
*

Ex. 9.92-1   Ex. 9.92-2   from

Some classical precedents for Brucknerian techniques

> The lack of the *organic* . . . Of *compositional technique* there is no trace . . .
> Each moment is an end unto itself . . . With Bruckner all of this [thematic
> association] lies *right on the surface* . . . His technique is defective . . . [19]

Schenker's haunting critical comments do identify certain essential
aspects of "compositional technique": – i.e. how to solve what he considered perhaps the greatest musical problem – that of *coherently* achieving
length.[20] For in an "organic" work, foreground events ("each moment")
must be placed on an underlying, motivically associated middleground.
This makes possible a motivic continuity in which the "thematic association" may not necessarily "lie right on the surface." It is probable that
Schenker, relying on his experience of Bruckner's teaching and trusting
his general impressions of Bruckner's music, was simply not inclined to
concern himself further with any thoroughgoing analytical study of
Bruckner's music – the kind of careful study which is Schenker's hall-
mark. (If he had, he might have altered his condemnatory position.)
Ironically, Schenker's criticisms do not stand up to Schenkerian criticism. Indeed, the organic nature of Bruckner's technique, the cogent
prolongation procedures, and the subtle and sophisticated motivic links
and associations are at the heart of every analytical sketch presented here.

In this study, *elisions* have figured prominently as a Brucknerian technical feature. Of course Bruckner did not invent the notion. Indeed, the
procedure had been explained in C. P. E. Bach's *True Art of Playing
Keyboard Instruments*. It may be helpful to conclude by citing a few
instances of elision in classical works, to suggest how Bruckner enlarged
upon and, so to speak, took possession of this somewhat infrequent classical procedure.

In ex. 9.93, (Beethoven, Symphony No. 1, Op. 26) elision comes about
by omitting a *note* of the chord of origin. In ex. 9.94 (Schumann,
Davidsbündlertänze, Op. 6) the entire *chord* of origin is withheld. Thus, in
the Beethoven the c^2 of the 8–♭7 is omitted: the initial I is deliberately
indefinite, and the sense is that of starting *in medias res,* leading to
V. In ex. 94, the line beginning with the initial understood g^1
(g^1–a♭^{1}–a♮^{1}–b♭^{1}–b♮^{1}–c♯^{2}) has subsequent motivic consequences, as if what
had been at first only suggested later comes into the open (ex. 9.95).

In exx. 9.96 and 9.97 (Beethoven, Symphony No. 1, Op. 26, Scherzo) not
the chord of *origin,* but a *due* chord, or chord of *resolution,* is omitted. A V
must be read at the NB: though f^1 is not actually present, it is nonetheless

---

[19] Abridgment of note 4 above.   [20] Federhofer, "Schenkers Bruckner-
Verständnis," 207.

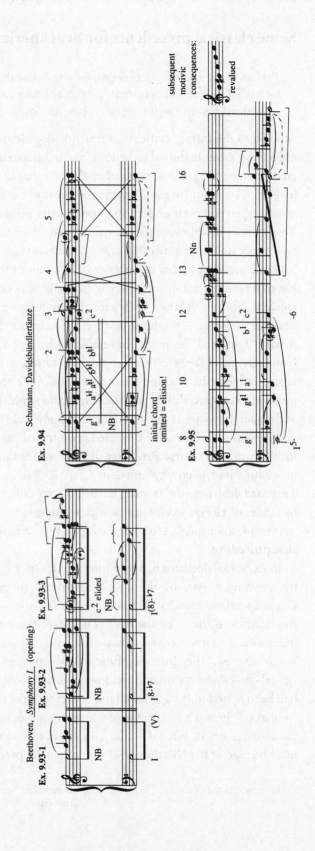

Beethoven, *Symphony 1* (opening)

Ex. 9.93-1   Ex. 9.93-2   Ex. 9.93-3

Schumann, Davidsbündlertänze

Ex. 9.94

Ex. 9.95

subsequent
motivic
consequences:

revalued

initial chord
omitted = elision!

c^2 elided

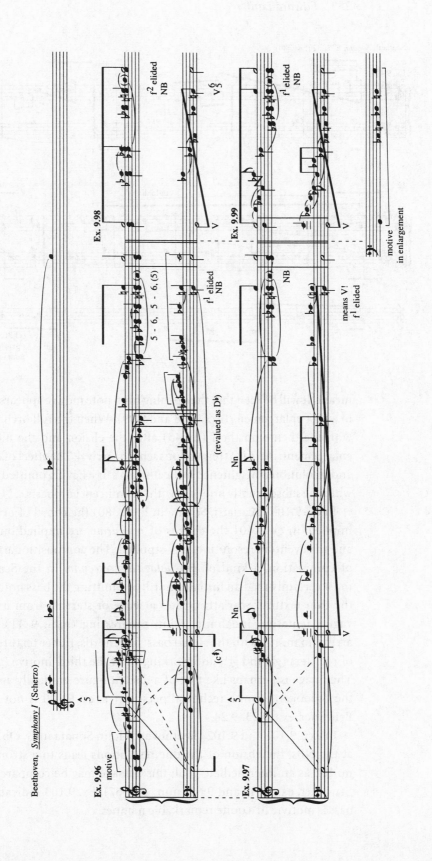

Beethoven, *Symphony I* (Scherzo)

Scarlatti, *Sonata, E* (L. 23; K. 380)

Ex. 9.100

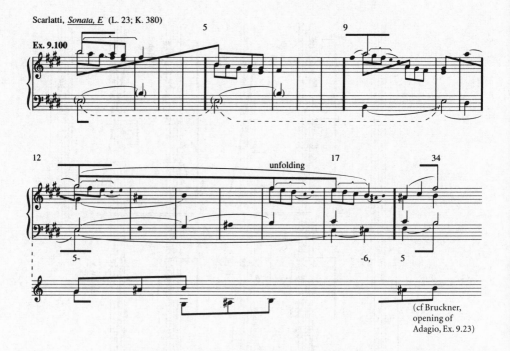

(cf Bruckner,
opening of
Adagio, Ex. 9.23)

meant. It will be seen that the opening four-note motive appears in the bass in a vast enlargement (exx. 9.98 and 9.99)! When the full orchestra enters with the theme on the I (m. 43) after the elision and the hidden bass-enlargement, there is a tremendous sense of arrival. The effect of expectancy and resolution is heightened by Beethoven's first having omitted something which he subsequently provides with magnificent emphasis.

In ex. 9.100 (Scarlatti, Sonata in E, K. 380) the chord of *origin* is only implied; in ex. 9.101 the chords of *resolution* are implied but withheld and the eventual resolution is postponed. The compositional idea is one of cumulation, a kind of *psychological crescendo*. In the Scarlatti, one must certainly read an initial I chord; by omitting the bass notes and with the thin texture, Scarlatti creates a sense of starting from a somewhat vague, tentative, indefinite point, progressing (mm. 9–11) to a clear arrival in m. 12 (with the stated bass, full chords, richer texture, coupling of registers ($g\#^2$ and $g\#^1$) and working-in of the third-motive ($g\#^1$–$a\#^1$–b^1). The image is perhaps like that of a distant figure gradually approaching the onlooker. From a technical perspective, ex. 9.100 is not unlike the Bruckner, exx. 9.23–9.24.

In exx. 9.101 and 9.102 (Beethoven, Violin Sonata in G, Op. 30, No. 3) at the NBs, the elision of the due resolutions leads to a strong sense of m. 105 as an intermediate goal; this passage may be compared with the Bruckner, exx. 9.47 and 9.62 (mm. 159–67). Ex. 9.103 indicates that the bass is motivic in a quite remarkable manner.

Beethoven, *Violin Sonata, Op. 30/3*

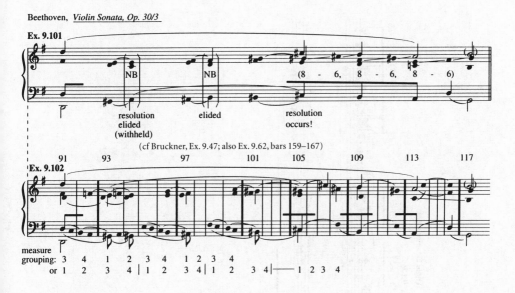

Ex. 9.106 shows very strange and atypical elisions in Mozart (Quintet for Piano and Winds, K. 452, II). The character, that of anguished recitative to be dispelled by serene aria, suggests an operatic or programmatic interpretation. Ex. 9.104 provides a first step in coming to terms with the odd $^6_4$ chords and arriving at a reading. As in ex. 9.105, to account for the $^6_4$ chords, it is necessary to understand *two* elisions, which enhance the quasi-recitative character. Ex. 9.106 then presents the whole development.

Ex. 9.107 (Chopin, Nocturne, Op. 27, No. 1) is an instance of an unsupported $\hat{2}$ in the final descent, somewhat as in the Bruckner, exx. 9.89 and 9.90. Whereas the background would show the $\hat{2}$ supported by the V, in the middle and foreground this is no longer the case: the $\flat\hat{2}$ is

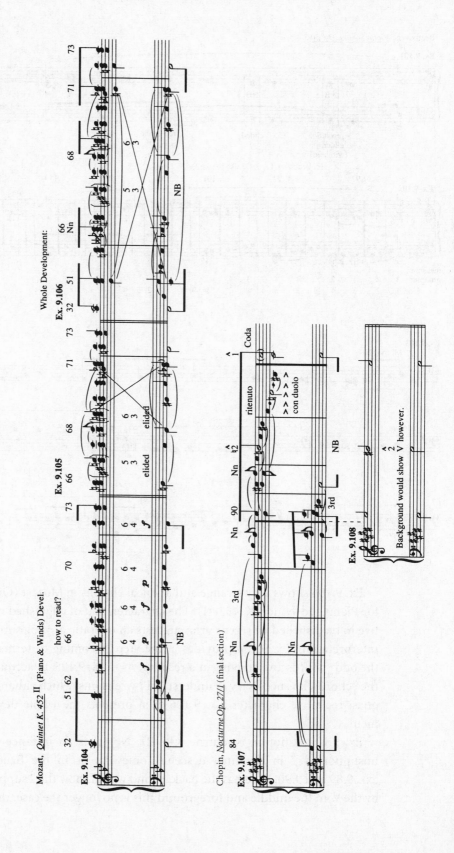

supported only by the I (pedal). With $\flat\hat{2}$ and no V, it is not a very convincing descent. Chopin compensates for this with the *con duolo* indication, the accents, and the *ritenuto*. The ending of the Nocturne is deliberately indefinite, as a reminder of the opening which (likewise) had been tentative, hesitant, and indefinite.

In classical practice such elisions are special events, expressing certain compositional or even programmatic intentions. In Bruckner's work they are more stock in trade. Perhaps the extent of their usage in Bruckner was perceived by Schenker as manneristic, if not ambiguous and, therefore, weak. As suggested earlier, it is possible that Schenker's dismissive critical remarks do not really reflect his mature thought – or rather, they indicate his unwillingness to apply his more mature insights to music about which he had already made up his mind as a student.

Surely Bruckner's compositional technique of repeatedly working in certain motivic ideas beneath the surface, in a more or less concealed manner, and making these motives form the guiding framework upon which the foreground is placed is at the heart of Schenker's concept of the organic nature of a great work of art. If Bruckner could shock Schenker by saying, "This is the rule, gentlemen, but of course *I* don't compose like that," we might acknowledge that there was a higher, deeper principle beyond whatever rule to which he was referring: indeed, it was the principle of organic prolongation. He did compose in *that* way, even if his characteristic modifications were so individual as to have us think otherwise.

10 Bruckner's sonata deformations

Warren Darcy

A major stumbling block for Bruckner analysis has been the composer's approach to sonata form. Donald Francis Tovey complained that "it is Bruckner's misfortune that his work is put forward by himself so as to present to us the angle of its relation to sonata form."[1] Robert Simpson agreed, adding that the Finale of the Fourth Symphony was a failure largely because Bruckner had "not yet shaken off the confusing influence of sonata," and had not "consistently felt the larger momentum that renders sonata strategy irrelevant."[2] This attitude led these and other critics to downplay the importance of the sonata concept in Bruckner's symphonic music. At the same time, the strong schematic aspect of Bruckner's symphonic movements led analysts at the other end of the spectrum to attempt to describe them within the confines of a narrow, prescriptive view of sonata form, derived largely from nineteenth-century *Formenlehre* paradigms. Far from marginalizing the sonata concept, these critics reified it.[3] Not surprisingly, neither approach has revealed the full richness of these works.

The past decade of musicological research has been characterized by a search for new explanatory strategies. Among the most promising is the theory of "sonata deformation" developed by James Hepokoski in a recent series of writings on Strauss and Sibelius.[4] This chapter sets forth

---

[1] Donald Francis Tovey, *Essays in Musical Analysis*, 6 vols. (Oxford University Press, 1981), *Symphonies and Other Orchestral Works*, p. 254.

[2] Robert Simpson, *The Essence of Bruckner* (New York: Crescendo Publishing, 1967), pp. 98 and 100.

[3] This approach is particularly evident in the work of German-speaking scholars. See, for example, Constantin Floros, "Die Fassungen der Achten Symphonie von Anton Bruckner," in *Bruckner-Symposion Bericht "Die Fassungen,"* ed. Franz Grasberger (Graz: Akademische Druck- und Verlagsanstalt, 1981), pp. 53–63.

[4] James Hepokoski, "Fiery-Pulsed Libertine or Domestic Hero? Strauss's *Don Juan* Revisited," in *Richard Strauss: New Perspectives on the Composer and His Work*, ed. Bryan Gilliam

(Durham, N.C.: Duke University Press, 1992), pp. 135–75; "Structure and Program in *Macbeth*: A Proposed Reading of Strauss's First Symphonic Poem," in *Richard Strauss: and His World*, ed. Bryan Gilliam (Princeton University Press, 1992), pp. 67–89; *Sibelius: Symphony No. 5* (Cambridge University Press, 1993), especially pp. 1–9 and 19–30; "The Essence of Sibelius: Creation Myths and Rotational Cycles in *Luonnotor*," in *The Sibelius Companion*, ed. Glenda Goss (Westport, Conn.: Greenwood Press, 1996), pp. 121–46; "Elgar" and "Sibelius" chapters in *The Symphony 1821–1914*, ed. D. Kern Holoman, *Studies in Musical Genres and Repertoires* VI, series ed. R. Larry Todd (New York: Schirmer Books, 1996), pp. 327–44 and 417–49; and "Three Documents on Analysis"

and expands upon seven hermeneutic concepts central to the theory: the redemption paradigm, teleological genesis, the rebirth paradigm, rotational form, the "alienated" secondary theme zone, the non-resolving recapitulation, and *Klang* as *telos*. Each concept is illustrated through references to the first and fourth movements of Bruckner's symphonies.

Preliminaries

In 1861, Bruckner began to study musical form with the conductor Otto Kitzler. Kitzler reports that they used Ernst Friedrich Richter's *Grundzüge der musikalischen Formen* as a textbook. The facts of the matter were probably far more complex.[5] What is certain is that Bruckner was well versed in standard nineteenth-century *Formenlehre* prescriptions.

It is well known that Bruckner characteristically divided his expositions into three parts: a primary theme zone, with a modulation during a second statement or "counterstatement" of the main theme; a contrasting secondary theme zone or, as Bruckner called it, a *Gesangsperiode*; and a closing zone that usually reenergizes the rhythmic momentum and often reinvigorates primary theme material. In the following discussion, I shall refer to these three parts as P, S, and C.

Hepokoski has proposed that, by the last third of the nineteenth century, an array of "deformations" of the *Formenlehre* structures had come into being, and that certain "sonata deformational" procedures were both common and readily recognizable. These structures are "in dialogue with the generic expectations of the sonata, even when some of the most important features of those expectations are not realized."[6] Thus a deformation "contravenes some of the most central defining traditions, or default gestures, of a genre while explicitly retaining others"; the "reified defaults" which the deformation overrides are those

(unpublished manuscript, 1993), including "Sonata-Deformation Families," "Principles of the Symphony in the Period of its Centering Phase, c. 1780–1820," and "One Approach to Musical Hermeneutics: Thoughts on Music Analysis."

[5] Ernst Friedrich Richter, *Die Grundzüge der musikalischen Formen und ihre Analyse* (Leipzig: Verlag von Georg Wigand, 1852). Göllerich–Auer, III/1, p. 144, reports that Bruckner also used volumes III and IV of Adolf Bernhard Marx's *Die Lehre von der musikalischen Komposition* (Berlin, 1837–47, rev. 1860–63), primarily for its sections on orchestration. Stephen Parkany's engaging account of Bruckner's studies in *Formenlehre*

is based upon the assumption that the composer studied Richter's book; see "Bruckner and the Vocabulary of Symphonic Formal Process" (Ph.D. diss., University of California at Berkeley, 1989), pp. 146–57. At one point, Parkany claims that "Bruckner was one of the first significant composers to learn classical forms from a textbook (or at least to admit to it)" (ibid., 151). In a personal communication Paul Hawkshaw, who is currently researching the origins of Bruckner's conception of musical form, has told me that many of the exercises Bruckner did for Kitzler cannot be traced to any of these texts.

[6] *Sibelius: Symphony No. 5*, p. 5.

"urged by the *Formenlehre* traditions."[7] The most prominent deformational procedures stem from key works of, among others, Beethoven, Schubert, Mendelssohn, Schumann, Liszt, and Wagner.[8] Although it is difficult to pinpoint exactly which works Bruckner may have studied, we can assume that he was cognizant of both the *Formenlehre* default gestures and the means by which composers had sought to override these defaults. Armed with this knowledge, he developed his own characteristic set of deformational procedures.

It is likely that the complex set of procedures we came to call "sonata form" developed during the eighteenth century in part as an expression of certain aspects of the world-view of the Enlightenment and concomitantly emerging modernism. Thus "sonata form" came to represent a perfect "action" within this new world: it emphasized balance, symmetry, closure, and the rational resolution of opposing tensions. Hepokoski has suggested that, when nineteenth-century composers began to deform some of the most characteristic features of this genre, they were subjecting the genre itself to a critique, perhaps to suggest that facile Enlightenment symmetries were no longer appropriate or casually available to a more vigorously modernizing society.[9] This is particularly evident when the "sonata-form" portion of a larger movement "fails" in some respect to solve its musical/tonal problems.[10] Such a "failure" – for example, an apparent "inability" of a secondary theme to secure the tonic key in the recapitulation (as in Beethoven's *Egmont* Overture, Glinka's Overture to *Russlan und Ludmilla*, and so on) – is of course no compositional shortcoming. On the contrary, this situation is normally a powerfully expressive, purposely intended feature of the musical narrative of any sonata of which it is a part. When a sonata is made to run into such difficulties in its recapitulation, it typically must be amended or "rescued from outside," usually in a corrective coda. This, too, is part of the expressive logic of the piece, and the coda can sometimes be perceived as a metaphor for the composer.

As we shall see, such ideas are particularly relevant to Bruckner. Nearly all the sonata-form portions of Bruckner's first and last movements are constructed in such a way as to "fail" to solve the problems they pose. These "problems" usually stem from Bruckner's deformation of the so-called "redemption paradigm," to which we now turn.

---

[7] "Fiery-Pulsed Libertine," p. 143.
[8] *Sibelius: Symphony No. 5*, p. 5.
[9] "One Approach to Musical Hermeneutics," 8, and private communication.
[10] By "sonata-form portions," I mean the expositional, developmental, and recapitulatory spaces of the movement. Although the coda is certainly an integral part of the movement, it is not, strictly speaking, a part of sonata space. As is the case with an introduction, a coda occupies a separate musical space; it is, in a sense, "not-sonata."

The redemption paradigm

In its simplest form, the *per aspera ad astra* narrative trajectory so important to the nineteenth-century symphony entails the "redemption" of a movement out of the minor mode into the major, usually by means of a secondary theme that appears first in the relative major, then is recapitulated in the tonic major. The first movement of Haydn's Symphony No. 95 in C minor offers a typical example. In a multi-movement work, redemption is often postponed until the Finale; the first movement "fails" to deliver the promised redemption by closing in minor. Beethoven's Fifth Symphony is the *locus classicus* here. The redemption paradigm can also be extended to major-mode works; here the task is to purge the piece of minor-mode elements such as ♭$\hat{3}$, ♭$\hat{6}$, ♭$\hat{7}$, or ♭$\hat{2}$. In such a case, the first movement ends in major, and the two middle movements often restore the minor scale degrees, suggesting that the first movement's apparent "success" was either temporary or an illusion; the Finale may actually begin in the minor mode.[11] Brahms's Third Symphony follows this pattern.

While each of Bruckner's symphonies is in dialogue with the redemption paradigm, most of them "deform" it in significant ways. For one thing, the sonata-form portions (i.e. the exposition, development, and recapitulation) of nearly all Bruckner's outer movements fail to deliver the promised redemption by closing either in the minor mode or in a non-tonic area, leaving the ultimate fate of the movement to the coda. For another, Bruckner generally isolates the secondary theme zone (*Gesangsperiode*) from the main line of the default symphonic discourse; instead of functioning as an agent of redemption, it often represents a visionary world that is incapable of being realized. Bruckner always postpones the redemptive moment until the coda of the Finale, after the sonata-form portion of that movement has once again 'failed' to deliver it. According to sonata deformation theory, this coda must be understood as drawing its strength from *outside* the sonata form and, in a sense, must *transcend* that form in order to succeed.

Teleological genesis

Hepokoski defines teleological genesis in its broadest sense as follows:

> As an individual composition's processes unfold, the [composer] often uses
> them as a matrix within which something else is engendered, usually a

---

[11] Brucknerian examples include the Fourth and Sixth Symphonies.

decisive climax or final goal (*telos*). The concept of a composition as gradually generative towards the revelation of a higher or fuller condition is characteristic of the modern composers.[12]

The process may unfold on various structural levels, from that of the individual theme to that of the movement as a whole. This formulation of the concept suggests two subcategories, which I call "teleological thematic genesis" and "teleological structural genesis."

In its most basic form, a "teleological theme" features a generative *crescendo* that leads to a thematic/tonal goal or *telos*. The theme is *end*-oriented; its musical processes flow inexorably towards the *telos*. Because Bruckner reserves this procedure almost exclusively for his primary theme zones, it is convenient to refer to the two components as P^{gen} (the generative *crescendo*) and P^{tel} (the *telos*).[13]

Bruckner's teleological themes are of two types, which I will call the "creatio ex nihilo" type and the "double theme" type. In the former, the *crescendo* is shaped as a generative matrix within which motivic fragments materialize out of the void and gradually coalesce into the fully formed thematic statement of the *telos*. The generative matrix is often tonally unclear; the *telos* frequently begins as a *fortissimo* unison statement, and breaks into cadential harmonies that clarify and confirm the tonic. Bruckner's model here was probably the first movement of Beethoven's Ninth Symphony; as is well known, his most obvious recasting of this model opens his own Ninth Symphony, although his generative *crescendo* is much longer than Beethoven's.[14]

The second type of teleological theme, the "double theme" type, also follows the pattern of generative *crescendo* plus *telos*. In this case the *crescendo* itself (P^{gen}) contains a more or less fully formed thematic statement, while the *telos* (P^{tel}) presents a different theme as goal. Here we are dealing not so much with the organic evolution of a single theme, as with the use of one theme to engender or give birth to a second, to which it is at least temporarily subordinated. Often the apparent thematic closure and well-formedness of P^{gen} begins to break down through motivic fragmentation and sequence; it ultimately loses its identity until, at the crucial moment of the generative process, it forcibly expels P^{tel}. A classic

---

[12] *Sibelius: Symphony No. 5*, p. 26.

[13] A teleological theme should be distinguished from an expository theme, which places its most characteristic or strongly articulated element at the beginning.

[14] An earlier example opens the 1880 version of the Finale of the Fourth Symphony: over a pulsating B♭ pedal and darkly sinuous string figurations, a slowly moving three-note motive evolves through intervallic expansion and rhythmic diminution into an apocalyptic unison outburst; the impetus continues through an extended *Sturm und Drang* passage to an affirmation of the E♭ major tonic. A still earlier example opens the Finale of the Third Symphony; in this case the *crescendo* (propelled by a repeated tetrachord over sustained open fifths) is short, and the *telos* is fully harmonized from the beginning.

example opens III/1: against a swirling nebula of string figurations, the trumpet theme (m. 5) appears as a fully formed melodic entity.[15] Its continuation is derailed; it becomes stuck harmonically and ignites a mighty "sound-sheet" which finally brings forth the fortissimo unison statement of P^{tel} (m. 31).[16]

The use of a teleological primary theme carries implications for the future course of a movement. When the "creatio" type recurs, Bruckner often expands its generative *crescendo*. In the first movement of the Ninth Symphony, he stretches it out across the entire length of the development, so that the eventual arrival of the *telos* marks the onset of the recapitulation (m. 333). On the other hand, a movement based on the double theme type may attempt to turn the generative P^{gen} theme into a *telos*, thus converting this theme's chronological priority into structural priority; this occurs in both III/1 (1877, m. 629) and IV/1 (1878, m. 557).

Although a different manifestation of the same idea, "teleological structural genesis" operates over longer compositional spans than "teleological thematic genesis." As was the case with thematic genesis, structural genesis takes two related forms. In the first, a thematic seed planted early in the piece evolves into a fully formed *telos*. In the second, a fully formed theme is gradually transformed into something different; this transformed shape constitutes the *telos*. Both types are usually associated with the process to be identified as "rotational form," which I shall discuss later.

A celebrated example of the first type – teleological genesis proper – occurs in the chorale that crowns the Finale of the Fifth Symphony. The seed of this *telos* is planted as early as the introduction to the first movement, where, after the opening slow processional, a solemn rhetorical flourish (m. 15) announces a brief, striking brass chorale (m. 18). The development, which can be understood as an enormous expansion of this introduction, also concludes with a powerful double statement of the chorale phrase (m. 338). The chorale texture returns during the closing zone of the Finale's exposition, now joined to a well-profiled melodic line

---

[15] III/1 = Symphony No. 3, first movement. This format will be employed to refer to individual movements. In most cases, I cite Leopold Nowak, ed. *Bruckner Sämtliche Werke B*; Fourth and Seventh Symphony citations refer to Robert Haas, ed., *Bruckner Sämtliche Werke A*, 4 and 7. Where more than one published version of a symphony exists, the date is specified in parentheses.

[16] The opening of IV/1 (1878) also follows this model: P^{gen}, the famous horn theme, initially achieves cadential closure, but its restatement (m. 19) begins to disintegrate into modulating sequences; gradually the two-plus-three "Bruckner rhythm" creeps into the *crescendo* and leads to P^{tel}, a *fortissimo* melodic shaping of this rhythmic pattern over the regained tonic (m. 51). Other examples open II/4 and VI/4, as well as the first two versions of IV/4 (which began life as a "double theme" type, but was ultimately converted into a "creatio ex nihilo" type through the substitution of a different generative *crescendo*).

(m. 175). During the Finale's development, this melody is detached from its chorale setting and employed as the subject of an imposing double fugue (m. 223). Its reassembly into a chorale does not occur, as expected, at the conclusion of the recapitulation; only at the climax of the coda does the chorale recur, now fully unfurled as the ultimate *telos* of the entire work (m. 583).[17]

The second type of structural genesis – the "transformation" variant – is represented by several of Bruckner's Finales. Often the chief task of a Finale is to transform its primary theme back into the initial idea of the first movement. Usually the potential for this transformation can be sensed in an obvious melodic and/or rhythmic affinity between the two themes; however, the Finale theme often lacks tonal clarity or stability. When the transformation finally takes place, it coincides with a long-delayed confirmation of the tonic. Bruckner first attempted this transformation technique in III/4; his most skillful application of it occurs in VII/4. In the latter, the primary theme follows the pitch sequence of the arpeggiated idea that opened the first movement, dressing it in dotted rhythms and seemingly capricious modulations that refuse to cadence in the tonic E. Throughout the movement, this theme makes several strenuous efforts to evolve into its noble forebear, notably through *fortissimo* unison outbursts (mm. 93 and 191). All these attempts fall short. Only at the end of the movement, after the theme finally learns how to cadence in E, is this evolution allowed to take place, and the resulting transformation (m. 331) is all the more overwhelming for having been so often thwarted.[18]

The rebirth paradigm

The rebirth paradigm, which is my own contribution to sonata deformation theory, derives from the concept of teleological genesis. According to the rebirth paradigm, a symphonic movement passes through a series of metaphorical "deaths" and "rebirths" on its way toward a final revelation; each rebirth signifies a higher level of understanding. The revelation may be construed as positive or negative depending upon the outcome of the redemption paradigm.[19]

[17] In my reading of the Finale the coda begins at m. 496.

[18] A somewhat different application of the "transformation" procedure occurs in the Fourth Symphony. As mentioned, both outer movements begin with teleological themes, the first with the "double theme" type, the Finale with the "creatio ex nihilo" type. In both, a portion of the primary theme begins to evolve during the development into a chorale; in the first movement it is P^{gen} that undergoes this transformation, in the Finale P^{tel}. In both movements this transformation is undone during the recapitulation.

[19] The aspects of feminine gendering or encoding scarcely need elaborating here.

A Brucknerian exposition typically begins with an image of gradual emergence: after the preceding silence has been set into motion through a string tremolo or some other rhythmic effect, the primary theme unfolds. This is often structured as a teleological theme of either the "creatio" or the "double theme" variety. The listener bears aural witness either to the cosmic creation of a single theme out of impersonal natural forces or to the, perhaps more human, phenomenon of one theme engendering another. Bruckner also uses a third type of opening, where a complete theme is slowly unfolded at a low dynamic level. In this case, the generative period is bypassed altogether, and the thematic entity emerges fully formed; it then often rears up and flexes its orchestral muscles in a *fortissimo* restatement. The opening of VI/1 provides a good example.

Bruckner's secondary theme zones or *Gesangsperioden* are often circular, repetitive, rotational, and tonally alienated – aspects that I will consider later. These characteristics frequently conspire to *suspend* or *defeat* linear time, creating what I will refer to as a "suspension field." Linear time is then rejoined (often rather abruptly) at the beginning of the closing zone which, not infrequently, begins by continuing the development of the primary theme.[20] Whether or not it uses the same material, the closing zone usually gives the impression of bringing to a full flowering the musical entity born during the primary zone. This flowering is followed by decay, and the exposition closes quietly with a metaphorical "death," or laying to rest. This cycle (birth, suspension, full flowering, decay, and death) is common to most Brucknerian expositions.

The development typically is initiated by a rather static "dormant zone," usually based upon the material that closed the exposition. This procedure suggests a return to the earlier state of preparation, and a quiet, gentle nurturing of the thematic seed. It is succeeded by a "reawakening zone" – a gradual return to life or period of more active preparation that initiates the rebirth process. In a movement based upon a teleological theme, this section usually expands either the generative *crescendo* or the engendering first theme. If the movement begins with a fully formed theme, that theme is now reassembled from fragments, thus tracing the preparatory process bypassed in the exposition.[21] The actual moment of rebirth (the arrival of the *telos* or the reconstitution of the primary theme) often marks the onset of the recapitulation.[22] Immediately thereafter it is common for a recapitulatory crisis to set in, one that leads to further decay and a second metaphorical death.

---

[20] For example, IV/1 (1878, m. 119); 0/4 (m. 92); V/4 (m. 137); and VII/4 (m. 93).

[21] A particularly clear instance occurs in VI/1: the generative process begins at m. 159, and the reconstituted theme appears in the tonic at m. 209.

[22] This rebirth can be painful, as in VIII/1 (1890), m. 225ff.

The coda often begins with another long generative period similar to that in the development and culminates in a final rebirth, usually based upon the primary theme over the tonic *Klang*.[23] The implication of this ultimate revelation – positive or negative – depends upon the musical processes of the individual movement.

Rotational form

One of the most important types of sonata deformation involves rotational form, where a movement cycles through the same thematic material several times, usually (although not always) in the same order.[24] Such a rotational process may simultaneously define a sonata–strophic hybrid in which several rotations of a multithematic pattern correspond to exposition, development, recapitulation, and perhaps even a coda. Because Bruckner's use of rotational structure to define a sonata-form pattern found ample precedent in the work of earlier composers, it is worthwhile to examine several works which may have served as models.[25]

An example by Mozart is the first movement of his Piano Sonata in F Major, K. 533. As outlined in ex. 10.1a, this movement features a triple rotation in which R1 corresponds to the exposition and R3 to the recapitulation, while R2 cycles through the main expositional themes by treating first P then S.[26] In this case, the second rotation is less than half the length of the others, and there is no coda; all oppositions are resolved and all problems solved within the sonata form proper.

Example 10.1b displays the rotational structure of the first movement of Beethoven's Fifth Symphony. The extended coda makes this piece a

---

[23] The concept of *Klang* is discussed on pp. 276–77 below.

[24] Hepokoski, *Sibelius: Symphony No. 5*, pp. 23–26.

[25] Bruckner experimented with rotational structures in his liturgical music long before his studies in sonata form. For example, the *Dies Irae* of his 1849 Requiem suggests a double rotation, in which each rotation begins with the same choral music (the second time transposed to the dominant); an incipient third rotation functions as a coda. Nor did he abandon rotational structures in his later choral works: the "Qui tollis peccata mundi" of his Mass in F Minor (1867–68) is a clear triple rotation, its three musical strophes aligned with (and motivated by) the threefold exhortation of the text.

[26] In addition to P^{gen} and P^{tel}, the following abbreviations are used in exx. 10.1–4: R = rotation (e.g. R1 = first rotation); [R] = incipient or partial rotation; P = primary theme zone (or, in the development, material drawn from this zone); S = secondary theme zone (or, in the development, material drawn from this zone); C = closing zone (or, in the development, material drawn from this zone); Tr = transitional zone; Rt = retransitional Zone; T = telos;, I = introductory material; ------ = a significant expansion (e.g. P------ = P expanded); Exp = exposition; Dev = development; Recap = recapitulation; Int = introduction; Coda = coda. Arabic numerals above the brackets refer to the number of measures in each bracketed segment; arabic numerals beneath the brackets refer to measure numbers.

Ex. 10.1   (a) Mozart: Piano Sonata in F Major, K. 533, first movement (triple rotation)
(b) Beethoven: Symphony No. 5 in C Minor, Op. 67, first movement (quadruple rotation)
(c) Beethoven: Piano Sonata in C♯ Minor, Op. 27, No. 2 ("Moonlight"), Finale (quadruple rotation)
(d) Beethoven: Piano Sonata in F Minor, Op. 57 ("Appassionata"), first movement (quadruple rotation)

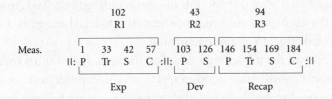

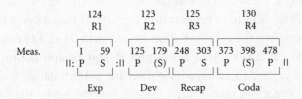

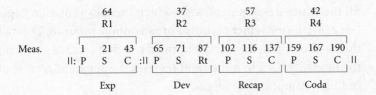

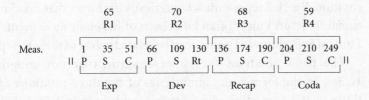

quadruple rotation that plays out the minor-mode redemption narrative.[27] Here the redemptive S in the development is incapable of being realized; it is summoned by the horn motive (m. 179) but fails to appear. Although the recapitulation (R3: m. 248) temporarily succeeds in

[27] Quintuple if one counts the repeat of the exposition.

turning the mode to major, its apparent success is overturned by the onset of the coda (R4: m. 373), which reverts grimly to minor. The movement concludes with a return of P in its original form (m. 478), in effect cycling back to the opening of the piece and underscoring the failure of the preceding redemption paradigm. Other Beethovenian examples include the Finale of the "Moonlight" Sonata and the first movement of the "Appassionata" Sonata (Exx. 10.1c and d). Again, these are quadruple rotations that play out the minor-mode redemption narrative; in each case, the continual recycling of thematic material suggests a repeated, frustrated effort to attain redemption.[28]

In each of the preceding examples, the second and third rotations are congruent with the development and recapitulation respectively. Sometimes the development and recapitulation are merged into a single rotation. Consider, for instance, the Finale of Schumann's Fourth Symphony (ex. 10.2a).[29] Here the development (m. 62) works primarily with P, and the dominant preparation (m. 105) is based upon the transitional theme (Tr); the recapitulation begins with S (m. 113) and continues with C (m. 141). Thus development and recapitulation together constitute a second rotation, whose thematic pattern parallels that of the first.[30] An even more interesting example is provided by the first movement of Schubert's "Unfinished Symphony." Here the brief opening phrase for low strings (marked "X" in ex. 10.2b) replicates perniciously to fill the entire development, after which the recapitulation begins with P (m. 218); the movement is thus a broad double rotation. The malignant X theme also initiates an incipient third rotation (m. 328), which wrenches the modality back to minor and reverses the apparent success of the preceding redemption paradigm.

Bruckner's rotational forms are either double or triple, depending upon whether or not development and recapitulation are fused into a single rotation. Ex. 10.3 represents schematically the forms that Bruckner's rotational structures most often take. Each of his outer movements after the Student Symphony in F minor can be related to one of these four patterns.

The triple rotations are either congruent or non-congruent (ex. 10.3a). In the former, the boundaries of the three rotations agree with those of the exposition, development, and recapitulation; the develop-

---

[28] In the Finale of Op. 27, No. 2, S appears in the dominant minor, in effect negating even the *possibility* of redemption. In the first movement of Op. 57, the customary repeat of the exposition is omitted.

[29] In my reading P begins at m. 1 (*Lebhaft*), Tr at m. 9 (new 'transitional theme' at m. 11), S at m. 23, and C at m. 51.

[30] The actual model behind this movement is a more infrequent type of eighteenth-century sonata paradigm found in the works of Stamitz, J. C. Bach, C. P. E. Bach, Mozart, and others. James Hepokoski and I are currently preparing an extended study of this "Type-2" sonata.

Ex. 10.2   (a) Schumann: Symphony No. 4 in D Minor, Op. 120, Finale (double rotation)
(b) Schubert: Symphony No. 8 in B Minor ("Unfinished"), first movement (double rotation)

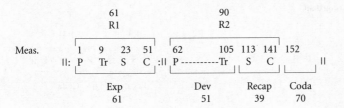

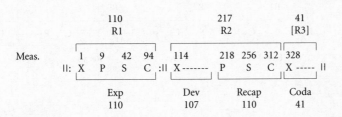

ment may or may not include a discussion of closing zone material (hence the parentheses around C in ex. 10.3a,1). Examples of congruent triple rotations include I/4, III/1 and 4, IV/1, and VIII/1. Movements I/1, 0/1, and II/1 also follow this model, but each reorders its thematic material during R2.[31] Movement II/4 offers an extremely complex working-out of this pattern.[32] In a non-congruent triple rotation, the end of the development overlaps the beginning of R3 (ex. 10.3a,2). Usually this means that, following R2, the primary theme is reassembled from fragments, unfolding in a generative process that culminates in the rebirth of the entire theme in the tonic; this rebirth initiates the recapitulation. The paradigmatic example here is VII/1.

A double rotation may be based upon either a teleological or a fully formed primary theme (ex. 10.3b). In the first case (ex. 10.3b,1), R2 begins by expanding the generative *crescendo* (P^{gen}) to fill the entire

[31] For example, in II/1 the P S C pattern of R1 (mm. 1, 63, and 97 respectively) is reordered in R2 as P C S (mm. 185, 233, and 275). It appears that R3 never reorders its material (certain interpretations of VII/1 to the contrary; see the final paragraph of this section).

[32] The Brucknerian coda almost always functions as an incipient "extra" rotation. As Ex. 10.3 suggests, it usually begins with P, expanded to lead towards the final *telos* of the movement. Only in V/4 does the coda (m.

496) attain the status of a complete rotation, making the movement as a whole a "Beethovenian" quadruple rotation. In all these rotational patterns, R2 usually begins with a transition, or "dormant zone," often based upon the material which concluded R1. In a congruent triple rotation, R2 may end with a retransition, or preparation for R3. These transitions and retransitions are not shown in the schematic representations of exx. 10.3–4.

Ex. 10.3   Bruckner's rotational patterns
            (a) Triple rotations
            (b) Double rotations

1. Congruent

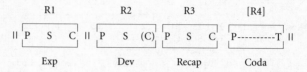

2. Non-congruent

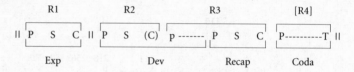

1. Teleological primary theme

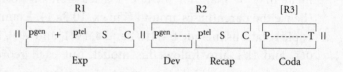

2. Fully-formed primary theme

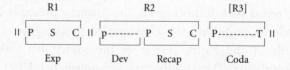

development; the arrival of the *telos* (P^{tel}) begins the recapitulation, which continues with S and C. The clearest examples are found in IX/1 (based upon a "creatio" theme), and VI/4 (based upon a "double" theme). In the case of a double rotation based upon a fully formed theme (ex. 10.3b,2), the development is filled by the gradual reassembly of P from fragments; the rebirth of the entire theme signals the beginning of the recapitulation. Movement VI/1 offers the most concise example of this, while VIII/4 plays out the same pattern in Promethean proportions.[33]

[33] To devote the development of a movement to a discussion of P does not automatically make that movement a double rotation; the generative process must flow unimpeded into the rebirth of the complete theme if development and recapitulation are to merge into a single rotation. Bruckner's early Overture in G Minor and the outer movements of his Student Symphony in F Minor devote their developments solely to P material; none of these pieces is rotational.

Obviously these patterns may be slightly varied for expressive purposes. For example, IV/4 (1880) varies the non-congruent triple rotation. As mentioned, this movement is based upon a teleological theme of the "creatio ex nihilo" variety. R2 reorders the material of R1 by inserting a "suspension field" based upon S (m. 237) between a reworking of the generative *crescendo* (P^{gen}: m. 203) and an expansion of the *telos* (P^{tel}: m. 295), during which the latter is transformed into a chorale (ex. 10.4a). After a sudden collapse, R3 begins with an unsuccessful attempt of P^{gen} to regenerate itself (m. 351); P^{tel} bursts in to begin the recapitulation (m. 383), but is seriously derailed and precipitates a recapitulatory crisis. Thus the two components of the teleological theme (P^{gen} and P^{tel}) straddle the development/recapitulation divide, so that the beginning of R3 overlaps the end of the development.

Exx. 10.4b and c display the structure of two movements that vary the double rotation pattern. In 0/4 (ex. 10.4b), each rotation begins with a slow introduction (marked "I," mm. 1 and 132); the development (m. 148) expands the fugal primary theme, leading to a *fortissimo* tonic restatement at the beginning of the recapitulation (m. 182); the latter features a significant expansion of S (mm. 210–78); and the movement lacks a coda, atypically resolving its issues during the closing zone (m. 279).[34] Movement V/1 also features an introduction, which is later greatly expanded to fill the entire development, into which primary and secondary zone material is poured; thus a "framing" introduction is absorbed into the sonata process (ex. 10.4c).

Finally, ex. 10.4d displays the structure of VII/4, a movement that has been analyzed by Leopold Nowak as containing a "reverse recapitulation" (that is, C S P), but which I prefer to consider a double rotation.[35] In this case, the closing zone of the exposition contains two components: C^1, a *fortissimo* unison transformation of the head motive of P (m. 93); and C^2, a restatement of the cadential portion of P (m. 113). During R2 (m. 163), these components are separated by the return of S (m. 213); both C^1 (m. 191) and C^2 (m. 247) here represent unsuccessful attempts of P to transform itself into the opening idea of the first movement; they also mark the endings of the development and recapitulation. The incipient third rotation (m. 275) begins again with P and finally achieves this long-thwarted transformation (m. 331). Nowak's "reverse recapitulation" interpretation depends upon his writing off the reappearance of C^2 as an

[34] This use of an introduction that stands outside the sonata form proper, yet initiates each rotation, looks forward to certain works by Mahler, such as III/1 or VI/4.

[35] Leopold Nowak, "Das Finale von Bruckners VII. Symphonie," in *Über Anton Bruckner. Gesammelte Aufsätze 1936–1984* (Vienna: Musikwissenschaftlicher Verlag Wien, 1985), pp. 30–34.

Ex. 10.4   Rotational variants

(a) Bruckner: IV/4 (1880) (non-congruent triple rotation variant)

(b) Bruckner: O/4 (double rotation variant)

(c) Bruckner: V/1 (double rotation variant)

(d) Bruckner: VII/4 (double rotation variant – not "reverse recapitulation")

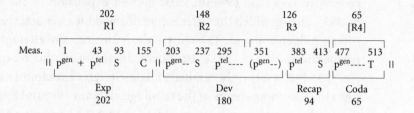

```
              202                148                126             65
              R1                 R2                 R3             [R4]
Meas.    1    43   93   155 | 203  237  295 | 351  383  413  477   513
     || p^gen + p^tel  S   C || p^gen-- S  p^tel---- (p^gen--) p^tel  S  p^gen---- T ||

              Exp                Dev                Recap          Coda
              202                180                94             65
```

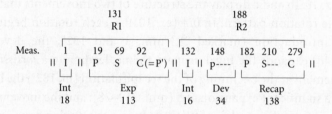

```
              131                188
              R1                 R2
Meas.    1    19   69   92 | 132  148  182  210  279
     || I || P   S  C(=P') || I || p----  P   S---  C ||

       Int        Exp        Int    Dev        Recap
       18         113        16     34         138
```

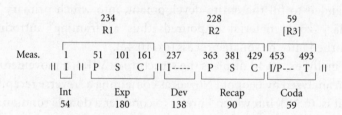

```
              234                228             59
              R1                 R2             [R3]
Meas.    1    51   101  161 | 237  363  381  429  453   493
     || I || P    S   C || I-----  P   S   C  I/P--- T ||

       Int        Exp        Dev        Recap       Coda
       54         180        138        90          59
```

```
              144                130             65
              R1                 R2             [R3]
Meas.    1    35   93   113 | 163  191  213  247  275   331
     || P    S   C^1 + C^2 || P   C^1  S   C^2  P---- T ||

              Exp        Dev        Recap       Coda
              144        68         62          65
```

'Einschub' and understanding the final appearance of P as an ending
rather than a rebeginning.[36]

The alienated secondary theme zone

As mentioned earlier, Bruckner's *Gesangsperioden* frequently suggest that
linear time has been temporarily suspended or defeated, creating a
"suspension field" between the primary and closing zones.[37] This effect is
created in two ways. First, secondary theme zones are often repetitive, circular, and rotational. For example, in III/1 (1877) S begins with a two-bar
thematic complex that is stated three times over local tonic harmony (m.
103), followed by several iterations of its first bar alone (m. 109); after
inflecting to minor and modulating up a half step, the repetitions begin
anew in the key of the Neapolitan (m. 115). The secondary theme of IV/1
(1878) comprises four rotations (mm. 75, 83, 97, and 107), each beginning at a different pitch level with a double statement of the two-bar
motive; the continuation is somewhat different in each case, allowing a
thematic seed planted in the first rotation to flower melodically in the
third (cellos, mm. 99–106), then decay in the fourth (teleological structural genesis). Movement IV/4 (1880) begins its secondary zone with
dirge-like material (m. 93) which, in key and character, recalls the main
theme of the second movement; it then continues with three rotations
(mm. 105, 125, and 139) based upon the incessant reiteration of two
short folk-like ideas.[38]

Second, Bruckner frequently employs the technique Hepokoski has
termed "tonal alienation," where a secondary theme occurs in a key other
than the expected one – and is thus kept from the place of resolution.[39]
Although Hepokoski has discussed only recapitulatory alienation, I have

---

[36] As is the case in the Finale of Schumann's
Fourth, this movement appears to be based
upon the "Type-2" sonata paradigm. A
frequent feature of "Type-2" sonatas is the
recurrence, towards the end of the movement,
of the primary theme as a coda. As the study
cited in n. 30 above will demonstrate, most of
the pieces commonly adduced as instances of
sonatas featuring "reverse recapitulations" are
actually "Type-2" sonatas ending with "P-as-
Coda." At least in the eighteenth century, the
"reverse recapitulation" does not appear to
have been an available formal option; the
"Type 2" sonata, on the other hand, has a
demonstrable compositional history. It is my
contention that this history continues into the
nineteenth century, and includes the

movement under discussion.
[37] A Brucknerian exposition is usually
characterized by extreme contrast between the
primary and secondary theme zones; this
corresponds to what Hepokoski has termed
the "Dutchman-type exposition," after
Wagner's *Fliegender Holländer* Overture
("Structure and Program in *Macbeth*," 72).
[38] Beginning with II/4, almost all of
Bruckner's secondary theme zones are
rotational, and contain anywhere from two to
six rotations. The exceptions are III/4, V/1,
and VII/4, which suggest ABA ternary forms;
even these themes are highly repetitive at the
surface level.
[39] "Sonata Deformation Families," 18; and
Sibelius: Symphony No. 5, p. 94.

broadened the concept to include expositions. For Bruckner, the "expected" key is that in which the exposition or recapitulation is "supposed to" end, according to the *Formenlehre* model: the exposition must conclude in the dominant or mediant major (depending upon the mode of the movement), and the recapitulation in the tonic. In fact, all of Bruckner's minor-mode expositions end in III and all of his major-mode expositions (except the Finale of the Seventh) in V; therefore, when a secondary theme zone occurs in a key other than III or V, it is felt to be tonally alienated from the overall i–III or I–V progression. It must find its way, as it were, to the proper key. A secondary theme that is *recapitulated* in a key other than the tonic inevitably signals a recapitulatory crisis and triggers the onset of what Hepokoski calls "sonata-process failure."

Beginning with III/4, most of Bruckner's expositions make a point of presenting S in the "wrong" key or mode; most recapitulations do as well.[40] This "wrong" key represents a tonal dissonance that must be resolved, either within the secondary zone itself or later; if the secondary zone gravitates toward the "proper" key, we may say that it is gradually "dealienated," or at least absorbed into expectation or default resolution.

I have elaborated Hepokoski's concept of tonal alienation by recognizing three different types: primary, secondary, and double. In primary alienation, an unexpected key is prepared by its own dominant; in secondary alienation, the expected key is prepared by a different dominant; and in double alienation, an unexpected key is prepared by a chord other than its own dominant – perhaps by the dominant of the expected key. One may also speak of *modal* alienation, in which the expected tonal center is subverted by the wrong mode.

An early example of primary *expositional* alienation occurs in 0/4 (D minor), where the *opera buffa*-like secondary theme begins, not in the expected F major (III of D minor), but in C major (m. 69), prepared by its own dominant G (mm. 67–68). The consequent phrase (m. 79) destabilizes this C, turning it into a dominant of F, in which key the theme cadences (mm. 91–92); thus, S is gradually dealienated.[41] A striking instance of *recapitulatory* alienation occurs in IV/4 (1880: E♭ major): after the recapitulation of P breaks off on V⁹/F♯ minor (m. 411), S begins in this rather remote key and, after several unsuccessful attempts to dealienate towards the tonic, finally collapses on the dominant of E♭ minor (m. 473).

[40] Bruckner's early orchestral works bow to tradition in this respect. The Overture, the Student Symphony, the first two numbered symphonies, and the first movement of the Third are all minor mode works; each follows the redemption paradigm of first presenting S in the mediant major, then recapitulating it in the tonic major.

[41] In Schenkerian terms, this secondary zone is a large auxiliary cadence in F; the exposition moves by falling fifths (D–G–C–F) from the D minor of the primary theme to the F major of the closing zone.

In V/1 and VI/1, S is recapitulated entirely in the submediant minor, and one does not encounter any attempts to pursue its dealienation.

The second type of alienation – secondary alienation – prepares the proper key with the wrong dominant; this produces a momentary effect of tonal "distancing" and usually requires that the key be stabilized by the future course of the secondary zone. For example, the exposition of I/1 (1866: C minor) prepares the E♭ major secondary theme with an inverted dominant ninth of G♭ (mm. 39–44); in a brilliant musical pun, the dissonant ninth (E♭) becomes the stable tone of the new key. In the exposition of II/1 (1877), V^7 of the tonic C minor is followed directly by the secondary zone in E♭ major (m. 63); during the recapitulation, this same V^7 leads instead to the tonic major (m. 368). In II/4 (C minor), Bruckner prepares the tonic recapitulation of S with V^7 of the Neapolitan (mm. 423–31); this chord is retrospectively understood as a German augmented sixth in the tonic key. Something similar occurs in the exposition of III/1 (1877: D minor), where the F major of the secondary zone is preceded by V^6_5 of G♭ (mm. 99–102).[42]

Most of Bruckner's secondary theme zones display the third type of alienation – double alienation – in which an "unexpected" key is prepared by a chord other than its own dominant – possibly by the dominant of the "expected" key. This begins as early as 0/1 (D minor): the primary zone moves from D minor to C major, which the listener assumes will function as V of F; in this case, the secondary zone begins unexpectedly in A major (m. 33) and turns towards F only in its consequent phrase (m. 43).[43] A more extreme case occurs during the exposition of II/4 (1877: C minor): the expected mediant E♭ is replaced by its tritone A (m. 76), prepared by V^7 of D♭; the secondary zone gradually resolves this tonal dissonance by moving from A through C (m. 90) to E♭ (m. 112) and cadencing in the "proper" key. The secondary theme of III/4 (1877: D minor) (the famous "polka plus chorale") occurs in F♯ major (m. 65) instead of the expected mediant F, and is prepared by V^9 of G minor; it gradually dealienates toward F (m. 125).[44] In IX/1 (D minor) the secondary zone "should" appear in the mediant F; instead it unfolds in the dominant A (m. 97), prepared by an altered V^7 of E♭.[45] Many more examples of double alienation could be cited, including the exposition of IV/1

[42] This preparation of a key by its enharmonic German sixth becomes a common procedure in the later symphonies.
[43] Thus the falling fifth C–F is arpeggiated by its third-divider A; the resolution to F is postponed until the closing zone, which reinvigorates P material.
[44] In the recapitulation this theme appears first (m. 433) in A♭ major (a tritone away from the tonic D!) prepared by V^7/C minor, and gradually moves towards A (m. 467); although this A begins vaguely to suggest V/D minor (m. 473), no real dealienation occurs.
[45] The closing zone begins in D minor (m. 167); because this key has been prepared by V of A, it sounds like a tonal dissonance rather than a tonic, and is gradually dealienated towards F.

(1878: E♭ major), where a strong dominant preparation for the "proper" key of B♭ (mm. 67–74) is succeeded by a tonally closed secondary zone in D♭ (m. 75), after which the closing zone picks up in B♭ (m. 119).

The net result is to isolate the secondary theme zone from the main line of the default symphonic discourse. If the movement is playing out a minor-mode redemption paradigm, the secondary zone presents, in effect, a visionary world – perhaps Utopian, Arcadian, or eschatological – but in any case, an alternative world which, Bruckner seems to say, cannot possibly be realized in the here and now. This does not mean that the movement as a whole will necessarily "fail," but it does suggest that "success" is not to be won along the traditional lines of sonata discourse.

Sonata process failure and the non-resolving recapitulation

If the redemption from minor to major or the purging of minor elements from the major mode is unsuccessful, the result is "sonata-process failure." This may be signaled in various ways. In a minor-mode work, the recapitulation of the secondary zone sometimes begins in the tonic major, then decays to minor; or the decay occurs during the closing zone. If the movement features recapitulatory alienation, the secondary zone appears in a major key other than the tonic, while the closing zone restores the tonic minor. In both cases, the coda acts either as a "sealer of fate" by reaffirming the minor mode (in a first movement), or as an agent of redemption by working through to major (in a Finale).

Sometimes the recapitulation closes in a key other than the tonic; this "non-resolving recapitulation" signals an even more serious case of sonata-process failure, and it may occur in both major- and minor-mode works.[46] Sometimes S closes in the tonic, while C is derailed tonally and collapses in a non-tonic key; or S is alienated and C proves incapable of regaining the tonic. Again the coda bears the burden of restoring at least the proper tonal level, if not the major mode.

Let us consider several examples. In the first movement of the F minor Student Symphony, S is first presented in the mediant major (m. 85), then recapitulated in the tonic major (m. 432); C (m. 493) decays to minor and ends on a dominant preparation for the coda (m. 561), which "seals the fate" of the piece by concluding in the tonic minor. Something similar occurs in I/1 (1866: C minor), except that the decay to minor occurs within the secondary zone itself (m. 249). A more complex situation

---

[46] Hepokoski, "Sonata Deformation Families,"
18; and "Elgar," 331.

characterizes VIII/1 (1890: C minor), where sonata-process failure is linked to alienated secondary theme zones. In the expositional space, S (m. 51) unfolds in the dominant major instead of the expected mediant; C begins in the mediant minor (m. 97) but eventually breaks through to major (m. 125). S is recapitulated (m. 311) in the mediant major (the key in which it "should" have appeared in the exposition); C begins in the tonic minor (m. 341), but its expected course to major is thwarted by a serious recapitulatory crisis (mm. 368ff.), and the movement closes quietly in minor *without* a coda. In VIII/4 (1890: C minor), S appears in the major submediant in *both* exposition (m. 69) and recapitulation (m. 547); during the latter, C (m. 583) restores the tonic minor, and ends on a dominant preparation for the redemptive coda (m. 647).

The first instance in the Brucknerian canon of a non-resolving recapitulation occurs in I/4 (1866: C minor). The secondary theme begins in C major (m. 301), then decays to minor; the closing zone quickly corrects this to C major (m. 315), and then is derailed, breaking off in E minor; the coda (m. 338) begins quietly on E and finds its way back to C.[47] In the recapitulation of III/1 (1877: D minor), the modal decay occurs at the beginning of the closing zone (m. 549), which then derails tonally and ends on the dominant major (mm. 583–90); again, the coda (m. 591) reinstates the tonic minor. IX/1 (D Minor) recapitulates S in the tonic major (m. 421). The closing zone begins in B minor (m. 459) and climaxes in B♭ minor (m. 493); a chorale-like transition (m. 505) leads to the dominant of D, after which the coda (m. 517) grimly reasserts the tonic minor.

As mentioned, non-resolving recapitulations can also appear in major-mode works. In IV/1 (1878: E♭ major) the recapitulation of the closing zone begins in the tonic (m. 485), then suddenly collapses; the coda begins in the minor submediant (m. 501) and eventually pulls back to the tonic. In VI/4 (A major), the recapitulation of S begins properly in the tonic (m. 299), and derails towards the dominant E; the closing zone (m. 333) leads from E to V⁷ of F; while the coda (m. 371) begins in F minor and finds its way back to A. Other non-resolving recapitulations may be found in V/1, V/4, VI/1, VII/1, and VII/4.

The end result of all these failed sonatas and non-resolving recapitulations is to place an enormous burden upon the coda of the Finale. This, of course, is precisely what Bruckner wishes to do. The coda is the music's final chance to attain the redemption that traditional sonata methods

---

[47] A similar situation occurs in II/1 (also in C minor), where again the recapitulation of S (m. 368) decays from major to minor; in this case, the closing zone first retains the minor modality (m. 402), then moves to E major (m. 460), and finally collapses on the borders of F minor (mm. 480–87); the coda (m. 488) returns to the tonic and concludes in C minor.

have been unable to secure; hence the air of hushed expectancy that often attends the beginning of a Brucknerian coda. It is a "do or die" situation: somehow the music must draw strength from *outside* the sonata form proper and, in a sense, *transcend* that form in order to achieve a breakthrough from darkness into light.

The Brucknerian coda: *Klang* as *telos*

Bruckner was one of the first composers after Wagner to exploit the concept of *Klang* or *Klangfläche*: a "soundsheet" that is outwardly static but inwardly in constant motion.[48] Although such a "soundsheet" may flare up anywhere and involve any harmony, it is apt to occur most prominently at the end of a movement, where the tonic *Klang* functions as the ultimate *telos* towards which the entire piece has been driving. In fact, the fundamental gesture underlying each Bruckner sonata deformation is just such a drive towards this final *telos*, and much of the drama in the work arises from the way in which this drive is delayed, blocked, or hindered. The *telos* itself constitutes the final rebirth or revelation of the movement and perhaps of the entire symphony.

In the early symphonies, the concluding tonic *Klang* is usually coupled with the primary theme of the movement or at least a motive or rhythm derived from that theme.[49] Beginning with III/4, Bruckner begins to combine the *Klang* with a recall of the primary theme of the *first* movement; as mentioned previously, this generally represents a transformation and tonal stabilization of the main theme of the Finale.[50]

The formal structure of the Brucknerian coda varies. It might comprise a single long crescendo to the *telos*, as in III/1, V/1, VI/1, VIII/4, and IX/1. Some codas are rotational, as in I/1, I/4, 0/1, II/1, II/4, IV/1, IV/4, and VI/4; because the usual number of rotations is two, a rotational coda represents a double drive to the *telos*, of which the initial attempt is unsuccessful. A few codas are bipartite but not rotational, as in V/4, VII/1, and VII/4. Finally, two movements lack codas altogether: 0/4, where the *telos* appears at the end of the closing zone; and VIII/1, whose concluding *fortissimo* restatement of P was excised during the 1890 revision.[51]

Many codas contain a lament for the failure of the preceding sonata

[48] See Carl Dahlhaus's discussion of *Klang* and *Klangfläche* in *Nineteenth-Century Music*, trans. J. Bradford Robinson, *California Studies in 19th Century Music*, V, series ed. Joseph Kerman (Berkeley: University of California Press, 1989), pp. 307–09.

[49] Specifically, Symphonies I, II, 0, and III/1.

[50] The *telos* that concludes III/4 (1877) spans an amazing forty-two bars (mm. 597 ff.), an extravagance Bruckner was not to repeat.

[51] III/4 is unique in that its coda is synonymous with the forty-two–bar *telos* (1877: m. 597).

form. In the earlier symphonies this occurs during a suspension field, usually placed just before the concluding *telos* (although in II/4 it occurs between the two rotations: R1=m. 590, lament=m. 640, R2=m. 656). This suspension of linear time often allows for the recall of earlier themes, possibly from previous movements as in II/4 and III/4 (1873); thus, in its final moments, the work reviews its musical "life." In the later symphonies these laments occur in real time and eschew thematic reminiscence. For example, in IV/4 (1880) the first rotation of the coda comprises the lament and is based upon a chorale-like transformation of P^{gen} (m. 477). In VII/1 the first part of the coda (m. 391) laments the failure of the preceding sonata, and the second part (m. 413) looks forward to the ultimate triumph of the Finale.

It should now be clear why, as is often remarked, the final moments of a Bruckner symphony create such an overwhelming sense of ecstatic release. They mark the simultaneous realization of all those tendencies that have been so obstinately blocked throughout the work: the resolution to and revelation of the tonic *Klang*, the unfurling of the thematic *telos*, the final rebirth and tonal stabilization of the primary theme, the redemption into the major mode – Bruckner causes all these achievements to converge and resonate sympathetically in a climactic moment of sonorous splendor. *This is nothing less than the moment the entire work has been constructed to produce.* Yet such a moment is not bought cheaply, and the long buildup to the *telos* usually suggests a tremendous exertion of will, during which the musical *persona* summons every last ounce of strength. In fact, this effort costs the piece dearly: the bright flame of glory soon burns itself out, and the work is over, its life force extinguished. It is not difficult to imagine the final chord being followed by total collapse into silence, a post-work silence that paradoxically may also be regarded as part of the work itself; indeed, this collapse is sometimes actually composed into the final bars, as in the falling gestures that conclude the second versions of III/4 and VIII/4.

To summarize: Bruckner seems to suggest that sonata activity is incapable of bringing about the redemptive moment on its own terms; redemption must be sought outside sonata space, in the coda. The whole sonorous fabric may be interpreted as a statement of the inadequacy of merely human activity and the necessity of redemption from outside. And having uttered this statement of faith, Bruckner throws himself onto the mercy of the silence that follows.

11 Phrase rhythm in Bruckner's early orchestral Scherzi

Joseph C. Kraus

Although some writers have categorized the Scherzo of a Bruckner symphony as the most "Austrian" movement, it would be more accurate to describe only the middle section in this manner, because it conveys the spirit of the *Ländler*. The "weight and bluntness" which Robert Simpson ascribes to the outer sections call to mind the more powerful symphonic conceptions of Beethoven.[1] Here, as Philip Barford points out, Bruckner, like Beethoven, "destroys the regular periodicity of the reiterated 3/4 bars to stamp the movement with hurtling dynamism."[2] The irregularities to which Barford refers occur more frequently in Bruckner's early symphonies, particularly the First, Second, and Third (composed 1865–66, 1870–72, and 1872–73, respectively).

In this chapter I will examine phrase rhythm in the initial sections of the Scherzi from these three symphonies, analyzing the interaction of phrase structure, hypermeter, and pitch structure, using techniques employed by Carl Schachter and William Rothstein.[3] For the Scherzi of the First and Third Symphonies, I will compare earlier and later versions to demonstrate how Bruckner's revisions affect matters of phrase length and the pacing of tonal events. Contrary to common wisdom, this music contains many interesting examples of expansion and contraction which create irregular units. In addition, certain passages which have a conventional length of eight bars – the normative *achttaktige Periode* – display internal irregularities. My investigation will also reveal striking similarities between the movements in question.

---

[1] Robert Simpson, *The Essence of Bruckner* (London: Victor Gollancz, 1967), p. 38.
[2] Philip Barford, *Bruckner Symphonies* (London: British Broadcasting Corporation, 1978), p. 25.
[3] Carl Schachter, "Rhythm and Linear Analysis: A Preliminary Study," *The Music Forum* 4 (1976), 281–334; "Rhythm and Linear Analysis: Durational Reduction,"

The Music Forum 5 (1980), 197–232; and "Rhythm and Linear Analysis: Aspects of Meter," *The Music Forum* 6/1 (1987), 1–59. William Rothstein, *Phrase Rhythm in Tonal Music* (New York and London: Schirmer, 1989). Scores consulted for this study are found in Leopold Nowak, ed., *Bruckner Sämtliche Werke B*, vols. I/1, I/2, I/3, II, III/1, III/2, and III/3.

Symphony No. I/3

Ex. 11.1 illustrates the string and timpani parts for the opening of the Scherzo from the First Symphony in both the Linz and Vienna versions. The timpani part provides the rhythm of the winds which have been omitted to conserve space. The original version of the opening phrase contains several interesting irregularities. Note the hemiola in mm. 3–4 and 6–7. The single-ton pattern in m. 5 can be heard as an expansion inserted between the hemiolas; a normal eight-measure unit has been lengthened to nine measures![4] When Bruckner revised this passage more than two decades later, he engaged in what Thomas Röder calls *metrische Regulierung*, normalization of the unit to create an even number of measures.[5] As illustrated by the bottom system of the example, the hemiolic pattern in mm. 3–4 has been removed by fashioning m. 4 as an exact repetition of m. 3. Bruckner then states this pattern again in m. 5 to give the old m. 5 (new m. 6) a partner, forming a new duple hypermeasure in mm. 5–6 of the revision. Notice that Bruckner produces an even-numbered (ten-measure) unit by a further *addition*, rather than by removing the old expansion. This "expanding of the expansion" is a common procedure during the revision process.

The rhythmic and metrical structure of the entire A section of the Scherzo is illustrated in ex. 11.2. The first sketch is a reduction produced by cutting the original note values in half; each bar of score is a single dotted quarter-note beat. The groupings of strong and weak bars into two- and three-bar units (called hypermeasures) are now shown as single measures in 6/8 or 9/8 time. Changes and irregularities in the hypermeter are now easily recognizable because they are now changes or irregularities in the notated meter. Sketch "b," a detailed Schenkerian graph of the A section, demonstrates the interaction between the hyper-meter and pitch structure. The summary in sketch "c" indicates a basic motion from tonic to dominant, with an anticipation of scale degree $\hat{2}$ in the soprano, harmonized by V of V. The motion from I to V/V is composed out by a 10–6 voice exchange, where g^2 is inflected to $g\#^2$ to produce an augmented sixth chord; this method of progressing from I to V/V is typical in sonata form expositions and has been pointed out by Carl Schachter, Edward Laufer and others.[6] In this case the voice

---

[4] This interpretation is reinforced by the timpani and wind parts, where the constant quarter notes in mm. 6 and 7 (an intensifying gesture) form a duple grouping of strong and weak bars.

[5] Thomas Röder, *Auf dem Weg zur Bruckner Symphonie. Untersuchungen zu den ersten beiden Fassungen von Anton Bruckners Dritter*

Symphonie (Stuttgart: F. Steiner, 1987), pp. 163–64.

[6] Carl Schachter, "The First Movement of Brahms's Second Symphony: The Opening Theme and its Consequences," *Music Analysis* 2 (1983), 63–66; Edward Laufer, "The Way to the Second Subject," paper read at *Mozart: 200 Years of Research and Analysis*, Hofstra University, 10 February 1991.

Ex. 11.1 Symphony No. 1/III, comparison of Linz and Vienna versions of opening phrase

exchange is accompanied by a chromatic ascent out of the inner-voice d^2, as shown.

A comparison of sketches "a" and "b" demonstrates the pacing of tonal events. The bar lines in system "a" designate hypermeasures; the thick barlines separate large hypermeasures consisting of combinations of smaller units. Only one of these large hypermeasures (mm. 32–39) is a prototypical eight-measure unit; all of the other large units are longer than eight measures, due to some irregularity. The one-measure expansion of the introductory phrase (mm. 1–9) gives the second measure of the proportional reduction three beats rather than two. The next large hypermeasure (mm. 10–21) is even longer due to the consistent use of triple hypermeasures in the main theme, which introduces scale degree $\hat{3}$ of the fundamental line. An expansion of the dominant at m. 19 lengthens the unit further, though the hypermeter shifts back to duple in mm. 20–21, when the music recalls the introductory G minor chords of mm. 8–9.[7] Bruckner's use of triple as opposed to duple hypermeter in this phrase, as well as the expansion, demonstrates a rhythmic flexibility which is both interesting and perplexing. It might even be said that the conflict between the triple hypermeter of the main theme and the duple hypermeter of the introduction constitutes a type of metrical "plot" for this movement, reminiscent of the conflict between "ritmo di tre battute" and "ritmo di quattro battute" in the Scherzo of Beethoven's Ninth Symphony.

The after-phrase in mm. 22–31 is even more subtle: the hypermeasure beginning at m. 25 is duple due to the omission of its last measure (which would have corresponded to the upbeat figure in m. 15). This omission occurs just as the inner voice d^2 begins its stepwise ascent, sounding eb^2 in m. 25. The E♭ is then prolonged by its lower neighbor, D, supported by a B♭ $^6_4$ chord, itself embellished by a common-tone diminished seventh at bar 28. The resolution of this diminished seventh is elided with the B♭ $^4_2$ chord in m. 29, its pseudo-bass A♭ passing from a tenor B♭ in the previous measures; thus, another triple hypermeasure (starting at m. 27) becomes duple. Sketches "a" and "b" show the overlapping measures separately, in order to clarify the voice leading of this passage.[8] In the only normal eight-measure unit, mm. 32–39, the inner voice completes its chromatic ascent to g^2. The final large hypermeasure (mm. 40–52) is thirteen measures in length because of the massive expansion of the D minor $^6_4$ in mm. 44–48. Note that this insertion juxtaposes three- and two-measure

[7] One might be tempted to combine mm. 19–21 into a final three-bar unit for the phrase. This interpretation contradicts the change of harmony from dominant at m. 19 to tonic at m. 20.

[8] Rothstein discusses overlapping (elision) in *Phrase Rhythm*, pp. 44–52.

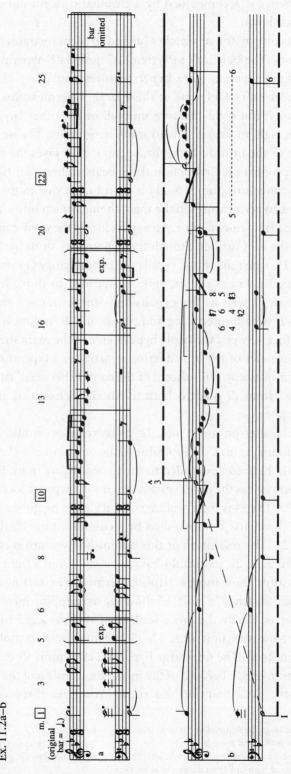

Ex. 11.2a–b

Ex. 11.2a–c

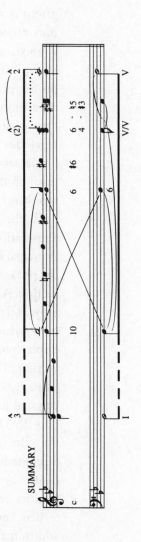

groups, as defined by the octave descent in the melody from d^3 to d^2 in mm. 44–46 and the addition of the woodwinds at m. 47. The conflict between triple and duple groupings is heard at the dramatic high point of the section.

In the B section of the Scherzo the triple hypermeter of the main theme is questioned, in preparation for its eventual suppression in a duple hypermetrical environment (ex. 11.3). The dialogue between bassoon and flute beginning in m. 65 establishes duple hypermeter as the norm, and a regular pattern of eight-measure units prevails for the remainder of the section. The introductory measures (53–56) are also duple in their orientation, since the soprano B♭ at m. 53 is reharmonized by G♭ major at m. 55. When the main theme enters in cellos and basses at m. 57 it is reduced to five measures in length: only a single three-measure group is sounded before its contradiction by a two-measure group in mm. 60–61. The situation is replicated in mm. 62–64 and 65–66. In this context, and given the subsequent preponderance of eight-measure units, it is possible to reinterpret mm. 57–66 in terms of four-measure prototypes with duple hypermeter; mm. 59 and 64 function as internal expansions. In this way the metrical identity of the main theme is called into question as it undergoes a compositional reduction. In fact, the principal idea is further reduced to two measures at 65–66, this clearly duple group serving as the basis for the imitation between bassoon and flute through the remainder of the section. Any reference to triple units has now been completely eliminated.

In the A′ section of the Scherzo the process of questioning and elimination heard in the B section is applied to the restatement of the principal theme. Although the first phrase returns unaltered, its answering phrase (ex. 11.4, m. 110) is reduced to five bars, as at the start of the B section. Again, the viability of the three-measure unit is placed in jeopardy, and the phrase might be heard as a four-measure unit with an internal expansion. Recall that the subsequent ascending sequence in clear duple hypermeter was the only regular eight-measure unit in the A section. This situation changes in the A′ section: in its last large unit (mm. 123–35 of the Linz version, not shown) Bruckner shortens the original five-measure expansion (subdividing 3 + 2) to four measures (2 + 2). The duple hypermeter remains undisturbed at the extension of the climactic $^6_4$ chord, the reference to triple having been removed. Strengthening the duple environment for the restatement of section A could be interpreted as a victory of sorts, if one ascribes a conflict–resolution archetype to the metrical "plot" for this movement.

Bruckner's final revision of the Scherzo damages the plot. In addition to regularizing the introduction from nine measures to ten

Ex. 11.3   Symphony No. 1/III, mm. 53–88 (Linz version)

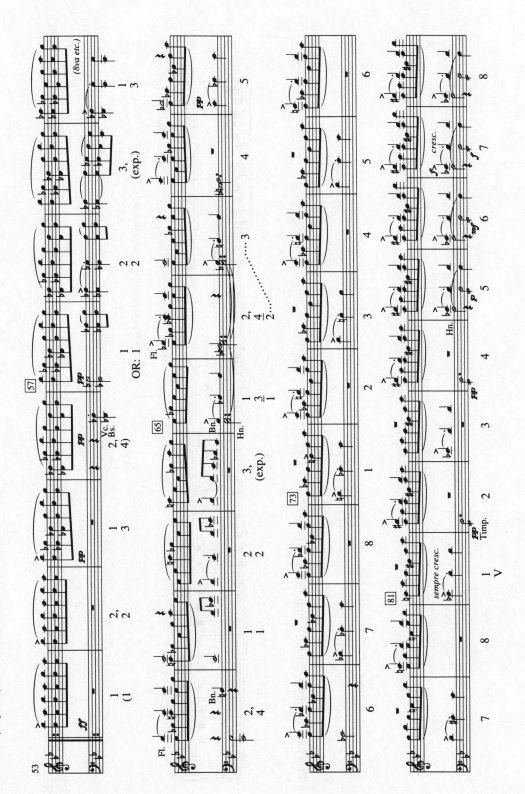

Ex. 11.4 Symphony No. 1/III, mm. 110–18 (Linz version)

(ex. 11.1), he adjusts the massive five-measure expansion of the $^6_4$ chord at the conclusion of the A section, adding a measure to produce an expansion of six measures in duple hypermeter. He restates the expansion in the A′ section, destroying the contrast between the five-measure expansion in A and its four-measure counterpart in A′ of the Linz version. Bruckner's "expanding of the expansion" not only reduces the metrical flexibility of the Scherzo, but also harms the development of its metrical plot. This perspective could be added to the many others which strongly recommend the Linz version of the First Symphony over its Vienna revision.

Symphony No. II/3

Although the Scherzo of Symphony No. 2 appears to be more conventional in its phrase rhythm, it contains several interesting irregularities and exhibits some striking similarities to its counterpart in Symphony No. 1 on a deeper level (ex. 11.5). The opening twelve measures subdivide evenly into 4 + 4 + 4 and present a clear duple hypermeter. Mm. 13ff. display a regular organization into eight-measure units (the *achttaktige Periode*) sounding C minor (mm. 13–20) and A♭ $^6_3$ (mm. 21–28). The next unit contains a motion from G minor $^6_3$ (m. 29) to a dramatic C♯$^{\sharp 0}_{}$ $^6_5$ (m. 35), the latter prolonged for an extra two measures to produce an expansion at mm. 36–37. The eight-measure prototype is lengthened to ten measures. A similar expansion of a chromatic embellishing chord occurs in the next large unit (mm. 39–48). The startling chromatic sound at m. 43 is extended (mm. 44–45) to create another ten-measure unit. The chord at m. 43 sounds like C♭ major, but Bruckner's idiosyncratic spelling (C♭–E♭–F♯) is hardly accidental. As illustrated on the bottom staff in mm. 43–45, the C♭ may be viewed as an inflection of C♮, part of a conventional F♯^{07} chord in the local area of G minor. This inflected chord is an example of Ernst Kurth's concept of *Alterationsstil,* where one or more notes of a conventional sonority are subjected to chromatic modification.[9] If one were to reinterpret the bass C♭ as B♮ leading to an implied C, an alternative analysis would consider the bass B as an example of Kurth's "neighbor-note insertion," involving "the interpolation of foreign tones striving into the chord."[10] Then B♮ would "strive into" C, an

[9] See Ernst Kurth, *Romantische Harmonik und ihre Krise in Wagners "Tristan,"* 3rd ed. (Berlin: Hesse, 1923; repr. Hildesheim: Georg Olms, 1985), parts 3 and 4. Lee Rothfarb provides a translation of passages from these sections in *Ernst Kurth: Selected Writings* (Cambridge University Press, 1991), pp. 99–147.

[10] Kurth, *Romantische Harmonik,* p. 186; trans. Rothfarb, *Kurth: Selected Writings,* p. 112.

Ex. 11.5   Symphony No. 2/III, mm. 1–48

Ex. 11.5 (cont.)

actual chord tone.[11] Though the expansion of Bruckner's altered chord (mm. 44–45) intensifies its effect, its two-measure length does not upset the prevailing duple hypermeter; the same is true for the expansion in the previous unit.

The pitch structure of the Scherzo's A section (ex. 11.6b) is similar to that of the First Symphony: a motion from tonic to dominant through V/V, with $\hat{3}$–($\hat{2}$)–$\hat{2}$ in the soprano. Again the initial tonic is extended by a voice exchange into m. 34, followed by chromatic inflection in m. 35. Several details differ. First, the motion from e♭^{2} (m. 1) to c^2 (m. 34) is filled in with a passing d^2 at m. 29, harmonized by G minor $^6_3$. Second, the extension of V/V, mm. 39–47, involves much more than a simple repetition of the cadential $^6_4$ chord. In the later work, the Ds in soprano and bass are each prolonged by neighbor notes; further neighbor motion at m. 43 in bass and alto produces the apparent C♭ major chord.[12] The interesting prolongation of V/V in mm. 39–47 is motivically related to the main theme, the bass motion D–C–D in these bars enlarging the $\hat{5}$–$\hat{4}$–$\hat{5}$ pattern heard in mm. 1–2 of the movement.

Sketch "a" provides details which again recall the Scherzo from the First Symphony. The arrival of the structural $\hat{3}$ in the soprano is delayed until m. 25; the First Symphony also contained such a delay, though it lasted only ten measures. The 5–6 exchange in mm. 1–21 embellishes the initial tonic; in the earlier Scherzo a similar exchange is employed, again over a shorter time span (mm. 22–25). Finally, the ascent in mm. 33–34 from inner-voice g^2 to c^3 echoes a similar motion out of the inner voice in the First Symphony, approaching the climactic $^6_4$ chord. In the Second Symphony this ascent takes place much more quickly, in the space of two measures, as compared to seventeen measures in the First. To summarize, in the Scherzo of Symphony No. 2 Bruckner reuses the tonal "plot" from the Scherzo of Symphony No. 1, but adjusts its pacing.

Symphony No. III/3

Ex. 11.7 compares the opening phrase of the 1873 and 1877 versions and is based on Thomas Röder's discussion of the same passage.[13] Bruckner's

---

[11] A comparable example in Kurth's *Romantische Harmonik* is the famous Fate motive from Wagner's *Ring* cycle, where an apparent D minor triad is spelled D–E♯–A; both the D and the A are upper neighbors displacing notes of the C♯ dominant seventh chord that follows. Refer to Kurth, *Romantische Harmonik*, p. 210; Rothfarb,

Kurth: Selected Writings, p. 117 (his ex. 4.16).

[12] In this broader voice leading context, an even stronger case can be made for Kurth's concept of neighbor-note insertion, since the neighbor motion in the bass (C–C♭–C) would suggest a respelling of C♭ as B♮.

[13] Röder, *Weg zur Bruckner Symphonie*, pp. 163–64.

Ex. 11.6

Ex. 11.7   Symphony No. III/3, comparison of 1873 and 1877 versions of opening phrase (after Thomas Röder)

metrical numbers are reproduced below the staff of each version; my own interpretation is placed in parentheses above each staff.[14] With respect to the first version, Bruckner considered the opening eight measures to be a normative eight-measure unit; I would suggest a different reading, based on the pacing of tonal events in the passage. The melody prolongs D in three different registers, the initial d^3 being embellished by neighbor notes in the first pair of measures and by arpeggiation in mm. 3–4. Note the rhythmic intensification of the falling arpeggio in m. 4, compared to m. 3 (indicated by the curved arrow).[15] The same combination of arpeggiation and intensification occurs in mm. 5–6 for the embellishment of D in the two-line octave. The repetition of the intensification in m. 7, therefore, can be heard as an expansion which prolongs d^2 for an extra bar, before the motion to d^1. D in the one-line octave only sounds for a single measure instead of the expected two; its duple partner has been eliminated by a contraction. Even though the eight-measure unit appears to be normative upon first hearing, its tonal pacing suggests an irregular seven-measure phrase with an internal expansion.[16]

Bruckner's initial rethinking of this passage is reflected in the second set of metrical numbers below the staff of the top system. For the purpose of *metrische Regulierung*, the composer repeated mm. 3–4 as 5–6 and eliminated the fifth measure. As a result the cadential d^1 (m. 8) fell on the first measure of the next eight-measure unit, causing the metrical structure to be "off track," according to Röder.[17] Bruckner abandoned this plan in favor of the revision shown on the lower staff. The quarter-note arpeggio of m. 3 in the original version is maintained and extended into m. 4, while the original combination of two eighths and two quarters in m. 4 of 1873 is stated twice in mm. 5–6 (see the right-branching dotted arrow). Measure 5 is eliminated, while weak m. 6 and strong m. 7 of the first version are shifted to become strong m. 7 and weak m. 8. The note d^1 (m. 9) still falls on count one of the following group; Bruckner remedies this problem by inserting an additional measure at m. 10, creating an independent two-measure unit.

In my own interpretation of the second version (shown above the

[14] Timothy Jackson points out that Bruckner probably added metrical numbers to the manuscripts of the 1873 and 1877 versions of the Third Symphony at a later time; however, the issue of exactly when these numbers were entered into the manuscript is not crucial to the present analytical discussion. Timothy L. Jackson, "Bruckner's Metrical Numbers," *19th-Century Music* 14 (1990), note 13.

[15] Measures 3 and 4 are grouped together *not* by identity of pattern, but by intensification of

pattern. This rationale is appropriate, given Kurth's emphasis on "wave" and "intensification" in his analyses of Bruckner's music. Rothfarb, *Kurth: Selected Writings*, pp. 151–207. Stephen Parkany has extended Kurth's ideas: "Bruckner and the Vocabulary of Symphonic Formal Process" (Ph.D. diss., University of California, Berkeley, 1989).

[16] There will be more about the "missing" eighth bar in the discussion below.

[17] Röder, *Weg zur Bruckner Symphonie*, p. 163.

staff), the extended arpeggiation (m. 4) and the repetition (m. 6) are expansions indicated by the plus signs. If this is indeed the case, mm. 9–10 are no longer "extra measures," but rather the seventh and eighth measures of the phrase. In particular, Bruckner's addition at score m. 10 supplies the measure which (in my opinion) was "missing" in his earlier version of the phrase; it is only now in the second version that the first phrase is truly "complete."[18]

Ex. 11.8a is a proportional reduction of the A section, similar to the one for the Scherzo from the First Symphony; exx. 11.8b and c are Schenkerian voice-leading graphs for the section. Graph "c" explains the tonal structure in several stages in order to clarify its interesting aspects. The structure (in graph "c1") is similar to that found in the two Scherzi already analyzed: a motion from I to V with an initial ascent delaying the arrival of $\hat{3}$ in the soprano. At the same time, a passing motion downward in the bass introduces VI as part of a 5–6 exchange from the tonic; to avoid parallel fifths as VI resolves to V, a vertical tenth is inserted. In sketch "c2" bass unfoldings add f and g, the latter supporting a consonant C major $^6_4$, which then resolves to C$^5_3$. As shown in graph "c3," the opening bass progression d–f–g is filled in by chromatic passing tones, producing a chromatic ascent into the consonant $^6_4$ at m. 43; in the music, this consonant $^6_4$ serves as the dramatic goal of an ascending sequence, much like the cadential $^6_4$ chords in the previous Scherzi. The passing bass C♭ at m. 49 creates a non-coincidence between soprano and bass, harmonized by a startling D♭ major-minor $^4_2$ – another likely candidate for Kurth's *Alterationsstil* (in relation to the B♭ $^5_3$ which follows).

A comparison of sketches "a" and "b" elucidates Bruckner's tonal pacing for this passage. In sketch "b," the motion in the soprano from D to E is composed out as a ninth in mm. 26 (d^2) through 43 (e^3); the ascent, which involves many reachings-over, is regular in its phrase rhythm, shown in sketch "a" as two large hypermeasures (each consisting of four duple hypermeasures, equivalent to eight score measures – see the thick bar lines). This is similar to the metrical regularity of the ascending sequences in the previous two Scherzi. Note the presence of several triple hypermeasures in mm. 43–48, as the chord is extended for dramatic effect. These triple groups accommodate the octave descents in strings and horns. Despite the presence of "extra" measures, the large hypermeasure in mm. 43–52 still divides into only four hypermeasures, sustaining a hypermetrical regularity which embraces the whole section. Even mm. 17–26 are based on four duple pairs, though an expansion (described in detail in ex. 11.7) involves the insertion of mm. 20 and 22 as

[18] Even though Bruckner may have inserted this bar for a different reason, it is indeed a happy coincidence that he did so, if my reading of the phrase rhythm is a valid one.

Ex. 11.8a–b

Ex. 11.8c

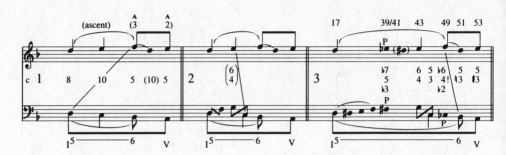

extra hypermetric "beats," placed after the first and second beats of hypermeasure number two, as shown. With respect to the soprano structure as a whole, notice how much time is taken with the initial ascent – 49 measures – as compared to a mere five measures for the descent from f³ to e³ at the end of the passage. As a result, the expressive curve of this section is perhaps the most intense of the three movements under consideration.

The difference between the Scherzo of the "Wagner" Symphony and the earlier ones goes beyond mere intensification. The background pitch structure of its soprano (including B and A′ sections) is substantially different from its two predecessors, as illustrated in ex. 11.9. A strict Schenkerian would consider the f²–e² motion in the A section (bottom system) as belonging to an inner voice, with A (5̂) as the head note.[19] The primary tone 5̂ never descends (since it serves as the final goal of the A′ section), and no interruption scheme is present, as in the previous examples. Moreover, this movement lacks a structural V–I at its conclusion; instead, the chromatic descent from bass C to A in the A section (see bracket) is transposed upward by a fourth in A′, so that it leads directly to D major (I) in the closing bars. These differences in the fundamental structure suggest that the Scherzo of the Third, despite its surface references to the earlier examples, represents a type of "turning point" in the development of the third movement in Bruckner's symphonies. Thomas Röder has made the same claim in his survey of all the Scherzi, citing melodic and rhythmic differences in the Scherzo of the "Wagner" Symphony as indication of a change of direction in Bruckner's compositional approach to the genre.[20] My own comparison of the pitch structures of the first three Scherzi offers further support for his thesis.

In summary, this study of phrase rhythm in the Scherzi of the First,

[19] Black notes are used for the 3̂–2̂ motion in sketches "b" and "c" of ex. 11.8: since no background soprano pitches are shown, no white notes can be included.

[20] See Thomas Röder, "Anton Bruckner's 'Scherzo,'" paper read at *Perspectives on Anton Bruckner: An International Symposium*, Connecticut College, 22 February 1994.

Ex. 11.9

Second, and Third Symphonies has revealed Bruckner's artful use of phrase expansion. The analysis has suggested that, from a rhythmic point of view, the Linz version of the Scherzo from Symphony No. 1 is more subtle and interesting than the Vienna revision. Schenkerian sketches have also shown a similarity in tonal "plot" for the three movements, but the pacing of events in each piece is varied, as are many of its musical details. The "hurtling dynamism" of which Barford spoke is indeed present in the Brucknerian Scherzo, if we simply know where to look for it – in Bruckner's early symphonic utterances.

Index